Dover Memorial Library

W9-BFC-762

The Way We Work

*Contemporary Writings
from the American Workplace*

The Way We Work

*Contemporary Writings
from the American Workplace*

Peter Scheckner and M. C. Boyes, *Editors*

Vanderbilt University Press | Nashville

Compilation and introduction © 2008
by Peter Scheckner and M. C. Boyes

Copyright for the individual selections resides
with the author, agent, or original publisher.
For more information, see the credit that
accompanies each selection.

Published 2008 by Vanderbilt University Press
Nashville, Tennessee 37235
All rights reserved

12 11 10 09 08   1 2 3 4 5

This book is printed on acid-free paper made
from 30% post-consumer recycled content.
Manufactured in the United States of America

Library of Congress Cataloging-in-Publication Data

The way we work : contemporary writings from the American
workplace / Peter Scheckner and M. C. Boyes, editors.
p. cm.
ISBN 978-0-8265-1608-4 (cloth : alk. paper)
ISBN 978-0-8265-1609-1 (pbk. : alk. paper)
1. Work—Social aspects—United States.
2. Occupations—United States.
3. Industrial sociology—United States.
I. Scheckner, Peter, 1943–   II. Boyes, M. C. (Mary C.)
HD6957.U6W29 2008
306.3'60973—dc22
2008019023

Contents

Acknowledgments

WE WOULD LIKE TO ACKNOWLEDGE the following people: Patricia Keeton, for patience, graciousness, and support throughout the six years it took to complete this book; Barbara Kalina, for her invaluable services as an intern; Lee Boyes, for helping us screen the four hundred submissions we received; Joy Ross, for her ideas and help with creating our introduction; Katie Doman, for her superb proofreading skills; Laura Browder, for her sage guidance on sources about work; Barbara Foley, for being a supportive reader and friend; Claudia Menza, our excellent agent, who, staying loyal to this project, navigated us to its completion; and Michael Ames, our editor and the director of Vanderbilt University Press, whose belief in this anthology has made it a reality. Finally, we would like to thank the contributors to *The Way We Work*. Many of these writers reduced their fees or gave us their stories or poems for free, demonstrating a commitment to a shared endeavor beyond their personal gain.

Introduction

IN 1819, "WHILE THE COUNTRY was yet a province of Great Britain," Washington Irving published "Rip Van Winkle"—possibly the first and most enduring American short story in which work plays a central role. In it, the title character sought to avoid two things: his wife and work. "The great error in Rip's constitution," wrote Irving, "was an insuperable aversion to all kinds of profitable labor." Thirty-four years later, Herman Melville wrote "Bartleby, the Scrivener," in which a clerk makes an existential decision about what he does for a living by replying to his boss's every request, "I would prefer not to."

The personal narratives, poetry, and short stories in this anthology, *The Way We Work: Contemporary Writings from the American Workplace,* reveal that "it's a living" is an expression still fraught with great ambivalence. As recently as March 2007, the Gallup Employee Engagement Index Poll found that only 29% of workers are truly "engaged"—that is, they work with passion and feel a profound connection to their company. Fifty-four percent are "not engaged," and at least 20% of employees are either actively or passively job hunting. The net effect of these numbers has been low employee retention and high absentee levels.

The Way We Work also shows that a seismic change has occurred in the workplace and in the distribution of wealth since the 1974 appearance of Studs Terkel's *Working: People Talk about What They Do All Day and How They Feel about What They Do. Working* revealed that workers felt shortchanged by their jobs. But Terkel's subjects also had a sense of themselves as workers and, despite their pervasive feeling of resentment at being belittled by their employers or alienated by the nature of their jobs, the men and women who spoke to Terkel felt that at least in the workplace they were part of a community. On the job they had co-workers with whom they could commiserate and identify.

The people Terkel interviewed were highly class-conscious in a way that today, more than a quarter of a century later, seems radical and even anachronistic. Nearly all the expressions of class anger, social consciousness, and rebelliousness articulated throughout *Working* have been dissipated. When the Cold War ended, so did the language of social class. Furthermore, toward the end of the first decade of the twenty-first century, Americans may have as much luck in the lottery as in putting in extra hours at work to climb the social ladder.

WHEN HORATIO ALGER PUBLISHED *RAGGED DICK* in 1867, he fueled the hopes and desires of a nation hungry to believe in the American dream of prosperity. Alger was a second-generation Harvard man and former minister who turned to fiction after abandoning his church post due to a sexual scandal, but the stories he told were mesmerizing to those born into lives considerably less privileged. Then, as now, Alger's works were often described as rags-to-riches stories. Americans simplified these stories significantly to accommodate a widely held belief—that they could be transformed through pluck, optimism and, most of all, hard work.

In fact, it is not hard work that saves the street urchin from his plight. Instead, as most of Alger's stories go, a poor boy is rescued by a wealthy gentleman who notices the boy as a result of some heroic act of bravery or honesty. The protagonist is rescued by a combination of luck and virtue.

Typically, the boys in Alger's stories do not become tycoons or millionaires. They become respectable, solid, middle-class citizens. The simplification of Alger's tales into rags-to-riches stories is telling—as a nation, we still want to believe that hard work, not luck, will lead us to wealth, success, and stability. While the rags-to-riches myth may still have a stronghold in the hearts and minds of many Americans, there is little evidence that this leap in social class by dint of hard work is actually occurring.

New York Times editorial writer Bob Herbert summed up the economic malaise now facing American workers:

> On the home front, a two-tiered economy has been put in place in which a small percentage of the population does extremely well while a majority of working Americans are in an all-but-permanent state of anxiety about job security, pensions, the economic impact of globalization, the cost of health care, college tuition, and so on. ("The Fading Dream," November 13, 2006)

The men and women in Terkel's *Working* spoke of themselves as members of an amorphous community—as employees—but as many of the writings in *The Way We Work* illustrate, today's workers—especially the nonunion, younger ones—hardly see themselves as a collective, even within a particular workplace. As contributor Mark Slouka writes in "Quitting the Paint Factory,"

> Look about, the business of business is everywhere and inescapable; the song of the buyers and the sellers never stops; the term "workaholic" has been folded up and put away. We have no time for our friends or our families, no time to think or to make a meal. We're moving product, while the soul drowns like a cat in a well.

By 1945, more than one in three American workers belonged to a union, but today fewer than one in eleven are organized. This ratio is reflected in *The Way We Work*. Only a handful of pieces, such as Ha Jin's "After Cowboy Chicken Came to Town" and Marcial González's "The River Bottom Ranch," are framed around organized struggle.

This economic malaise and unfairness are manifested in ways both obvious and complex in *The Way We Work*. While some of the narrators feel passionate about their work, others are barely conscious that they are "workers." In transit from one job to another, some workers find it hard to take either their co-workers or their job situation too much to heart. Psychic or geographical dislocation and insecurity in a global marketplace replace any semblance of the simpler class anger or class solidarity of the past. One pronoun rarely used by the narrators of the works in this anthology is "we." Individualism and passivity have largely replaced class-consciousness.

While many reasons exist for all the economic inequities described above, two factors not so apparent in Terkel's time dominate: globalization and privatization. They are the five-hundred-pound gorillas responsible for the general transformation of the American workforce: the relocation (or offshoring) of the transnational corporations in the search for cheaper labor and an eager consumer market, and the outsourcing of what used to be unionized labor with multi-year contracts and benefits. With globalization, Americans can file their taxes from India, get help with their computers from Canada, review their credit card statements with specialists in Brazil; public colleges that once employed only unionized custodial workers now outsource to private companies.

Even the quintessential American industry, automobile manufacturing, has succumbed to globalization. By 2006, Toyota had become the world's largest automaker, and in that same year the German DaimlerChrysler, having just laid off 13,000 workers, sold its Chrysler Group, the third-largest car manufacturer in the United States, for a pittance to a private equity firm. Whatever certainty, romance, or centrality that may have once accrued to Americans in their workplace is gone.

The story in *The Way We Work* that explicitly addresses the effects of a now thoroughly global corporate economy on its workers is "After Cowboy Chicken Came to Town," by Chinese-born writer Ha Jin. Behind the scenes in such writings as "Chicken 81," "Livelihood," "The Women Who Clean Fish," "The Basement," and "McDonald's—We Do It All for You" is the sense that given the realities of globalization, privatization, and, most of all, the inexorable bottom line of profitability, many workers are now wholly expendable. Barbara Garson offers an example of a less than super-sized employment opportunity in "McDonald's—We Do It All for You":

> "Look, there," said Damita as the teenage job applicant left and the manager went behind the counter with the application. "If I was to say I can't come in at 7, they'd cut my hours down to one shift a week, and if I never came back they wouldn't call to find out where I was."

THE WORKERS IN *THE WAY WE WORK* are divided in a myriad of ways—part-timers, temps, and full-timers; those with sophisticated information skills and those with only a high school education or a college education from a lower-tier school. *The Way We Work* demonstrates that the nature of work during this era has changed dramatically. Some 13% of all jobs created have been in the temporary employment industry. This is part of a larger trend called "nonstandard employment." Those people who fall into the category of nonstandard employment work part-time, are self-employed, or are under contract. These jobs typically pay about 10% less than their full-time counterparts, and they are much less likely to have benefits such as health insurance—adding to the numbers of the forty-five million without health care coverage. Salespersons, customer service representatives, nurses, post-secondary school teachers, janitors and cleaners, waiters, food preparers, home health aides, orderlies and attendants, and general and operations managers, many of whom have a story to tell in *The Way We Work,* have all seen a shift to nonstandard employment.

Those who are more privileged—more immune from being outsourced or marginalized—often like their work. In the writings from *The Way We Work,* Amercans with "good" jobs—those who know themselves as doctors, social workers, police officers, or owners of their own businesses—find a secure sense of self; they do not view themselves merely as employees but as crucial, even exuberant, participants in American life. These relatively lucky few come alive at work. Much of this enthusiasm is evident in the Rick Bass short story, "The Fireman":

> But after a fire—holding a can of cold beer and sitting there next to the hearth, scrubbed clean, talking to Mary Ann, telling her what it had been like—what the cause had been, and who among his men had performed well, and who had not—his eyes water with pleasure at his knowing how lucky he is to be getting a second chance, with every fire.

In the majority of the selections in *The Way We Work,* however, the narrators spend most of their time in work that is stultifying. These speakers lack attachment to co-workers or to the company (which has already expressed its lack of attachment and commitment to them). For many in these essays, stories, and poems, a job gives little positive meaning to the narrator's life. Its dehumanizing demands translate into idiosyncratic behavior, violence, or just plain craziness manifested on the job.

"My mother had charge of three chicken houses, 48,000 chickens to a house, and several thousand Cornish hens besides," writes Sarah Courteau in "Chicken 81." "She had three main duties: feed them, water them, and kill any of the chicks that weren't uniform and spry." And in Daniel Orozco's "Orientation," a new worker has the job laid out for him:

> You must pace your work. What do I mean? I'm glad you asked that. . . . That was a good question. Feel free to ask questions. Ask too many questions, however, and you may be let go.

The type of dark humor manifest in Orozco's story is one way the writers of the pieces in *The Way We Work* deal with the absurdity of the psychic dead-end of work in America. The knowledge that workers are disposable, that transnational corporations with no loyalty are boss, that work leads to more work—not happiness, security, or respectability—permeates many of the stories, poems, and essays in *The Way We Work.*

The Way We Work: Contemporary Writings from the American Workplace might just as accurately be called "The Way We Are," since Americans work longer hours and many more weeks than others in the developed world. American workers are often lauded as more productive—in part because of these longer hours, and because some of us continue to work even during vacation periods, short though these breaks may be compared to those in other countries. For some, such as Charles Bowden in "Torch Song," the job consumes the worker's life:

> For the next three years I live in a world where the desire of people, almost always men, to touch and have their way with others makes them criminals. Gradually I began to lose the distinction between the desires of criminals and the desires of the rest of us. I am told I can't get off this kind of beat, because most reporters won't do it.

In "Quitting the Paint Factory," Mark Slouka argues that all work and no play has a material benefit to America's economic and political managers: an obsessive work ethic prevents citizens from thinking critically about what kind of society they want to live in.

And this process of getting busy starts early, even for the middle class. Since the cost of college now requires *both* parents to earn what a GM worker made thirty or forty years ago (adjusted for inflation), the typical college student works part-time and sometimes full-time in order to help pay tuition. On many campuses American students spend as much or more time at work as they do at their studies. According to a 1998 U.S. Department of Labor statistic, over half of college students under the age of twenty-five had jobs, and nearly two-thirds of the students at two-year colleges worked for pay. Eight years later the picture had hardly changed for the better: of full-time college students, 40.8% were in the labor force, either working or looking for work, and 81.0% of part-time college students participated in the labor force.

"IT'S A LIVING." THAT WAS HOW WORK was once described. It was a living in at least two senses: a job provided a livelihood and also an identity—a life worth living. Nowadays being at the office, working in a factory or a restaurant, or attending to someone's children offers millions of Americans considerably less than the invigorating Horatio Alger fantasy would suggest. In fact, *The New York Times'* fourteen-part series called "Class Matters" (2005) concluded that, since the 1970s, there had actually been an increase in the percentage of families staying in the same income group and that social mobility has declined during the last twenty years. The *Times* study in effect suggested that the Horatio Alger myth had been turned upside down:

> Nearly every economic indicator points to the conclusion that the share of the aggregate income in America is more unequal than ever, with more and more wealth being concentrated at the top. The typical American CEO earns 300 times the average wage, up tenfold from the 1970s, and no other country

has seen such dramatic shifts in economic inequality. By 2000, only Brazil had greater income inequality than did the United States.

Despite the evidence—dry statistics set against an all-encompassing cultural bootstraps myth—one can only wonder how many Americans continue to believe that hard work and a good education are more important to getting ahead than connections or wealthy parents.

THE WAY WE WORK IS AN ANTHOLOGY of literature, not a sociological survey. The writings in *The Way We Work* were chosen for their literary quality and variety of voice. Of the forty-two pieces in this anthology, we selected only fifteen from magazines, books, and journals we had read. The rest of the writings were chosen from more than four hundred submissions we received based on a modest advertisement in *Poets and Writers* magazine soliciting short stories, poetry, and essays about work. The table of contents reflects this process, in that it is arranged by an assortment of narration and genre rather than by occupational group. The job classifications in the table of contents refer to the topic of the piece and not necessarily to the author.

The Way We Work demonstrates how we create, how we imagine, and what stories are worth telling about our nine-to-five lives. Whatever else we dedicate our lives to—friends, family, religion, sports, and hobbies—we still work a third of our lives' worth. As Mary Malinda Polk writes in her essay, "At Work,"

> It is eight hours of my day, five days a week. Sleeping is the only thing I spend as much time doing in a week. I don't know how not to let that much of my week matter. And I wish I did.

When you read the pieces in *The Way We Work*, you'll realize that no definitive answer presents itself to the question, "How does work define us in the twenty-first century?" The narratives, short stories, and poems in this collection are first and foremost excellent examples of contemporary literature—literature that shows us to be complex, contradictory, ironic, self-reflective, and often very funny. These forty-two writers, who represent nearly as many occupations, look closely and passionately at individual American women and men and at the variety of cultures, ideologies, and mindsets they represent. How Americans make a living and what they think about their jobs is as varied and idiosyncratic as we are as a people. We may come alive rather crazily on the job, but we sure do come alive.

—Peter Scheckner and M. C. Boyes

The Way We Work

*Contemporary Writings
from the American Workplace*

Chicken 81

Sarah L. Courteau

MY MOTHER IS A KILLER.

She knows how to pull a chicken's head off under her size-ten shoe, but she prefers to lay it gently on a chopping block and lop off its head with a clean stroke of the ax. Then she swings the flapping body away from her so its red life spatters the yard.

She's grabbed up a shovel, an ax, a hoe, to hack the heads off copperheads and occasional rattlesnakes that have confused their territory with ours. Once she dispatched an unfortunate black snake with a knot in his middle. He'd swallowed the white stone we kept in the chicken coop to fool the hens into thinking we weren't taking all their eggs.

She has stood in the barn and dropped five of a litter of nine puppies with the blunt side of an ax head. We had nothing to feed them but a gruel my mother cooked each day on the stove. Her winsome sketches on handbills and the tearful calls my younger sister Darcy made to numbers in the phone book had failed to turn up any takers for the puppies. The guy at the pound said no one would adopt redbone-hound mix pups, and the pound would charge $5 a head to dispose of them.

My father kills with a gun, which my mother knew would terrify the puppies in their last moments. She did the killing because her weapon of choice is an ax wielded with a skill honed by many mornings of chopping kindling for the stove. When he ended up using the gun anyway on the last three puppies, he knew—though she didn't ask—to save the pup with one blue eye. Annie, as we came to call her, had sat down and looked frankly up at my mother instead of nosing the decoy food bowl. My mother set down the ax and would do no more killing that day.

Other killings I can't remember or she's lied to us about. Years after our mutt Brodie had run away and been replaced in short order with an Australian shepherd puppy, my mother let the truth slip at the dinner table. They went for a walk, and my mother shot Brodie in the head with a .22 pistol. I used to kiss little Brodie on the nose, but strangers made her nervous. When a friend's child bent to pet and coo, Brodie bit the girl in the face. On our farm, a dangerous bull might be tolerated, but not a dangerous pet.

Death is supposed to be matter-of-fact on a farm. A flick of the wrist, an arc of the ax, a squeeze of the trigger, and the wriggling animal becomes just another lump of flesh to be plucked, skinned, or buried.

Not for my mother.

This is a woman who has nursed along innumerable baby birds fallen from their nests, foundling rabbits quivering with the anxiety of existence, a hairless baby mouse she tucked away in an old sock, a wild fawn found by the roadside, goats heaving with the effort of holding in their own guts after a dog attack, a calf that lived in a corner of the front room after my father cut it from the womb of its dying mother, a small king snake with a broken back that lacked the prudence to stay out from underfoot. For weeks, I remember, she carried bits of food out to him in a protected brush pile behind the house as he wasted slowly toward death.

I've asked her how she forced past that moment of hesitation when, ax in hand, she eyed the chicken and it eyed her back with the uneasy sideways look a chicken gets when it knows something bad is going to happen. The answer is always the same: it had to be done. We had to eat, she had to protect us, an animal's pain had to be extinguished.

When our neighbors gave us several white geese to butcher one fall, Darcy stood in the haymow while my mother and father killed them, wailing over and over, "Can't we keep just one?" The answer was as inevitable as the coming winter. Survival was not negotiable.

My mother doesn't kill much anymore. Maybe it's because my grandmother died a few years ago and left my father a little nest egg. Maybe it's because the last of my six siblings is in school and my mother's job as a part-time sculptor has vaulted her into the ranks of moneymakers who buy their hamburger in plastic instead of on the hoof. But the chief reason, I think, is her summer job three years ago at a chicken farm a mile up the road.

"I went into it with the same attitude as a Quaker going into the medical corps in Vietnam," she says. She wasn't there to send these chickens to the swift, steely deaths she had witnessed working at a Campbell Soup factory before she met my father. She was just there to care for them and make a little money at a job close to home.

The neighbors paid her $25 a day to shepherd the chickens through six weeks of life, until their muscles were just the right consistency for Tyson chicken patties and nuggets. Then the chicken catchers would descend in big trucks, stuff the three-and-a-half-pound birds into crates, and haul them away to processing plants, from which they would emerge breaded and boxed.

My mother had charge of three chicken houses, 48,000 chickens to a house, and several thousand Cornish hens besides. She had three main duties: feed them, water them, and kill any of the chicks that weren't uniform and spry.

She didn't discover that she would have to kill until her first day on the job, but she learned quickly enough. The man I'll call Alvin Smith, who owned the operation along with his wife, would scoop up a runty chicken. "He'd be talking but I'd be watching that chicken in his hand, small and soft as an egg yolk," she said. "Without looking down, he'd squeeze its head and it would loll limp in his hand, and all the while he'd be talking. Alvin was completely opaque."

It was easy to spot the deviants, the ones that weren't quite big enough or vigorous enough to reach the water line that was raised every two days in accordance with the growth plan plotted by Tyson, a company that has engineered the six-week life span of a chicken to the point where it considers its chicken-feed formula a trade secret.

When Alvin or the woman who trained her was around, my mother killed, snapping the necks of as many as forty-five chickens a day. When I could picture the scene at all, I imagined her sweeping through the chicken houses like a cross between the Angel of Death and Little Bunny Foo Foo.

My mother had always been a sucker for the underdog, the slow starter, the runt. Now she was to cull any birds that didn't conform to the Tyson life plan. They wrecked the feed conversion ratio, wasting resources better consumed by chickens that would fit Tyson specs come collection day. If she put off killing them when they were young, she wasn't doing them any favors. The further they fell behind the other birds' growth, the harder their life of scavenging became. And, in the end, this was not a system that rewarded game survival. To put off the day of reckoning meant only that the mature chicken would be less easily and painlessly snuffed out.

I WAS LIVING IN ST. LOUIS THEN. When I called home, I started hearing little cheeps in the background. They were just a few at first, but they swelled to a chorus over the course of the summer. Within a few days of starting work, my mother had become an Oskar Schindler of the chicken farm. Once left alone to do the job, she started smuggling chickens home, a few at a time.

She couldn't save them all, but she chose the birds she called little champions, like the one that would leap up and peck a drop of moisture from the water line when it wasn't tall enough to reach otherwise. One chick she brought home had a leg that stuck out sideways. She had lifted him up to the water line once, and he had the pluck to call to her the next time she made her rounds so she could help him again.

I started hearing scrappy tales of chicken survival during my calls home. She admired the way the misfits scratched for food on the chickenhouse floors or sought out condensed moisture on the door of the chicken house when they couldn't compete with the bigger birds at the feeders. In her enthusiasm, she held the chick with the sideways leg to the phone receiver so that I could hear his reedy chirps, a triumph of life over science.

EVEN WITHOUT WHAT HAPPENED THAT summer, I think my mother's association with big agribusiness would have been short-lived. Where before the force of necessity had borne her through each time she took an animal's life, now she was merely a hired killer.

It was a hot summer. Old folks who were too thrifty or poor to turn on their air-conditioners were dying in their rocking chairs. Then one of the Tyson plants shut down to fix a wastewater problem, and the chicken catchers stopped coming to pick up birds for slaughter. The temperature controls where my mother worked were crude, and the chickens began to pant in the heat.

The birds passed the three-and-a-half-pound mark and the Tyson pickup date. As they closed in on four pounds, they began to run out of room. They started going lame, and my mother tracked down a Tyson field representative who diagnosed the problem as femur-head necrosis, a disease caused when bacteria fester in a chicken's equivalent of our hip joint. The birds lost even what little range of movement they'd had in the cramped houses. Everything from space allotment to bird weight was controlled by adherence to the Tyson schedule. Now that the schedule was disrupted, the precise equations began to jumble. The chickens started to die.

My mother made her rounds day after day, picking up the dead. The freezers in each chicken house that preserved the dead chickens before transport began to overflow, and when they gave out the dead birds inside started to ferment. The chickens that lived couldn't keep cool as they put on weight, and they panted miserably.

Chicken 81 clinched my mother's decision to leave. She was fastening chicken wire across a doorway so that the chickens could get a little more air from outside while she did her chores. One chicken followed my mother as she moved from one side of the doorway to the other, and finally settled between her feet. She reached down and rubbed its head with her finger. All the other thousands of chickens that summer had run from her or avoided her. When she rubbed the head of this one, she could see the chicken enjoyed it.

My pathologically honest mother decided to commit seventeen cents' worth of larceny—the profit the Smiths made on each bird. She resolved to come back to collect this chicken and take it home after she'd finished her rounds in the house. Even among those tens of thousands of white birds, she knew she'd find it again. Most chickens confined themselves to a fairly small area, and this one had distinctive charcoal feathers on its neck and wing.

When she returned to the spot, she had collected eighty dead chickens. She counted and recorded the dead each time she passed through a house to track the attrition for Alvin. She searched all over for the affectionate chicken, convinced that it couldn't have shuffled far. Finally, she gave up. She started to lift the makeshift screen she'd lashed across the door and discovered Chicken 81. In the half hour she was gone, her chicken had crawled partway beneath the screen and died.

My mother wept.

She gave her notice that afternoon but agreed to stay on until the Smiths could find someone else. Ten days past schedule, the Tyson trucks rolled in and the catchers hauled away the chickens in a flurry of feathers. Most of the chickens, anyway. In each house several hundred were left—those too small or too crippled to meet the Tyson specs. In the past, Alvin had orchestrated a chicken roundup, closing in on the rejects with a circle of chicken wire. Then he had immobilized them any way he could—snapping their necks, stomping on them—to clean out the house for the next shipment of dandelion-puff chicks. This time, he was working at his job in town and the press was on to prepare the houses.

My mother went alone, at night, when she knew the chickens would be sleeping. She left on her car's parking lights to shine into the house and silhouette the birds where they slept clustered in puddles of white. The water lines, the feeders, all the chickenhouse equipment, had been hoisted to the ceiling to clear the way for the chicken catchers earlier that day.

She started down the first cavernous house. The chickens had become accustomed to the occasional bump or nudge as part of life in close quarters. My mother would sidle up to one and try to grab it by the neck and give a quick twist before it could utter a sound to alert the others. A clean grab the first time was essential. Even if the chicken flapped afterwards, if it didn't squawk, its companions didn't suspect a death spasm. By the time my mother reached the end of the chicken house, though, the few birds that were left knew a predator was among them. She had to stalk them and chase them down as she pounced and twisted, pounced and twisted.

She stood in the dark to catch her breath, her hands and shoulders sore from her kills. And she started to feel that she wasn't alone anymore.

"It began to grow in me, this feeling that someone else was in this long, dark building. I shouted out loud, 'Who's there?' I felt for a moment as though a shark spirit was there, drawn by the blood itself."

My mother fought down her panic. She finished the job that night by promising herself she would never do it again. The few chickens she missed and discovered the next day she took home.

By mid-August she had trained a young man who lived near the Smiths to tend the chickens, and she was up to her elbows in clay at Terra Studios, where she'd been offered a sculpting job. She'd stopped buying chicken in the stores. The chickens she had rescued grew and grew. With a little feed and the run of the place, their bantam-size bodies grew far beyond the three and a half pounds at which their brethren had perished, and they lumbered around the farm producing noises closer to a bellow than a cluck.

A brother of mine dubbed one of the roosters Boots, after its large, muscled legs. Boots had arrived nearly grown, one of the refugees from the final night of extermination. He strutted around the farm and, when he hit puberty, started a reign of terror. He lay in wait in the yard and jumped out at my little brothers. And he raped the hens so often and so viciously that one finally died, sealing Boots's own fate as surely as Brodie's snap at a child had sealed hers.

My mother put on a kettle of water to boil and brought out her ax.

"Boots, he had seen me killing the other chickens, and he never trusted me after that. In the end, he was fully justified."

————————

Sarah L. Courteau was born in Fayetteville, Arkansas, not many miles from the chicken farm where this essay is set. Her nonfiction and reviews have appeared in *Witness, The Wilson Quarterly, The American Scholar, Washington Post Book World, The Iowa Review, Delmar,* and elsewhere.

As a child, Courteau milked cows, pulled weeds, slopped pigs, helped stretch fences, and did the other chores that help keep a farm going. She has worked as a corn detasseler, library aide, waitress, restaurant hostess, janitor, legal news writer, business reporter, deli sandwich maker, teaching assistant, standardized test evaluator, and office temp. Currently, she is literary editor of *The Wilson Quarterly* and does nothing that leaves her hands rough.

She confesses to a hint of shame that she will likely never live by the sweat of her brow. "To write this essay, I didn't pour chicken feed or collect dead birds. I didn't see the mordant absurdity of it all as I picked my way through the chicken shit, or decide to preserve life even as I functioned in a massive apparatus of death. I picked up my pen. But my mother did the work."

"Chicken 81" was originally published in *Witness* (Fall 2001) and reprinted in *Harper's Magazine* (2002). Copyright © 2001 by Sarah L. Courteau. It is reprinted here by permission of the author.

Orientation

Daniel Orozco

THOSE ARE THE OFFICES AND these are the cubicles. That's my cubicle there, and this is your cubicle. This is your phone. Never answer your phone. Let the Voicemail System answer it. This is your Voicemail System Manual. There are no personal phone calls allowed. We do, however, allow for emergencies. If you must make an emergency phone call, ask your supervisor first. If you can't find your supervisor, ask Phillip Spiers, who sits over there. He'll check with Clarissa Nicks, who sits over there. If you make an emergency phone call without asking, you may be let go.

These are your IN and OUT boxes. All the forms in your IN box must be logged in by the date shown in the upper left-hand corner, initialed by you in the upper right-hand corner, and distributed to the Processing Analyst whose name is numerically coded in the lower left-hand corner. The lower right-hand corner is left blank. Here's your Processing Analyst Numerical Code Index. And here's your Forms Processing Procedures Manual.

You must pace your work. What do I mean? I'm glad you asked that. We pace our work according to the eight-hour work day. If you have twelve hours of work in your IN box, for example, you must compress that work into the eight-hour day. If you have one hour of work in your IN box, you must expand that work to fill the eight-hour day. That was a good question. Feel free to ask questions. Ask too many questions, however, and you may be let go.

That is our receptionist. She is a temp. We go through receptionists here. They quit with alarming frequency. Be polite and civil to our temps. Learn their names. Invite them to lunch occasionally. But don't get close to them, as it only makes it more difficult when they leave. And they always leave. You can be sure of that.

The men's room is over there. The women's room is over there. John LaFountaine, who sits over there, uses the women's room occasionally. He says it is accidental. We know better, but we let it pass. John LaFountaine is harmless, his forays into the forbidden territory of the women's room simply a benign thrill, a faint blip on the dull flat line of his life.

Russell Nash, who sits in the cubicle to your left, is in love with Amanda Pierce, who sits in the cubicle to your right. They ride the same bus together after work. For Amanda Pierce, it is just a tedious bus ride made less tedious by the idle nattering of Russell Nash. But for Russell Nash, it is the highlight of his day. It is the highlight of his life. Russell Nash has put on forty pounds, and grows fatter with each passing month, nibbling on chips and cookies while peeking glumly over the partitions at Amanda Pierce, and gorging himself at home on cold pizza and ice cream while watching adult videos on TV.

Amanda Pierce, in the cubicle to your right, has a six-year-old son named Jamie, who is autistic. Her cubicle is plastered from top to bottom with the boy's crayon artwork—sheet after sheet of precisely drawn concentric circles and ellipses, in black and yellow. She rotates them every other Friday. Be sure to comment on them. Amanda Pierce also has a husband, who is a lawyer. He subjects her to an escalating array of painful and humiliating sex games, to which Amanda Pierce reluctantly submits. She comes to work exhausted and freshly wounded each morning, wincing from the abrasions on her breasts or the bruises on her abdomen or the second-degree burns on the backs of her thighs.

But we're not supposed to know any of this. Do not let on. If you let on, you may be let go.

Amanda Pierce, who tolerates Russell Nash, is in love with Albert Bosch, who sits over there. Albert Bosch, who only dimly registers Amanda Pierce's existence, has eyes only for Ellie Tapper, who sits over there. Ellie Tapper, who hates Albert Bosch, would walk through fire for Curtis Lance. But Curtis Lance hates Ellie Tapper. Isn't the world a funny place? Not in the ha-ha sense, of course.

Anika Bloom sits in that cubicle. Last year, while reviewing quarterly reports in a meeting with Barry Hacker, Anika Bloom's left palm began to bleed. She fell into a trance, stared into her hand, and told Barry Hacker when and how his wife would die. We laughed it off. She was, after all, a new employee. But Barry Hacker's wife is dead. So unless you want to know exactly when and how you'll die, never talk to Anika Bloom.

Colin Heavey sits in that cubicle over there. He was new once, just like you. We warned him about Anika Bloom. But at last year's Christmas Potluck, he felt sorry for her when he saw that no one was talking to her. Colin Heavey brought her a drink. He hasn't been himself since. Colin Heavey is doomed. There's nothing he can do about it, and we are powerless to help him. Stay away from Colin Heavey. Never give any of your work to him. If he asks to do something, tell him you have to check with me. If he asks again, tell him I haven't gotten back to you.

This is the Fire Exit. There are several on this floor, and they are marked accordingly. We have a Floor Evacuation Review every three months, and an Escape Route Quiz once a month. We have our Biannual Fire Drill twice a year, and our Annual Earthquake Drill once a year. These are precautions only. These things never happen.

For your information, we have a comprehensive health plan. Any catastrophic illness, any unforeseen tragedy is completely covered. All dependents are completely covered. Larry Bagdikian, who sits over there, has six daughters. If anything were to happen to any of his girls, or to all of them, if all six were to simultaneously fall victim to illness or injury—stricken with a hideous degenerative muscle disease or some rare toxic blood disorder, sprayed with semi-automatic gunfire while on a class field trip, or attacked in their bunk beds by some prowling nocturnal lunatic—if any of this were to pass, Larry's girls would all be taken care of. Larry Bagdikian would not have to pay one dime. He would have nothing to worry about.

We also have a generous vacation and sick leave policy. We have an excellent disability insurance plan. We have a stable and profitable pension fund. We get group discounts for the symphony, and block seating at the ballpark. We get commuter ticket books for the bridge. We have Direct Deposit. We are all members of Costco.

This is our kitchenette. And this, this is our Mr. Coffee. We have a coffee pool, into which we each pay two dollars a week for coffee, filters, sugar, and Coffee-mate. If you prefer Cremora or half-and-half to Coffee-mate, there is a special pool for three dollars a week. If you prefer Sweet'N Low to sugar, there is a special pool for two-fifty a week. We do not do decaf. You are allowed to join the coffee pool of your choice, but you are not allowed to touch the Mr. Coffee.

This is the microwave oven. You are allowed to *heat* food in the microwave oven. You are not, however, allowed to *cook* food in the microwave oven.

We get one hour for lunch. We also get one fifteen-minute break in the morning, and one fifteen-minute break in the afternoon. Always take your breaks. If you skip a break, it is gone forever. For your information, your break is a privilege, not a right. If you abuse the break policy, we are authorized to rescind your breaks. Lunch, however, is a right, not a privilege. If you abuse the lunch policy, our hands will be tied, and we will be forced to look the other way. We will not enjoy that.

This is the refrigerator. You may put your lunch in it. Barry Hacker, who sits over there, steals food from this refrigerator. His petty theft is an outlet for his grief. Last New Year's Eve, while kissing his wife, a blood vessel burst in her brain. Barry Hacker's wife was two months pregnant at the time, and lingered in a coma for half a year before dying. It was a tragic loss for Barry Hacker. He hasn't been himself since. Barry Hacker's wife was a beautiful woman. She was also completely covered. Barry Hacker did not have to pay one dime. But his dead wife haunts him. She haunts all of us. We have seen her, reflected in the monitors of our computers, moving past our cubicles. We have seen the dim shadow of her face in our photocopies. She pencils herself in the receptionist's appointment book, with the notation: To see Barry Hacker. She has left messages in the receptionist's Voicemail box, messages garbled by the electronic chirrups and buzzes in the phone line, her voice echoing from an immense distance within the ambient hum. But the voice is hers. And beneath her voice, beneath the tidal whoosh of static and hiss, the gurgling and crying of a baby can be heard.

In any case, if you bring a lunch, put a little something extra in the bag for Barry Hacker. We have four Barrys in this office. Isn't that a coincidence?

This is Matthew Payne's office. He is our Unit Manager, and his door is always closed. We have never seen him, and you will never see him. But he is here. You can be sure of that. He is all around us.

This is the Custodian's Closet. You have no business in the Custodian's Closet.

And this, this is our Supplies Cabinet. If you need supplies, see Curtis Lance. He will log you in on the Supplies Cabinet Authorization Log, then give you a Supplies Authorization Slip. Present your pink copy of the Supplies Authorization Slip to Ellie Tapper. She will log you in on the Supplies Cabinet Key Log, then give you the key. Because the Supplies Cabinet is located outside the Unit Manager's office, you must be very quiet. Gather your supplies quietly. The Supplies Cabinet is divided into four sections. Section One contains letterhead stationery, blank paper and envelopes, memo and note pads, and so on. Section Two contains pens and pencils and typewriter and printer ribbons, and the like. In Section Three we have erasers, correction fluids, transparent tapes, glue sticks, et cetera. And in Section Four we have paper clips and push pins and scissors and razor blades. And here are the spare blades for the shredder. Do not touch the shredder, which is located over there. The shredder is of no concern to you.

Gwendolyn Stich sits in that office there. She is crazy about penguins, and collects penguin knickknacks: penguin posters and coffee mugs and stationery, penguin stuffed animals, penguin jewelry, penguin sweaters and tee shirts and socks. She has a pair of penguin fuzzy slippers she wears when working late at the office. She has a tape cassette of penguin sounds which she listens to for relaxation. Her favorite colors are black and white. She has personalized license plates that read: PEN GWEN. Every morning, she passes through all the cubicles to wish each of us a *good* morning. She brings Danish on Wednesdays for Hump Day morning break, and doughnuts on Fridays for T.G.I.F. afternoon break. She organizes the Annual Christmas Potluck, and is in charge of the Birthday List. Gwendolyn Stich's door is always open to all of us. She will always lend an ear, and put in a good word for you; she will always give you a hand or the shirt off her back, or a shoulder to cry on. Because her door is always open, she hides and cries in a stall in the women's room. And John LaFountaine—who, enthralled when a woman enters, sits quietly in his stall with his knees to his chest—John LaFountaine has heard her vomiting in there. We have come upon Gwendolyn Stich huddled in the stairwell, shivering in the updraft, sipping a Diet Mr. Pibb and hugging her knees. She does not let any of this interfere with her work. If it interfered with her work, she might have to be let go.

Kevin Howard sits in that cubicle over there. He is a serial killer, the one they call the Carpet Cutter, responsible for the mutilations across town. We're not supposed to know that, so do not let on. Don't worry. His compulsion inflicts itself on strangers only, and the routine established is elaborate and unwavering. The victim must be a white male, a young adult no older than thirty, heavyset, with dark hair and eyes, and the like. The victim must be chosen at random, before sunset, from a public place; the victim is followed home, and must put up a struggle; et cetera. The carnage inflicted is precise: the angle and direction of the incisions; the layering of skin and muscle tissue; the rearrangement of the visceral organs; and so on. Kevin Howard does not let any of this interfere with his work. He is, in fact, our fastest typist. He types as if he were on fire. He has a secret crush on Gwendolyn Stich, and leaves a red-foil-wrapped Hershey's Kiss on her desk every afternoon. But he hates Anika Bloom, and keeps well away from her. In his presence, she has uncontrollable fits of shaking and trembling. Her left palm does not stop bleeding.

In any case, when Kevin Howard gets caught, act surprised. Say that he seemed like a nice person, a bit of a loner, perhaps, but always quiet and polite.

This is the photocopier room. And this, this is our view. It faces southwest. West is down there, toward the water. North is back there. Because we are on the seventeenth floor, we are afforded a magnificent view. Isn't it beautiful? It overlooks the park, where the tops of those trees are. You can see a segment of the bay between those two buildings there. You can see the sun set in the gap between those two buildings over there. You can see this building reflected in the glass panels of that building across the way. There. See? That's you, waving. And look there. There's Anika Bloom in the kitchenette, waving back.

Enjoy this view while photocopying. If you have problems with the photocopier, see Russell Nash. If you have any questions, ask your supervisor. If you can't find your supervisor, ask Phillip Spiers. He sits over there. He'll check with Clarissa Nicks. She sits over there. If you can't find them, feel free to ask me. That's my cubicle. I sit in there.

Daniel Orozco's stories have appeared in *Best American Short Stories*, *Best American Mystery Stories*, and *Pushcart Prize* anthologies, and in *Harper's Magazine*, *Zoetrope*, *McSweeney's*, and others. He is the recipient of a National Endowment for the Arts fellowship. He teaches in the creative writing program at the University of Idaho.

Prior to returning to school in his thirties to study fiction writing, Orozco worked as an administrative assistant in Human Resources for about ten years, then as an office temp during his summers in graduate school. "It was for the most part very tedious work with very nice people," about whom he knew either very little or far more than he ever wanted to. Out of this clerical sojourn, "Orientation" was born.

"Orientation" was first published in *The Seattle Review* and was then selected for *Best American Short Stories 1995*. Copyright © 1994 by Daniel Orozco. It is reprinted here by permission of the author.

That Joy That Packs the Body

Andrew Miller

2:32 a.m. We stood along the line,
the conveyor switch-backing
past hands we hardly knew were our own,
sealed tightly in surgical gloves.
Into tins we packed the curds-n-whey
of what had been, an hour before,
mackerel, tuna, blue fish or shark.
Once done, we did it again,
keeping time to the steel strings
from the foreman's country station
and/or the spiritual of the canner,
and/or both there in the hull
of *The White Czar*, a high-yield
factory-ship out of Anchorage.
We worked side by side—Wade and I—
worked to cut and pack the hunks
until it came thoughtlessly in one
motion and our thoughts rose up
like breath to linger first
around swaying bulbs but then out
of the hold altogether. We drifted,
dreaming of women and money,
the horizon of our nearby country,
golden with morning—as it was said to be—
on the verge of our minds. There
two army-green cots awaited us
like wives, and we saw ourselves
diving for them in love, felt
their hard canvases flattening
against our faces until the night
brought freedom. Was it daydreaming?
or the two of us horsing around
with fish guts and knives—aping,
under that pure noise? The gestures—
flexed arms, fancy knifework—

of the veteran canners around us,
men we mocked because we were not them
and wished to be. Whatever it was,
when he heard the crisp shunk
of his cleaver,
Wade didn't scream. He stood,
marveling a minute
at the shortness of his index
and middle finger, stood regarding
the jets of blood shooting straight up
from the stumps. "Holy shit!"
someone was crying. "Holy shit!"
I was crying, letting the steel cans fall—
white metal and fish clattering
on the grating, tearing my sleeve,
knotting the already blood-soaked cloth
around those keys of bone
and all the while still crying,
"Holy shit. Holy shit."
Until the foreman finally came,
his machines not halting, not slowing,
fish piling on the floor in raw red lakes
and islands of heads and fins, and Wade,
"Where's my thumb? Where is it?"
Whole hours turn their backs
tonight, and the time's foremen
yells up from midship: "So be it."
Still, what was it that same morning
when we stood on the Texas-deck
after the ship's surgeon had sewn back
all we could find on the grated floor—
our blue country, sliding up to us
across the steel colored sea—
that demanded our happiness?
Not relief that more of Wade
was saved than lost, but happiness,
that joy that packs the body
without reasons, or plans, or sense
all for the habit the sun has
of striking us with a new day—
dawn obliterating day.

Andrew Miller was born and raised in Fresno, California. His poems have appeared in journals such as *Iron Horse, The Tusculum Review,* and *Hunger Mountain,* as well in the anthology *How Much Earth* (Heyday 2001). He now lives in Copenhagen, Denmark.

Miller writes, "Before becoming college-educated, I did the kinds of stupid jobs that most suburban kids do: fast-food, retail, service. These jobs allowed me to rub shoulders with those who would never graduate out of that kind of work. But to say that I gained insight into the lives of those people—many of whom were and are friends—would be a lie. Always I was a dilettante to true work, and now that I am a teacher of English, in many ways I still am.

"When I wrote 'That Joy That Packs the Body,' I wasn't thinking about the subject of working but about friendship. The work described in the poem was just the location in which that friendship occurred, and it offered the circumstances from which that friendship achieved its greatest and most absurd memory."

Copyright © Andrew Miller

Hatchet Man

Leo Parascondola

THE HUNTS POINT TERMINAL MARKET in the Southeast Bronx—or Hunts Point, as it has come to be known—replaced the old and dilapidated Washington Street Market in lower Manhattan as the primary terminal for the arrival of fresh fruit, produce, and other foods into the Port of New York. The lower precincts of Manhattan were being cleared for anticipated demolition and development— construction of the World Trade Center—and the Hunts Point Market opened for business in the mid-1960s. A decade or so later, I was a bus operator on MaBSTOA's Bx6 line, which stretched from Riverside Drive and West 157th Street in Manhattan, past Yankee Stadium in the Bronx, all the way to East 163rd Street, crossing Bruckner Boulevard and stopping only when it reached the immense stretch of redeveloped land provided by the Port Authority of New York for the Hunts Point Market.

The majority of men and women employed at the Market were dependent on public transportation. Rush hour trips into and out of Hunts Point were packed with passengers going to or returning from work in one of the dozens of establishments contained beyond the terminal gates. In the morning, bus stops from Yankee Stadium to Bruckner Boulevard were filled with people traveling into the Market. In the evening rush, hundreds of workers eager to get home would pour out of the various exit gates into the street, running to board the buses lined up to receive them.

Those bus drivers unlucky enough to be receiving Hunts Point passengers at the peak of the rush hour were in a particularly unenviable position. The trips were crowded and difficult, and traffic was always at its worst. And if it was summer and the Yankees were scheduled for a home game, the streets of the Bronx and Washington Heights were even more congested than usual, resulting in a snarl that could double the time of one's trip from one end of the line to the other.

THE BUS DRIVERS WITH WHOM I worked came to know their regular passengers and their habits. This might not necessarily include any intimacies (although nearly all male bus drivers thought of themselves as Lotharios), but it certainly resulted in a nodding acquaintance with who was on time, who was habitually late and had to run for the bus, who was regularly weighed down with packages, who boarded with children, who was silent or, alternatively, who talked too much, who had his/her fare ready, and who diddled with change for two or three blocks before returning to the front of the bus to deposit money into the farebox. While substituting for another Bx6 driver away on vacation, I discovered that one of the finer points of knowledge about the line was who paid the fare, who didn't pay the fare, and who paid the fare after a fashion.

What I mean is that some workers had made arrangements with this particular driver, completely illegally and without the knowledge of management, to pay their bus fare in small packages of fruits and vegetables obtained inside the Market. How they obtained these packages remains a mystery, but one could reasonably guess that these comestibles had been obtained by application of the five-finger discount. Before he left for his vacation, this driver had warned me to be alert for particular passengers who were in the habit of relying upon the aforementioned "discount" in lieu of cash payment of their fare. The most astounding of these individuals, and by far the most astounding passenger I can remember ever encountering, was Hatchet Man.

The regular driver on this particular route, an African American man with considerable seniority in the system, said to me, "Leo, watch out for Hatchet Man. He don't pay no fare. Sometimes he pays with fruit, but whatever he do, don't give him no shit. Mind your own business." Hatchet Man, you have probably guessed, was not his real name. I don't know his real name, and I don't imagine anyone ever did, except his parents. Hatchet Man was an enormous black man, well over six feet in height, weighing in at around 300 pounds, with a wild, unkempt mane of hair that radiated out from the globe that was his head as if he had been electrocuted only moments ago. He looked mean and ugly, and he smelled so bad that other passengers would automatically give him the right of way. Hatchet Man defined his own space without fear of contradiction or argument. People were just plain afraid of Hatchet Man, and with good reason. His appearance was that of an angry ogre; he never spoke to anyone and conveyed a palpable sense of doom or danger. Hatchet Man just looked crazy. If you had any ideas about fucking with Hatchet Man, his mere appearance would wipe those ideas right out of your mind. In fact, you would have to be out of your mind to think about fucking with Hatchet Man.

Hatchet Man always boarded the bus with three or four large shopping bags full of stuff, much like the array of shopping bags that have come to be associated with certain homeless people in large cities. This is not to say that Hatchet Man was a homeless person. He was, from all the evidence, employed within the Hunts Point Terminal Market and made the same evening rush hour trip out of the Market every day with the same driver, the man for whom I was now substituting. The considerable crowd waiting to board the bus parted like the Red Sea did for Moses, and the person who I knew could only be Hatchet Man walked up the front stairs of the bus. He looked down at me, temporarily confused, blinked, and walked to the back of the bus without paying his fare.

The other passengers boarded in the more conventional way, and I didn't see him again until he got off the bus on East 163rd Street. So far, so good.

My second encounter with Hatchet Man began in much the same way as the first. Red Sea . . . climb the stairs . . . confused glare . . . walk to the back of the bus. End of story. Or so I thought. When the bus was full and the trip begun, well away from the Market, I approached the bus stop just before the one for Bruckner Boulevard. This corner was a major drug market, with addicts, dealers, hookers, and cruisers from other neighborhoods, constantly bustling back and forth across the sidewalk. On this occasion, several young guys, looking tough and defiant, jumped on the bus after a few people got off. They walked right by me without paying their fare or acknowledging any intention of doing so. In these cases, I had been instructed by veteran drivers simply to announce loudly that the person or persons had "forgotten" to pay their fare and to ask them to come forward to pay it. After that announcement, the affair was officially closed as far as I was concerned. I was paid to drive a bus, not to enforce the laws of the City of New York. Whether they paid or didn't pay, I had been schooled by many other drivers, was none of my business. I had been warned many times that the only trouble you had on this job was the trouble you made for yourself. I thought I had successfully negotiated yet another catastrophe. No such luck.

These same guys, upon hearing my comment, charged back to the front of the bus spoiling for a fight. They circled the driver's area, hanging over the metal bar that served as a grab-rail and also separated the driver from the passengers. Apparently they took great offense to either the idea that they had to pay a fare or that I should remind them of this obligation. In short, they seemed about to kick my ass. They actually started the process by leaning over the bar and smacking the top of my head while I tried to explain that I didn't care if they paid, that I was just doing "my job." To their thinking, my job was to drive the bus and shut up.

Just when I was convinced that my ass was done for, there was an enormous racket from the back of the bus: a primordial kind of roar, a sound so loud and shocking that all of us—my assailants, the other passengers, me—turned our heads to see what had created this unnatural sound. Hatchet Man stood alone in the middle of the aisle, like a great Colossus astride Rhodes. Upon hearing his scream, people had jumped away from him in fear, not knowing the meaning of his bellowing or the intention behind it. Hatchet Man screamed from the back of the bus, "I want to go home." One of the young guys, momentarily frozen by the novelty of the sight, screamed back, "Mind your own fucking business, old man."

Hatchet Man was struck by this response, as if vaguely offended. He reached down with one hand into one of his shopping bags. When it came out, at the end of his fist was a bright shiny hatchet, glowing in the interior lights of the bus. He took a few steps forward and repeated, "I want to go home." He quickly followed this with a warning: "Get off the bus." The young guys laughed until Hatchet Man began to stride toward the front of the bus, hatchet raised high in his right hand. Passengers jumped out of his way, once more imitating the Red Sea. When Hatchet Man got to about the midpoint of the bus, the fare-beaters scrambled out the front door and ran in the opposite direction. Hatchet Man stopped next to me, looked down at me, and said, "Drive the bus." I obeyed.

When Hatchet Man departed the bus at his usual stop, he came all the way to the front of the bus and, before exiting, turned to me, reached into another of his shopping bags and handed me two grapefruits. Paid!

"Hatchet Man" represents a small slice of **Leo Parascondola**'s experience of twenty-one years working as a bus driver in New York City. From 1973 until 1994, Parascondola "drove a twenty-ton vehicle around Manhattan and the Bronx, delivering people to their daily destinations, getting to know them like a bartender—from the comfortable distance that encourages intimate anonymity."

Since then, Parascondola has attended graduate school and worked at various levels of higher education, including teaching college-level writing, American and world literature, and administering a college preparation curriculum for adult learners. His publications include a chapter in *Tenured Bosses, Disposable Teachers: Writing in the Managed University* (Southern Illinois University 2004), an anthology he co-edited, as well as a variety of articles and interviews in *Workplace: A Journal of Academic Labor*.

Parascondola writes, "While driving a bus, I was doing a different kind of learning work—collecting stories about people's lives (as I variously came to know and/or imagine them), discovering many fascinating individuals, some famous, some eccentric and interesting, others quite crazy and threatening. Along these borders—eccentric, interesting, crazy, threatening—you will find Hatchet Man."

Copyright © Leo Parascondola

Coins

Mona Simpson

I ALWAYS SAY, WE ARE the second-oldest profession. That is because we serve the needs of women. And what we do is harder. Because we are giving more than only our bodies. Our bodies too—I carry him, he is now already forty pounds.

We may be selling our time—we are here in America for the money, that is our purpose—but still we give our love. Some things they are not for sale.

DEE TOLD ME, WHEN I first came here, I don't need to teach you children. You have been a mother to five, she said, you know. Children, they are not hard.

But most you need to think about the mother. Here, the mothers are the ones who throw the tantrums.

You may have had nannies, but you have not before been a nanny.

Dee has always been my teacher, of America. I was never the only one learning. No, in the house of Dee there is always a crowd. After only one month, I was no longer even the newest. But I understood that I was the teacher's favorite pupil. I had never before been the favorite of any teacher; I used to be the favorite of the class. When the teacher turned around to the blackboard, I stood up and made the face that caused everyone to laugh. Dee believed I had the talent for baby-sitting, because of the schools my children attend in Manila. Even in the provinces, people know the names of our best colleges. I was the only one Dee ever asked for a job from her employer. "The others, they are not for Beverly Hills," she said, quiet because that is Dee's way of talking.

I HOLD MY HANDS OPEN in front of me to take away whatever my employer is beginning. If she starts to sew a button, I finish. If she runs water to rinse a lettuce, I say, I will be the one. When the husband spills something and pounds a wet napkin at the spot, I reach out my hands and say, Give it to me. I will make it clean.

All the while with a smile. It is not hard. No. Not when you have a purpose. And I have five purposes, the youngest seventeen, entering medicine.

But I have a good job. The parents of Ricardo get him in the morning, while they eat their breakfast. I fix their bed, take the glass of water from the side table, pick up Kleenexes.

Always the parents first, Dee said. A kid cannot fire you. Even here. They can love you but they cannot pay you. And anyway, they will forgive.

WHEN I STARTED WITH RICHARD, Dee said, I'm not going to tell you how to love, because either that will happen or it won't. And in six jobs, twenty-five years, she said, only once it did not happen to her. And then you need to quit. Because you cannot do the job if you do not love the baby.

But children, they are easy to love. Especially if you have them from a baby. Ricardo, they put him in my hands the first day at the hospital. They gave him to me.

Call me Lola, I whispered. That will be my name for you. (I was two years in America, I had been only a housekeeper. He is my first baby here.)

For me it is the parents who are more hard to love.

No, DEE SAID, AT THE beginning, I will not tell you how to love. I wouldn't if I could, because what I would tell you if I knew would be how not to so much. Because you will love him the same as your own and he never will. They love you, but it is not the same.

"I know, I know," I told her then. "I am a mother, too."

But now I think, if you can keep them until they are five, then they will not forget you. I ask Ricardo, "Will you remember your Lola?"

"Why? You are not going away," he says.

"Some day," I tell him, "I will return to my place."

"And what will you do there?"

I will just sit in my house. Look at my kids' diplomas.

"COMEON COMEON COMEON COMEON COMEON. CometoLola. I have something for you," I say. Because he is very angry.

Usually, it is the dad. But today, it was the mother he was hitting. She has her hand on her eye and I dab ice, the way I do with his boo-boos. My employer when she is hurt she sounds like an animal.

So I take him in my arms, away. We turn on ground now in the yard and he is strong, three years old, I cannot so easily hold him. And Lola told a lie. I do not have anything for him. So I make promises.

"Some day," I whisper, "I am going to take you home with me. And there we will make the ice candy."

He lies still in my arms, not any longer fighting. His bones they feel different now, not pushing to get out. They fall in a pattern, like the veins of a leaf.

"I will put you in my pocket and I will feed you one candy every day. And you will be happy. Because the ocean at our place it is very blue. The sky, higher than here. And the fruits that grow on trees, very sweet. Durians, mangos, atis."

His head hangs down between his knees, but he is listening.

"In my pocket I will give you one lichee. You can bounce it for a ball."

"If you were a kangaroo you would have a pouch," he grumbles. He is better now, slower his heart.

Through the window I see my employer on the telephone. She holds the ice to her eye and thumps around the kitchen talking to her friend, long-distance, a woman who reads many books about the raising of children. When my employer becomes upset she calls this friend, the full-time mother.

My employer works and she has the American problem of being guilty. But you should not be guilty to your children. It is for them that you are working. I am here for my own, to pay for their professional education.

He is better now. Only his mouth smears outside the edges. He will come with me. I lift him into the stroller and promise candy, not the ice candy, just candy we can buy here. "But-ah, do not tell your mother." I call, "Excuse but, we are going now."

"Is that okay? Thanks, Lola." This is how my employer believes she cannot live without me. She is telling her friend who reads the books that he is better with me than with her.

And her friend will say to her that it is perfectly normal.

"Play date," she says into the phone cross-country. "I can't even stand the word."

SMELL," I SAY. "DO YOU have a poo-poo?" I pull his diaper back. I am paid to smell that. By the time I change him and we are ready to leave, the mother is going too.

Claire walks out into the world, away from us, holding keys in front of her, ready to start her car.

With a child small small it is a little like a ball and chain. You are never free. Not even sleeping. So with her it is a prance almost, an escape. She can walk under the old pines of the university, talking about an even older book.

But what she said to her friend on the phone is true. With me, he is no problem. When she takes him with her, it is not the same for me. Some weight is lifted off my lap. I have no purpose. For me alone here, I am too light.

My employer she says, When a baby comes home from the hospital, a Filipina should arrive with him. That, for her, would make a perfect world.

I TAKE RICARDO TO THE store to show him our place on the map.

I say, Where is Lola from, and he points.

Very good.

I told my employers already, When they go to Europe to celebrate their tenth anniversary, I will take Ricardo to the Philippines. We are already saving for the tickets. I have one hundred twenty-five put away. I cannot save much because every month I have many tuitions. I even wrote in a letter to my husband that I will bring Ricardo home. Only my kids, they do not yet know. They are a little jealous, especially BongBong, my son, who has two children. And it is true. I am closer to Richard than I am to my own grandchildren. Because I see him every day.

He is my albino grandson.

WE ARE JUST ALONE. This neighborhood is ours, during the daytime. You do not see the white mothers walking. Only sliding in and out of cars, carrying shopping bags. In my place, I was, at one time, one of these ladies. Now that I see from afar, it looks like a lot of work.

I push him in the stroller and he sits. That is the good of fighting: it makes them very tired. The sun is solid, like many small weights on our arms. We pass the park, and in the distance we see baby-sitters and children, so I roll him under the tall trees.

All the while, I keep talking to him. Dee told me, You have always to talk to him. Even a baby, it is very important that they hear words. And I always talked to him, more than to my kids, because my kids I had one after the other, five in ten years. But with Richard, I talk and talk, I tell him everything, and see, now, he is very *madaldal.* He understands more than one hundred words Tagalog.

In the class of 2020, at Harvard University, which is where the parents of Ricardo would like him to go, there will be six Santa Monica boys saying to the cooks in the cafeteria, Excuse, where is my adobo?

Lola by then will be swaying in a hammock, back in the Philippines.

"What for?" he says to me.

He is young. He does not yet understand the importance of rest.

"THEY CHANGE WHEN THEY MOVE to the big house," Rita says, kneeling in the sandbox, holding a sieve, "they really change."

For your salary, I am thinking, let them change! Rita gets one hundred dollars a day. Six months ago, her employers transferred to a fourteen-room mansion they had custom-built for themselves. My employer's house is the smallest. We compare jobs, the same as women will compare their husbands. Usually, you would trade a part of what you have, but not all. If you are wanting to trade all, then there is trouble.

"But-ah, your employers, they are good," I say. I am always the one telling baby-sitters to stay in their jobs. Because too much change, it is bad for children. I look at the two little girls in the sandbox. Of all of our kids, those two of Rita are the best behaved. Maybe because they are Asian (Chinese, adopted).

"They don't think I will leave but I can leave," Rita says. "Lot of people they are looking Filipinos."

"The richest people all want Filipinos," Kitkat says.

"Like a BMW," I say. "We are status symbols." With only women, I can make them laugh.

"No, you know why? You know what Prudence told me?" Rita whispers. "It is because we are quiet. Prudence told me in the hospital they have a joke: What does 'yes' mean in Tagalog? 'Yes' means fuck you."

"That is right. Fuck you." Kitkat says out loud.

"Shhh," I say. Ricardo is a mynah bird, and sure enough the head springs up.

"What?" he says. Always, What? He is very intelligent.

I have never said out loud but I have thought before, I am not the same as other baby-sitters. A part of me, I want to be known for what I can do. I want to be seen alone. At a few certain things, maybe I am the best.

The baby-sitters stand and brush sand off their laps, ready to go. "Tomorrow at the house of Rita," Kitkat calls, hitting me in the stomach.

"I want to go there now," Ricardo says. "To Ritahouse."

In their voices, that is the only time it is our house.

BACK HOME, I HAVE READY a project. We put into cardboard all the coins we can find. His mother told us we could have the pennies for the choo-choo bank, our place to save for tickets to the Philippines.

We also find nickels, dimes, and quarters, and I have brown tubes from the bank for those too. There is always money in this house, little puddles, where people empty their pockets. "It is a hunt," I tell Ricardo, and we discover nests in the carpet, piles on counters, little dishes filled. If someone came to the door with a pizza and I needed ten dollars, I could always collect, in coat pockets and cups, next to little slips of paper with writing. My house in the Philippines is like this, too. I leave money places I forget. That way if I become very low I can dig.

That is what Lola calls her secret garden. People who too much like order, they do not have this security, the many seeds.

Richard is a very good worker. We pile the tubes of coins. We build with them an American log cabin, using Richard's Play-Doh for the mortar. If we can also keep the quarters and dimes and nickels, we will have a lot already. The pennies they are ours already. But the rest I will have to call and ask.

Claire answers her office phone, "Hey."

"We are wanting," I explain. "Can we have the money also for the silver coins we find?"

"Sure, Lola," she says. Usually she will say to me, "Sure, Lola." There are certain people in life, you know, they will always say to you yes.

AT THE BANK, WE WAIT in line a long time. Then when we go to the front, the lady acts all business, making a total of the rolled dimes. I say to her, "This little man rolled the nickels by himself."

While she finishes the silver coins, I lift a bag of pennies from his wagon. It is very heavy. We have many pennies. We took apart the fort and the log cabin. We counted forty dollars from nickels, twenty-seven dollars from dimes, and one hundred and three dollars from pennies. I lift Ricardo up so he can see.

But the lady pushes our tubes out of the cage. "We cannot take pennies," she says.

Richard picks one roll in his hand, to give it back to her. I remember this moment, again and again. It is like the giving of a flower. He does not yet understand.

"We don't take these," she says.

For a second, then, his face changes, what his mother calls berry-with-a-frown. Cartoon looks, they are really true on children. The upside-down smile, an open mouth, then he is bawling. And he throws the roll of pennies at the lady's face.

Her hand goes to a place above her eye. "I cannot help you," she says, setting the teeth. She has already given us the paper money for the other coins. She looks at me with hate. I have seen real hate only a few times in my life. The shape of diamonds, it is shocking. But she is hurt above the eye and I am not white.

"Come, Ricardo." I fight him down into the wagon. I will have to pull all the rolls of pennies and him. "We will make our getaway."

But he runs dragging pennies to a garbage can and begins dumping the tubes in the open top. Still crying but he is mad now. Also mad. I have to stop him. This is not right. All our effort. With him what I do is almost tackle. Lola is not a big person. But I get on the floor and hold him until the fight is out. Then I tell him a story, keeping him in my lap.

"Once upon a time," I say, "I work in Beverly Hills. In a house that is very fancy. Three layers. Floors like a checkerboard. All marble.

"When I was first here, new, the lady she open the door and saw me and right away she said, You are hired. She told me, she knew like that—and when she said that she snap her fingers—you will never guess from why. She said, because of the way I tie my sneakers."

"How did you, Lola?"

"She thought Lola was a tidy person. But Lola is not so very tidy, not really. I can be. If I have to. And for her I was neat. I clean everything. But that is not the way I live my life. It is too much time, always straightening. I would rather see people, taste some part of life.

"The lady's husband, he had an office, and she wanted that to be neat too. She hired me extra to go on the Saturday and straighten. He was there working while I clean. And he had one jar like this, up to my waist, full with pennies. I asked him did he want me to get tubes from the bank. And he said, 'You can take the pennies.' But I could not lift.

"And so I came back Sunday, my day off, and I sat on the floor out of his way and put all the pennies into tubes. He stepped around me when he went down the hall to use the rest room or the machines. He'd ask me how much money it was as he went by, and I'd tell him the total so far.

" 'Thirty-six dollars,' I said.

" 'Good job, Lola.'

"The next time it was ninety-two.

"By the last time he passed, I was at two hundred and six. That time his face looked strange, like two lines cross over it. He went down the hall and I heard xeroxing.

"On his way back, he stopped over my legs and said, 'Maybe you better leave the pennies.'

" 'Whatever you say. It is up to you.'

"When he was back in his office on the phone, I stood and left it all there, the rolled pennies, the pile on the floor, the jar turned over. I took the bus to the place of Dee, and I never went back to that house. That was the end of my career for a Beverly Hills nanny."

"Is that when you came to me?"

"That is before," I say. "You were not yet born. Still I had to wait one year more. But-ah, when the husband took the pennies I rolled to the bank, you know what they are telling him? They are telling him, too, what they are telling us. 'We cannot help you.' And you know what he will do then?"

"He shouldn't have taken your pennies, Lola. He is a bad man."

"A little bad. Listen, you know what he will do? He will throw the pennies in the garbage and walk away in a hurry, he is always in a hurry. He is too busy, see?"

Now I fish with my arm in the garbage, feeling among wet things for our tubes, the ones Ricardo threw.

"But we will do something else. Come. You watch Lola." I pull him in the wagon out of the bank into the bright air. We go to the five-and-dime. And then the candy shop. And then the Discovery Store, where we study the globe. Each place, I count out the money in pennies. I put in piles of ten on the counter, so it is easy for the register clerk.

My father always told me, Spend your small money first. He remembered in our place when money became light, the smaller denominations would not buy anymore. And still at that time, he told me, there was so much wealth.

In the wagon, Ricardo is eating long orange and green candy worms.

"See, in the bank it is nothing, but out here in the world it is money. Not for the Philippines, but we can still buy. Every day a little. It is our own private fund. Our trust fund. I trust you and you trust me. You have your candy. Now, we will use some pennies to buy Lola her cup of coffee."

That is what my kids and Ricardo, they will remember. That Lola loved her coffee.

WHEN WE RETURN HOME, THE hallways round to caves, warm, dark already. I hear the mother of Richard making dinner in the kitchen.

I take the tomatoes from my employer. "I will be the one," I say. That is our way. My employer did not grow up living with helpers. She cannot easily ask. Also, my employer is a very good cook. I am happy to chop chop, while Ricardo plays on the floor with his action figures.

Tonight, Claire's eye, where he hit, shines black-and-blue, there is yellow also. Over it, she has applied makeup.

"Now he's fine," she sighs when I bend to look closer. "I don't know what I'm doing wrong."

"It is the age too," I say. But my children, they were not like this, not even my boy. Here in America, they are different. They are also taller.

My employer whispers, "Maybe I should find a psychologist for him. Do you think this is all still normal?"

Really, I do not know. The hitting, too, I worry. I cannot tell her about the woman at the bank. "You are talking to the wrong person," I say. "Because-ah, I like naughty boys."

She sighs, but she is better. We are like magicians. With us, too, there is what the employer sees and there is sleight of hand.

I FEED HIM HIS DINNER because that is easier for the baby-sitter.

Then, when Ricardo has eaten enough, I get out of the way and let the family sit together. My employer gives me my plate, covered with a napkin, and I carry it back to my own place.

At first, they used to ask me to eat with them, but I always said no.

Dee advised me, Don't, even if they ask. Americans do not know what they want. They will invite you, and then later on they will pine for their privacy. Americans need very much privacy. Because it is a big big land.

And the parents of Richard work all day, it is their only time together. Also, if I was eating with them, when Ricardo needed more milk or the salt was not on the table, I would be the one getting up and down. I like to put my feet up, watch the TV. It is important to have hours in the day when you are comfortable.

Later on, he can come back to my place, but then it is not my job anymore, he is a visitor, my buddy-buddy. And he is very good in my house. He never breaks anything. He looks at my pictures, he knows the names of my children, and we study the map.

We will save for the globe, on a layaway plan. Each day, we will give the man fifty pennies. It will help teach Ricardo counting.

The parents do not come out here. My work is done. They leave the dishes, I do them in the morning. My money is earned. I can sit. That is my day.

So, some people across the Pacific; they had better be studying.

Mona Simpson is the author of the following novels: *Off Keck Road* (Knopf 2001), which was a finalist for the PEN/Faulkner Prize and winner of the Chicago Tribune's Heartland Prize; *A Regular Guy* (Knopf 1997); *The Lost Father* (Knopf 1992); and *Anywhere But Here* (Knopf 1986). Her stories and articles have been published in *Atlantic Monthly, Harper's Magazine, Granta, Pushcart Prize* anthologies, *The Paris Review Anthology*, and *London Review of Books*. Simpson is the recipient of a Whiting Writer's Award, a Guggenheim grant, a grant from the Lila Wallace–Reader's Digest Foundation, and the Hodder Fellowship at Princeton University. She lives in Santa Monica, California, with her two children.

Simpson writes, "I started working for money at age thirteen, claiming I was fourteen. I landed a two-week job wrapping Christmas presents in a Beverly Hills clothing store. My mother helped me out by fudging the year of my birth to the Social Security office. I suppose, if the system holds, I'll receive benefits a year early. To this day, I can make a tight package and a plausible bow. My career as a capitalist continued through high school. In the early years, I scooped at an ice cream store, eventually rising to the rank of assistant manager, which meant I got to stay after the front doors were locked. I sat and counted the money in a back booth while the cool, long-haired boys who worked as dishwashers mopped the floor. This provided my first education in Top 40 music; I often find myself chattering my teeth along to those popular songs of the 70s.

"All those years, I watched the numbers rise in my bank account. It's probably fitting that I've ended up working in the least worldly profession and going about it in the least profitable way. The novel from which 'Coins' is excerpted, has been in the making ten years and is still not finished. . . .

"Often, I think, displaced people imagine themselves leading double lives. So a portion of my identity has always been privately siphoned into what would have been if I had stayed in Wisconsin. A whole imaginary path emerged—who my young loves might have been, where I'd have gone to college, even what I would have become."

"Coins" was first published in *Harper's Magazine* (August 2002); it was then anthologized in *Best American Short Stories* and excerpted on *This American Life*. Copyright © 2002 by Mona Simpson. It is reprinted here by permission of the author.

Morrison's, 1968

Rick Campbell

In the Riviera Beach black morning
where the secret cold is hidden
from tourists, where only workers
and fishermen on an early mackerel tide
know freezing is a South Florida word,
a 17 year old boy walks to the back door
of Morrison's Cafeteria. Rats scatter
as he mumbles past bloody fryer boxes
and through the greasy backdoor smell.
He hits the lights at the breaker box,
stumbles to the bathroom for starched
white work pants. Ten more minutes
he figures he can steal,
so he sits on the toilet and leans his head
on the sticky wall. Chef Narville bangs
the door as he walks down the hall
to change in the black bathroom.
Saturday begins. This is it.
In another world the sun will rise
over the sea. Lovers and drunks sleep
in the sand. His girlfriend is wrapped
in blankets, home. Her touch
still on his hands, but even that
won't save him, so he struggles out
to the stockroom. One more day, he thinks.

Rick Campbell was born in 1952, in Baden, Pennsylvania. Baden was across the Ohio River from a Jones and Laughlin steel mill, and most of the Beaver Valley owed its financial existence to mills—U.S. Steel, American Bridge, and many others. Campbell lived in Baden until 1966, when he moved to Florida with his mother. "Perhaps because of this dislocation," Campbell writes, "when I started writing poetry, many years later at the University of Florida, I was almost obsessed with the mills, mill towns, and the Ohio River as my subjects."

Campbell had a number of "dirty and stupid" jobs after high school. "I usually worked a while, then left to hitchhike or travel by van across the country. I worked temp jobs in Denver, Houston, and San Diego. I was a land surveyor, a bricklayer, a pool boy, and a factory worker."

Campbell's poem "Morrison's, 1968" is about his time as a stock boy at Morrison's Cafeteria when he was in high school. "Finally, after years of this life, I went to college, got a few degrees, and ended up being a teacher and a writer." Campbell now lives in North Florida, Gadsden County, outside of Tallahassee, Florida, where he teaches at Florida A&M University and runs Anhinga Press. Campbell's books include *Setting the World in Order* (Texas Tech University Press 2001), *The Traveler's Companion* (Black Bay 2004), and *Dixmont* (Autumn House 2008).

"Morrison's, 1968" originally appeared in *Setting the World in Order* (Texas Tech University Press 2001). Copyright © 2001 by Rick Campbell. It is reprinted here by permission of the author.

The Midnight Tour

Marcus Laffey

WHEN I WENT TO WORK midnights a few months ago, it was discovered that I didn't have a nickname. You need one, to talk casually over the radio: "Stix, you getting coffee?" "Chicky, did you check the roof?" "O.V., T., G.Q., can you swing by?" Nicknames never stuck to me, for some reason, and I always thought that nicknaming yourself was like talking to yourself, something that made you look foolish if you were overheard. So Hawkeye, the Hat, Hollywood, Gee Whiz, Big E., the Count, Roller Coaster, and Fierce pitched a few:

"'Hemingway'—nah, they'd know it was you."

"'Ernest' is better."

"Or 'Clancy'—he'd be a good one to have."

"What about 'Edgar'?"

"What from?"

"Edgar Allan Poe."

"What about 'Poe'?"

As I thought about it, the fit was neat: Poe, too, in his most famous poem, had worked, weak and weary, upon a midnight dreary. He moved to New York City in 1844, the same year that legislation created the New York City Police Department. And he wrote the first detective story ever, "The Murders in the Rue Morgue," in which the killer turns out to be a demented orangutan with a straight razor. There is also a brilliant detective, an earnest sidekick, and a mood of languor and gloom—all now hallmarks of a genre that has endured for a century and a half. Poe spent his last years in the Bronx, living and working in a cottage that is midway between where I live and where I work. I am a police officer in the Bronx, where kids sometimes call the cops "po-po." And so "Poe" it was.

Midnights for Edgar Allan Poe seemed less a time than a territory, a place of woefully distant vistas, as if he were stargazing from the bottom of a well. A lot of that has to do with needing sleep, I think. Everyone on the late tour lacks sleep, and this state of worn-out wakefulness while the rest of the world is dreaming tends to stimulate thoughts that meander. Each precinct has a list of "cooping-prone locations," which are out-of-the-way places, under bridges and by rail yards and the like, where bosses are supposed to check to make sure patrol cars haven't stopped in for a nap. The list is posted in the station house, and when you're tired it reads like a recommendation, a Zagat guide for secret sleep, as if it might be saying, "St. Mary's Park, with its rolling hills and abundant trees, offers superb concealment in a pastoral setting—we give it four pillows!"

On midnights, we talk about sleep the way frat boys talk about sex. Did you get any last night? How was it? Nah, nah, but this weekend, believe me, I'm gonna go all night long! Although I've asked practically everyone on the tour how long it takes for your body to adjust to an upside-down life, only three people have given precise answers, which were "Two months," "Four years," and "Never." Nevermore.

I went to midnights after my old narcotics team split up. It seemed like a good interim assignment, a way station until something better came along, and I thought I could use the free time during the day. Mostly, you drive around and check things out until a job comes over the radio. There are fewer jobs than during the other tours of duty—although the jobs tend to be more substantial—and even on weekend nights they tend to taper off after two or three in the morning. You usually have to check a few buildings, and you'd probably get into trouble if you never wrote a ticket, but you have more time to yourself than on any other tour. My uncle finished his thirty-three years as a cop working midnights in the Bronx; he would have said that he liked it because the bosses leave you alone. Still, to be back on patrol feels odd sometimes, and when I think about my past and the past of this place I wonder where I'm going. It can bring on a terminal feeling.

One night, I drove with my partner to the corner of 132nd Street and Lincoln Avenue—a cooping-prone location, though that wasn't the reason for the visit—which is a dead end at the very bottom of the Bronx, with a warehouse on one side and a parking lot on the other. Across the black shimmer of the river you can see Harlem and the salt piles along the FDR. The Bronx begins here physically, and it began here historically as well; this was the site of Jonas Bronck's farmhouse. Not much is known about him: he was a Swedish sea captain who was induced to settle the area by the Dutch West India Company. A peace treaty signed at Bronck's house ended years of sporadic but bloody skirmishes between the Dutch and the Weckquasgeeks. Bronck didn't have much to do with it, but his house was the only one around. "When did he move?" my partner asked. It was a funny question, because it made me think of the Bronx as a place where people come from but not where they stay, if luck is on their side.

The Bronx was a place of slow beginnings: Bronck came here in 1639 to homestead, and at the beginning of the twentieth century there was still farmland in the South Bronx; it became citified only as the subway was built. A person alive today could have witnessed the borough's entire metropolitan career: two generations as a vibrant, blue-collar boomtown, and one as a ravaged and riotous slum. When Jimmy Carter visited Charlotte Street in September 1977, he saw vacant and collapsing buildings inhabited by junkies and packs of wild dogs. A week later, during a broadcast of the World Series at Yankee Stadium, there was a fire at a school a few blocks from the game. Millions watched it as Howard Cosell intoned, "The Bronx is burning." One of my uncles was a fireman here at the time, and he told me that they were busier than the London fire department during the Blitz.

My partner and I cruised up to 142nd Street between Willis and Brook Avenues, a block with a row of little houses on one side and a school on the other. I used to chase a lot of junkies down that street when they were buying heroin with the brand name President from the projects on the corner. A hundred years ago, the Piccirilli brothers, sculptors from Pisa, had a studio here, where they carved the statue for the Lincoln Memorial, but I don't suppose the dope was named in any commemorative spirit. Four blocks up and two over, Mother Teresa's order runs a soup kitchen and a shelter next to the Church of St. Rita, a boxy old building painted robin's-egg blue. The work the order does is holy and noble, but for us there is something embarrassing about it: nuns reassigned from leper duty in Calcutta to lend us a hand. There was a picture in the *News* a few years back of Mother Teresa and Princess Diana visiting the mission together, and one of my old partners was there, standing guard, just out of the frame. A little farther out of the frame is the building where Rayvon Evans died: a little boy whose parents kept his corpse in a closet until the fluids seeped through to the floor below and the neighbors complained. No one was ever charged with the murder, because there wasn't enough left of him to determine how he died. There is a garden dedicated to Rayvon, but no sign of the Princess or the sculptors. Memory is short here, but the past is visible all around you—at least until the present calls you back. It can take time for your eyes to adjust.

MIDNIGHTS TEND TO MAGNIFY THINGS, to set them in sharp relief against the empty night, like gems on a black velvet cloth. You meet lonely people who seem more solitary and sorrowful at night, such as the chubby little woman who reclined in her armchair like a pasha after attempting suicide by taking three Tylenol PMs. Or the woman with dye-drowned blond hair going green, who denied trying to hurt herself, though her boyfriend confided that she had: "She slapped herself, hard." Domestic disputes are all the more squalid and small-hearted when they take place at five in the morning—like the one between two middle-aged brothers who were at each other's throats hours before their mother's funeral. The place stank and the walls seethed with roaches. One brother had a weary and beaten dignity; he was sitting on the couch with his overcoat and an attaché case when we arrived, like a salesman who'd just lost a commission. The other brother shouted drunkenly, jerking and flailing like a dervish afflicted with some unknown neurological misfiring. They had argued because he had started drinking again.

I took the jerky one aside, to let him vent a little. His room was littered with cans of Night Train; military papers and alcohol rehab certificates were taped to the wall. As he punched the honorable discharge to emphasize that his had been a life of accomplishment, a burst of roaches shot out from underneath. I wanted to punch his rehab diploma, to show that he still had some work to do, but I thought better of it.

My partner and I knew that we would be back if both brothers remained there, and we dreaded the idea of having to lock one of them up before the funeral, so we asked the sane brother if he wouldn't mind leaving for a while. He agreed that it was the best thing to do; we agreed that it was deeply unfair. He used to work as a security guard, and he offered us his business card. "If there's anything I can do for you gentlemen," he said, and he went out to walk until daybreak.

If some people call because they need someone—anyone—to talk to, there are others for whom we're the last people they want to see. For them, we arrive the way the Bible says judgment will: like a thief in the night. It felt like that when we showed up to take a woman's children away. We were escorting two caseworkers from the Administration of Children's Services who had a court order to remove the one-, two-, and three-year-old kids of a crackhead I'll call Pamela. The midnight visit was a sneak attack, as she had dodged the caseworkers the day before. We were there—not to put too fine a point on it—as hired muscle.

When we knocked, a woman answered ("Who?") and then delayed ten minutes, muttering excuses ("Hold on," and "Let me get something on," and "Who is it, again?"), before surrendering to threats to kick the door down. She was just a friend, she said, helping to clean up—probably in anticipation of such a visit, Pamela was out. Yes, there were kids in the back, but they were Pamela's sister's kids, and the sister was out, too. As we looked in on the sleeping children, another woman emerged from a back bedroom, and she was equally adamant: "But those are my kids, and I'm not Pamela, I'm her sister, Lorraine! I can show you you're making a mistake!"

We grilled both women, but they never deviated from their story, and we could find no baby pictures or prescription bottles or anything else that would tie these children to the case. So when "Lorraine" said she could prove that they were hers if we'd let her call her mother to get her ID we agreed, as it would clearly demonstrate whether we were professional public servants doing a difficult job or dimwitted repo men hauling off the wrong crack babies.

But she didn't call for her ID, she called for reinforcements, and the apartment was soon flooded with angry women. We held the baby boy while Pamela managed to grab the two girls; then a neighbor took one of the girls as Pamela tried to get out with the other, making it all the way into the hall. More cops came, and one started after her, telling her to stop, but a neighbor blocked his way, howling, "Call the cops! Call the cops and have him arrested! He ain't leaving till the cops come and arrest him!"

The sergeant called for backup, and even more cops arrived, two of them running up twelve flights of stairs—but then one had to lie down in the stairwell, and the other was rushed to the hospital with chest pains. The press of angry bodies made the apartment hot, and some women yelled for everyone to calm down, and some women yelled the opposite, and as we tried to dress the crying kids some women tried to help in earnest, finding their jackets and socks, while others were still plainly angling to spirit them away.

When Pamela's last child had been taken, she swung at a cop, but then another cop grabbed her wrists, and her friends took her aside, and after a few more eruptions of screaming we got the kids out. One woman yelled, "This is why people hate the cops!" Although I thought very little of her and the rest of them—Mothers United for Narcotics and Neglect—she had a point: no one likes people who steal babies in the middle of the night. And we had just started our tour.

The midnight tour is also called the first platoon, the second being the day tour and the third being the four-to-twelve. You begin at 2315 hours and end at 0750. If you have Tuesday and Wednesday off one week, say, you have Tuesday, Wednesday, and Thursday off the next, and then Wednesday and Thursday the week after that. It takes some getting used to, because if you're working a Friday you don't come in Friday—you come in Thursday night. Another depressing thing about midnights is that when you finish work in the morning, at ten minutes to eight, you don't say, "See you tomorrow," which would seem soon enough; you say, "See you tonight." Tonight began yesterday, and tomorrow begins tonight, and the days become one rolling night.

When I first went on the job, I started out on steady four-to-twelves, Sunday to Thursday, working in a project called Morris Houses, which, with Morrisania, Butler, and Webster Houses, make up a huge complex of thirty apartment buildings called Claremont Village, in the heart of the South Bronx. On that beat, I was generally busier than I am now, when I might cover an entire precinct. I knew less local lore then, and the landmarks I navigated by were of recent relevance: the pawnshop to check after a chain snatch; the crack house where a baby overdosed; the rooftop where they fought pit bulls, sometimes throwing the loser to the street below. I still occasionally drive through this area with my partner, but even with my grasp of the neighborhood's history I'm not sure why things turned out as they did, and still less what led me here.

Morris Houses was named after Gouverneur Morris, a Revolutionary War hero, who was with Washington at Valley Forge and later established the decimal system of United States currency, proposing the words "dollar" and "cent." His half-brother Lewis was a signer of the Declaration of Independence, and tried to get the Founding Fathers to establish the nation's capital on the family estate, but the idea was more or less a nonstarter. The Morrises owned most of the South Bronx for nearly two centuries, and their name is everywhere: Morrisania, the neighborhood in the Forty-second Precinct, where my beat was; Morris Heights; Port Morris; Morris High School, which the industrialist Armand Hammer and General Colin Powell graduated from. Yet I couldn't say it means much to anyone here. The kids that Bernhard Goetz shot in 1984—four thugs who failed to recognize a subway-riding vigilante—came from Morrisania. One of them remains confined to a wheelchair, and I'd sometimes see him around; I locked up another one's sister for robbery, after a nasty girl-gang fight. I can't imagine that her mother said, upon her return from jail, "Gouverneur Morris and his half-brother Lewis must be rolling in their graves!" The Morrises made this place and helped make this nation, but they might as well have knocked up some local girls and split after the shotgun wedding, leaving nothing behind but their name.

On midnights, there is a risk of drifting within yourself, trailing off on your own weird train of thought, so that when the even weirder world intrudes it is hard not to laugh. One night not long ago, it was so slow that three patrol cars showed up for a dispute between two crackheads over a lost shopping cart. To pass the time, we conducted an investigation, asking pointed questions: What color was the cart? Do you have a receipt? It was cold, and after a while one of the cops said we should leave. But I was bored enough to want to talk to the crackheads, who relished the attention. I said to the cop, "They have issues, we can help them work through them, the relationship can come out even stronger than it was before." He looked at me and said, "Hey, I'm no Dr. Zhivago—let's get out of here."

On another job, we received a call for help from an old man and his sick wife. They seemed like good people: he had an upright, military bearing, and she was a stick figure, with plum-colored bruises all over, gasping through a nebulizer, "*Ayúdame, ayúdame, ayúdame.*" We made small talk, in broken English and Spanish, while waiting for EMS. On a shelf, there was a photograph of a young man in a police uniform, who the old man said was his son, a cop in San Juan who died at the age of thirty-four from cancer. The entire apartment was a Santeria shrine: cigars laid across the tops of glasses of colorless liquid; open scissors on dishes of blue liquid; dried black bananas hanging over the threshold; Tarot cards, coins, and dice before a dozen statues of saints, including a huge Virgin Mary with a triple-headed angel at her feet. Suddenly, I thought, They keep the place up, but it's more *House Voodooful* than *House Beautiful*. The line wouldn't leave my head, so I had to pretend to cough, and walk outside.

You get in the habit of reading these scenes for signs, whether forensic or sacramental, of sin and struggle in the fallen world. Santeria shrines and offerings are often placed in the corner of a room near the entrance, and in just that corner of one apartment we found a black-handled butcher knife next to blood that had not just pooled but piled, it lay so thick on the floor: dark, sedimentary layers with a clear overlay, like varnish, which I was told came from the lungs. The woman responsible for this handiwork explained why she had tried to sacrifice her brother at the household altar: "Two years ago, he broke my leg in five places. I came in tonight, he sold my couch. He killed my mother. Well, she died from him and all his nonsense." She stopped talking for a moment and tried to shift her hands in her cuffs as EMS took her brother out in a wheelchair, pale and still. "I didn't stab him," she went on. "He stabbed himself by accident, in the back, during the tussle."

Some objects tell simple stories of fierce violence, like the two-by-four, so bloody it looked as if it had been dipped in the stuff, that a woman had used to collect a fifty-dollar debt, or the rape victim's panties in the stairwell, covered with flies. Others are more subtle and tentative, like the open Bible in the apartment of a woman whose brother, just home from prison, had suffered some sort of psychotic break. "He sat there reading the Bible for a while, and then he just looked up and said he was going to kill me," she said. The Bible was open to Proverbs 1:18, which states, "These men lie in wait for their own blood, they set a trap for their own lives." Maybe he'd read only the first part of the sentence. The woman's husband had just died, and next to the Bible there was a sympathy card from someone named Vendetta.

As a cop, you look for patterns—for context and connections that tell a fuller truth than a complainant may be willing to tell. Sometimes, though, the parts belong to no whole. So it was with a pair of attempted robberies, only twenty minutes and four blocks apart. Each perp was a male Hispanic, tall, slim, and young, in dark clothes, with a razor blade, though in the second robbery the perp wore a mask and a wig. And so when we came upon a tall, slim, young male Hispanic in dark clothes with a wig, mask, and razor in his pocket, in a desolate park between the two crime scenes, I reasonably expected to have solved at least one crime. Both complainants were sure, however, that he wasn't the man responsible, and we let him go.

In such cases, the solution seems out of sight but within reach, like the winning card in three-card monte. But there are other, older mysteries, and if there is a hint of a game in what unfolds you feel more like a piece than like a player. One night, we went to a routine "aided case," an old woman with a history of heart trouble, whose breath was rapid and shallow. She moaned, "Mami!" as she sat on a red velvet couch, flanked by two teenage girls. As the old lady left with EMS, my partner told me that she was raising her two granddaughters. An hour or so later, we had another aided case, a "heavy bleeder." When we went inside, a woman said, "She's in bed," and then, "It's in the tub." We checked on a teenage girl in the bedroom, who said she was fine, and then looked in the bathtub; there, nestled in the drain, was a fetus the size and color of a sprained thumb. The head was turned upward and the eyes were open and dark.

When the EMTs came—the same guys we'd met on the previous job—they asked for some plastic wrap or tinfoil, and were provided with a sandwich bag to pick it up. As we helped them put the teenage girl in the ambulance, they told us that the old lady had gone into cardiac arrest and wouldn't make it. Nothing else happened that night, and as we drove around I kept thinking that for everyone who dies another isn't necessarily born. It was late but also too early, not yet time to go home.

FROM THE SIXTIES THROUGH THE eighties, the landscape of the Bronx was a record of public failure, high and low—from Robert Moses, who moved through the Bronx like Sherman through Georgia, evicting thousands in order to build highways, to the scavengers and predators who made ordinary life impossible for ordinary people. I've often wondered what Poe would have thought of the South Bronx at its worst—what his ghost would make of our ghost town. He wrote about loves lost to death at an early age, and set his tales in ancestral houses gone to ruin, but he might have taken to the abandoned factories and the tenements whose graffiti-covered walls had collapsed, leaving them open like doll houses. He might have said, "Don't change a thing!" Then again, such a landscape might have left little room for the imagination, or offered too much.

Since then, the landscape has changed for the better, and the record has been rewritten, often quickly and well. Of course, when something returned from the dead in Poe's world no good came of it, like the hideous beating of that telltale heart. On the other hand, the phrase "with a vengeance" does come to mind when I look at Suburban Place, one block from Charlotte Street, which is now the center of several blocks of well-tended ranch houses. There is something surreal about this development, with its fences and lawns, given both the area's past and its surroundings, which are still rough. You could look at it as a plot twist as unexpected as anything in Poe. You have to wait for it, and be accepting of surprise.

ONE NIGHT, WE RACED TO the scene of "shots fired" from an elevated subway platform—a call that EMS workers had put over as they were driving past. A number of passersby confirmed it, but the shooter was long gone. Four hours later, with little to do in the interim except drive around in the dark we received another job of shots fired, from an apartment right next to the El. Inside, a lovely old couple pointed out a hole in the window, and the neat chute that the bullet had cut through a hanging basket of African violets, littering stems and leaves on the floor. "I love my plants, they're my babies," the woman said, more concerned about what had happened than about what might have happened. The woman was a kind of grandmother to the neighborhood, and had been for more than a generation. There was a picture on the wall of her with Mayor Lindsay, who she said had let her have a house for a dollar a year to take care of local children. "Give your plants a big drink of water," I said. "And I'll play them some nice soothing music, too," she added. We saw where the bullet had hit the back wall—not far from Mayor Lindsay—but then had to dig around in the kitchen for a while before we found it, under the refrigerator. The heat and speed and impact had transformed the sleek missile into an odd-shaped glob, like a scoop of mashed potato, harmless and pointless. It was a big slug, probably from a .45, and had she been watering her plants it would have taken her head off. It frightened her, to be sure, but she had slept through its arrival and she would sleep again now that it was gone.

The bullet had taken less than a second to travel from the barrel into the couple's home, but in my mind the journey had taken four hours—from when the bullet was heard to when it was found—and I could picture it in slow motion, floating like a soap bubble on a windless night. Both perspectives seemed equally real, the explosive instant and the glacial glide, and I was glad to be able to see each of them, in the luxury of time. The old couple, I'm sure, were glad of it as well. My partner and I took the bullet with us, and morning arrived as we left.

Marcus Laffey is the pen name used by **Edward Conlon** in his "Cop Diary" pieces, published in *The New Yorker*. His memoir, *Blue Blood* (Riverhead 2004), was a *New York Times* Notable Book of the Year and a finalist for the National Book Critics Circle Award. He is working on a novel.

Edward Conlon is a New York City native and a graduate of Regis High School and Harvard College. He joined the NYPD in 1995 and was assigned to the South Bronx, where he worked as a beat cop in housing projects and in the Narcotics Division. He is presently a precinct detective in the Yankee Stadium area.

"The Midnight Tour" originally appeared in *The New Yorker* (2000) and was reprinted in *Best American Essays 2000*. Copyright © 2000 by Marcus Laffey (Edward Conlon). It is reprinted here by permission of William Morris Agency, LLC, on behalf of the author.

Dirty Talk

Amanda Scheiderer

FRIDAY NIGHT WHEN I GET into work, Angela, one of the day shift girls, is on the main stage dancing to Journey's "Lovin', Touchin', Squeezin'." She smiles at me from the stage. Liz, the day shift manager, is talking on the phone, and Zye, another dancer, is sitting at the bar smoking a cigarette and drinking a cup of coffee. Zye is half Puerto Rican and into Wicca. Years before I entertained the thought of becoming a dancer, my husband and one of his friends saw her dance at a small club on the east side of town. She says she remembers them because they were the only guys in the audience who appreciated her taste in music.

I pass her as I head for the dressing room. "Just you two today?" I ask, nodding toward Angela.

Zye blows smoke away from me. "Is it seven?"

"Little after," I say, maneuvering my dance bag around the bar stool.

"Well, thank fucking God," Zye says, crushing out the cigarette. She follows me into the dressing room and grabs a baby wipe from a box on the counter.

I hang my dance bag on the hook next to my locker, then clear my brain as I open the lock. I know from high school that if I think too hard about the combination, I'll never recall it.

"You want to hear something fucked up?" Zye asks as she bends over in front of the big wall mirror with her t-bars (stripper talk for thong panties) pulled aside. She's checking her butt, a ritual we all perform about a hundred times a shift to check not only our butts but our crotches too, for toilet paper, lint, discharge, extruding tampons, or anything else that'll glow underneath the black and red lights around the main stage.

She straightens up and throws the wipe into the trash can next to the toilet. "This dude came in today and was all like, 'Yo, baby! I'd take care of you if you was my woman.' And I was like, '*Yo,* asshole, I don't need no nigger with a gerry-curl taking care of me.'"

I laugh as I kick off my street shoes. "Did he really have a gerry-curl?"

She raises a hand. "This dude was greased *up.* And then," she says, slapping her thigh—the one with The Misfits' crimson ghost tattoo—"he wouldn't even tip me a dollar."

"That *is* fucked up," I say, stepping out of my jeans and underwear. Fucked up, but not uncommon. I've heard the same line from customers more times than I can count. I hang my pants, with my underwear shoved in the front pocket so I won't lose them, over the door of my locker. I pull on a pair of t-bars and fish my shoes out from underneath the blanket I use during private shows.

The soft cotton makes crawling around on the glass-bottomed stage more bearable.

The music stops and Zye pauses for a moment at the door before heading out. "Dude, my feet are so tired, I think they're gonna fall off."

I hear Zye's song start to play—"Summer Breeze" by Type O Negative (which doesn't sound anything like the Seals & Crofts version my mother listened to when I was a kid)—and I sit on the back toilet in front of the big wall mirror to slip into my dance shoes, silver, open-toed platforms with five-inch stiletto heels. They're the sexiest things I've ever owned. Seventy dollars at the local stripper store, Stepping Out, but well worth the money. I've had them for over a year and aside from the awful stink (nothing's funkier than a stripper's shoes) they're still in great shape.

I'm almost always the first night shift girl to show up. I come in a full hour early. My husband thinks this is compulsive behavior, but I have a practical reason. Most of the other girls don't show up until quarter till or even eight-fifteen, which means I can have the dressing room to myself.

It's really just a restroom—a cramped space tucked between the two private stages. The dressing room is P-shaped, just a little bigger than one of those kiosks in malls that sell gold chain by the inch. The walls are lavender, the color muted by years of dirt. There are two toilets, both doorless, on opposite ends of the room; two stacks of lockers, decorated with stickers that say *Girl Power*, *Chicks Rule*, and *Princess*; and two sinks which shoot out scalding hot water and are frequently clogged with cigarette butts and hair.

The narrow counter that runs along the stem of the P is the only one in the whole dressing room. On a typical night, with half a dozen or more girls, the clutter is severe: a phalanx of curling irons (all plugged into one outlet thanks to a dangerously handy six-plug converter), makeup bags, Caboodles, cans of hair spray, bottles of body spray, jars of glitter, and overflowing ashtrays.

When I'm dressed (black t-bars, black strapless bra, black spandex micro-miniskirt, and a black and white striped vest that zippers down the front), I go out front to wait for eight o'clock. I still have five minutes, so I sit at the bar and scan the prospects as Angela dances to Lords of Acid's "Pussy." There's Larry, the attorney, sitting at the stage with his arms hanging over the chair railings, knuckles dragging. A couple of suits over by the cigarette machine nursing Cokes and checking their watches. A day shift regular at the other end of the bar peeling the label off of a water bottle. And an older guy in a flannel shirt and ball cap with a bushy beard sitting alone at the stage. Angela sits down on the ledge of the stage in front of him. She's a tiny thing with long legs and dimples that make you want to pinch her cheeks forever. She has a three-year-old kid, a boyfriend who burns her with cigarettes, and a drinking problem I find especially unsettling because she's so young; I don't think she's even twenty-one. Angela wraps her legs around the guy's neck and smiles. He just sits there and looks grumpy.

For my first set of the evening, I play something on the slow side—"You Showed Me" by The Turtles and "Oh My Lover" by PJ Harvey—giving my muscles time to warm up and stretch. We play our music on a jukebox and it costs us a dollar each time we dance. There are a hundred CDs to choose from and eight of them are mine: Red Hot Chili Peppers, Macy Gray, PJ Harvey, a 60s collection, Cake, the *Natural Born Killers* soundtrack, Fiona Apple, and a mix CD that one of the girls' boyfriends burned for me off of Napster. Ten bucks and I got fifteen of my favorite songs, including "Crazy" by Patsy Cline and "Wish You Were Here" by Pink Floyd.

I step around Angela, who's sitting on the three wooden steps, and climb onto the stage. "Make some money, babe," she says to me, unstrapping her heels and rubbing her feet. "I'm out of here."

As I dance, I make eyes at the two suits, but I can tell from the stage they're not going to buy. They're more interested in talking to each other than looking at me. I make my way over to Larry and give him some obligatory attention. I can't stand him anymore. He's the kind of customer who'll only buy ten-dollar drinks, but expects fifty dollars worth of reassurance about how he's not a loser, all the while spitting on you as he talks. The last straw came over a year ago when he kept asking, "I bet I'm your favorite customer, aren't I? I bet you think about me when you're not in here, don't you?" Finally, I just couldn't take it. "Larry," I told him. "I don't ever think about you." Nothing makes me madder than when people push me to be mean. Despite this negative history, I feel bad for him as a human being. He's pathetic and lonely. If anyone owns a can of fake sweat, it's Larry.

As I gyrate my hips in front of him, he grabs onto the edge of the stage with his long, hairy hands. "Hey, Amanda."

"How are you, Larry?" Through the music I hear him grunt.

I crawl over to Grumpy and lean down close to his face, letting my hair brush against his cheek. He's my last chance of making a drink after this set, but that doesn't seem likely. When I smile at him and say, "Hey there, sweetie," not only does he not say anything back, he grimaces.

Well, so much for this, I think. I stand up and twirl around the poles. When my second song starts I ignore the guys altogether and watch myself in the mirrors, trying to decide if white t-bars might make my ass look a little smaller, and admonishing myself for eating that bag of Combos earlier in the day.

WHEN I BECAME A STRIPPER, I couldn't dance a stitch. This is true of most girls. There's no training to becoming an exotic dancer. Fortunately, most customers don't distinguish good dancing from bad, so even new dancers who look like they're picking potatoes can make money. It took me about a year before I considered myself a good dancer. Even now, almost two years into it, there are things I wish I could do. I still can't do the splits, or one of those really great high kicks. I can't move very fast on my feet because I'm afraid of toppling over. In these stilettos I wear, it's a miracle just to walk around.

Despite these shortcomings, I love this kind of dancing and think I'm fairly good at it. When I'm on stage, I let the music take over and I just ride along. When I was eleven, all gangly and shy, I watched *Grease 2* over a dozen times on HBO. I thought if I could just be cool, tough, and pretty like Michelle Pfeiffer then some boy would like me. All the popular girls at Gulf Middle in Cape Coral, Florida, had boyfriends. My best friend Erica, who carried a purse and drank vodka out of an Aqua Net bottle at school, told me she once gave Chris Durham head during a boat safety assembly. Even my mother, who went crazy when I was nine, had boyfriends traipsing in and out of our house. So, I bought pink and black sweatshirts at Goodwill and cut off the sleeves. I danced around the duplex and sang "Cool Rider" under my breath in front of the TV. I snuck glimpses of myself in the mirror that hung above the piano and longed for someone to notice me.

The club where I work is a nude club, ranked the best nude club in Columbus, Ohio, by several Web sites I've seen. It's just about the exact opposite of a go-go bar, which, at least here in Columbus, is a club that can serve alcohol because the girls don't get completely naked. These are generally the big, glitzy show bars that everyone thinks of when they hear the term strip club. These clubs have featured porn stars, DJs, and dozens of dancers who are tan, long-legged, hipless, and cosmetically enhanced. Nude clubs in Columbus, on the other hand, are homey places where the music is pumped out of a jukebox and the girls—for better or worse—come in all shapes and sizes.

My club is cozy when it's not crowded. When it is crowded, on weekends, the smoke is as thick as steam and the only way to ventilate the place is to turn on the air conditioner. This means that even in the middle of winter the club is a crisp fifty-eight degrees. Nestled between three of Columbus's nicer residential communities (Hilliard, Dublin, and Upper Arlington), the clientele are mostly mild-mannered and middle-class. A sign in the parking lot displays a Havelock Ellis quote, proclaiming dance "the loftiest of the arts." Inside, the club is lodge-like, with its walls half wood-paneled/half mirrored and its ceiling low. You almost expect to see a moose head hanging over the faux fireplace along the north wall instead of the framed print of the buxom blond stripper in ballet shoes. The carpet is black with pink and purple and blue swirls that must have glowed underneath the lights back in the days before disco died.

By THE TIME I GET my t-bars and bra back on and walk around for tips, the two suits have scooted out the door without even leaving a dollar. Larry shoves a couple bucks into my underwear, poking me in the stomach with them as he does, and says, "Hey, Amanda," like a kid trying to be cool. I'm willing to bet he's been shoved into a locker or two in his day, and I feel bad again, remembering the times in grade school when Phyllis Smith and Cody James would shove me into the girls' room trash can for kicks.

I don't bother asking the guy at the bar for a tip because he had his back turned the entire time. When I get to Grumpy, he slips a bill in and I say, "Thanks, sweetie," with a big smile, giving it another go with the charm. He looks up and says, "Yep," in a voice as flat as a forgotten glass of pop.

I go back to my seat at the bar and wiggle into my skirt. Amber, the waitress, stands in front of me twirling a strand of her long, curly hair around one finger. She's an ex-dancer who now goes to Columbus State where she is studying veterinarian science. She's bitter and mean to customers, but she raises pit bulls and loves dogs, so she gets points in my book for that. I've asked her if she hates being in the club so much, why she just doesn't leave altogether. "It's not the kind of job you can just quit," she told me. "You have to wean yourself off the money and the attention."

I sometimes dread the day I'll have to retire. I work three nights a week and am told I'm beautiful and sexy and wonderful a gazillion times an hour. That's a tricky fix to kick. Sure, I believe there's more to me than what's on the outside, but it's nice to get compliments on a regular basis. Not that my husband doesn't give me his share of praise, but after almost seven years of marriage, it's kind of like your mother telling you you're pretty.

The money will be hard to give up too. If I broke it down hourly—twenty-four hours per week —I make, on average, over forty bucks an hour. It feels good to know I can do something on my own. I've been able to support my husband and myself for the last three years and still have time to pursue my writing interests. I like being the breadwinner.

It's probably the attention I'll miss the most, though. I always feel beautiful in here. When I look in the big wall mirror in the dressing room, I am amazed at what I see. That girl is so pretty! Even her nose looks good—that same big, fat nose that sits on my face, the one that made me skip school and hide in my room time and again as a teenager, so the world wouldn't see what an atrocity I had become. In here, no one ever calls me "monkey" or tells me that I look like the flying dog-dragon from *The Neverending Story*.

Amber points to Grumpy as I shove the money into my small purse. "Ever sit with him?" she asks.

"That guy?"

"He used to buy for Delilah. Big. Hundreds."

I look at him again. Then at her. "You sure?"

"Totally."

The few times Amber has steered me, she hasn't been wrong, so I stand up and shrug. "Guess I got nothing to lose."

My strategy for dealing with sourpusses like Grumpy is excessive cheerfulness. It's been my experience that these kinds of men are rarely mean.

They're just stoic. It's the guys who smile so big their dogteeth show that you've got to watch out for. They're usually assholes.

I plop myself down in the seat next to Grumpy and give him a smile, nudge him in the side with my elbow, and ask in my cutest voice, "You ready for some private shows, darlin'?" I normally don't say "darlin'" but this guy looks real down home, West Virginia or Kentucky maybe. He smells surprisingly pleasant, warm and smoky, like an old wood stove.

He turns his head a little my way and grimaces again. "You think so, huh?"

I look at him closer. The corners of his mouth twitch a little, and I realize that Grumpy's not grimacing at all. That's just his way of smiling.

I rub my knee against his leg and bat my eyes a bit. "You sure do look ready."

He grimaces—no, smiles—again. "You sure?"

"Are you funnin' with me?" I ask, noticing I've lapsed into a slight drawl.

"Why? You havin' some fun, are ya?"

I laugh. I find out his name's Vernon and he buys me a fifty-dollar drink, which in here translates into three private dances. We move from the stage to a small two-seater booth in the corner. Vernon takes up three-quarters of it, so I'm forced to teeter on the edge.

"You been working here long?" he asks.

"About a year," I say.

He asks (like almost everyone does) what got me into dancing, and I give him the easiest answer, the one everyone seems to expect and therefore understands: money. But that's not entirely true. Before I ever walked into a strip club I had a decent job processing loans at a mortgage company. I didn't make near what I make as a dancer, but my husband was earning good money as a loan officer at the same company, so we weren't hurting. We both got tired of the business, though, and when he decided to go back to school to finish up his BA (the one he had begun at Ohio Wesleyan University where we met), I got it in my head that I could be a stripper. I had been bored and unsatisfied at my job for months, feeling much older than twenty-six, and yearning for some excitement, some new challenge, something that would make me feel more alive than working fourteen hours a day in a cubicle.

One night, my husband and I went into The Toy Box, a nude club on the north side that's closed down now. I had seen an ad for *dancers wanted* in the local paper. *No experience necessary.* We bought a dancer named Austin a ten-dollar drink, and within two songs' worth of time she had given me a fairly detailed run-down of the job. I filled out an application that night and started a week later. My first night was a Sunday, I made $98 (a sum I would bitch about today), and I quit my processing job the following week. It was the craziest thing I'd ever done, and, although I was terrified my first time on stage (more because I knew I couldn't dance than because I was naked), I've never regretted it.

When Vernon asks if I do anything else, I tell him this is it. Because of his dark blue pants, his plain, gray pocket Tee, and the dirt underneath his finger-nails, I figure he's working-class, so I don't mention my writing courses at Ohio State or my plans for graduate school. I don't want to introduce a gulf between his way of life and mine. To him, I just want to be a gal trying to earn a living. This doesn't require acting on my part, just tapping into my working-class roots. I was raised in a trailer park in Southwest Florida by my single, working mother. She dated men like Vernon (and many others unlike him), had them over to the house for supper, dessert, *and* breakfast as thanks for fixing our busted window screens and backed-up toilet. Vernon reminds me of these men who used to tap my mother on the rear and call her "sweet cheeks" when they thought my older sister and I weren't looking. These men who, after a couple of beers had loosened them up, would stand beside the piano, their thick fingers drumming against the wood, as my mother played "Sunday Morning Coming Down."

"What do you do?" I ask Vernon, sipping on my big glass of water, taking the spotlight off me for a while.

"Heavy machinery," he says.

"Like cranes and stuff like that?"

He nods.

"That sounds like fun."

He nods again.

"I bet it pays good."

"I'm union."

Then it's my turn to nod and I sip on my drink some more. We sit in silence for a good half a song. He looks at me, his expression indiscernible underneath all that facial hair.

"What?" I say, smiling.

"Nothing," he says, looking away again.

After the next song ends, I point to the girl who's about to go up on stage. "Rose always plays really good stuff," I say. "You want to head back and get me naked?"

"What's your hurry?" he says.

I twirl the straws around in my glass and wonder what this girl Delilah talked about during all those hundred-dollar drinks.

"So, do you live around here?" I ask, tapping my foot to "Love Her Madly" by The Doors.

"Out east," he says, uncrossing, then recrossing his arms on top of his large belly.

"Where out east?" I ask. "Reynoldsburg? Canal Winchester?"

He looks at me. He has this way of pausing before answering.

"Pataskala."

"Pa-tas-ka-la," I say, drawing out the syllables. "I love that name. Know what other name I love? Wapakoneta. Isn't that a great name?" I don't know why I'm saying any of this but it's better than silence. The way he's looking at me is unnerving. I'm starting to wonder if he isn't a bit touched. "There's an astronaut from Wapakoneta," I say. "What's his name?"

Vernon stares at me for a long time. "I got a feeling about you," he says.

When we finally do go back to do our private shows, three songs later, Vernon gets more talkative.

"Oh, yeah," he says. "I could lick that. I could lick Baby all night long."

"Baby," I figure out, is Vernon's name for what I euphemistically call "my stuff" (other terms among us girls are "my cootch," "my cookie," "my shit"—all terms I prefer hands down to what my mother insisted I call it: "my giny," pronounced with a soft "g").

In return, I find myself calling Vernon's stuff "Pocket." As in, "Vernon, quit playing with your pocket! You know you're not allowed to do that in here." Contrary to what Jerry Springer had my mother convinced of ("Do you have to pleasure these men?" she asked me when I first broke the news), not all strip clubs are dens of illicit sexual activity. Our club is a no-touch environment, thanks, no doubt, to the owner, an ex-dancer and recovering drug addict turned Scientologist. The customers can't touch us. They can't play with or expose themselves. We can't touch them. The stages are in full view of the bar, and the managers keep an eye out. We can't even touch ourselves "down there," although the laws on this in Columbus are a little fuzzy, and some girls push the envelope. Those girls who do, though, are ridiculed and looked down upon by the other girls. This no-touch rule mainly applies to sexual touch. We can get away with rubbing our calves against men's faces, shaking their hands, patting their backs, and giving them hugs. We can even give birthday boys and bachelors pecks on the cheek if we're so inclined.

As far as customers copping casual feels on us girls, it normally depends on money. I'm less likely to get pissed off by a customer touching my thigh if he's tipping me a five or higher. Rules on casual, non-sexual touching are often self-made and on-the-spot. Some girls simply tolerate more than others. My tolerance depends on the guy. With Vernon, it's low, mainly because I don't think he can handle the excitement.

"I'm gonna have to go out to my truck when we're done," Vernon says during our last song, leaning over the ledge of the private stage.

I smile and shake my head, knowing damn well he wants me to ask him why.

"Want to know why?"

"That's okay, Vernon."

"C'mon, you think there's something wrong with me jerking off while I think about Baby?"

"No, but you don't have to tell me about it."

"Why not?"

"Because it's none of my business," I tell him, laughing a little, to show him I'm not offended, just embarrassed. I'm not even embarrassed, really, just grossed out. I don't want to begrudge the man his sexuality, but I don't really want to think about him beating off in his truck. So I feign modesty and hope I don't hurt his feelings.

"Don't you want to know how I'm gonna shoot it all over the steering wheel?"

"Vernon! You're making me blush."

After our show, I tell Vernon I'll meet him out at the booth, and I go into the dressing room to freshen up. I almost trip over Jay, who's sitting on the floor reading a Dave Barry book and eating a box of Teddy Grahams.

I step over her carefully so I don't kick her in the head with my shoe, then I sit on the back toilet and start to pee.

"Must be nice," Jay says, not looking up from her book. I know she's talking about the shows I just did. Jay has a hard time making drinks and usually spends a good part of the shift in the dressing room, coming out on the floor only when it's her turn to dance. She thinks it's because she's black (the clientele here is predominantly white), but it could also be because she's over six feet tall in her seven-inch heels and is built like R. Crumb's fantasy woman—fertility goddess breasts, muscular thighs, meaty ass—all perfectly proportioned but unfortunately unappreciated by the majority of the customers. Of course, no one ever makes money in this business by sitting in the dressing room.

"Not that nice," I say, feeling the need to mitigate my luck. "He's a dirty talker."

Jay puts her book down. "What's he say?"

I do my best imitation of Vernon, complete with syrupy drawl.

"Eeeww!" she says, making a face. " 'Baby'? What the fuck is that all about?"

"It wouldn't be so bad, except he only tipped a dollar." I wipe, flush the toilet, then bend over in front of the big mirror to check my butt.

"I don't know what makes them think we want to hear that shit," Jay says, going back to her book.

When I'm dressed again, I meet Vernon out front in the small booth. He's crunching on the ice in his empty glass, and I ask him if he'd like a refill.

"Sure," he says, reaching for his wallet.

"Do *I* want a refill?" I ask, tapping on the side of my own empty glass. It's my coy way of waiting on myself. Some girls like to have the waitress come over to ask the customer if he would like another round, but I like to keep the money moving, especially with guys like Vernon who are hard to talk to, dirty or not.

"Get yourself a hundred," he says and hands me a credit card.

I take the card up to the bar and give it to Amber to run. "Did Delilah ever say anything about this guy?" I ask.

"Oh, yeah," she says. "He's a fucking pervert."

I bring our drinks over and Amber follows behind with the slip for him to sign and a bottle of nonalcoholic champagne that comes with the hundred-dollar drink (seven dances). Vernon asks her if he can keep the pen, and he writes his name and phone number on the bottle's white label. That would really annoy our owner, I think. No one's expected to keep the bottle. We don't even open it. It's just for show, a marker to let the other girls know you're sitting on a big drink. Normally, once a customer leaves, the bottle's put back on the shelf behind the bar to reuse.

"This is so you'll remember me," he says, handing it to me.

I take it and set it on the table.

"Read it," he says.

I pick it up again and pretend to read what I just watched him write. "Thank you, Vernon," I say, as though he'd just written me a poem. "That's so sweet." It is, I guess, in a weird, touched sort of way. Part of me feels bad because I know it's going to end up in the trash, probably just like Delilah's did.

"You call me any time you want."

"Okay." I hold the bottle in my hands, and wonder if enough time has passed to warrant setting it back on the table. "Hey," I say. "Weren't you gonna go out to your truck?" I laugh and poke him in the side with my elbow.

He shifts away from me and looks upset.

"What's the matter?" I ask, thinking, *oh no, I've pissed him off by not making enough out of the whole bottle thing.* Many times in my life I've been given gifts and have not gotten the significance they hold for the person giving them. I have a way of coming across as an ingrate. Even though this is just a dusty bottle of flat champagne, I wonder if it doesn't mean something to Vernon.

I run my fingers over what Vernon's written and smile at him. He still looks upset.

"I don't want you to think I only like you for your body," he finally says.

I set the bottle on the table, relieved. "Is that what's bothering you, Vernon? It's all right."

"No, it isn't."

"Really," I say, patting his arm. "It's okay."

"No, it's not okay. I'm sick. I just love sex and you're so beautiful."

"Really, it's okay. I don't mind you saying those things." I try to soothe him, try to convince him that this is a silly thing to get upset about. "Listen, Vernon," I tell him. "This is your dime. You can say whatever you want. You won't offend me."

I mean it. It's very hard to offend me, especially with words. I know some dancers who get angry when a guy so much as says she has a nice ass. Maybe I'm more realistic. I mean, let's not forget where we are. What we're doing. We're sticking our stuff right in their faces. Why wouldn't they comment on it? I remember one time I was on the main stage spread-eagle in front of some drunk in a Harley vest. He leaned over and sneered, "That's a mighty nice punching bag, little lady." All I could do was laugh. He had called me "little lady," for God's sake.

I FINALLY GET VERNON TO quit feeling guilty about the dirty talk, and the next time he comes in it's dirty talk all night long—in back and out front. I won't lie

and say it doesn't get tedious. Vernon's not very original. He tries to get me to
talk dirty back to him but I can't do it.

"Do you like to suck a man's cock?" Vernon asks as we sit in the booth I've
come to think of as ours.

"Now ain't that a fine question for a lady?"

"Just say it. Say, 'I like to suck a man's cock.'"

"I will not say it." I laugh, but not at him. Somehow he knows this because he
doesn't get angry. "Didn't you go fishing or something this weekend?" I ask.

"Don't change the subject."

"Tell me," I say. "What'd you catch?"

Reluctantly, he tells me of how he hooked a snapping turtle. "That big
around," he says, holding his hands up. "Damn thing bit me on the finger when I
tried to take the hook out."

"What did you do with him?"

"Threw him back in the river."

"Poor little guy."

"He'll be all right," Vernon says. He sips his Coke and looks at me. "Okay,
now. Say it."

"What?"

"Say you like to suck a man's cock."

"You like to suck a man's cock."

WHY CAN'T I TALK DIRTY? I don't know. I suppose I could if someone offered
me enough money. But that's not entirely true. Once, a guy the girls call Dirty
Dan came in and bought me a ten-dollar drink. He put a hundred on the table
and said it was mine if I'd sit there and "talk" to him. He told me the kinds of
things he wanted to hear: "Tell me how bad I am, what a dog I am, how you're
going to make me eat your shit, I'm such a low-life, filthy fuck." Of course, this
goes far beyond anything Vernon ever wants me to say but this was a hundred
dollars for ten minutes of verbal abuse. I gave it a shot. I forget exactly what I
said but after my third or fourth sentence Dirty Dan held up his hand. He took
the hundred dollar bill away and reached in his wallet. "You really suck at this,"
he said, handing me a twenty. "But you tried." I took the bill and asked him what
I'd done wrong. "You're not angry enough," he told me.

So, evidently, talking dirty just isn't my thing. But listening is. Interestingly,
the dancer who could always get mad money out of Dirty Dan was a girl named
Keenah. She was big and black and looked like Urkel. She was angry about that,
and about a host of other things. She was an expert dirty-talker.

OVER THE NEXT SIX MONTHS, Vernon comes in to see me about a half-dozen
times. I learn that he's never been married (although he came "real close a couple
times") and that he lives with his mother who recently lost her leg to diabetes.

"I bought her this little dog," he says to me one night. "About yea big. Just a fur ball of a thing. But it keeps her company while I'm at work, so I don't have to worry about her."

"You close to your mom?" I ask.

"Oh yeah," he says. "We been living together since Dad died. She still cooks supper and does the laundry."

"What's your favorite meal?" The question sounds idiotic, but I find myself asking many like it when we're together in an attempt to curb the dirty talk.

Vernon smacks his lips. "Mom makes this stuff with red beans and corn and rice." He makes a yummy noise and smiles. "Put a little hot sauce on and you're good to go."

"Sounds deadly," I say, laughing.

"Don't you like it hot?" he asks, nudging me.

I sip on my water and wave a hand at him.

"There's this girl lives next door," he says. "She's about twenty, twenty-one. Anyway, she comes over the other night and tells me she likes taking it in the ass."

His non sequitur, as always, amazes and tires me. I crane my neck toward the stage like I'm checking to see who's dancing. It's a lame diversion, but it works.

"What?" he says. "You up next?"

"I've got a couple more songs."

He chews on some ice and I ask him if he has any hobbies other than fishing. Anything to keep us off the topic of taking it up the ass.

"You know those figurines of Indian girls?" he asks.

I nod, even though I don't.

"Squaws," he says. "I collect figurines of squaws."

"Oh," I say, thinking of ads I've seen in *TV Guide* and *The Star*. "Like Franklin Mint?"

He looks at me like he doesn't know what I'm talking about. "I collect Indian stuff. Just the girls though. I don't like the man ones."

ONE NIGHT BACK ON THE private stage, when I'm slipping out of my t-bars, Vernon asks for something new.

"You got any real underwear back there?" He nods toward the dressing room door.

"Like full-back?"

"Just regular panties," he says. "Not those silky thong things that go up your ass. Nice white cotton panties."

"I thought you liked things going up my ass?"

"I do," he says. "But I like cotton panties too."

"All right," I say. "Give me a second." I go into the dressing room and dig the underwear I wore in out of my jeans pocket. The panties aren't white, but they are cotton. Purple with a white moon and stars on the front, the word *cosmic* spelled out in funky letters. They're part of a whole series I bought at Target: *starry, lunar, solar, atomic, spacey.* It always bugged me that there weren't seven of them.

"Them's some nice drawers," a voice says from behind me. Chris, one of the dancers, is sitting on the back toilet lighting matches. She's one of the old-school girls, has been dancing almost ten years, and is what I expected all strippers to be like when I first started: tough, rough, and secretly kind. "Why you got those goofy things on for?"

I stand in front of the big mirror and look at myself. The panties look ridiculous with my silver heels. "My regular wants me to wear them."

"Shit," she says, grabbing a wad of toilet paper off the roll. "Like your job ain't hard enough, you've got to run around in some silly-ass drawers for that hillbilly fool." She gets up, flushes, then says, "Excuse me, babe," as she bends over in front of the mirror.

"I don't really mind," I say. "At least they're comfortable."

"Man, I'd tell that motherfucker to kiss my ass."

When I go back out to the private stage, Vernon says, "Oh yeah. Pocket likes Baby's bottoms." I start dancing, and he leans on the ledge like it's holding him up. His eyes are half-closed and there are beads of spittle clinging to his moustache.

"You like that?" I ask, my legs spread around him.

He doesn't so much nod, as sways.

I like it too, dancing in my underwear, but not in the same way he does. Having danced for him back here close to a hundred times, it's a relief to do something different. The same old moves feel new again, and now when I lean back against the mirror with my legs spread wide—his favorite pose—I don't feel like I'm just lying there, like I'm just a thing he's gawking at. I hook my fingers around the waistband and tug this way and that. Play peepshow. Hide-and-seek. It's kind of fun, this teasing. It breaks the monotony.

After our seventh song is over, he hands me a dollar and asks me if he can keep the panties.

"As long as you don't tell me what you do with them," I say.

I START TO WONDER WHY Vernon, who makes very good money as a heavy-machine operator, would bother to come in and waste it on a bunch of dances with a girl who not only won't let him touch her, but won't talk dirty either. He's always saying how much he loves sex, how long it's been since he's had a woman, so why doesn't he take just a fraction of the five or six hundred he spends on me each visit and go get himself a prostitute?

It baffles me until one night he tells me a story of how one of the "niggers" at work called him a faggot.

"I don't go for that," says Vernon to me, hotly. "I'm no goddamn queer."

His anger takes me by surprise. Normally he's so laid back, almost cuddly.

"I was raped, you know, when I was in high school."

The foot I was tapping to the music stops.

Vernon shifts around in his chair and stares at the stage while he tells me. "I was about sixteen and went out drinking with a bunch of guys, older guys I thought were my friends. We was in a van getting pretty wasted. They drove out to the boondocks and told me to suck their cocks. They beat the shit out of me and left me in a ditch. I had to walk home."

I sit there stunned, wanting to ask how far it went before they dumped him but I can tell he's done talking about it. He coughs in his hand, sips his Coke. Then he points at the girl on stage, a tall blonde in pink go-go boots named Genie. "You ever think about eating her pussy?"

I DOUBT THAT VERNON HAS ever told anybody else that story. And I'm not sure why he told me. Maybe he knew I wondered why he kept coming back. Or maybe he felt that he could trust me. At any rate, my two-bit analysis says that Vernon is terrified of being gay. To quell that fear he comes in and pays to look at pussy, because what kind of man would pay to look at naked women but a straight man? Of course, I would think that paying a woman for intercourse would do the trick a whole lot better, but in the end I guess I am a safer alternative. After all, he knows that when he comes to see me he's not expected— not even permitted—to lay a finger on me. The pressure's off for him to actually perform, but he still gets the reassurance he needs. And perhaps this is where all this dirty talk fits in. Maybe when he's saying to me, "I want to lick that, I want to fuck that, I want to come on those," he's saying to himself, "I am not a fag. I like women. I don't like men."

"I WANTED TO ASK YOU something," Vernon says to me one night during our private shows. It's been almost five months since I last saw him. I was beginning to think he had disappeared forever, like so many regulars do. I had considered giving him a call a couple times, found myself missing him in a strange know-what-to-expect kind of way, but I had thrown out all the bottles he had written on.

Vernon's shaved his beard off and his face looks different: round and pink, newborn. I didn't even recognize him until I asked him for a tip.

He rests his arms on the stage ledge. "I want to ask you something. But you need to know I'm serious. I ain't playing around."

"What's up?"

"Well, I was gonna ask you to marry me tonight." His voice is soft and gentle, and an image comes to my mind of him standing in front of the mirror in his bathroom, straightening his shoulders, practicing those lines.

I lean back against the mirrors. "Nuh-uh," I say, trying my best to gloss over this moment, suddenly conscious like never before of my nakedness.

"C'mon, now," he says, looking like he might cry. "I ain't kidding. I love you."

I search my brain for the right thing to say. The intimacy that he's wanting makes me uneasy, because it's so much more than intimacy. It's affirmation he's after, and not just affirmation regarding his sexuality, but his very existence. I remember reading something years ago by a British writer named Arnold Ludwig, that by loving others we deny the potential meaninglessness of our own lives. And it doesn't even matter if we know the other person or whether the other person loves us back. In the very act of loving we keep all that nasty existential angst at bay. The fact that I am not the first dancer he's become infatuated with belies his need for someone, anyone. And this makes me uneasy too, this reminder that it's not really me he loves, that our—can we call this a relationship?—is just an illusion, that I could be any girl, that I am any girl. No, I don't want to marry Vernon, but I'd like him to want to marry *me*.

"Vernon, I'm sorry. I can't marry you."

He nods and straightens his hat. He doesn't ask why and I'm grateful. To tell him I'm married would be almost cruel now, like I was making excuses, insulting his intelligence.

We finish the rest of our dances in silence, and I find myself longing for the dirty talk. The easy talk. If he were to ask me to say something now, I think I would. Then I think, *no you wouldn't, you just want to think you would.*

Before he leaves, I give him a hug goodbye. It takes him by surprise, and me too. I've never done that before. I don't know why I do it now. Maybe to remind myself that we're real people. That the three hundred dollars I made off him tonight carries its own price. That what we're doing here has consequences bigger than ourselves. Then I think, *no, don't make too much out of this. You're just a girl making a living, and he's just a dirty old man who ought to learn some manners.*

When he's gone, I pick up the bottle of nonalcoholic champagne and check my watch. Twenty until four. Almost closing time. I pass by a table of three young guys who probably came in after the regular bars closed to sober up before going home. One of them is asleep with his head thrown back at an unnatural angle. If it weren't for the music, you could hear him snore.

Another one grabs my arm. "You got alcohol?" He looks no more than sixteen. He's wearing dark sunglasses.

I hold the bottle out of his reach. "Trust me," I tell him. "You don't want this."

The third one has his legs sprawled out and I have to step over them. "You're looking fine, girl," he says. He has a cell phone up to his ear, but I get the feeling there's no one on the other end. He winks at me. "Where you gonna be after work, baby?"

"Wherever you're not," I say. He doesn't hear me. I don't want him to hear me. It just feels good to say it.

Amanda Scheiderer (known also as Amanda Rush) got her first job washing dishes at a mom-and-pop diner in Cape Coral, Florida, when she was fourteen years old. She has been working ever since. Her job history has been varied and seemingly incongruous—cashier, assistant security alarm installer, part-time private investigator, office manager, real estate investor, mortgage loan processor, stripper, graduate student in creative writing, legal assistant, online bookseller, and psychiatric hospital volunteer. Scheiderer is currently a registered nurse working toward her master's in psychiatric nursing. She lives in Hilliard, Ohio, with her second husband and step-pets. "Dirty Talk" is Scheiderer's first published work.

Scheiderer writes, " 'Dirty Talk' came to be when I was a graduate student in creative writing at The Ohio State University. I was still dancing then and was interested in writing a collection of essays about my regular customers. In the three years I stripped, I came to know these men not as seedy, lecherous, dangerous perverts but as fellow human beings trying their best to make it through the world. I believe it was my experiences with these men in the club that prepared me for the work I do now as a psychiatric nurse."

Copyright © Amanda Scheiderer

Womanhood

Catherine Anderson

She slides over
the hot upholstery
of her mother's car,
this schoolgirl of fifteen
who loves humming & swaying
with the radio.
Her entry into womanhood
will be like all the other girls'—
a cigarette and a joke
as she strides up with the rest
to a brick factory
where she'll sew rag rugs
from textile strips of Kelly green,
bright red, aqua.

When she enters
and the millgate closes
final as a slap,
there'll be silence.
She'll see fifteen high windows
cemented over to cut out light.
Inside, a constant, deafening noise
and warm air smelling of oil,
the shifts continuing on . . .
All day she'll guide cloth along a line
of whirring needles, her arms & shoulders
rocking back & forth
with the machines—
200 porch size rugs behind her
before she can stop
to reach up, like her mother,
and pick the lint
out of her hair.

Born in Detroit in 1954, daughter of a school teacher and a newspaper reporter, **Catherine Anderson** grew up in the midwestern cities of Detroit and Kansas City. She spent twenty-five years on the East Coast, most of the time in Boston, where she worked with new immigrants and refugees as a teacher, newspaper editor, fundraiser, and community activist. She now lives and works in Kansas City, assisting that region's growing immigrant and refugee population. Anderson is the author of two collections of poems, *The Work of Hands* (Perugia 2000) and *In the Mother Tongue* (Alice James 1983).

Anderson writes, "Work is a strong theme in my poetry, a deep wellspring of drama and imagery. Though I think I work hard, I've always known people who have worked harder than I could ever imagine." The poem "Womanhood" was inspired by a friend, Victoria Byerly, who grew up in the mill region of North Carolina and writes movingly of African American and white women who worked in the mills in *Hard Times Cotton Mill Girls* (ILR 1986). Anderson's poem "is a glimpse of a young woman's initiation into her mother's life of labor, a strenuous form of work she both understands yet also resists."

"Womanhood" is reprinted from *The Work of Hands* (Perugia Press 2000) by permission of Perugia Press, Florence, Massachusetts. Copyright © 2000 by Catherine Anderson.

Concrete Men

Dan Pope

IN THE SUMMER OF 1978, when I was sixteen years old, I worked as a laborer for Carbonaro Construction Company in Hartford, Connecticut. I was part of a crew of fifty men—sheetrockers, carpenters, electricians, plumbers, roofers, painters, bricklayers—hired to renovate a concrete hulk of a building that used to be a Buick dealership.

I was the sweeper. I followed the workmen with a broom, dustpan, and garbage pail, listening to them curse and brag and fart and ridicule each other. Nearly all of the men had tattoos on their biceps and forearms, a litany of women's names or slogans like Semper Fi. Some had bullet scars. I picked up junk they threw onto the floor and carried it to the dumpster out back. For this, I received five dollars and fifty cents per hour.

The boss was a man named Sal Carbonaro. He and my father were longtime friends; they grew up together and used to be partners in a construction business. That's how I got the job.

During my first week, Sal Carbonaro said to me, "What's the rush, kid?"

I said, "What do you mean?"

"Don't work so fast," he said, gesturing with his hands. His fingers were stubby and creviced. "You're making the others look bad. It's a state job, you understand?"

I nodded, but he could tell I didn't know what he meant. He placed his hand on my shoulder. "No one's checking up on you," he said. "Slow and steady. That's the way to go. Okay?"

"Okay."

"Whatever you do, don't get hurt." He stressed every word. "That's the important thing. If you get hurt, your father will kill me."

I didn't see how it was possible to get hurt on a job like this one. Everyone was working half-days, stealing, overcharging. "It's a state job," they said, again and again, like a punchline. Sal Carbonaro sent crews of workmen out to his house in the suburbs—they told me about the swimming pool they dug, the new roof and skylight—all on the state's tit, as they said. The wealth got spread down the line. Grateful subcontractors gave him gifts—usually cases of scotch or cognac—which I loaded off their trucks into the trunk of his Lincoln Continental.

ONE DAY—IT WAS THE MIDDLE of July, hot and muggy, reeking of tar and exhaust fumes—Sal Carbonaro called me into the office he'd set up in the rear corner of the building. There were two desks: one for him and one for Gerald. Gerald was Sal Carbonaro's cousin. If the phone rang, he answered it and wrote down the message. That was his job. Mainly, he just sat in his swivel chair with his feet up, doodling pencil-and-paper drawings of naked women.

Sal Carbonaro told me, "The concrete men are coming today. You're going to work with them."

I said, "Okay."

"They're shorthanded. That means you're in for some hard work. That means no fucking around. You ready for that?"

"Sure," I said.

He pointed a thick index finger at my feet. He said, "Where's your workshoes?"

I looked at my Chuck Taylor Cons, the worn canvas.

"Those are no good," said Sal Carbonaro. "Those aren't OSHA. Something falls on you wearing those things, you'll break every bone in your foot. You got twenty bones in your foot, did you know that?"

"No."

"Most bones in your body, they're in your feet. Get a pair of steel-toed boots. You don't want to get hurt, remember. That's the golden rule."

I smiled. "Okay."

Sal Carbonaro leaned back in his chair and looked me over. "You're a smart kid," he said. "You go to college, right?"

"I'm in high school," I said. "I don't have to worry about it until next year."

"Trust me," he said. "College is the best thing in the world. That way, you get a good job. Lawyer, something like that."

He checked his watch, got up from the desk and left the office.

As soon as the door closed, Gerald turned toward me. He said, "Can you keep a secret?"

"Sure," I said.

He reached under the desk and pulled out a box labeled *Powder-Actuated Fastening Tool*. "It's a Hilti gun," he said. "Twenty-two caliber."

"What's it for?"

"Watch," said Gerald. He loaded a handful of four-inch metal studs into the barrel of the gun and slid a strip of cartridges into the magazine. Then he wheeled around in his swivel chair, reached down, pressed the gun against the floor, turned his head, and pulled the trigger. I flinched at the explosions, three blasts in quick succession. The spent copper cartridges popped out and clanked on the floor. He moved the gun aside to reveal the studs, embedded in the concrete.

"You gotta have a license to operate this thing. It's not legal otherwise," he said.

Gerald had a twitch to his right eye—not a wink, but something convulsive, uncontrollable, like a baby bird trying to fly.

"What's wrong with your eye?" I asked.

"Nothing," he said.

"Looks like you got something stuck in it."

"Nah. It does that sometimes. I can't help it."

"Why not?"

"This hippie broad I got mixed up with in Providence. She blew my brains out."

"What do you mean?"

"You know about blow jobs, right?"

"Sure," I said.

"Ten times a day, she did it. She blew me so much I didn't know my own name. She blew me at night when I was sleeping. I'd wake up and there she was, down there. I never been the same since."

"It made your eye twitch?"

"Yeah."

"That's impossible," I said.

"No," he said. "It's true."

The phone began ringing. It rang three, four, five times. There's something about a ringing phone. You can't think straight until it stops.

"Aren't you going to get that?"

Gerald said, "Nah." He flattened out a fresh piece of paper on his desk and began doodling.

AT LUNCHTIME, THE FOOD TRUCK parked on the street in front of the building, giving off greasy vapors. The workmen handed me dollar bills and I walked out to the truck and gave their orders, Cokes and hot dogs, usually. The youngest guy was always the "go-for," they told me. Some of them even started calling me that, Gopher. They let me keep the small change, which clinked in my pockets, adding up, a clump of pennies, nickels, and dimes.

After lunch, the concrete truck pulled up onto the sidewalk. A big man got out of the passenger side. He had square shoulders and a beer belly hanging beneath his soiled white T-shirt. There was a long scar along his left cheek, which looked like a lopsided grin. You thought he was smiling, but he wasn't.

He said, "Where's Numb Nuts?"

I said, "Who?"

The big man strode past me into the building. From behind he looked as trim as a football player.

The driver called from the truck: "That's Leroy." He was resting his arm on the top of the door, his head tilted back so that I could see only part of his face.

I watched the letters on the side of the truck go around and around: *Spara Spara Spara Spara*. I said to the driver, "Everybody's been waiting for you."

The driver said, "We're here, man."

I said, "When does the truck stop spinning?"

"Never, man. Never stops. Just keeps turning."

Leroy returned a couple of minutes later, cursing under his breath. He said, "Who the hell are you? You're the boss's kid, aren't ya?"

"No," I said.

"Bullshit. I know a shit-ass boss's son when I see one."

He turned toward the building and said, "Go find a wheelbarrow. Get me a load of concrete and bring it inside."

I called after him. "I'm supposed to sweep up."

He said without stopping, "Get moving. You're working with me."

I got the wheelbarrow from around the side of the building—a huge metal tub, dimpled from years of use. The tire needed air; it wobbled as I pushed the wheelbarrow to the truck. The driver swung the chute over the tub and pulled the lever. In a moment, the concrete slithered down, like soft-serve ice cream.

There were eight steps that ascended to the entranceway of the building. I picked up a wooden plank and placed it over the steps. As I pushed the wheelbarrow up the plank, the concrete shifted to the rear of the tub, nearly causing me to lose control.

I found Leroy in a small room, the tile floor ripped up. He was leaning against the wall, smoking a cigarette. I lowered the handles of the wheelbarrow and wiped the sweat from my brow.

He said, "You call that a load?"

"Huh?"

"That's all you can lift? A fucking quarter load?"

"It's what the guy gave me."

"Gimme that goddamn wheelbarrow," said Leroy, flicking aside the cigarette. He grabbed the handles and pitched the tub to the side, dumping the concrete onto the floor. Using one hand, he spun the wheelbarrow around and rolled it out of the room. I followed him outside, hurrying to keep up, and watched, shading my eyes from the sun, as the driver moved the chute over the tub and plopped in the concrete.

Leroy said, "Fill the fucking thing."

The driver added more.

Leroy said, "Did I tell you to stop?"

The driver kept filling until the concrete made a mound in the middle, some oozing over the sides of the tub. "That's too much," he said. "Nobody can push that."

Leroy ignored him. He bent his knees, grabbed the handles, and lifted. With a thump, he rolled the wheelbarrow onto the plank, his body bent forward, his legs pumping. He nearly reached the top of the plank before losing momentum, then stopping. He strained, leaning to one side, the tub tilting the other way, concrete spilling over the side. The driver jeered, calling out Leroy's name. In response, Leroy growled a great bellow of defiance, and pushed the load over the top and into the building.

WHEN I ENTERED THE ROOM, Leroy was on his hands and knees, smoothing wet concrete onto the floor with a trowel.

He said, "You know what this is, this room?"

"Bathroom."

"It's an executive bathroom," he scoffed. "They're bringing in special fixtures made of marble. Italian tile. Cost a fortune."

"So what?"

"That's the way it works, kid. We pay taxes so one old limp-dick state motherfucker can wipe his ass in style. Gimme a shovelful right here."

I stuck the shovel into the wheelbarrow and lifted some concrete and pitched it onto the floor. The concrete struck the floor and splashed up into Leroy's face.

He wiped his face with his shirtsleeve and said, "Not like that. Lay it down easy."

I pitched another load onto the floor, farther away from him, but the concrete splashed back, speckling his arms and legs.

He said, "What the fuck is wrong with you?"

"Sorry," I said.

"Do it like this." He moved on his knees toward me, took the shovel out of my hand, lifted some concrete, lowered the shovel to the floor and gently flipped it over, like someone turning the page of a book. The concrete made no splash.

He said, "Like that. Got it?"

"Yeah."

"Good. Now gimme one like I showed you."

I stuck the shovel into the wheelbarrow and lowered it but the handle slipped out of my sweaty hands and the shovel clattered to the floor, splashing concrete into Leroy's eyes and over most of his body.

He said, "Fucking kid. You fucking kid."

He lunged at me. I jumped back, but he kept coming. I took off, running out the door.

"Fucking kid," he panted. He chased me through the building, out the entranceway, down the plank and into the alleyway that led to the rear of the building. Then he stopped and bent over and grabbed his knees and exhaled and didn't move for a long time. I stood ten yards away, watching.

"You all right?" I said.

He panted, bent double.

"Go get me a Coke, will ya," he said.

UNDER THE SHADE OF THE food truck's awning, I watched people pass on the sidewalk—a tattooed street punk in a tank top, a bum talking to God or the devil or no one in particular, a legless man wheeling himself to the VA office located next door. A pretty girl walked by, causing a small, sharp pain somewhere in my guts, like a hunger pang. The disc jockey on the food truck radio announced the temperature. It kept getting hotter.

Sal Carbonaro was standing by the rear of his Lincoln Continental, which was parked on the lawn in front of the building. He always parked on the lawn, where everyone could see. It reminded you who he was, someone not bound to petty rules like parking meters. He was talking to two men dressed in suits and ties.

One of the men said, "You're not on our books and we're not on yours. That's the way I like to do business."

A few moments later, he said, "Lenny's taking in a million dollars a year and he's not keeping ten G for himself."

The other man said, "There's too many goddamn bosses, that's the problem with this business these days."

"He's in too deep," said Sal Carbonaro. "I always said that about Lenny." He looked up and saw me watching. He called, "Hey, kid. Come here."

I walked over and stood next to them, holding my two cans of Coke.

Sal Carbonaro introduced me to the men, telling them who my father was. They looked me up and down.

One of them said, "What's your father doing these days?"

"Real estate appraisal," I said.

"Who's he working for?"

"Himself. It's his own business."

"You see," he said, looking at Sal Carbonaro. "He got out. The smart ones always get out."

"You tell him we said hi," said the other man. "Sam and Mike, that's us. He'll remember us."

"Okay," I said.

Sal Carbonaro winked at me. "You working hard?" he said.

"I guess."

"Good for you," said one of the well-dressed men. "Put some hair on your chest."

The other man grunted. "Who you kidding? What do you know about hard work? You never worked a goddamn day in your life."

"The hell I didn't."

Sal Carbonaro laughed. "If you call pulling your pud work, then you're the hardest working son of a bitch I ever met."

When I got back to the alley, Leroy was sitting in the shade, with his back resting against the wall. I handed him the Coke.

He said, "You're pretty quick."

I said, "Fastest in my class."

"I used to be fast," he said. He took off his shirt and wrapped it around his head. He smacked his belly and began squeezing the fat like he was trying to rearrange his internal organs.

"Too fucking hot to chase you. Must be ninety-five degrees."

"It's a hundred and one," I said.

He said, "Hundred and one was a cool day in Nam."

"Is that where you got that scar?"

He touched his cheek, running his finger along the crease. "One of my own guys did that, with a Bowie knife."

"Why?"

"I cheated him."

"Did you get him back?"

"Nah. He was a friend of mine."

I said, "Did you kill anyone?"

He glanced at me for a moment, then looked away. "Sure. Lots."

"What was it like?"

"It was a job. Just like this one. They set you down in the jungle, you did your job."

Leroy popped the tab and glugged down half the can in one pull. Then he closed his eyes and reclined his head against the wall. I opened my Coke and took a few sips and looked around the alleyway—broken glass, stray newspapers, cracked asphalt, reflections of light from the windows of the VA office. Car noise came from the street, horns, engines.

"Why did they leave you in the jungle?" I asked.

"You don't want to know," he said.

"Sure I do."

He said, "War, kid. There is no reason."

"There had to be a reason."

He looked at me, smiling twice—his scar and his mouth. "You think so, huh? Don't be so sure."

He drank the rest of the soda and tossed the can aside. I watched it bounce down the alleyway. I said, "If you put a tooth in a can of Coke it'll be gone in a week. Disintegrated."

He said, "That true?"

"Yeah. We did it in science class."

He said, "I got diabetes. I ain't supposed to drink soda pop anyhow."

He rose to his feet. "Let's go," he said. "Gotta finish the rich man's shitter."

Then came the real work.

We had to dig a twenty-by-twenty-foot ditch on a patch of rocky earth behind the building. The ditch had to be three feet, six inches deep—below the frost line—to make a concrete platform for a large transformer that was being delivered the next day.

Leroy and I dug with shovels, with Sal Carbonaro watching over us. The surveyor had marked the lines with string tied to wooden posts, and Sal

Carbonaro made sure we kept the line plumb. It was an important job. "No fucking around," Sal Carbonaro kept saying. We worked under the full afternoon sun, sweat pouring into our eyes.

The ground was so rocky that Leroy put down his shovel and took up a pinch bar, stabbing with it, loosening the soil and rocks for me to take away. It wasn't like digging on the beach. I used the edge of the shovel, scraping out pieces of clay and pebbles and rocks and clumps of dirt, half of which fell back into the ditch. Before long, my hands started to blister and bleed against the rough wooden handle. Sal Carbonaro noticed, and he gave me a pair of heavy work gloves, which I put on.

He asked if I wanted to quit.

"No," I said.

"Good man," he said, without smiling.

Leroy and I grunted and mumbled stray phrases. "Hit here." "Get the rock." "Fucking root." "Use the pinch." Often I worked with my hands, bent over, flinging the rocks and dirt back between my legs like a dog digging, but no one laughed.

It took two hours to dig the ditch, and my back was so sore I could barely straighten up, but that was only the start. We then had to lay down the plywood forms that went around the sides of the ditch.

After that came the concrete, load upon load, which I fetched with the wheelbarrow from the truck in front of the building. Leroy pointed where he wanted it, and I dumped and shoveled the concrete into the ditch. He smoothed it into place with his trowel. He made a few trips with the wheelbarrow, but mostly it was me, wrestling the tub up the slope of the alleyway, going back and forth, getting the load from the driver, who stayed by the truck.

At one point, after I shoveled some concrete into the trench, Sal Carbonaro swore. I wondered what I'd done wrong. I felt, for a moment, like crying. He pointed his big fingers at me and said, "You tell that son of a bitch to stop adding so much goddamn water. You tell him I want a goddamn one-two-four mix. Look at this watery shit. How's he expect this to dry by tomorrow?"

I rolled the wheelbarrow back to the truck and told the driver, "Too much water."

"Says who?" He was leaning against the side of the truck, partially in the shade, smoking a cigarette. I envied him, his easy job, staying by the truck.

"Boss."

"Fuck him. He doesn't know what he's talking about," he said.

But he changed the mix, I noticed, by pulling a lever that cut off the water, which made the concrete clumpier.

The other workmen packed their gear and left, calling out insults. Even the sheetrockers—French Canadians who lived in a motel during the workweek and who were always the last to go—even they left, speaking in their own language.

Sal Carbonaro said, "We're almost done."

He worked alongside us the last half-hour, pushing the concrete around the ditch with a shovel, splattering his trousers.

"That's it," he said.

Leroy put down his trowel. I leaned against my shovel, unable to stand.

Sal Carbonaro put his hand on my shoulder. "It's six o'clock," he said. "Go sit inside for a couple minutes and get some water while I find Gerald and take care of a few things."

Leroy and I went into the basement of the building through the overhead garage door—there was a row of five of these doors, where they used to wheel in the Buicks for repair. Sal Carbonaro parked his fleet of pickup trucks inside, along with some heavy machinery.

We went into the corner room, which used to be the waiting area. There were posters of LeSabres and Regals, torn and yellowed now, still covering the plywood walls. I turned on a rusty faucet and stuck my head underneath the stream. I drank for a long time and filled a tin cup for Leroy and handed it to him.

We sat down in wooden chairs, facing each other.

"Cool in here," said Leroy.

There was a stink to the room from bums sleeping on the floor at night. They got in through the broken windows, Sal Carbonaro once told me. He found them here every morning. He'd turn on the fluorescent light and bang a metal pipe against a pillar until the bums groaned and got up and shuffled out the overhead doors, red faced and reeking.

I leaned back, feeling satisfied. I'd done the work, like Leroy, like the other guys—real work, not sweeping, not go-for work. I wasn't a shit-ass boss's son.

I caught Leroy's eye. For a moment I thought he was smiling back, feeling the same thing I was. But I was wrong. It was just his scar-grin, falsely smiling. There was no satisfaction on his face, just weariness.

He said, "They got this place in Florida where they wrestle alligators with their bare hands. The guy grabs him by the tail and straddles him and feeds him dead chickens. He's got scars all over his body and three fingers missing and a stump for a foot."

"That's worse than digging ditches," I said.

"No it ain't. It's the same thing." Leroy spat. "Three years ago, I had my own cleaning business, with three full-time workers. I had a wife. I had a nice little house and a backyard that ran against a creek. Ask me what happened."

I said, "What happened?"

He said, "I paid my bills. The only asshole in Connecticut who paid his bills on time, that's me. Sons of bitches didn't pay me. Sons of bitches never paid a dime. My wife left me for a plumbing contractor name of Paddy Bartone. Last I heard, she moved to Florida."

"Maybe she's wrestling alligators."

Leroy grinned his double grin. "I hope she is," he said.

He offered me a stick of gum. I reached forward to take it, and as I did, the blasts rang out. Five explosions, a couple of seconds apart. I heard something whiz past my ear and ricochet off the floor, kicking up shards of concrete.

Leroy jumped to his feet, sending his chair backward. He crouched low and looked all around. I just sat in my chair, flinching with each blast.

"What the fuck," said Leroy. He leaned over and picked up something. He held it toward me: a bent four-inch metal stud.

"It's the Hilti gun," I said.

"You're right. Who the fuck is shooting?"

It's Gerald, I wanted to say, but something kept me from telling.

"You're not hit, are ya?" he asked.

"No."

He looked up. There was a line of holes in ceiling tiles, with threads of insulation hanging down. "Coming from upstairs," he said.

He went outside and walked up the alleyway. I hurried to keep up, following his long strides.

We met Sal Carbonaro walking into the building, jiggling his keys. He had a six pack of Schlitz in one hand, which he held out toward Leroy.

Leroy said, "Who's using the Hilti gun?"

Sal Carbonaro said, "The Hilti? Why?"

"He almost killed us, that's why. We were down in the basement office. He shot right through the fucking ceiling."

Sal Carbonaro said to me, "Is that true?"

"Yeah. Five times."

Sal Carbonaro's face reddened and formed an expression that you didn't want directed at you. You could see how hard a man he was with that look. For a moment I thought he was going to punch me.

He said, "Son of a bitch."

He dropped the beer cans—one of them started fizzing out—and walked into the building, his leather shoes smacking against the floor. It was a long walk across that building, the concrete floor littered with pieces of wood and silver insulation ducts and metal rods and pipes, pieces of copper and wire and cord— all the material that makes up a building that you never see.

He headed directly for the office, us following, and pushed open the door. Gerald glanced up, a look of dumb surprise on his face. He was sitting on the floor with the Hilti gun in his hand. Sal Carbonaro took the gun out of Gerald's hand and slapped him across the face, two hard, ringing slaps on the same cheek.

Gerald said, "Hey."

Sal Carbonaro said, "Who told you to use the Hilti?"

Gerald said, "I wanted to try it out."

"You wanted to try it out?"

"Yeah."

Sal Carbonaro said, "You're firing through a goddamn hollow in the concrete."

"A what?"

"A hole, you dumb bastard."

"So what?"

Sal Carbonaro took a few deep breaths. "How many times have I told you not to play around on the job? Huh? You do a job, you do it serious. How many times have I told you that?"

"I don't know."

"Go home, Gerald." Sal Carbonaro said the words slowly. "I don't care how you get there. Just go."

Gerald said something that made no sense. He said, "Hey. If you can't laugh in the daytime. Right?"

Sal Carbonaro pointed to the door with his big fingers. "Don't come back till Monday morning. I don't want to see your face until then."

Gerald got up and left, his eye twitching.

SAL CARBONARO LOCKED THE BUILDING. He remained silent as he did so.

I followed him to the car, parked on the front lawn. He popped open the trunk, revealing cases of scotch and cognac. He tore open one of the boxes and took out a bottle—the label said *Hine Triomphe*—and handed it to me. "That's for your father," he said.

He reached into his pocket and pulled out a wad of cash and peeled off a hundred dollar bill. "That's for you, for working late."

I looked at the bill, something I'd never seen before.

"Get in," said Sal Carbonaro. "I'll take you home."

I opened the big door and sank into the leather seat.

Instead of starting the motor, Sal Carbonaro turned to me and said, "From now on, you come in on Friday afternoons to pick up your paycheck. That's it."

"What do you mean?"

"I mean, you stay home. You go swimming. You chase pussy. You do whatever you want to do. Don't worry about your check. You get the same amount no matter what."

"Why?"

"Why? It's a state job, that's why. Because I owe your father, that's why."

"But why can't I come to work?"

He glared at me. "You almost got killed today," he said. "Don't you realize that? That what you want? To end up like Gerald, with your eye twitching?"

"He got that from a hippie girl," I said.

"There was no hippie girl," said Sal Carbonaro. "He got hit on the head with a brick hod that fell off a roof. Knocked him into a coma for two weeks. That's what happened to Gerald."

He started the car, racing the big motor. He said, "This life's not for you, kid. You don't want any part of it. You go to college, like I told you."

I said, "You and my dad, you did it. You made lots of money."

"Your dad was smart," said Sal Carbonaro. "He got out. He doesn't owe anybody but himself. That's the way to live. You remember that."

Sal Carbonaro moved the gearshift and drove the car across the lawn onto the sidewalk, beeping the horn to let some pedestrians know he was coming. He eased off the curb onto the pavement, and the bottles of liquor clinked inside the trunk. In my hands, I held a bottle of cognac and a hundred dollar bill. This was the way things operated, I realized, on cash and booze and marble bathrooms and alligator skins, things people wanted. There was a whole secret commerce, a network of stealing that wasn't called stealing, that went on all the time, that no one told you about in the suburbs where I lived, where all the lawns were neatly trimmed and only sane people walked the streets.

We turned down the road, heading toward the concrete truck. Leroy and the driver were leaning against the rear of the truck, drinking from cans of Schlitz. They were sweating and dirty and splotched all over with gray dabs of concrete. It was still hot, the light starting to redden toward sundown.

I called out.

I said, "Leroy. Hey, Leroy."

Leroy looked up and saw me and grinned his double grin, his scar turned toward me. He raised his right fist above his head like an Olympian, and he roared. He said, "Arrrrrr!"—an animal growl, something never to be tamed.

Sal Carbonaro drove by without slowing down.

He said, "Don't talk to those slobs."

Dan Pope is the author of a novel, *In the Cherry Tree* (Picador 2003). His short stories have been published recently in *Harvard Review, Crazyhorse, Postroad, Iowa Review, McSweeney's, Shenandoah, Gettysburg Review, Witness*, and other magazines. He is a winner of the Glenn Schaeffer Award from the International Institute of Modern Letters and a grant in fiction from the Connecticut Commission on Culture and Tourism.

Pope writes, "My father was co-owner of a construction company in the sixties and seventies in Hartford, Connecticut. Mainly his company built and renovated industrial warehouses on Locust Street in the south end of the city, near the sewage treatment plant and Brainard Airport, an area that seemed isolated from most forms of humanity but is now seedy and fenced-in. When I turned thirteen, Dad started taking me to the job over the summers. He put me and my older brother on the payroll as laborers and gave us $6 per hour, which seemed an incredible sum of money in the mid-seventies. My brother and I tended to mess things up, so my father made us the demolition crew. Whenever something needed to be destroyed, he put us to the task—knocking down sheetrock walls with sledgehammers, say, or ramming a concrete post with a forklift. We were on a constant lookout for 'the OSHA guy' or the 'state inspector.' If such individuals showed up, we were supposed to report immediately to my father and then hide.

"A different construction crew would arrive on the job every week or so—the electricians, the carpenters, the sheetrockers, the plumbers—each bringing with them a whole new pool of amazement. A lot of these men were Vietnam vets. Many had knife or bullet scars and severe, untreated mental disorders, and almost all were tattooed, which was not common at that time. They delighted in teaching me the intricacies of such subjects as war, sex, infidelity, racism, drunkenness, and the inequities of American capitalism. They would give me cold beers—Schlitz or Pabst Blue Ribbon—at the end of the day, sitting by their trucks, smoking cigarettes. Drunk in the sun—an indelible first feeling.

"In school, my long-haired English teacher (a conscientious objector) lectured about the causes and effects of the Vietnam War, but Lenny the cement truck driver taught me the proper method of sticking a knife into an enemy soldier—thrusting upward from the hip so you couldn't miss and then turning the blade to tear out the other's intestines. It seemed the highest praise when Lenny deemed my father 'a good guy.'

"I remember thinking, when I returned in the fall to ninth grade, that my classmates knew nothing."

"Concrete Men" originally appeared in *Shenandoah* (2001). Copyright © 2001 by Dan Pope. It is reprinted here by permission of the author.

We Who Have Escaped

Leigh Hancock

1.

Tell stories
of industrial rumble, the clattering looms
and shellfish stink that stuck in our hair,
of slick floors, sharp knives
and bags of waste
spilling on the hospital floor.

It's not funny but we manage to laugh
at the boss who pinched on his way
to the bathroom and later sat
crotch forward on his pivoting throne,
saying *You don't like it*
you can leave, there's always another

girl with a couple of kids to feed,
another man with a mortgage,
or a dream of one, who wakes nights
sweating at the thought of *his* father,
that gruff man with broken nails
raising a family on a shovel blade,
another wiry kid who still believes
a good day's work will get him somewhere.

2.

More stories, mine
typing claims for Sterling Insurance,
caught between slime and ooze
while Mr. Sterling battles Dr. Lord
and somewhere someone with a bungled spleen
opens the letter my lips licked shut
and feels hope dissolve with the word *Denied.*

Still others: slinging hash at Sigma Chi,
tucking the corners at Rodeway Inn,
shucking corn, dialing phones, cleaning up messes
someone else made because work is noble
and we want to be.

3.

The man I love doesn't tell stories.
He rises silent, takes his coffee,
cigarette, shower, coffee again,
and only then, on better days,
feels a tremor of life return.

I watch him sugar his sugar pops,
a hard-muscled man with savage hands
scarred by his bloodie, rashed with chemicals
from the berber and pile he lays,
and can hardly believe that yesterday
those thick fingers put my glasses together,
twirling the screw in the tiny threads,
untangled the knotted jade plant roots and,
finding the knots in my white-collar back,
kneaded them away.

4.

Our stories of escape bear witness
to salaried jobs that opened sesame
just when we couldn't go one step more,
to chance encounters with someone
who miraculously knew someone big,
to job corps coaches who saw in our faces
a high school girl they secretly loved.

The password of the order we share
isn't hard work, isn't talent,
isn't ethics or perfect skill.
It isn't even education,
though that's what we've been told, and tell.

Luck, we whisper to each other,
careful our own children don't hear. Luck—

that whipcrack at the tailend of despair,
half dozen pulltabs on a sticky bar,
a sucker-hole that draws us in
with promises of one gold chance
to do good work and be human again.

But what—and this we never ask—
what if we weren't lucky? What if
we're never lucky again?

Leigh Hancock has spent much of her adult life trying to avoid paid work, in order to have time to write. In her less successful moments, she has been a bike messenger, prep school teacher, security guard, front desk clerk, college instructor, arts administrator, and counselor for men convicted of domestic abuse. Her current work includes taking care of her five-year-old son, grant-writing, and running the Gorge Writing Project, which sends writers into middle schools in the rural region where she lives.

She wrote the poem "We Who Have Escaped" in another life, when she was involved with a man who lay carpets for a living and subsequently immersed in issues of class and work. "I continue," she writes, "to feel terrifyingly lucky to live the life I do."

Hancock's poems and stories have been published in several anthologies, as well as in various magazines, including *Calyx, Mothering*, and *Sundog*. She has been the recipient of fellowships from the Henry Hoyns Foundation, the Helene Wurlitzer Foundation, and the Villa Montalvo Arts Center. She is currently at work on a memoir about her father, the artist Cordell Hancock.

Copyright © Leigh Hancock

Torch Song

Charles Bowden

I CAN'T TELL MUCH FROM her silhouette. She's sitting off to one side, her shoulders hunched, and toward the front is the box with the teddy bears. Or at least I think they're teddy bears. Almost twenty years have passed, and I've avoided thinking about it. There are some things that float pretty free of time, chronology, the book of history, and the lies of the experts. In the early eighties I went to a funeral as part of my entry into a world—a kind of border crossing.

It started as the gold light of afternoon poured through the high, slit windows of the newsroom. I had no background in the business and I'd lied to get the job. I was the fluff writer, the guy brought on to spin something out of nothing for the soft features and the easy pages about how people fucked up their marriages or made a quiche or found the strength to go on with their lives because of God, diet, or a new self-help book. Sometimes they wrote the book, sometimes they just believed the book. I interviewed Santa Claus, and he told me of the pain and awkwardness of having held a child on his fat lap in Florida as ants crawled up his legs and bit him. One afternoon the newsroom was empty, and the city desk looked out and beckoned me. I was told to go to a motel and see if I could find anything to say.

The rooms faced a courtyard on the old desert highway that came into town and were part of a strip of unhappy inns left to die after the interstate lanced Tucson's flank. When I was twelve this belt still flourished, and my first night in this city was spent in a neighboring motel with a small pool. I remember swimming until late at night, intoxicated with the idea of warm air, cool water, and palm trees. My sister was fourteen, and the son of the owners, a couple from the East with the whiff of Mafia about them, dated her; later, I read a newspaper story that cited him as a local purveyor of pornography. But the row of motels had since lost prosperous travelers to other venues and drifted into new gambits, most renting by the day, week, or month, as old cars full of unemployed people lurched into town and parked next to sad rooms where the adults scanned the classifieds for a hint of employment. The children always had dirty faces and anxious eyes. The motel I was sent to was a hot-sheet joint, with rooms by the hour or day, and featured water beds (WA WA BEDS, in the language of the sign), in-room pornographic movies, and a flock of men and women jousting through nooners.

The man at the desk had a weasel face and the small frame of the angry, smiling rats that inhabit the byways of America; the wife was a woman of some heft, with polyester pants and short-cropped hair. They seemed almost delighted to have a reporter appear, and after a few murmured words in the office, where I took in the posters for the featured films of cock-sucking, butt-fucking, and love, ushered me across the courtyard, with its unkempt grass, to the room. As we entered, she apologized and said she was still cleaning up. The linoleum floor looked cool, and the small chamber offered a tiny kitchenette and a small lavatory with shower, the old plastic curtain stained by years of hard water. The water bed, stripped of its sheets, bulged like a blue whale, and as the woman and I talked—he was quiet, she seemed nice, they didn't cause any fuss, the kid was a charmer—a dirty movie played soundlessly on the screen hanging off the wall and confronting the bed. I seem to remember a mirror of cheap, streaked tiles on the ceiling.

I walked around aimlessly and popped open the door of the old refrigerator—shelves empty—and then the little door to the freezer, where two bottles of Budweiser, frozen solid, nestled as if someone with a powerful thirst had placed them to chill in a hurry and then been distracted. I heard the woman's voice in my ear explaining how the mother had gone to work—she danced at a strip joint, one of the new gentlemen's clubs that featured college-looking girls instead of aging women with bad habits—and so was gone when it happened. I nodded, purred soothing words, closed the freezer door, and strolled back by the water bed; the blue of its plastic had the gaiety of a flower in the tired room. I looked at a big splotch on the cinderblock wall, and she said, "I haven't had time to clean that yet.'"

That's where the head had hit, the skull of the toddler just shy of two years, as the man most likely held him by the legs and swung him like a baseball bat. He probably killed the kid out of boredom or frustration with the demands of a small child, or because he'd been bopped around himself as a child, or God knows why. The man had taken off, then been caught by the cops, and was sitting in jail as they figured out what level of murder he'd scored. The dancer they'd found wandering in the desert, and they'd flung some kind of charges at her. As I stared at the block wall, the proprietress bubbled up in my ear again and said, with that small, cooing voice American women sometimes favor when indicating feeling, "We kind of made a collection and customers chipped in and we bought him an outfit for the burial." She told me they got the clothes at Kmart. I drove back to the paper, wrote an impressionistic piece pivoting on the frozen bottles and all the hopes and basic desires found in a beer chilling for a thirsty throat, and then phones started ringing at the city desk and I was hurled at the funeral.

So I sit through the service studying the mother's profile. She has fine hair, a kind of faint red. I once knew a woman with hair like that, and as I stare I can smell this other woman and feel my hands tracing a path through the slender strands. I can smell the soap, the scent of the other woman; the small smile and fine bones and clean, even teeth. In my memory the coffin is open, the boy's small face very pale and blank, and he is surrounded by donated teddy bears that came from a town that told itself these things are not supposed to happen, and if such things do happen they're not supposed to happen in our town.

Just before the service ends, I have a hunch that the cops are going to take the mother out the back so that the press cannot snap her image and I cannot scan her face. So I get up and leave the chapel of the cheap mortuary and go to the back, and, sure enough, suddenly the metal door opens and two cops burst through with the lap dancer handcuffed and sagging between their grip. The light is brilliant at 1:15 p.m. and merciless as it glares off the woman. Her face is small, with tiny bones, and her age is no longer possible to peg—somewhere between nineteen and one thousand. She is wearing tight pants on slender, girlish hips and a black leather vest over her blouse. The waist is small, the hair falls to her shoulders, the lips are very thin. A moan comes off her, a deep moan, and I sense that she is unaware of the sound she is making, just as she is unaware of what has happened to her. The only thing she knows is what I know. There is a toddler in a box with teddy bears, and the box sits in a room full of strangers from this town where she has bagged a job dancing for other strangers.

The cops look at me with anger, drag her slumping form away, and toss her into the back of a squad car. I stand still, make no notes. Then I go back to the newsroom and write up the funeral. That is when it begins. The toddler's death probably didn't have anything to do with child molestation, but for me this child became the entry point to rape and other categories of abuse. For the next three years I live in a world where the desire of people, almost always men, to touch and have their way with others makes them criminals. Gradually I began to lose the distinction between the desires of criminals and the desires of the rest of us. I am told I can't get off this kind of beat, because most reporters won't do it. This may be true, I don't really know, because those three years are the only ones I ever spent working for a newspaper and practically the only ones I ever spent working for anyone besides myself. I would quit the paper twice, break down more often than I can remember, and have to go away for a week or two and kill, through violent exercise, the things that roamed my mind. It was during this period that I began taking one-hundred- or two-hundred-mile walks in the desert far from trails. I would write up these flights from myself, and people began to talk about me as a nature writer. The rest of my time was spent with another nature, the one we call, by common consent, deviate or marginal or unnatural.

I can still see the woman coming through the metal door, slumping between the paws of the cops. I am standing northwest of her and about twenty feet away. It is 1:15 p.m., the glare of the sun makes her squint, her hips are bound in impossible pants, her face has never seen anything brighter than the dim lights of a strip joint, and her wrists, in the chrome gleam of cuffs, are tiny. I can remember this with photographic detail, only I can't remember what became of her or her lover. Just the boy, the splotch on the wall, the blue water bed, and the frozen Budweiser.

Until this moment, I've avoided remembering what became of me.

NIGHT, THE WARM NIGHT OF early fall, and they form up in the park, the women and their supporters, with candles and flashlights, banners and the will to take back the night. The green pocket of trees and grass hugs the road. They go a few blocks and swing down one of the city's main thoroughfares. Safety in numbers, group solidarity, sisterhood is powerful, protest, demands, anger, laughter, high spirits.

They find her later in a narrow slot between two buildings, more a gap in the strip of commercial facades than a planned path or walkway, the kind of slot that sees hard sun a few minutes a day and then returns to shadow. She is seven and dead. While the march to take back the night was passing through here, she apparently left her neighbor's yard nearby and came over to see the spectacle. The police and press keep back one detail: she has been eviscerated. That is part of what a newsroom feeds off—the secret facts that others do not know or cannot be told, the sense of being where the action is and where the knowing people gather. So we say to one another: opened up from stem to stern that night.

I come in the next morning ignorant of all this and am called into a meeting. The city editor, the managing editor, and the publisher are agitated. They have children; they want to do something, but they don't know what. I'm told to make a difference in the slaughter of our children. I nod and say, "You'll have to give me time." The exchange is very short; this paper has no long meetings. I go back to my desk and remember another night long ago: the man crying. And when I remember, I don't want to take this assignment, but I do.

HE SPEAKS IN A SMALL voice as his hands cradle his face in the hospital waiting room, and he says, "My baby girl, my baby girl." His wife looks on stoically. The call came in the middle of the night, and when I arrive there is the cool of fluorescent lights, the sterile scent of linoleum floors, and the memory of her going down the corridor on a gurney with her face pulverized into raw flesh. She had gone to visit a friend near campus and stepped out of her car onto the quiet street.

That is when he took her. He forced her back into her car, and they drove out of town into the open ground. He raped her, pistol-whipped her, pumped two rounds into her, and then left her for dead. She saw a house light and crawled toward it. The people inside feared her pounding in the night and did not want to open up. Somehow an ambulance came, and now she is in surgery as I sit with her weeping father and stoical mother. At the time, I am related by marriage. But that does not help. I am a man, but that does not help. I am not a rapist, and that does not help at all. Nothing really helps—not words, not anger, not reflection.

For days afterward, as the hospital reports come in, as the visits to the room present a bandaged and shaved head, as the unthinkable becomes normal for all of us, nothing really helps. We have stepped over a line into a place we refuse to acknowledge, a place of violence and danger, where the sexual impulses that course through our veins have created carnage.

I was in my late twenties then, and I remember my male friends all coming to me with visions of violence, scripts about what should be done to the rapist, what they would do to him, how these instances should be handled. I would nod and say very little.

I'm over at a house where friends live, the kind of male dormitory that has a dirty skillet festering on the stove, clothes tossed here and there, and empty beer bottles on the coffee table giving off stale breath. It is precisely 10:00 a.m., and one guy is just getting up from the mattress on the floor of his room. He is a Nam vet with a cluster of medals and has two interests after his war: hunting and women. A stack of skin magazines two feet high towers over the mattress, and a fine .270 with a polished walnut stock leans in the corner. He tells me they should take those guys out and cut their dicks off, and then he staggers down the hall with his hangover to take a piss. I feel that I am watching something happening on a screen but that I am not really here.

Eventually, a red-faced detective comes by to placate the victim's family and express his sense of urgency as we sit in the quiet kitchen. He explains all the things being done, but he convinces no one. How do you find a rapist when half the population is suspect? This is when I first hear the police read on rape: "Fifteen minutes for the guy, five years for the woman."

I had a vegetable garden then, and this was the only place where things made sense and fell into some kind of order. So I sit on the dirt amid the rows of bell peppers, tomatoes, eggplant, marigolds, and squash, sip red wine, and let my mind flow. I wonder if there is a monster lurking in all of us. I never cease, I realize, scanning faces when I prowl the city, and what I wonder is, *Are you the one?* I look over at the other cars when I am at a stoplight. This becomes an unconscious habit. Sometimes I think I have adopted the consciousness of a woman. Now I think like prey.

Later, a year or two later, a guy goes to a party near the campus, drinks and whoops it up, and leaves with a woman he meets there. He takes her out and rapes her and tries to kill her. Turns out he is the one, and they send him off to prison. By then, it hardly matters to me. I know he will be back and he will be older, and that that will be the only change. I bury the memories and go on pretty much as if nothing had ever happened. As does the woman who was raped, pistol-whipped, shot, and left for dead. You can know some things and the knowing seems to help you not at all.

"My baby girl, my baby girl." These memories resurface as I leave the editorial meeting with my instructions to figure out something for the paper to do about the slaughter of a seven-year-old girl during a march to take back the night. I sit at my gray desk and stare at the clock on the east wall. It is early in the morning, 7:00 or 8:00 a.m. I have no delusions that I will magically crack the case. But I decide to look into the world where such acts come from, though I do not consciously know what such a desire means in practical terms. I have no plan, just this sensation of powerlessness and corruption and violation and grief. I can feel my eyes welling with tears, and I know instantly that this feeling will do nothing for me or anyone else.

After that I follow my instincts, which is what the predators do also.

THERE ARE FIVE THINGS I KNOW to be true. These rules come to me out of my explorations.

1. No one can handle the children.

2. Get out after two years.

3. Always walk a woman to her car, regardless of the hour of the day or the night.

4. Don't talk about it; no one wants to hear these things.

5. No one can handle the children.

The fourth lesson is the iron law. We lie about sex crimes because we lie about sex. We lie about sex because we fear what we feel within ourselves and recoil when others act out our feelings. American society has always been more candid about murder ("I felt like killing him," we can say out loud) than about the designs we have on each other's bodies. What destroys people who have to deal with sex crimes is very simple: you lose the ability to lie to yourself about your feelings, and if you are not careful you fail to lie appropriately to others. When we are in bed with each other we find it difficult to say what we want, and when we brush up against sex crimes we find it difficult to stomach what we see and even more difficult to acknowledge the tug of our fantasies. In the core of our being live impulses, and these impulses are not all bright and not all as comfortable as an old shoe.

Soon after I embark on this assignment, I am at the home of a friend, a very learned man who is elderly. When we sit and drink he is open to any topic—the machinations of the Federal Reserve, the mutilation of young girls in Africa, male menopause, or the guilt/innocence of Alger Hiss. I have just written a story for the newspaper on child molestation that runs four solid pages without one advertisement because no merchant wants products next to such a story. I vaguely remember the lead. I must do this from memory, because regardless of the passage of years, with their gentle soothing effect, I cannot look at the clips yet: "The polite term is child molestation. The father said he had done nothing but fondle his son. The boy had gonorrhea of the mouth. The polite term is child molestation."

As I sit with my friend and we ponder the intricacies of the world and swap lifetimes of reading, he suddenly turns to me and says, "I want you to know I didn't read your story. I don't read things like that."

I am not surprised. After the story hits the press, women at the newspaper come up to me for soft conversations and want to have lunch or drinks. They murmur that they are part of the sisterhood or secret society of the maimed. The men avoid me, and I can sense their displeasure with what I have written and the endless and relentless nature of the piece. I realize that if I had not written it, I would avoid reading it, too.

Another revelation comes from having drinks with a retired cop. We are kind of friends: cops and reporters are natural adversaries and yet, in some matters, have no one else to talk with (see rule number four). I ask him how the local police handled rape during his time.

He says, "Well, the first thing we'd do is take the suspect out of the house and into the carport, and then we'd beat the shit out of him with our saps. Then we'd take him downtown and book him for assault." He does not read the piece either.

Then there is the woman who is passionately into nonviolence and vegetarianism and speaks softly as if she embodied a state of grace. She comes to my door one night after a couple of my stories have run, and we make love on the cement floor. Afterward, she tells me that when she was a girl her father, who was rich and successful, would sit around with his male friends and they would take turns fucking her in the ass. I walk her to her car.

I AM SITTING ON THE north end of a back row facing the west wall. The room is institutional and full of therapists, counselors, and other merchants of grief who have gathered to share their experiences treating victims of sex crimes. I scan the crowd, mainly women without makeup wearing sensible shoes. I listen for hours as they outline play therapy, describe predators (with children, usually someone close and accepted by the family; with rape, often as not the mysterious stranger), call for a heightened public consciousness about the size of this plague. Their statistics vary but basically suggest that everyone is either a victim of a sexual crime or the perpetrator of a sexual crime or a therapist treating sexual crimes. They all agree that children do not lie and that more attention must be paid.

Late in the day a woman walks to the podium. I have been noticing her for hours, because she does not fit in with the group. Her lips are lacquered, her hair perfect, and she wears a tasteful lavender dress—one I sense she has bought just for this occasion—and high heels. She is the only woman wearing high heels. She speaks with a southern accent and tells the group that she is not a professional person. She is a mother, and a neighbor molested her daughter, her very young daughter. And she wants something done about it. In her case, she continues, nothing was done. The neighbor still lives a few doors down, and her daughter still lives in terror—they have had to seal her window with duct tape so "he can't look in."

The woman at the podium is on fire and very angry. Her words slap the audience in the face. She has no theory, she says, and no program. She simply wants her government, her police, and her city to pay attention to the problem. And she will not rest. She reads her words off sheets of yellow legal paper, and her articulation is harsh, as if she were drumming her fingers on a Formica kitchen table.

Afterward, I cut through the crowd and find her. I say I am a reporter and would like to talk more. She is flustered. She is not used to talking to audiences and not used to talking to the press. She gives me her number, and we agree to meet. I notice her eye makeup and the sensual nature of her lips.

When I turn, another woman comes up to me. I vaguely noticed her enter when the woman whose child was molested was speaking. She is about thirty and wears leather pants and a motorcycle jacket. Her eyes are very intelligent, and she tells me she is a therapist. Her smile is generous. We walk out and go to a nearby café, which is empty and half-lit in the late afternoon, and sit at a round table with a dark top. We both sip longnecks.

Her life has not been simple lately. She is distancing herself, she explains, from a bad relationship. She has been living with a man, and he is very successful. He came home a few days ago and they made love. He told her she was the sixth woman he had had that day but that he liked her the best. *He never comes,* she says; *anything else, but he never comes. He withholds, don't you see?* she asks.

When I go to her place, she is in shorts and a shirt and is roller-skating in her driveway. She tells me she wanted me to see her that way, free and skating with delight. We lie on the floor. She says, "Squeeze my nipples hard, squeeze my titties as hard as you can." Later, we are in the bathroom, because she wants to watch us in the mirror. We go back to the bedroom and she rolls over on her stomach.

She says very softly, "Yes."

Somewhere in those hours my second marriage ends. I know why. I, too, tend to say yes. The marriage ends because I do not want to live with her anymore, because she is a good and proper person and this now feels like a cage. I do not want to leave my work at the office. I do not want to leave my work at all. I have entered a world that is black, sordid, vicious. And actual. And I do not care what price I must pay to be in this world.

The therapist has a lot of patients who are fat women, and they fascinate her. She herself has not an extra ounce of fat; she is all curves and muscle, her calves look like sculpture, her stomach is flat, her features are cute. She is very limber. Once at a party, she casually picked up one of her legs while talking to a couple and touched her ear with her foot. She was not wearing panties when she performed this feat. She runs daily, has been part of a female rock and roll band, takes showers three or four times a day, and is proudly bisexual. She tells me one of her best tactics for keeping boyfriends is to seduce and fuck their girlfriends. She smiles relentlessly.

What fascinates her about the fat women is their behavior. Not the eating. She cannot even fathom the eating part, since she never gains weight and eats whatever she wishes. Her place is always cluttered with bowls of macadamia nuts for guests. No, it's their sexual lives she is interested in. Their sexual lives are very simple: they will do anything. That, she tells me, is why men like fat women. They will do anything; name your fantasy, try out your imagined humiliation.

She tells me how she became a therapist. She went to visit her own therapist once and he questioned her openness, and she wound up doing golden showers in his office. After that she fled to an analytic center on the West Coast and studied very hard. No, she says, she is not bitter about it. She learned he was right; she was not open enough.

I find her smile addictive. We sit in her kitchen and she makes a Greek salad. She becomes a blur cutting up the feta cheese and dicing olives. And then we go to the bedroom. She tells me I have green blood and smiles with the promise that she will make it red.

HERE IS HOW PLAY THERAPY GOES. You look through one-way glass at very small children on the floor. The child holds anatomically correct dolls, ones with actual sexual organs, and acts out what has happened in the past. It is something to see. The dolls look like Raggedy Ann. And do pretty much exactly what adults do with each other. My guide in this place is a gray-haired woman who is very well-spoken and has the quiet calm of a Quaker lady. She used to work in a ward with terminally ill children. She tells me this work is harder. Ah, now the child is moving the two dolls.

WE TALK FOR TWENTY-TWO HOURS. Not all at once, no one can do that, but for very long stretches at a time. That is how the lady in the lavender dress with the hard words, the lady who stunned the seminar audience, begins. With talk.

We sit across from each other with the coffee table and a patch of rug between our chairs. She is cautious. This is her story and, like most people, she wishes to tell her story but only to the right person—the person who listens. I have no tape recorder, just a pen and a notebook, and we begin spiraling into the tale. It is night, her daughter is in the tub, she mentions pain and points. The mother hides her alarm, asks gentle questions, and it slowly comes out as the minutes crawl past. He is the older man, the pal of neighborhood kids. Always a smile, perfectly normal, you never would have guessed.

As she talks, her daughter, so very young and small, plays out in the yard, and from time to time I catch a glimpse of her as I look up from my notepad or glance away from the woman, her monologue flowing from her full lips. The child is in sunlight, gamboling about without a worry in the world. For a second, none of it ever happened. I see this apparition through the sliding glass doors, and then the woman's words pull me back to the night, the aftermath, the weeks and now months of coaxing the child back first from terror and then from a sense of betraying her special friend by telling—and, of course, she was warned not to tell, they always make sure to stress this warning.

When I am with the woman I enter, as she does, a kind of trance. When I am away the trance still holds to a degree, and I talk with no one about what I am doing. I make a point of filing other stories to disguise the hours I spend listening. I live in worlds within worlds, since the child's identity must not be revealed, and so for me things become generic and universal and yet at the same time, looking into one woman's face and taking down one woman's words, specific, exact, and full of color, scent, and feel.

I write the story in one long fury, and the printout runs about twenty feet. I crawl along my floor, reading it and making changes. Sometimes my therapist roller skater drops by and finds me crawling on the floor with my felt pen, and she does not approve of this act. It is too involved, not suitable for things that should be done at a desk with a good lamp and a sound chair. I sense I am failing her by falling into myself, and our sex grows more heated and yet more empty. This goes on for weeks. I don't know what to do with the story, and then finally I turn it in and they print it.

Fifty subscribers cancel in less than an hour, I am told.

I PROWL THROUGH THE POLICE blotter savoring the rapes of the night: The woman who leaves the bar at 1:00 a.m. with the stranger. No, can't sell her. The woman who decides at 3:00 a.m. to take a walk in short shorts and a halter to the all-night market for a pack of cigarettes and then gets bagged. She's out, too. The girl who goes into the men's room with her boyfriend to give him head and then his friends follow and gangbang her. No sale. I course through the dull sheets of pain, hunting for the right one—the one I can sell, the one to which readers cannot say, "Well, that could never happen to me," the one they can't run away from so easily.

A woman rides the freights into town and then hooks up with two guys at a cafe, and they say if you need a place to crash come with us. She does. She decides she needs a shower, and they say go ahead. When she comes out of what she calls "the rain closet" they're on her. She later goes to the cops, describes herself as a motorcycle mechanic, and tells them of the rape. The paper takes one look at my story and says forget it. And, of course, they're right. Rape, like many things, is kind of a class matter. You have to not deserve it for the world to care even a little bit. This I learn.

Sometimes, for a break, I drop in on a small bookstore where a heavy woman with a British accent sells used volumes. A gray cat is always nestled inside, and the place has the feel of afternoon tea in someone's living room. Then she is attacked and held hostage in her home one night. The store closes; I don't know what happens to the cat. Eventually, she leaves town and settles in a somewhat distant city. Finally, I hear she kills herself.

I keep hunting, talking with fewer and fewer people. Except for those who live in this world or at least understand its dimensions. I'll be somewhere, maybe kicking back, feet up on the coffee table, glass of wine in hand, and someone will play, say, the Stones' "Midnight Rambler," and my mood will sink and go black.

Best not to visit people.

THE DAYS OF THE WEEK CEASE to have meaning, as do the weeks of the month and the months of the year. My life went by clocks and dates and deadlines, but the order implied in paychecks, withholding taxes, dinner at six, and Sunday-morning brunch vanished with my consent. I did not lose control of my life; I gave up the pretense of normal life, and followed crime and appetite. I learned things on the run and without intention. Knowledge came like stab wounds, and pleasure came with the surprise of a downpour from a blue sky in the desert. I remember sitting with some women who had been raped after I wrote a profile of the rapist. Turns out all the guy's co-workers, mainly women, found him to be a polite, nice person.

One woman looked at me and said flatly, "He wasn't that way when I was with him."

Stab wounds.

I have become furious, but mainly with myself. Certain protocols in writing about such matters anger me. I decide never to write the phrase "child molestation" or "sexual assault" except in a context of deliberate mockery. I am angry at the pain I witness and listen to each day as I make my appointed rounds, and I am angry at the hypocrisy of it all. We want to believe that the intersection between sex and crime happens only in an alien country, one that does not touch our lives or feelings or lusts of the midnight hours.

A WOMAN IS AT THE DOOR and she has three balls on a string she wishes to insert in my ass, and then she will pull the string at the moment of orgasm.

A woman is at the door and she says she has cuffs.

A woman is at the door late at night and we make love, and as she leaves she says she can't see me again because she is getting married in the morning.

Two women are at the door . . .

We like to call things that disturb us a jungle, to wall them off from our sense of order and self. But we all inhabit that forest, a dense thicket of desire and dread, both burning bright. We want to categorize: victims or studs, seduced or seducers. And we can hardly look at people who we agree are criminals and admit we feel some of their passions and fantasies within ourselves. My life in those days erased boundaries and paid no attention to whether I was a predator or a victim or a newspaper savior with a byline. I was attractive to women because what I knew made me somehow safe. Ruined people were telling me things they never told anyone else, and the women dealing with ruined people were sharing secrets as well, and some of those secrets were fantasies they wished to act out. There is a way to go so deep into the secrets and hungers of your culture that you live without concern for the mores and with a keen sense of your own needs. I have seen this state most often in the old, who finally realize that the rules of conduct are optional and read what they wish, say what they think, and live in sin without a qualm. I didn't feel guilt. Then or now. I didn't feel love. I didn't seek a cure. Getting in bed with women was a pleasure but not the center of my life. The center of my life was crime. And sex was also an attempt to redeem or exorcise what I saw. As the crimes piled up and corroded my energy and will, I ceased to find even cold comfort in women, and everything in my life became perfunctory except for the crimes. I have hard memories of my life then, but not bad memories. But of the work, I still have nightmares. I still drive by commonplace haunts and see weeping women, bodies, a terrified child, an eviscerated girl. There are accepted ways of dealing with such experiences: the secular renunciation of a clinical visit to all the Betty Ford centers out there, the religious rebirth of being born again. I did neither. I simply continued plowing my way into that night.

She sits up in bed and asks, "Aren't my breasts beautiful? Aren't they the best you've ever seen?"

I nuzzle her hair. Time has passed, the story long gone, the woman in the lavender dress with the hard words and the maimed child is now the woman here.

She tells me her husband has been suspicious of me.

I ask her what she told him.

"Don't worry." She smiles. "I told him you were a queer."

Then she slides over, gets up, and rolls a joint.

RULE NUMBER ONE: No One Can Handle the Children.

I'll tell you something that, although not a trade secret, is not generally said to others outside the work. The rapes are bad but not that bad. The mind is protected from what adults do to adults. There is a squeamishness about the rapes, an embarrassment among the men who investigate them, and an anger among the women who treat the casualties. But the rapes can be handled to a degree. Of course, it's not as easy as homicide; people stay in homicide forever and never lose pleasure in their work. Sex crimes generally cycle people out in two years. And it is the kids who do it. No one can handle the kids. But then the highway patrol always dreads the car wreck with kids. It goes against nature as we know it.

Once I was helping a guy move—him, his wife, their two young daughters— and a box I was carrying out broke open and small paperbacks spilled to the ground in the bright sunshine. I gathered them up and then idly flipped through one, and then another and another. They were all cheap things from no-name presses about men—daddies, uncles, whoever—fucking kids. I was stunned and did not know what to do. I felt oddly violated, like it was wrong for me to have to know this. So I put them back in the box and put the box in the truck and said nothing and did nothing.

That is part of what I feel as I enter the gray police station and go to the offices where the sex-crimes unit works. They've got a treasure trove of child pornography seized from perps, and in my memory the stack rises six or seven feet. They leave me at a table with it, and what they want is for me to look at it and come out with an article recommending that people who possess such materials go to prison.

The collection mainly features boys—seven, eight, nine from the looks of them—and they are sucking off men, taking it in the ass, being perfect pals about everything. I am struck not by what I feel but by how little I feel. It is like handling the treasured and sacred icons of a dead religion. I have careful constitutional qualms filed in my mind—basically, that to think something is not a crime. Fucking kids and taking pictures—that is already against the law. So I stand firmly on the Constitution of the United States and look at photographs I do not believe should exist made by and for people I do not believe should exist. I look for hours and still feel nothing. I am in a place beyond the power of empathy.

A few months later I get a thick packet of fifty or sixty typed pages. The writer is facing a long prison sentence for having had sex with Scouts, as I recall. He writes with courtesy, clarity, and an almost obsessive sense of detail. Essentially, nothing ever happened except that he tried to comfort and love his charges. I doubt him on his details but come to sense that he means his general thesis about love. He loves children, totally, and locks onto them with the same feeling I have for adult women.

That is what I take away from the photos the police want outlawed and the autobiography of the man they eventually send away to be raped and possibly murdered by fellow convicts for being a child molester. A crime is being committed by people who see themselves as the perfect friend. Other things are being committed by people who see themselves as lovers. And, of course, a lot of things are being done by people who have no romantic delusions about their desires but are full of hate, who drag women off into the bushes or a corner because they hate them and are going to get even by causing pain, humiliation, and, at times, death. Cycles of abuse, the role of pornography, the denigration of women by Hollywood and glossy magazines—there is no single, simple explanation for sex crimes. But in the case of the men who use children for sex there is often this fixation, this sense of love, which always leads them to betray the very idea of love itself by using children for their own selfish ends.

During this period of my life my musical taste changes and slowly, without my awareness, starts sliding backward through the decades. One day I decide to look up a style of music I've been listening to in a big Merriam-Webster dictionary. Torch song: from the phrase "to carry a torch for" (to be in love); first appeared 1930; a popular sentimental song of unrequited love.

THE WALLS ARE BLOCK, HUMMING fluorescent lights replace windows, and we sit in rows forming a semicircle as the woman teaching the class speaks. She is very nicely done up in a sedate professional suit, tasteful hair, low-key makeup; she has a serious and clear voice. The prisoners mark time as I go through rape therapy in the joint. I am not here because of a story. I've come to find something beneath the stories or deep within myself. The boundaries between normal, accepted sexual appetite and crime are blurring for me. People get an erotic charge out of playing with consent—holding each other down, tying each other up—indulging in ritualized dominance. Rape is an eerie parody of accepted life, an experience using the same wardrobe but scratching the word "consent" from the script. I am obeying the law and the rules of consent, but I am losing a sense of distance between my obedient self and those who break the law. When I listen to women tell of the horrors they've experienced, the acts they recount are usually familiar to me, and what they recount as true terror, the sense of powerlessness, strikes chords within me also. I can't abide being in the joint even for this class. I can't take the bars, guards, walls.

The men, struggling to earn good time, feign attention. They answer questions appropriately and wear masks of serious thought. I don't believe them for an instant, and I think that this class is a farce and that nothing will deter my colleagues from their appointed rounds when they leave this place. The woman herself, from a good family and with sound religious values, has been attacked—"I am part of the sisterhood," she once told me shyly—and she has brought me here so that I will see hope and share her hope. So I sit with the current crop of convicted rapists. "There are no first-time offenders," a cop once snarled at me, "just sons of bitches that finally get caught"—and feel no hope. Of course, prison is rape culture—"just need a bunk and a punk," one local heroin dealer offered in explaining his lack of concern about doing time.

The session finally ends, and we bleed out the door of the room into the prison corridor. I am ambling along in a throng of convicts, the woman walking just ahead in her prim suit with her skirt snug on her hips. The guy next to me is singing some kind of blues about what he's gonna do to that bad bitch. I've blotted out the actual song. I can remember the corridor (we are strolling east), see her up ahead, hear him singing next to me, his lips barely moving as he floats his protest against the class and her fucking control and all that shit, but not the lyrics themselves. They're gone, erased by my mind, I suspect in self-defense. Afterward, she and I go to a truck stop and eat apple pie, and I can still see the whiteness of her teeth as she smiles and speaks brightly about her work.

Later, I taste child-molestation therapy, a regimen where men who have fucked their own children sit in a circle and talk while their wives run the show. It's either show up at such sessions or the joint—so attendance is rather good. Afterward, I go off with the boys and we have beers. In recounting his lapse from accepted behavior, each and every one of them describes the act itself as fondling. Apparently, there are hordes of diligently caressed children out there.

I nurse my beer and say little, pretending to try to understand. But I understand nothing at all. I have seen the end result of fondling, and it does not look at all like fondling to me. I cannot put myself in their place. I cannot see children as sexual objects, it does not seem to be in me. I fixate, I realize, on women. And my fixation is sanctioned, as long as I toe the line. Such thoughts lead to a place without clear light. We all share a biology and deep drives, and what we have created—civilization, courtesy, decency—is a mesh that comes from these drives and also contains and tames them. Whatever feels good is not necessarily good. But what I learn is that whatever is bad is not necessarily alien to me.

Or to you.

SHE LOVES PORNOGRAPHY. IT'S AROUND MIDNIGHT, and she is standing in the motel room clutching a bottle of champagne against her black garter belt and peering intently into the screen of the television as fornicating couples, powered by the handyman of American fantasy, the telephone man, frolic. This is one of the seedy motels that cultivate hourly rates, water beds, and hard-core cinema, a place much like the room where my life in this world began with the splotch on the wall left by the toddler's head. She is a counselor, one of the many I now deal with, and she likes sex and is fascinated by pornography. This is not unusual; another woman, a professional woman I deal with, has several hundred pornographic tapes. But the interests of the woman in the black garter belt are kept off the table at her work and left to the night hours and random bouts with me. Days are for the maimed—in her case, children with cigarette burns and sore orifices. Some nights are like this.

I glance at her naked ass, see the serene concentration of her face as she tracks the movie, and I am empty. She and I share the same country, and there is a big hole in us, so we come here. We live in a place past the moral strictures of sin and lust; we run on empty. For us, sex has been drained of its usual charge, delight is beyond our reach. This is a fact. As the months roll past, I feel this slippage within me. I will have lunch or dinner or a drink or coffee with someone and wind up in a place like this. Romance is not a consideration. There is seldom anyone to talk with, and when there is someone, a person like the woman in the black garter belt watching the porn movie, a person stumbling across the same terrain, there is nothing to say, since we both know. So we come here. A proper distance from our appetites has been denied us, so we seek moments of obliteration. I have never regretted those moments or fully understood them. I just knew then, and know now, that they come with the territory.

But the slippage bothers me. I seem to drift, and the drift is downward. Not into sin and the pit but into that emptiness. I am losing all desire and mechanically go through the motions of life. Food also does not tempt me. I flee into the wild country with my backpack, flee again and again for days and days, but increasingly this tactic does not work. Once I am lying by a water hole in

July and it is 104 degrees at 1:00 a.m. (I get up with my flashlight and check my thermometer.) I am crawling with crabs. When I go back I buy twelve bottles of the recommended cure and for a day have coffee or drinks with a succession of women, handing each a bottle. I take this in stride, as do they. One woman is briefly anxious because she fears I have called her only to deliver the medicine, but this feeling passes when I assure her that this is not true, that I really wanted to see her. I think we then go to bed. It turns out that this mini-epidemic has come from the therapist who showers three or four times a day. She also is quite calm about it and prefers to talk about her new favorite movie, something entitled *Little Oral Annie*. She tells me she resents the smirks of the male clerks when she rents it at the video store, and I politely sympathize.

The moments of my impotence increase. I am not alarmed by this fact but clinically engaged. I sense that I am walling off everything, all appetites, and have room for nothing but this torrent of pain and squalor that pours through me from the daily and weekly harvest of rapes and killings and molestations. I remember once reading a statement allegedly made by Sophocles in his old age, when sexual desire had left his loins; he said he was glad to be free of the mad master. So I am becoming classic and care not at all. I repeatedly try to leave the work, but the city desk always wins because a part of me feels bound to the crimes. So I protest, and then return. I tell myself it is a duty, but what I feel is the desire to run out my string, to see how much I can stomach and learn. And yet then, and now, I cannot really say what this knowing entails. I can just feel its burden as I lie with caring women in countless cheap motels, the movies rolling on the screen.

THE END BEGINS IN THE bright light of afternoon on a quiet street lined with safe houses. One moment an eight-year-old girl is riding her bicycle on the sidewalk near her home; the next moment the bicycle is lying on the ground and the girl is gone with no one the wiser.

This one is my torch song. The rudiments are simple. The alleged perpetrator is a man in his twenties from a very good home in another city; a man whose life has been a torment of drugs, molestation of himself by others and of others by himself; a man who has slipped from his station in life into dissipation and wound up roaming the skid rows of our nation. None of this concerns me, and I leave ruin in my wake. I fly to that distant city, talk my way through a stout door, and gut his mother like a fish. When I leave she is a wreck, and later that night her husband goes to the hospital for perturbations of his heart. I get into files—legal, psychiatric—that I should not have had access to, and I print them fulsomely. The child favored a certain doll, and I buy one and prowl the city with it on the truck seat beside me, a touchstone. I am standing in the backyard as the mother of the missing girl makes a plea to whoever took her daughter to bring her home safe and sound. The woman's face is grief made flesh, and I note its every tic and sag. It turns out that the alleged perpetrator stayed for a time with a couple in a trailer court. I visit; the man is facing child-molestation charges himself, the woman is a hooker with a coke habit. "Do I have to tell you that?" she whines. I remember leaving them, driving to a saloon, setting my small computer on the bar, and begging a phone for the modem. I sip my drink and write in one quick take. The story flits through the wires and descends into the next edition. The following night a local PTA meeting takes a recess, walks over to the trailer, and then it goes up in flames.

My temper is short, my blood cold. A young mother who works in the newsroom comes over to my desk and asks me what I think the chances are of the girl being alive. I snap, "Fucked, strangled, and rotting out there." And keep typing. The sheriff leaps into the public wound and starts leading marches of citizens holding candles and decrying violence and the rape of children. It is much like the time so long ago with a seven-year-old eviscerated while people marched to take back the night. I pay no notice to these marches; they are for others. The reporters on the story all speculate about the girl—even when the arrest comes and still the girl is missing. I do not. I know. Bones bleach out there. It is months and months before her remains turn up, but this hardly matters to me. I know. This is my country.

It ends several times, but at last it finally ends. The city desk asks my help to find a woman whose son, a famous local rapist, has just escaped. I leave, chat up some neighbors, and within an hour I am in a state office, a bullpen of women toiling over desks and processing forms. She has done everything she can—changed her name, told no one of her son, gone on and tried to fashion a life. I approach her desk and tell her my errand. She pleads with me, *Don't do this to me.* She leans forward and whispers that no one typing away at the other desks, none of them knows anything about this. *Leave me in peace,* she says. I look into her careworn eyes and I say yes. I tell her I will now leave and she will never read a word of my visit in the newspaper. Nor will I tell anyone of her identity.

When I enter the newsroom, the editor comes over and asks, "Did you find her?"

I say, "Yes."

"When can I have the story?"

"I'm never writing the story."

He looks at me, says nothing, then turns and walks away.

That is when one part of me is finished. I know I must quit. I cannot take the money and decide what goes into the newspaper. I do not believe in myself as censor and gatekeeper. And yet I know I will never write this story, because I have hit some kind of limit in pain. The phone rings. It is a woman's voice. She says, "Thanks to you she has had to go to the hospital. I hope you are happy."

I tell her I am not writing the story. I tell her I told the mother I would not write the story. She does not believe me. This does not matter to me. My hands are cold, and I know from past experience this means I can take no more. I am righteously empty.

THE OTHER ENDING IS MORE IMPORTANT, because it does not involve the work, the little credos and dos and don'ts of journalism. It involves myself. It happens the night the arrests come down for the missing eight-year-old snatched off her bicycle on that safe side street. Around three in the morning, I wrap the story and reach into my desk drawer, where I stashed a fifth of Jack Daniels bought earlier in the day. I do not drink hard liquor, and I bought the bottle without questioning myself and without conscious intent. So I finish the story, open the drawer, take the bottle and go home. I sit in my backyard in the dark of the night, those absolutely lonely hours before dawn. I drink, the bite of the whiskey snapping against my tongue, and drink in the blackness.

After a while I feel a wetness and realize that I am weeping, weeping silently and unconsciously, weeping for reasons I do not understand. I know this is a sign that I am breaking down, this weeping without a moan or a sound. I feel the tears trickle, and step outside myself and watch myself clinically in a whiskey-soaked out-of-body experience. That is the other ending.

I quit the paper, never again set foot in a newsroom, and go into the mountains off and on for months and write a book about them. That helps, but not enough. I sit down and in twenty-one days write another book about the land, the people, and the city. That helps, but although I barely touch on the world of sex and crimes in this book, it broods beneath the sentences about Indians and antelope and bats and city streets. Nothing really helps.

That is what I am trying to say. Theories don't help, therapies don't help, knowing doesn't help. The experts say they have therapies that are cutting recidivism, and maybe they do, but I doubt it. I live with what I am and what I saw and what I felt—a residue that will linger to the end of my days in the cells of my body. I have never been in an adult bookstore. Two years ago I was at a bachelor party in a lap-dancing place and lasted fifteen minutes before I hailed a cab and fled. This is not a virtue or a position. I have no desire to outlaw pornography, strip joints, blue movies, or much of anything my fellow citizens find entertaining. Nor have I led an orderly life since my time in sex crimes. I write for men's magazines and pass over without comment their leering tone and arch expressions about the flesh. I am not a reformer. So what am I?

A man who has visited a country where impulses we all feel become horrible things. A man who can bury such knowledge but not disown it, and a man who can no longer so glibly talk of perverts or rapists or cretins or scum. A man who knows there is a line within each of us that we cannot accurately define, that shifts with the hour and the mood but is still real. And if we cross that line we betray ourselves and everyone else and become outcasts from our own souls. A man who can be an animal but can no longer be a voyeur. A man weeping silently in the backyard with a bottle of whiskey who knows he must leave and go to another country and yet never forget what he has seen and felt. Just keep under control. And try not to lie too much.

JUST BEFORE I QUIT, I AM IN A BAR in a distant city with a district attorney. He shouts to the barkeep, "Hey, give this guy a drink. One of our perverts whacked a kid in his town."

The bartender pours and says, "Way to go."

And I drink without a word. Nobody wants to hear these things.

Charles Bowden is the author of twenty-one books, including *A Shadow in the City: Confessions of an Undercover Drug Warrior* (Harcourt 2005); *Down By the River: Drugs, Money, Murder, and Family* (Simon & Schuster 2002); *Juárez: The Laboratory of Our Future* (Aperture 1998); *Blood Orchid: An Unnatural History of America* (Random House 1995); *Desierto: Memories of the Future* (Norton 1991); *Red Line* (Norton 1989); *Blue Desert* (University of Arizona 1986); and *Inferno* with photographer Michael Berman (University of Texas 2006). He is a contributing editor of *GQ*, and his work has appeared in *Harper's Magazine, Mother Jones,* and *Esquire,* among others. Winner of the 1996 Lannan Literary Award for Nonfiction, he lives in Tucson, Arizona.

"I was having a drink with an editor at *Harper's* when I idly mentioned my years covering sex crimes for a paper and how this experience was toxic. She said, 'Write that.' So I did."

"Torch Song" was originally published in *Harper's Magazine*, vol. 297, no. 1779 (August 1998): 43. Copyright © 1999 by Charles Bowden. It is reprinted here by permission of Anderson Literary Management.

When I Was Eleven

Ed McManis

I wasn't supposed to hear
Mom whisper,
"He's lost his job"
to my oldest sister.
He wore a t-shirt to dinner,
scooped slowly, seconds
of vanilla ice milk, said
in a low voice, "Better enjoy it."
Thick as chalk, we swallowed
hard, and I made
Jack lick his bowl clean.

No one complained
when Mom turned off the TV
and we all pitched in
on the dishes as he dragged
himself and a pillow
up the stairs, closed the bedroom door.

Asleep, sitting up on the couch,
I woke tingling with fear
against the stubble of his chin.
"You're getting too heavy," he whispered,
thinking I was still asleep.
I wanted to walk, but he held
me too tight. It was late
and I couldn't find the words
to wake myself, make myself
light in his tired arms.

_____

Ed McManis was born and raised in Denver. His writing career has ranged from journalism to poetry to songwriting to writing greeting cards. McManis's most recent chapbook is *Sister Mary Butkus* (Červená Barva 2007). Currently McManis teaches at Denver Academy, a school for students who learn differently.

McManis writes, "I grew up in a huge Catholic neighborhood. We had ten kids; across the street had eight. Murphys had seven, Piersons had ten. There were eighty kids in two blocks, not a pagan in the bunch. Coupled with the hard line of the church was the backhand of my strict Catholic father. There were lots of rules, not much tenderness."

"When I Was Eleven" is part of a larger collection, *Working for My Old Man*, which speaks to this time and examines the poet's subsequent multiple firings and rehirings.

Copyright © Ed McManis

McDonald's—We Do It All for You

Barbara Garson

Jason Pratt

"THEY CALLED US THE GREEN MACHINE," says Jason Pratt, recently retired McDonald's griddleman, " 'cause the crew had green uniforms then. And that's what it is, a machine. You don't have to know how to cook, you don't have to know how to think. There's a procedure for everything and you just follow the procedures."

"Like?" I asked. I was interviewing Jason in the Pizza Hut across from his old McDonald's.

"Like, uh," the wiry teenager searched for a way to describe the all-encompassing procedures. "O.K., we'll start you off on something simple. You're on the ten-in-one grill, ten patties in a pound. Your basic burger. The guy on the bin calls, 'Six hamburgers.' So you lay your six pieces of meat on the grill and set the timer." Before my eyes Jason conjures up the gleaming, mechanized McDonald's kitchen. "Beep-beep, beep-beep, beep-beep. That's the beeper to sear 'em. It goes off in twenty seconds. Sup, sup, sup, sup, sup, sup." He presses each of the six patties down on the sizzling grill with an imaginary silver disk. "Now you turn off the sear beeper, put the buns in the oven, set the oven timer and then the next beeper is to turn the meat. This one goes beep-beep-beep, beep-beep-beep. So you turn your patties, and then you drop your re-cons on the meat, t-con, t-con, t-con." Here Jason takes two imaginary handfuls of reconstituted onions out of water and sets them out, two blops at a time, on top of the six patties he's arranged in two neat rows on our grill. "Now the bun oven buzzes [there are over a half dozen different timers with distinct beeps and buzzes in a McDonald's kitchen]. This one turns itself off when you open the oven door so you just take out your crowns, line 'em up and give 'em each a squirt of mustard and a squirt of ketchup." With mustard in his right hand and ketchup in his left, Jason wields the dispensers like a pair of six shooters up and down the lines of buns. Each dispenser has two triggers. One fires the premeasured squirt for ten-in-ones—the second is set for quarter pounders.

"Now," says Jason, slowing down, "now you get to put on the pickles. Two if

"McDonald's—We Do It All for You" is reprinted here by permission of Simon & Schuster Adult Publishing Group, from *The Electronic Sweatshop: How Computers Are Transforming the Office of the Future into the Factory of the Past* by Barbara Garson. Copyright © 1988 by Barbara Garson. All rights reserved.

they're regular, three if they're small. That's the creative part. Then the lettuce, then you ask for a cheese count ('cheese on four please'). Finally the last beep goes off and you lay your burger on the crowns."

"On the crown of the buns?" I ask, unable to visualize. "On top?"

"Yeah, you dress 'em upside down. Put 'em in the box upside down too. They flip 'em over when they serve 'em."

"Oh, I think I see."

"Then scoop up the heels [the bun bottoms] which are on top of the bun warmer, take the heels with one hand and push the tray out from underneath and they land (plip) one on each burger, right on top of the re-cons, neat and perfect. [The official time allotted by Hamburger Central, the McDonald's headquarters in Oak Brook, Illinois, is ninety seconds to prepare and serve a burger.] It's like I told you. The procedures make the burgers. You don't have to know a thing."

McDONALD'S EMPLOYS 500,000 TEENAGERS AT any one time. Most don't stay long. About 8 million Americans—7 percent of our labor force—have worked at McDonald's and moved on.* Jason is not a typical ex-employee. In fact, Jason is a legend among the teenagers at the three McDonald's outlets in his suburban area. It seems he was so fast at the griddle (or maybe just fast talking) that he'd been taken back three times by two different managers after quitting.

But Jason became a real legend in his last stint at McDonald's. He'd been sent out the back door with the garbage, but instead of coming back in he got into a car with two friends and just drove away. That's the part the local teenagers love to tell. "No fight with the manager or anything . . . just drove away and never came back. . . . I don't think they'd give him a job again."

"I WOULD NEVER GO BACK TO McDONALD'S," says Jason. "Not even as a manager." Jason is enrolled at the local junior college. "I'd like to run a real restaurant someday, but I'm taking data processing to fall back on." He's had many part-time jobs, the highest paid at a hospital ($4.00 an hour), but that didn't last, and now dishwashing (at the $3.35 minimum). "Same as McDonald's. But I would never go back there. You're a complete robot."

"It seems like you can improvise a little with the onions," I suggested. "They're not premeasured." Indeed, the reconstituted onion shreds grabbed out of a container by the unscientific-looking wet handful struck me as oddly out of character in the McDonald's kitchen.

"There's supposed to be twelve onion bits per patty," Jason informed me. "They spot check."

---

* These statistics come from John F. Love, *McDonald's Behind the Golden Arches* (New York: Bantam, 1986). Additional background information in this chapter comes from Ray Kroc and Robert Anderson, *Grinding It Out* (Chicago: Contemporary Books, 1977), and Max Boas and Steve Chain, *Big Mac* (New York: Dutton, 1976).

"Oh come on."

"You think I'm kiddin'. They lift your heels and they say, 'You got too many onions.' It's portion control."

"Is there any freedom anywhere in the process?" I asked.

"Lettuce. They'll leave you alone as long as it's neat."

"So lettuce is freedom; pickles is judgment?"

"Yeah but you don't have time to play around with your pickles. They're never gonna say just six pickles except on the disk. [Each store has video disks to train the crew for each of about twenty work stations, like fries, register, lobby, quarter pounder grill.] What you'll hear in real life is 'twelve and six on a turn lay.' The first number is your hamburgers, the second is your Big Macs. On a turn lay means you lay the first twelve, then you put down the second batch after you turn the first. So you got twenty-four burgers on the grill, in shifts. It's what they call a production mode. And remember you also got your fillets, your McNuggets . . ."

"Wait, slow down." By then I was losing track of the patties on our imaginary grill. "I don't understand this turn lay thing."

"Don't worry, you don't have to understand. You follow the beepers, you follow the buzzers and you turn your meat as fast as you can. It's like I told you, to work at McDonald's you don't need a face, you don't need a brain. You need to have two hands and two legs and move 'em as fast as you can. That's the whole system. I wouldn't go back there again for anything."

June Sanders

McDonald's french fries are deservedly the pride of their menu; uniformly golden brown all across America and in thirty-one other countries. However, it's difficult to standardize the number of fries per serving. The McDonald's fry scoop, perhaps their greatest technological innovation, helps to control this variable. The unique flat funnel holds the bag open while it aligns a limited number of fries so that they fall into the package with a paradoxically free, overflowing cornucopia look.

Despite the scoop, there's still a spread. The acceptable fry yield is 400 to 420 servings per 100-pound bag of potatoes. It's one of the few areas of McDonald's cookery in which such a range is possible. The fry yield is therefore one important measure of a manager's efficiency. "Fluffy, not stuffy," they remind the young workers when the fry yield is running low.

No such variation is possible in the browning of the fries. Early in McDonald's history Louis Martino, the husband of the secretary of McDonald's founder Ray Kroc, designed a computer to be submerged in the fry vats. In his autobiography, *Grinding It Out*, Kroc explained the importance of this innovation. "We had a recipe . . . that called for pulling the potatoes out of the oil when they got a certain color and grease bubbles formed in a certain way. It was amazing that we got them as uniform as we did because each kid working the fry vats would have his own interpretation of the proper color and so forth. [The word "kid" was officially replaced by "person" or "crew person" in McDonald's management vocabulary in 1973 in response to union organizing attempts.] Louis's computer took all the guesswork out of it, modifying the frying to suit the balance of water to solids in a given batch of potatoes. He also engineered the dispenser that allowed us to squirt exactly the right amount of catsup and mustard onto our premeasured hamburger patties. . . ."

The fry vat probe is a complex miniature computer. The fry scoop, on the other hand, is as simple and almost as elegant as the wheel. Both eliminate the need for a human being to make "his own interpretation," as Ray Kroc puts it.

Together, these two innovations mean that a new worker can be trained in fifteen minutes and reach maximum efficiency in a half hour. This makes it economically feasible to use a kid for one day and replace him with another kid the next day.

June Sanders worked at McDonald's for one day.

"I needed money, so I went in and the manager told me my hours would be 4 to 10 p.m." This was fine with June, a well-organized black woman in her early twenties who goes to college full time.

"But when I came in the next day the manager said I could work till 10 for that one day. But from then on my hours would be 4 p.m. to 1 a.m. And I really wouldn't get off at 1 because I'd have to stay to clean up after they closed. . . . Yes it was the same manager, a Mr. O'Neil.

"I told him I'd have to check first with my family if I could come home that late. But he told me to put on the uniform and fill out the forms. He would start me out on french fries.

"Then he showed me an orientation film on a TV screen all about fries. . . . No, I still hadn't punched in. This was all in the basement. Then I went upstairs, and then I punched in and went to work. . . . No, I was not paid for the training downstairs. Yes, I'm sure."

I asked June if she had had any difficulty with the fries.

"No, it was just like the film. You put the french fries in the grease and you push a button which doesn't go off till the fries are done. Then you take them out and put them in a bin under a light. Then you scoop them into the bags with this thing, this flat, light metal—I can't really describe it—scoop thing that sits right in the package and makes the fries fall in place."

"Did they watch you for a while?" I asked. "Did you need more instruction?"

"Someone leaned over once and showed me how to make sure the fry scooper was set inside the opening of the bag so the fries would fall in right."

"And then?"

"And then, I stood on my feet from twenty after four till the manager took over my station at 10:35 p.m.

"When I left my legs were aching. I knew it wasn't a job for me. But I probably would have tried to last it out—at least more than a day—if it wasn't for the hours. When I got home I talked it over with my mother and my sister and then I phoned and said I couldn't work there. They weren't angry. They just said to bring back the uniform. . . . The people were nice, even the managers. It's just a rushed system."

"June," I said, "does it make any sense to train you and have you work for one day? Why didn't he tell you the real hours in the first place?"

"They take a chance and see if you're desperate. I have my family to stay with. That's why I didn't go back. But if I really needed the money, like if I had a kid and no family, I'd have to make arrangements to work any hours.

"Anyway, they got a full day's work out of me."

Damita

I WAITED ON LINE AT my neighborhood McDonald's. It was lunch hour and there were four or five customers at each of the five open cash registers. "May I take your order?" a very thin girl said in a flat tone to the man at the head of my line.

"McNuggets, large fries and a Coke," said the man. The cashier punched in the order. "That will be . . ."

"Big Mac, large fries and a shake," said the next woman on line. The cashier rang it up.

"Two cheeseburgers, large fries and a coffee," said the third customer. The cashier rang it up.

"How much is a large fries?" asked the woman directly in front of me.

The thin cashier twisted her neck around trying to look up at the menu board.

"Sorry," apologized the customer, "I don't have my glasses."

"Large fries is seventy-nine," a round-faced cashier with glasses interjected from the next register.

"Seventy-nine cents," the thin cashier repeated.

"Well how much is a small fries?"

As they talked I leaned over the next register. "Say, can I interview you?" I asked the clerk with glasses, whose line was by then empty.

"Huh?"

"I'm writing a story about jobs at fast-food restaurants."

"O.K. I guess so."

"Can I have your phone number?"

"Well . . . I'll meet you when I get off. Should be sometime between 4 and 4:30."

By then it was my turn.

"Just a large fries," I said.

The thin cashier pressed "lge fries." In place of numbers, the keys on a

McDonald's cash register say "lge fries," "reg fries," "med coke," "big mac," and so on. Some registers have pictures on the key caps. The next time the price of fries goes up (or down) the change will be entered in the store's central computer. But the thin cashier will continue to press the same button. I wondered how long she'd worked there and how many hundreds of "lge fries" she'd served without learning the price.

DAMITA, THE CASHIER WITH THE glasses, came up from the crew room (a room in the basement with lockers, a table and a video player for studying the training disks) at 4:45. She looked older and more serious without her striped uniform.

"Sorry, but they got busy and, you know, here you get off when they let you."

The expandable schedule was her first complaint. "You give them your availability when you sign on. Mine I said 9 to 4. But they scheduled me for 7 o'clock two or three days a week. And I needed the money. So I got to get up 5 in the morning to get here from Queens by 7. And I don't get off till whoever's supposed to get here gets here to take my place. . . . It's hard to study with all the pressures."

Damita had come to the city from a small town outside of Detroit. She lives with her sister in Queens and takes extension courses in psychology at New York University. Depending on the schedule posted each Friday, her McDonald's paycheck for a five-day week has varied from $80 to $114.

"How long have you worked at McDonald's?" I asked.

"Well, see I only know six people in this city, so my manager from Michigan . . . yeah, I worked for McDonald's in high school . . . my manager from Michigan called this guy Brian who's the second assistant manager here. So I didn't have to fill out an application. Well, I mean the first thing I needed was a job," she seemed to apologize, "and I knew I could always work at McDonald's. I always say I'm gonna look for something else, but I don't get out till 4 and that could be 5 or whenever."

The flexible scheduling at McDonald's only seems to work one way. One day Damita had arrived a half hour late because the E train was running on the R track.

"The assistant manager told me not to clock in at all, just to go home. So I said O.K. and I left."

"What did you do the rest of the day?" I asked.

"I went home and studied, and I went to sleep."

"But how did it make you feel?"

"It's like a humiliating feeling 'cause I wasn't given any chance to justify myself. But when I spoke to the Puerto Rican manager he said it was nothing personal against me. Just it was raining that day, and they were really slow and someone who got here on time, it wouldn't be right to send them home."

"Weren't you annoyed to spend four hours traveling and then lose a day's pay?" I suggested.

"I was mad at first that they didn't let me explain. But afterwards I understood and I tried to explain to my sister: 'Time waits for no man.' "

"Since you signed on for 9 to 4," I asked Damita, "and you're going to school, why can't you say, 'Look, I have to study at night, I need regular hours'?"

"Don't work that way. They make up your schedule every week and if you can't work it, you're responsible to replace yourself. If you can't they can always get someone else."

"But Damita," I tried to argue with her low estimate of her own worth, "anyone can see right away that your line moves fast yet you're helpful to people. I mean, you're a valuable employee. And this manager seems to like you."

"Valuable! $3.35 an hour. And I can be replaced by any [pointing across the room] kid off the street."

I hadn't noticed. At a small table under the staircase a manager in a light beige shirt was taking an application from a lanky black teenager.

"But you know the register. You know the routine."

"How long you think it takes to learn the six steps? Step 1. Greet the customer, 'Good morning, can I help you?' Step 2. Take his order. Step 3. Repeat the order. They can have someone off the street working my register in five minutes."

"By the way," I asked, "on those cash registers without numbers, how do you change something after you ring it up? I mean if somebody orders a cheeseburger and then they change it to a hamburger, how do you subtract the slice of cheese?"

"I guess that's why you have step 3, repeat the order. One cheeseburger, two Cokes, three . . ."

"Yeah, but if you punched a mistake or they don't want it after you get it together?"

"Like if I have a crazy customer, which I do be gettin', 'specially in this city, and they order hamburger, fries and shake, and it's $2.95 and then they just walk away?"

"I once did that here," I said. "About a week ago when I first started my research. All I ordered was some french fries. And I was so busy watching how the computer works that only after she rang it up I discovered that I'd walked out of my house without my wallet. I didn't have a penny. I was so embarrassed."

"Are you that one the other day? Arnetta, this girl next to me, she said, 'Look at that crazy lady going out. She's lookin' and lookin' at everything and then she didn't have no money for a bag of fries.' I saw you leaving, but I guess I didn't recognize you. [I agreed it was probably me.] O.K., so say this crazy lady comes in and orders french fries and leaves. In Michigan I could just zero it out. I'd wait till I start the next order and press zero and large fries. But here you're supposed to call out 'cancel sale' and the manager comes over and does it with his key.

"But I hate to call the manager every time, 'specially if I got a whole line waiting. So I still zero out myself. They can tell I do it by the computer tape, and they tell me not to. Some of them let me, though, because they know I came from another store. But they don't show the girls here how to zero out. Everybody thinks you need the manager's key to do it."

"Maybe they let you because they can tell you're honest," I said. She smiled, pleased, but let it pass. "That's what I mean that you're valuable to them. You know how to use the register. You're good with customers."

"You know there was a man here," Damita said, a little embarrassed about bragging, "when I was transferred off night he asked my manager, 'What happened to that girl from Michigan?' "

"Did your manager tell you that?"

"No, another girl on the night shift told me. The manager said it to her. They don't tell you nothing nice themselves."

"But, see, you are good with people and he appreciates it."

"In my other McDonald's—not the one where they let me zero out but another one I worked in in Michigan—I was almost fired for my attitude. Which was helping customers who had arthritis to open the little packets. And another bad attitude of mine is that you're supposed to suggest to the customer, 'Would you like a drink with that?' or 'Do you want a pie?'—whatever they're pushing. I don't like to do it. And they can look on my tape after my shift and see I didn't push the suggested sell item."

McDonald's computerized cash registers allow managers to determine immediately not only the dollar volume for the store but the amount of each item that was sold at each register for any given period. Two experienced managers, interviewed separately, both insisted that the new electronic cash registers were in fact slower than the old mechanical registers. Clerks who knew the combinations—hamburger, fries, Coke: $2.45—could ring up the total immediately, take the cash and give change in one operation. On the new registers you have to enter each item and may be slowed down by computer response time. The value of the new registers, or at least their main selling point (McDonald's franchisers can choose from several approved registers), is the increasingly sophisticated tracking systems, which monitor all the activity and report with many different statistical breakdowns.

"Look, there," said Damita as the teenage job applicant left and the manager went behind the counter with the application. "If I was to say I can't come in at 7, they'd cut my hours down to one shift a week, and if I never came back they wouldn't call to find out where I was.

"I worked at a hospital once as an X-ray assistant. There if I didn't come in there were things that had to be done that wouldn't be done. I would call there and say, 'Remember to run the EKGs.' Here, if I called and said, 'I just can't come by 7 no more,' they'd have one of these high school kids off the street half an hour later. And they'd do my job just as good."

Damita was silent for a while and then she made a difficult plea. "This might sound stupid, I don't know," she said, "but I feel like, I came here to study and advance myself but I'm not excelling myself in any way. I'm twenty years old but—this sounds terrible to say—I'm twenty but I'd rather have a babysitting job. At least I could help a kid and take care. But I only know six people in this city. So I don't even know how I'd find a babysitting job."

"I'll keep my ears open," I said. "I don't know where I'd hear of one but . . ."

Damita seemed a little relieved. I suppose she realized there wasn't much chance of babysitting full-time, but at least she now knew seven people in the city.

Jon DeAngelo

JON DEANGELO, TWENTY-TWO, HAS BEEN a McDonald's manager for three years. He started in the restaurant business at sixteen as a busboy and planned even then to run a restaurant of his own someday. At nineteen, when he was the night manager of a resort kitchen, he was hired away by McOpCo, the McDonald's Operating Company.

Though McDonald's is primarily a franchise system, the company also owns and operates about 30 percent of the stores directly. These McOpCo stores, including some of the busiest units, are managed via a chain of command including regional supervisors, store managers and first and second assistants who can be moved from unit to unit. In addition, there's a network of inspectors from Hamburger Central who make announced and unannounced checks for QSC (quality, service, cleanliness) at both franchise and McOpCo installations.

Jon was hired at $14,000 a year. At the time I spoke with him his annual pay was $21,000—a very good salary at McDonald's. At first he'd been an assistant manager in one of the highest volume stores in his region. Then he was deliberately transferred to a store with productivity problems.

"I got there and found it was really a great crew. They hated being hassled, but they loved to work. I started them having fun by putting the men on the women's jobs and vice versa. [At most McDonald's the women tend to work on the registers, the men on the grill. But everyone starts at the same pay.] Oh, sure, they hated it at first, the guys that is. But they liked learning all the stations. I also ran a lot of register races."

Since the computer tape in each register indicates sales per hour, per half hour or for any interval requested, the manager can rev the crew up for a real "on your mark, get set, go!" race with a printout ready as they cross the finish line, showing the dollars taken in at each register during the race.

The computer will also print out a breakdown of sales for any particular menu item. The central office can check, therefore, how many Egg McMuffins were sold on Friday from 9 to 9:30 two weeks or two years ago, either in the entire store or at any particular register.

This makes it possible to run a register race limited to Cokes for instance, or Big Macs. Cashiers are instructed to try suggestive selling ("Would you like a drink with that?") at all times. But there are periods when a particular item is being pushed. The manager may then offer a prize for the most danish sold.

A typical prize for either type of cash register race might be a Snoopy mug (if that's the current promotion) or even a $5 cash bonus.

"This crew loved to race as individuals," says Jon of his troubled store, "but even more as a team. They'd love to get on a production mode, like a chicken pull drop or a burger turn lay and kill themselves for a big rush.

"One Saturday after a rock concert we did a $1,900 hour with ten people on crew. We killed ourselves but when the rush was over everyone said it was the most fun they ever had in a McDonald's."

I asked Jon how managers made up their weekly schedule. How would he decide who and how many to assign?

"It comes out of the computer," Jon explained. "It's a bar graph with the business you're going to do that week already printed in."

"The business you're going to do, already printed in?"

"It's based on the last week's sales, like maybe you did a $300 hour on Thursday at 3 p.m. Then it automatically adds a certain percent, say 15 percent, which is the projected annual increase for your particular store. . . . No, the person scheduling doesn't have to do any of this calculation. I just happen to know how it's arrived at. Really, it's simple, it's just a graph with the numbers already in it. $400 hour, $500 hour. According to Hamburger Central you schedule two crew members per $100 hour. So if you're projected for a $600 hour on Friday between 1 and 2, you know you need twelve crew for that lunch hour and the schedule sheet leaves space for their names."

"You mean you just fill in the blanks on the chart?"

"It's pretty automatic except in the case of a special event like the concert. Then you have to guess the dollar volume. Scheduling under could be a problem, but over would be a disaster to your crew labor productivity."

"Crew labor productivity?"

"Everything at McDonald's is based on the numbers. But crew labor productivity is pretty much the number a manager is judged by."

"Crew labor productivity? You have to be an economist."

"It's really simple to calculate. You take the total crew labor dollars paid out, divide that into the total food dollars taken. That gives you your crew labor productivity. The more food you sell and the less people you use to do it, the better your percentage. It's pretty simple."

Apparently, I still looked confused.

"For example, if you take an $800 hour and you run it with ten crew you get a very high crew labor percent."

"That's good?"

"Yes that's good. Then the manager in the next store hears Jon ran a 12 percent labor this week, I'll run a 10 percent labor. Of course you burn people out that way. But . . ."

"But Jon," I asked, "if the number of crew you need is set in advance and printed by the computer, why do so many managers keep changing hours and putting pressure on kids to work more?"

"They advertise McDonald's as a flexible work schedule for high school and college kids," he said, "but the truth is it's a high pressure job, and we have so much trouble keeping help, especially in fast stores like my first one (it grossed $1.8 million last year), that 50 percent never make it past two weeks. And a lot walk out within two days.

"When I was a first assistant, scheduling and hiring was my responsibility and I had to fill the spots one way or another. There were so many times I covered the shifts myself. Times I worked 100 hours a week. A manager has to fill the spaces on his chart somehow. So if a crew person is manipulable they manipulate him."

"What do you mean?"

"When you first sign on, you give your availability. Let's say a person's schedule is weeknights, 4 to 10. But after a week the manager schedules him as a closer Friday night. He calls in upset, 'Hey, my availability isn't Friday night.' The manager says, 'Well the schedule is already done. And you know the rule. If you can't work it's up to you to replace yourself.' At that point the person might quit, or he might not show up or he might have a fight with the manager."

"So he's fired?"

"No. You don't fire. You would only fire for cause like drugs or stealing. But what happens is he signed up for thirty hours a week and suddenly he's only scheduled for four. So either he starts being more available or he quits."

"Aren't you worried that the most qualified people will quit?"

"The only qualification to be able to do the job is to be able physically to do the job. I believe it says that in almost those words in my regional manual. And being there is the main part of being physically able to do the job."

"But what about your great crew at the second store? Don't you want to keep a team together?"

"Let me qualify that qualification. It takes a special kind of person to be able to move before he can think. We find people like that and use them till they quit."

"But as a manager don't you look bad if too many people are quitting?"

"As a manager I am judged by the statistical reports which come off the computer. Which basically means my crew labor productivity. What else can I really distinguish myself by? I could have a good fry yield, a low M&R [Maintenance and Repair budget]. But these are minor."

As it happens, Jon is distinguished among McDonald's managers in his area as an expert on the computerized equipment. Other managers call on him for cash register repairs. "They say, 'Jon, could you look at my register? I just can't afford the M&R this month.' So I come and fix it and they'll buy me a beer."

"So keeping M&R low is a real feather in a manager's cap," I deduced.

"O.K., it's true, you can overspend your M&R budget; you can have a low fry yield; you can run a dirty store; you can be fired for bothering the high school girls. But basically, every Coke spigot is monitored. [At most McDonald's Coke doesn't flow from taps that turn on and off. Instead the clerk pushes the button "sm," "med" or "lge," which then dispenses the premeasured amount into the appropriate size cup. This makes the syrup yield fairly consistent.] Every ketchup squirt is measured. My costs for every item are set. So my crew labor productivity is my main flexibility."

I was beginning to understand the pressures toward pettiness. I had by then heard many complaints about slight pilferage of time. For instance, as a safety measure no one was allowed to stay in a store alone. There was a common complaint that a closer would be clocked out when he finished cleaning the store for the night, even though he might be required to wait around unpaid till the manager finished his own nightly statistical reports. At times kids clocked out and then waited hours (unpaid) for a crew chief training course (unpaid).

Overtime is an absolute taboo at McDonald's. Managers practice every kind of scheduling gymnastic to see that no one works over forty hours a week. If a crew member approaching forty hours is needed to close the store, he or she might be asked to check out for a long lunch. I had heard of a couple of occasions when, in desperation, a manager scheduled someone to stay an hour or two over forty hours. Instead of paying time-and-a-half, he compensated at straight time listing the extra hours as miscellaneous and paying through a fund reserved for things like register race bonuses. All of this of course to make his statistics look good.

"There must be some other way to raise your productivity," I suggested, "besides squeezing it out of the kids."

"I try to make it fun," Jon pleaded earnestly. "I know that people like to work on my shifts. I have the highest crew labor productivity in the area. But I get that from burning people out. Look, you can't squeeze a McDonald's hamburger any flatter. If you want to improve your productivity there is nothing for a manager to squeeze but the crew."

"But if it's crew dollars paid out divided by food dollars taken in, maybe you can bring in more dollars instead of using less crew."

"O.K., let me tell you about sausage sandwiches."

"Sausage sandwiches?" (Sounded awful.)

"My crew was crazy about sausage sandwiches. [Crew members are entitled to one meal a day at reduced prices. The meals are deducted from wages through a computerized link to the time clocks.] They made it from a buttered English muffin, a slice of sausage and a slice of cheese. I understand this had actually been a menu item in some parts of the country but never here. But the crew would make it for themselves and then all their friends came in and wanted them.

"So, I decided to go ahead and sell it. It costs about 9¢ to make and I sold it for $1.40. It went like hotcakes. My supervisor even liked the idea because it made so much money. You could see the little dollar signs in his eyes when he first came into the store. And he said nothing. So we kept selling it.

"Then someone came in from Oak Brook and they made us stop it.

"Just look how ridiculous that is. A slice of sausage is 60¢ as a regular menu item, and an English muffin is 45¢. So if you come in and ask for a sausage and an English muffin I can still sell them to you today for $1.05. But there's no way I can add the slice of cheese and put it in the box and get that $1.40.

"Basically, I can't be any more creative than a crew person. I can't take any more initiative than the person on the register."

"Speaking of cash registers and initiative," I said . . . and told him about Damita. I explained that she was honest, bright and had learned how to zero out at another store. "Do you let cashiers zero out?" I asked.

"I might let her in this case," Jon said. "The store she learned it at was probably a franchise and they were looser. But basically we don't need people like her. Thinking generally slows this operation down.

"When I first came to McDonald's, I said, 'How mechanical! These kids don't even know how to cook.' But the pace is so fast that if they didn't have all the systems, you couldn't handle it. It takes ninety seconds to cook a hamburger. In those seconds you have to toast the buns, dress it, sear it, turn it, take it off the grill and serve it. Meanwhile you've got maybe twenty-four burgers, plus your chicken, your fish. You haven't got time to pick up a rack of fillet and see if it's done. You have to press the timer, drop the fish and know, without looking, that when it buzzes it's done.

"It's the same thing with management. You have to record the money each night before you close and get it to the bank the next day by 11 a.m. So you have to trust the computer to do a lot of the job. These computers also calculate the payrolls, because they're hooked into the time clocks. My payroll is paid out of a bank in Chicago. The computers also tell you how many people you're going to need each hour. It's so fast that the manager hasn't got time to think about it. He has to follow the procedures like the crew. And if he follows the procedures everything is going to come out more or less as it's supposed to. So basically the computer manages the store."

Listening to Jon made me remember what Ray Kroc had written about his own job (head of the corporation) and computers:

We have a computer in Oak Brook that is designed to make real estate surveys. But those printouts are of no use to me. After we find a promising location, I drive around it in a car, go into the corner saloon and the neighborhood supermarket. I mingle with the people and observe their comings and goings. That tells me what I need to know about how a McDonald's store would do there.*

By combining twentieth-century computer technology with nineteenth-century time and motion studies, the McDonald's corporation has broken the jobs of griddleman, waitress, cashier and even manager down into small, simple steps. Historically these have been service jobs involving a lot of flexibility and personal flair. But the corporation has systematically extracted the decision-making elements from filling french fry boxes or scheduling staff. They've siphoned the know-how from the employees into the programs. They relentlessly weed out all variables that might make it necessary to make a decision at the store level, whether on pickles or on cleaning procedures.

It's interesting and understandable that Ray Kroc refused to work that way. The real estate computer may be as reliable as the fry vat probe. But as head of the company Kroc didn't have to surrender to it. He'd let the computer juggle all the demographic variables, but in the end Ray Kroc would decide, intuitively, where to put the next store.

Jon DeAngelo would like to work that way, too. So would Jason, June and Damita. If they had a chance to use some skill or intuition at their own levels, they'd not only feel more alive, they'd also be treated with more consideration. It's job organization, not malice, that allows (almost requires) McDonald's workers to be handled like paper plates. They feel disposable because they are.

I was beginning to wonder why Jon stayed on at McDonald's. He still yearned to open a restaurant. "The one thing I'd take from McDonald's to a French restaurant of my own is the fry vat computer. It really works." He seemed to have both the diligence and the style to run a personalized restaurant. Of course he may not have had the capital.

"So basically I would tell that girl [bringing me back to Damita] to find a different job. She's thinking too much and it slows things down. The way the system is set up, I don't need that in a register person, and they don't need it in me."

"Jon," I said, trying to be tactful, "I don't exactly know why you stay at McDonald's."

"As a matter of fact, I have already turned in my resignation."

"You mean you're not a McDonald's manager any more?" I was dismayed.

"I quit once before and they asked me to stay."

"I have had such a hard time getting a full-fledged manager to talk to me and now I don't know whether you count."

"They haven't actually accepted my resignation yet. You know I heard of this guy in another region who said he was going to leave and they didn't believe

---

*   Ray Kroc and Robert Anderson, *Grinding It Out* (Chicago: Contemporary Books, 1977), p. 176.

him. They just wouldn't accept his resignation. And you know what he did? One day, at noon, he just emptied the store, walked out, and locked the door behind him."

For a second Jon seemed to drift away on that beautiful image. It was like the kids telling me about Jason, the crewman who just walked out the back door.

"You know what that means to close a McDonald's at noon, to do a zero hour at lunch?"

"Jon," I said. "This has been fantastic. You are fantastic. I don't think anyone could explain the computers to me the way you do. But I want to talk to someone who's happy and moving up in the McDonald's system. Do you think you could introduce me to a manager who . . ."

"You won't be able to."

"How come?"

"First of all, there's the media hotline. If any press comes around or anyone is writing a book, I'm supposed to call the regional office immediately and they will provide someone to talk to you. So you can't speak to a real corporation person except by arrangement with the corporation.

"Second, you can't talk to a happy McDonald's manager because 98 percent are miserable.

"Third of all, there is no such thing as a McDonald's manager. The computer manages the store."

Barbara Garson wrote her first play, *MacBird*, while collecting unemployment insurance of $25 a week. That was in 1965 and she hasn't held a paid job since. Yet she has written two books—*All the Livelong Day* (Doubleday 1975) and *The Electronic Sweatshop* (Simon & Schuster 1988)—and dozens of articles about work.

"Labor stories are so often about long hours, low pay, toxic chemicals, or even worse, unemployment," Garson says. "I write such pieces too because one has to. But the reason I'm still with the subject is because work is wonderful: concentration is the most spiritual human expression. To me the great crime isn't forcing people to work but robbing them of real work with all its satisfactions." Indeed, Garson's classic book, *All the Livelong Day*, in print since 1975, is subtitled *The Meaning and Demeaning of Routine Work*.

Her other works include *Money Makes the World Go Around: One Investor Tracks Her Cash Through the Global Economy* (Viking Penguin 2000); the OBIE-winning children's play *The Dinosaur Door*; *The Department*, a comedy about an office being automated; *Going Co-op*, a 1970s play about gentrification (before it had that name); and most recently, *Security*, a farce about our increasing economic insecurity.

For her playwriting, journalism, and non-fiction, Garson has been awarded a Guggenheim Fellowship, a National Endowment for the Arts Fellowship, two OBIEs, a National Press Club Citation, a New York State Council for the Arts Grant, The Library Journal's Best Business Book of the Year Award, and a research grant from the John D. and Catherine T. MacArthur Foundation. Garson lives in New York City.

The River Bottom Ranch

Marcial González

POP CAME TO THE U.S. from Mexico before the rest of us, crossing the border in '42 to follow the crops. In '46, he got a job at a cold storage plant in Kingsburg. Walking on ice all day was better than working in the fields. The wages were higher and the work was steady. Two years later, when I was twelve, he fixed his papers and brought our whole family to live in California, and the next year is when the incident—the one I want to tell about—took place.

There were eight children in our family. I was the third, with an older brother and sister. We settled three hundred miles north of the Mexican border in the town of Parlier—a small town then, not much more than a labor camp. But a school and a store had been built by the time we moved there. To the south and east of town ran the Kings River; to the north and west, tributaries snaked their way through the cultivated fields like the veins in a person's arm. Workers walked behind the tilling disks of tractors, picking up large stones that had once formed the bottom of riverbeds. The alluvial flood plains had created a fertile soil—a dark sandy loam that sponged in your fist when you squeezed it. Growers became rich farming peaches, plums, nectarines, and grapes in this part of the great San Joaquin Valley.

Right from the start, Mama didn't like the U.S. "Everyone here works too much, especially the women," she said. "Too much work will kill you."

Early in our second summer in California, Pop suffered a stroke. It happened at home while we all watched. At first we thought he was fooling, but when we saw that he was choking on his tongue, we knew it was serious. His face twisted as if some invisible hands were strangling him. Mama grabbed him as he fell, dragged him to the sofa, laid him down, and unbuttoned his shirt. That's when we saw the blood on Mama's chest. When she'd grabbed him, Pop scratched her with his fingernails from her neck down to her breast. Not on purpose, of course. But the scratches were deep, and Mama's blood oozed from the wounds and stained the material of her blouse. She was the only calm one among us—we children were all screaming and crying, terrified as much by Pop's condition as by the lines of blood that crossed Mama's heart. She sent my brother running to the corner store to call an ambulance since we didn't have a telephone. Pop's skin turned blue, the color of an ugly bruise, and Mama wiped his face with a damp cloth till the ambulance came. The driver looked at the blood on her body and asked if she wanted to come to the hospital, too. But she said she'd better stay with her children. It wasn't till after the ambulance had left that Mama cried.

The ambulance took Pop to a hospital in Fresno, twenty miles from Parlier.

We visited him there but saw that he was in bad shape. Half his body was paralyzed, and his face sagged on the right side as if it had melted. A week later they sent him to a hospital in San Francisco. The insurance from Pop's job paid his hospital expenses, but nobody gave Mama anything for his lost wages. He'd been gone more than a month that summer when I got the job at the River Bottom Ranch.

We'd always been poor, but times got worse after Pop's stroke. My older brother was arrested for stealing cars. He had this foolish idea he could help pay the bills by selling car parts, and ended up spending a year in juvenile hall. My older sister, just as foolish, ran off with a man who promised to marry her. But the man lied and it would be many years before we saw her again. With both my brother and sister gone, I suddenly found myself the oldest child at home.

I was thirteen years old that summer and wanted to play baseball in the youth league. I'd played shortstop for the school team, and the coach said I had an arm like a gun and a natural swing at bat. Whether this was true or not, his words filled my head with dreams of the big leagues. The problem was that Mama said I had to work, and the only place where a Mexican boy could work was in the fields. Mama couldn't leave the younger children to go to work. It would have cost almost as much to pay a sitter for so many children as she would have made working. So instead she stayed home taking care of other people's children but didn't earn much.

Forced to choose between baseball and work, I tried to ignore Mama's reasoning. "How will we eat?" she asked.

I shrugged my shoulders.

"Well, you have no choice," she said. "It's either work or starve."

That wasn't the only problem. It cost money to be on the team. We couldn't afford to buy a glove and shoes, even though I expected Mama to come up with the money somehow. I confronted her about it at the dinner table. "I need money. I need a glove and shoes." I told her how much they cost, and that I wanted to play baseball.

She didn't say anything, just sat eating her dinner silently. With no screens on the windows and no wind, a dense heat thicker than Tule fog entered the room as easily as did the flies.

I got mad and yelled, "Why do you and Pop have to be so poor? Why did you have to be so stupid?"

Mama still said nothing but stopped eating. My sisters and brothers sat frozen. After a minute, Mama got up from the table and walked to her bedroom. I followed. She opened the top drawer of her dresser and took out a box that had envelopes and papers in it. From the box she took a handkerchief, knotted on the corners. She untied the handkerchief and spread the cloth on the bed, exposing a small amount of money—some bills and coins. She separated the amount I had asked for and handed it to me, but I couldn't put my hand out to take it. So she took hold of my hand and placed the money in my palm. "Take it," she said. "But don't ever ask me for anything again."

Too ashamed to look into her eyes, I looked down at the flowery bedspread and saw that only a few coins were left on the handkerchief. She walked away and left me standing there alone in the bedroom, the money still clutched in my hand. The money she'd given me was what she'd been saving to visit Pop at the hospital. No one had to tell me, I knew it. That night, when everyone was asleep, I slipped quietly into Mama's bedroom and placed the money on top of her dresser where I was sure she'd notice it. Then I went to sleep. She never said a word about the money. And neither did I.

I decided to work instead of playing baseball. The easiest place to get a job was with the farm labor contractors who parked their buses in town every morning between three and four o'clock to load them up with workers. The antique buses were death traps—engine fires, exhaust fumes, accidents, you name it. Sometimes they'd break down in the morning on the way to the field, and we'd all parade the long road to town after losing a day's work, or they'd break down on the way home, and it was midnight before another would come get us.

The advantage, though, was that the contractors paid every day in cash. Sometimes it meant pushing and shoving to get on a bus because there were always more people looking for work than there were available seats. I joined the ranks of workers competing for a job, and before long I learned to push and shove my way into the buses like the rest. The buses worked every day, Sundays included. After a while I got tired of it.

One morning I met a man who was looking for workers to pick peaches at a farm called the River Bottom Ranch, and he had enough work to last all summer. The fields were near Parlier, which meant I wouldn't have to get up so early. What's more, the pay was a buck twenty an hour, twenty cents more than the best wages the contractors were paying. Ten hours straight, a half hour for lunch, and we'd be paid in cash promptly after work each day. I wasted no time agreeing to work with the man, whose name was Juan. The workers piled into the back of two vans. One of the vans pulled a trailer with ladders and buckets. The other pulled a portable toilet.

I didn't know a thing about picking peaches, but when Juan asked me, "Have you done this work?" I said, "Yes, sir." I could tell by his frown that he knew I was lying. When we got to the field, the only instructions he gave me were, "You'd better not scratch your neck." I had to watch the other workers to see what I was supposed to do. They all worked so expertly, moving the ladders with ease, placing them just right so they wouldn't fall, scampering up and down with a bucket in each hand, knowing which fruit to pick by color and size. The ladders were fourteen feet tall, with rings fastened to the sides of the ladder on which to hang the buckets while picking. The buckets had to be balanced or the ladder would fall. Each bucket held twenty pounds of fruit. After filling the buckets, the picker hurried down the ladder, dumped the peaches in boxes stacked next to the road, and hurried back to fill more buckets. There was a knack to handling the ladders, especially since the ground was weedy and muddy, with irrigation trenches between the rows. There were twenty men in the crew. Each man worked a row of trees. Everyone was expected to keep up, and no one liked to stay behind, much less to help someone who had fallen behind. I was the youngest and was quickly given the nickname, "Peach Fuzz," which was soon shortened to just plain "Fuzz."

My ladder fell a few times and I fell with it. I tried not to look at the men when they laughed at me for falling or when they called out, "Hey, Fuzz. Watch out for the ground. It's moving under your ladder." Juan told one of the workers to take the row next to me so he could help if I fell behind. The worker's nickname was El Gato Negro, or "Gato" for short. He was a black man with green eyes like a cat's, though his name probably had as much to do with his personality as with his eyes. He was the fastest picker and didn't let anyone forget it. He was the loudest talker in the crew, too, and no conversation took place without someone yelling through the trees, "Hey, Gato, what do you say?" And Gato would answer as if his was the final word. Gato was popular, big, dark, strong and fast, but something about him made me feel uneasy.

Gato complained to Juan. "Why do I have to help the kid? If he's old enough to work, let him work on his own. How else can he learn?"

Unlike Gato, Juan was levelheaded. "If someone falls behind, the boss will fire the whole crew."

But Gato was a rebel. "Then why hire the boy?" he said. "Send him to school with the children where he belongs."

"You forget that you were young once," Juan replied.

"Oh, I'm young still," Gato said, speaking louder so all the men could hear. "Just ask my girl about that."

The men laughed and joked about Gato's lovemaking abilities, but when the joking stopped, Juan reminded Gato, "Make sure the boy doesn't fall behind."

The first day was rough. I quickly learned what Juan meant about not scratching. When peach fuzz falls on your sweaty neck it itches terribly, but if you scratch, you'll get a rash that itches ten times worse. You have to button your shirt up to your neck and wear a handkerchief around your face like a bandit. And no matter how bad you itch, don't scratch. Yet that wasn't the worst of it. I tried with all my might to keep up with the crew so Gato wouldn't have to help me, but my eyes couldn't select the fruit fast enough and my hands were too slow. My legs and back tired quickly, carrying the buckets of fruit up and down the ladder. I fell behind, and when I tried to catch up, I made more mistakes and got frustrated and fell farther behind. Gato helped me but made a public announcement of it each time he did.

When I got home from my first day of work at the River Bottom Ranch, I took off my shirt before entering the house, not wanting to get peach fuzz and dust on everything, and washed myself down outside with a water hose.

Once inside, Mama asked, "How was your first day?"

I pretended it went well. She didn't ask why the men had called me "Fuzz" as they drove away. After dinner I proudly counted twelve dollars even for ten hours of work and gave the money to my mother—an act I'd repeat every day that summer. Then I took a bath and knocked out until it was time to get up again in the morning.

The next day I quickly fell behind and felt like crying because I knew Gato would soon begin complaining.

"Imagine that!" Gato said. "Fuzz can't tell the good fruit from the bad. How will he ever pick a pretty girl?"

"What do girls have to do with peaches?" someone yelled.

"They're exactly the same," Gato yelled back. "They're sweet and they make you itch."

"Don't be so hard on the boy," Juan said.

"How do you expect Fuzz to keep up with the crew?" Gato replied. "He can't even grow a beard yet."

"Don't you remember when you couldn't grow a beard?" Juan asked.

Gato was never without witty answers at the tip of his tongue. "I was born with a beard. It tickled my mother to death during the delivery."

The crew laughed and someone said, "Ah, qué, Gato!

Gato was hard to figure out. As much as he complained, he wouldn't let me fall behind, but he'd still scold me.

"When are you going to learn to work fast, Fuzz?"

There was nothing I could say. I feared that if I talked back, he'd stop helping me. Then I'd be out of a job. I almost wanted to like Gato, despite the control he had over me. I admired his confidence, the way the men listened to him as if listening to an authority, and how he mastered his work—how he made picking peaches look like a breeze. He was a handsome man too. Dark as ripe olives. Lean and sleek like a panther.

On my second day of work at the River Bottom Ranch, the farmer came to the field. He didn't walk into the orchard because, I suppose, he didn't want to get his boots muddy. He parked outside the field on the road. Everyone knew a honk of the horn meant the farmer wanted a word with us, and automatically the men headed for the edge of the field. I began to go too but was stopped by Gato, who grabbed my arm from behind.

"Don't go out there, Fuzz," he said. He let go of my arm and rested his hand on my shoulder. "Get back up on your ladder as high as you can and hide in the branches. Don't let yourself be seen." He spoke these words softly, almost in a whisper, and then followed the other men out of the field. Maybe I'd been wrong about Gato, I thought. Maybe he wasn't such a bad guy after all. When the men came back to their ladders, they were all grumbling. The farmer had scolded them for not working fast enough. This was not good news. I couldn't keep up before. Now the boss wanted us to go even faster. No one else liked the new orders either, but everyone obeyed.

The camaraderie I had briefly felt toward Gato quickly faded when I heard him shout, "I had to tell that kid to stay in the tree. He could've got us all fired."

"I thought you were protecting Fuzz," one of the men said.

"What do I care about Fuzz? I'm protecting my own skin, not his."

That night I was more tired than the first, and I tried not to think about Gato's words but couldn't erase them from my mind.

On the third day we finished picking fruit from a row of trees and were drinking water from a large can that Juan had placed at the back of his van. A shiny new pickup truck sped by on the dirt road. Dust showered our bodies and we covered our mouths and coughed the dirt out of our throats.

"He's the farmer's son," Gato said. "Not much older than you, Fuzz. His father bought him that truck to check up on his workers. Stay out of his way. He's like an animal trainer learning to use a new whip."

I drank more water and watched as the new truck came back down the dusty road again, this time cruising slowly. As the boy in the truck passed, I recognized him. I'd seen him before at school. He might have been a grade or two ahead of me. I didn't think he recognized me, but to make sure I pulled my handkerchief up around my eyes and lowered the brim of my hat.

In the evening after work, some boys from the baseball team came to my home and invited me to play ball. "We told the coach you had to work," one friend said. "He said you could be on the team and play whenever you're able to."

Another said, "I have extra shoes."

Still another, "I'll lend you a glove."

I thought about playing. The sun still shone in the west, but magnificent shadows of giant walnut trees shaded the yard where we stood. We picked up green walnuts that had fallen to the ground and threw them like baseballs as far as we could into a field. Even if I'd convinced myself to play, my body resisted. The fatigue was unbearable.

"I can't go," I told them. They nodded and kicked at the ground and picked up more walnuts but cracked them in their hands instead of throwing them. Shortly after they'd gone, I was asleep on my bed. And that's the way it was all week long. From work to bed. From bed to work. Day after day.

On my seventh day at the River Bottom Ranch, a Sunday, I cried in bed before getting up. When Mama came to wake me, I couldn't hold it back. With my face against the pillow, I wept the way babies weep when they want their mother's breast. I was tired, but worse yet, I could no longer bear to hear Gato's constant complaints that I was too slow. He made me feel inferior to the men in the crew. The thing was, I didn't want to be like the men. I wanted to be like the boys on the team who didn't have to work at all. When Mama heard me crying, she said, "Shut your mouth! The van will be here soon."

After a while, I stopped crying, got up, put on my clothes, and tried not to make noise because the children were still asleep. I got my lunch and went outside to the cool air of the morning to wait for Juan. The stars glittered like the eyes of a million babies laughing. I stood looking up to every point where the stars gathered in thick clumps, pivoting on my feet like a soldier doing an about-face. Juan came and the men laughed, "What were you looking at up there, Fuzz?"

The day started off bad but got worse. We began to work at daybreak and before eight o'clock the temperature had climbed to over one hundred degrees. A suffocating humid air rose from the stagnant water in the trenches. Our clothes clung to our bodies with sweat. The field was particularly weedy, the grass reaching above my waist. I stayed farther behind on that day than on any previous day. My ladder fell several times, and I fell with it, spilling the fruit. Gato practically had to pick two rows at the same time, and I still couldn't catch up.

I heard Gato complain to Juan. "Do I get paid double to pick two rows? Or do I get half of the kid's wages?"

Juan didn't answer Gato, but he came and asked me what was wrong. "You've got to work faster," he said.

But I couldn't work faster, no matter how hard I tried. It was more than I could handle just to stay on the ladder and to stay awake. When lunchtime came, I didn't go to the van to eat but lay down right there in the middle of the field where we stopped working and rested on top of a border so as not to get wet from the moisture in the furrows. I folded an armful of weeds so that it made a sort of pillow for my head, and, lying down, all I could see was the grass to my sides, the leaves and fruit of the peach tree straight above, and bits of blue sky filtering through the branches of the tree I was under. I could hear the voices and laughter of the men as they walked out of the field toward the van and to their lunches. Their voices got farther and farther away until they sounded like the last part of an echo or like a dream you remember when you wake up in the morning but after a while you don't remember any more. Soon I couldn't hear their voices at all but listened instead to the buzzing of the gnats near my ears. Brushing them away, I put my straw hat over my face and smelled the dried sweat and the leather lining on the inside of the hat, where it was dark, except for the specks of light that shone through the ventilation holes. In the darkness, I saw my friends dressed in bright new uniforms, playing baseball at a stadium, while fans cheered them on. They called me to play with them and I walked on to the field, shyly. They put a bat in my hand and it was my turn to hit. Stepping up to the plate and noticing that I too was dressed in a new uniform, I felt proud because the crowd was cheering me on. I swung the bat over the plate. I swung and I swung and I swung, and the voices of the fans kept ringing in my ears.

I COULD HEAR THE VOICES. They came from far away. I listened then opened my eyes and took the hat off my face. The voices were those of the men in the crew, but they weren't getting closer. I heard Juan tell the men to select the best fruit and to work faster, but his voice was faint.

I sat up and saw my ladder next to the tree where I had stopped working before lunch, but the ladders of the rest of the crew were gone. I stood up and looked under the trees up ahead to where the men were picking. They were a good ten trees in front of me. I must have slept for two hours. Why didn't Juan wake me? How could I catch up now? I went to my ladder and checked my tree but noticed that it had been picked. I quickly moved the ladder to the next tree, but that one too was finished. I moved to the next, and it was finished too. I walked with my ladder, hurriedly, slipping in the grass and the mud, tree by tree. They were all picked. All finished. I caught up with Gato, who was talking and arguing as usual. I placed my ladder next to his and began picking nervously, wondering what Juan and Gato would tell me for having fallen asleep on the job—for making them do my work. They said nothing and kept working as if I wasn't there.

I didn't know what to make of all this. I was flattered they had helped me, but afraid that I'd be fired. As it turned out, it was a good thing I woke when I did, for no more than ten minutes passed until the farmer got there with his son at his side. They didn't honk the horn of their pickup truck. They walked right out to the field where we were working.

The farmer told Juan to gather the crew—he had something to say to us. We formed a half circle in front of the farmer and his son. Juan asked a worker who knew English to interpret, and he signaled me to hide my face. I stood behind the men as the farmer spoke. He was mad as hell because the fruit we were picking was either too small or didn't have enough color. "I'm losing money," he said. "If you can't pick my peaches right, I'll fire the whole bunch of you."

"Tell them about the boy, Dad," the farmer's son said.

The farmer nodded, and then said, "It seems there's a boy in this crew too young to work."

The interpreter relayed these words in Spanish.

"I don't give a damn if you put wetback boys to work," he said. "It's no sweat off my back. But I'll only pay half wages for half a man."

The interpreter lowered his head at these words.

No one said a thing, and I wanted to turn myself in because I knew the boss could fire the whole crew, and I'd be to blame for it.

"What'll it be?" the owner said.

I was about to speak when Gato cleared his throat and raised his finger in the air, as if in some kind of official meeting, requesting the right to speak.

"Patrón," Gato said. "I have something to say, but I want you to know I'm speaking only for myself."

The interpreter kept up, talking directly to the owner.

"As far as I'm concerned," Gato went on. "I have to protect myself. Why risk my job for someone who doesn't yet know how to work? Ask anyone. I'm the fastest picker."

All the men of the crew hung their heads, anticipating what Gato was going to say next, even Juan, who seemed to have shrunk in the presence of the farmer.

Gato gathered confidence the more he spoke. "But just as I'm the fastest worker, Patrón, I'm also against those who don't do their share. Why should I help a boy who should be in school instead of out here working?"

The farmer took a watch from his pocket and looked at it. Then he put his watch away, crossed his arms, and stared at Gato. The farmer's son shifted his weight from one leg to the other, put his hand in his pocket, and jingled some keys.

"See these hands, Patrón." Gato stuck out his hands and spread his fingers apart wide. I hadn't noticed until then how long his fingers were. They looked like thick asparagus shoots. "These are my livelihood. They're the bread on my table and my rent."

Although Gato's words didn't surprise me, knowing him to be unpredictable, it angered me thinking he'd actually turn me in. I noticed the faces of the other workers and their expressions of dismay at Gato's words. The interpreter's expression was the worst of all, perhaps because he had to repeat the words.

Gato still stood with his fingers stretched out into the air. "Do you think I'd give these up to some boy who can't wipe his nose?"

The owner interrupted Gato abruptly. "What are you babbling about? If you got something to say, say it! I got business to take care of."

Gato spat on the ground. "You were asking about wetback boys and half men. I was going to tell you about that."

"What's your name?" asked the farmer.

"Gato," Gato said. "They call me Black Cat because no one crosses my path."

"All right, Cat," the boss said. "Spit it out."

Gato took a step forward. He stood half way between the workers and the boss, in the middle of the circle. "What I'm saying is that if there's a boy working here in this crew, you'll know it, because I'll be the first to tell you. I'm not about to risk my job for some snot-nose kid. I take care of myself first. You can count on me. But as you can see, there are no wetback boys here. We are all men."

A fly landed on the farmer's son's face. He didn't shoo it away. Mouth gaping, his eyes hung on the green-eyed black man at the center of the circle.

"And you can be sure of that," Gato said, "because Gato doesn't lie."

The boss looked at Gato, apparently taken back by his boldness. Gato looked back at him, and I couldn't tell if the look on Gato's face was one of humility, defiance, or mockery. And I don't think the farmer could tell either.

Without taking his eyes off the farmer, Gato spoke back over his shoulder, "Isn't that right, compañeros?"

Everyone in the crew answered at once, nodding their heads and shouting, "That's right!" Even Juan. I felt my face redden. The farmer stared back at Gato silently for it must've been a whole minute. Then without saying another word, he turned and left. The farmer's son took a last look at us with his scanning eyes, and then followed his father, his big boots plastering the weeds as he went. Before they were too far away, Juan yelled loudly, "Let's go! Get back in those trees!" Everyone obeyed. And I did too.

I climbed up the ladder and began to work. All that had just happened was still not very clear in my mind. As I was trying to figure it out, something strange was happening to my hands. I could move them faster. I felt light-footed on the ladder, and the buckets weren't heavy at all. Better yet, it didn't matter to me any more if I kept up with the crew or not. It didn't matter if I picked the right size fruit or the right color. It didn't matter if I picked a hundred buckets an hour or ten or one or none. Something had just happened, something very minor but significant nonetheless. There are things in this life, I thought, much more important than picking fruit. Yet my hands moved rapidly with a newfound speed and confidence I hadn't known before, and they fluttered through the leaves of the peach trees uninhibited by fear.

Juan shouted to pay closer attention to the fruit. "Better color, better size," he said. He walked up and down between the rows of trees and when he got to Gato's tree he stopped.

"So you are against snot-nosed kids, eh, Gato?" Juan said.

"That's right, Juan. You show me one, and I'll be the first to turn him in to the patrón."

"You forget that you were young once," Juan said.

Gato answered loudly, "Who me? I was never young. But that's the thing. I'll never get old either."

Then Gato and Juan laughed. They laughed loudly, so loud that if you had been standing on the opposite end of the field you would have heard them. The rest of the men joined in the laughter, and it lasted a long time. Gato pointed at me and said, "Look at Fuzz! He's not laughing!" He stood on his ladder, pointing his asparagus finger at me, and laughing, and everyone else stopped working to look at me, too. And they all pointed their fingers at me and shouted, "Fuzz is not laughing!" Then something had broken loose in my heart and I began to laugh. I laughed with the rest of the men, loud and hard, until tears came to my eyes. The laughter lasted a long time. It lasted all day. It lasted all summer, echoing over the grasses and through the branches of those peach fields, and I'll leave it up to you whether or not to believe me when I say that to this very day I can still hear the laughter of the men in that crew.

A lifetime has passed since the incident at the River Bottom Ranch. Mama never did get to visit Pop in San Francisco. He died that autumn. We used the money she'd been saving and brought him back to Parlier to bury him. Mama lived a long, fruitful life, though, remarrying twice and outliving all her husbands. After burying the third, she stayed single. It wasn't until shortly before my fiftieth birthday—a dozen years ago this spring—that she finally passed away, taking the scars on her chest with her to the grave. As for the men of the crew, I never saw any of them again after that summer. I don't know what became of Gato and Juan or the others. For all I know, Gato may still be as young as he claimed he'd always be. But young or old, one thing is certain. What took place in those peach fields at the River Bottom Ranch during that tender time of my youth will remain embedded in my memory for as long as I live—the way river stones are embedded in the river's bottom, holding firm against the currents of water and years.

Marcial González was born in Fresno, California in 1953—the son of Mexican farm workers and the fifth of seven children. He worked as a farm laborer in the San Joaquin Valley until the age of thirty-six. He has also worked as a political activist, helping to organize an independent, anti-racist farm workers union in the 1980s. At the age of thirty-seven, he began taking college courses at a junior college, and ten years later received his doctorate degree from Stanford University. González is currently Associate Professor of English at the University of California, Berkeley, and the author of *Chicano Novels and the Politics of Form: Race, Class and Reification*, a book of literary criticism forthcoming from the University of Michigan Press.

Of "The River Bottom Ranch," González writes, "The story is a coming-of-age narrative that explores the psychological pains produced by the exploitation of child labor. It also attempts to understand the relation between emotions and ideology—i.e., how a young boy's memory of a small act of compassion by co-workers can form the basis of his class consciousness years later."

An earlier version of "The River Bottom Ranch" was published by *The Americas Review*, vol. 22, nos. 1–2 (1994): 32–46. Copyright © Marcial González. It is reprinted here by permission of the author.

One Woman Watching

Linda Kantner

IT'S A NORMAL DAY. THE way twenty-four degrees below zero is normal in the winter in Minnesota. The way children play outside even though spit freezes on the sidewalk in forty-seven seconds. The way frozen fingertips hurt when they're getting warm again, when it's safe to hurt, but too late to do anything about it.

Their voices are loud early in the morning. Winter coats carry the smell of home. Grease that fried chicken, eggrolls, and ham. Exotic smells of curry and coriander. All kinds of sweat. Bus sweat—where should you sit, who will let you, who's going to trip you and laugh? Fear sweat that enters your flesh and sours in your bones. Staying sweat that penetrates polyester, rayon, nylon and down, living in pockets, armpits and collars. The raw stink of cigarette smoke. Nicotine rises from seven-year-old bodies like chain smokers in rehab.

The kids stroll to breakfast as though leisure is their right. As though childhood hadn't already slipped from their grasp. The free breakfast kids are poor and pissed; they swagger with attitude or shuffle, heads down.

"HURRY! FIVE MINUTES!" shouts a haggard woman who isn't paid enough to take any crap. "KEEP EATING! IT'S GOING INTO THE TRASH IN THREE MINUTES."

It's free, but no one said it would be pleasant. "KEEP YOUR HAT ON. DON'T TAKE OFF YOUR COAT. YOU CAN EAT IN SNOWPANTS. THIS ISN'T A PARTY. JUST EAT AND GO. YOU KNOW THERE IS NO TALKNG AT BREAKFAST. THIS IS A PRIVILEGE."

Breakfast is a privilege. There has been no recess in eight days because the wind chill is thirty-nine and fifty-eight and sixty-two below zero. The school secretary says we are making wimps out of the children. A run in the fresh air will do them good. What will happen if we raise a generation of weather wimps?

It's a normal day.

"CYRUS GOT HIT LAST NIGHT," his teacher says.

"For real this time?"

"He's got a bruise."

"I'll come and get him; give me five minutes."

I take off my coat, shove my purse in a drawer, grind coffee beans, and start a killer pot of four cups that will keep me wound until noon when I switch to Diet Coke. Grinding beans brings pleasure you would not believe.

The computer lab is crowded with eight-year-olds. Sticky hands pound the keys. Number munchers. Letter jugglers. Punctuation pirates. Decimal daredevils. A poet and two would-be songwriters hum a tune and search for a catchy phrase. Two Hmong boys are surfing the net; their straight black hair hangs close to the keys. They whisper with excitement and high five each other. My cynical mind wonders if they've found the Totally Nude Girls on Unicycles website.

"Hey, Cyrus, can you come with me?"

He's with his new buddy Neal. They're making monsters eat numbers and spit out the answers. "Watch, Linda. He pukes when we do it wrong."

"Cool."

"Can Neal come with me? We wanna play Twister."

"Not this time, buddy. But soon. Okay, Neal?"

Neal shrugs like it doesn't matter, which is better than when he pretends I don't exist or mutters "bitch" loud enough for the class to hear.

IN THE HALL, CYRUS STARTS to whisper. It's the old Cyrus, not the new and improved version we have been working on. This is the Cyrus who was hit last year. That time I could count fingers on his flesh. I could see his dad wore a ring on his pinky. The next two times Cyrus lied. He told me he'd been hit, but when the police came he said he fell off his bike. The next time he said his brother tripped him. The police mentioned something about their job being to fight crime, not babysit liars.

After I filed the first abuse report, Cyrus's dad, Ruddy, called me and asked who was giving Cyrus sugary cereal at school. Cyrus said a nice lady gave him Captain Crunch and then the police came. Didn't I know that Cyrus would lie for a bowl of cereal without milk and the chance to talk? "Don't ya know that shit makes him hyper?" I apologized. I knew Cyrus was hyper, but I believed he lied because he was afraid and would say anything to avoid getting hit. I wasn't aware that all of Cyrus's problems could be traced back to Captain Crunch. What in the world was I thinking when I fed him? I wasn't thinking. I was being a Norwegian grandmother who fixed problems with chicken soup, or Captain Crunch.

I didn't ask Ruddy what he was thinking when he squeezed Cyrus's neck so hard the bruise stayed purple for two weeks. But I didn't apologize for calling the police either. I said I'd watch the sugar. I said, "Thanks for calling. Let me know if you have other concerns." I didn't call him any of the names he deserved.

"I GA' A WHIPPIN'," CYRUS whispers. His shoulders sag forward like a scarecrow that has lost most of its stuffing. He drops words like solitary stones at my feet. In my poetic moments I imagine he is Hansel dropping breadcrumbs, hoping to find a way home. If you remember, the birds ate the breadcrumbs.

"We can talk even if you didn't get hit."

He looks at me like I'm crazy. "I ga' a whippin'."

"Let's wait and talk in my office." I prefer to start out gently, with small talk; it makes *me* feel better. I want to pretend we are having a nice chat and child abuse happens to come up.

"It's cold outside. What's for lunch?" I try, but Cyrus doesn't care about my feelings. Once he gets started, he could be on stage with the whole school watching. I walk quickly for his privacy while he talks.

"I ga' a whippin'," he starts again, since I clearly missed the point the first time.

"Who hit you?"

"Ma."

"What did she hit you with?"

"A belt, folded over."

"What were you wearing when you got hit?"

"I put on some boxers, just before."

Routine questions, when child abuse is part of your routine.

FINALLY WE REACH MY OFFICE and he bumbles in like a big bear cub. He looks in the direction of the cabinet where I keep treats and cereal.

"I kinda hungry."

"You had breakfast," I remind him.

He shakes his head "no," but I saw him there, laughing and stealing an extra milk to hide in his locker.

"I can't give you any food right now, Cyrus." If he'd lie for sugared cereal, what would he do for a Kit Kat bar? "Did anyone see you get hit?"

"My brotha' was der. He laff at me." I lean toward him to hear his voice. He crushes his words together like a stomped-on pop can. "My brotha say, 'you big fat baby.'" There are tears in Cyrus's eyes. His big brother is his hero.

"Where did you get hit, Cyrus, can I see?"

"On da back and on da leg." He lifts the back of his flannel shirt up over his ears and bends over like he's getting in position to be hit again. He shakes his butt so his huge pants slide down.

I stop him, "That's okay, Cyrus, I've seen enough for now. Thanks for showing me." His wide back has three red stripes about an inch wide and ten inches long—the size of a belt, folded over. One has been rubbing against the waist of his pants and looks raw. "What made your mom so mad?"

"Rayman live in my apartment buildin' and he fight me. My ma get mad at me. She say, 'A big boy like you can fight Rayman.'

"I got a bloody nose and some of da blood went on my new shirt."

"Your mom hit you because you got beat up?" I can believe it, but I don't want to. His mom is a great big woman with bushy black eyebrows and shoulders that push into a room first like a snowplow. I wouldn't want her to hit me. She's been understanding so far about the times I called the police and Cyrus has lied.

She advised me, "You can't believe everything that boy says. He lies, you know, and he steals." One day she called to ask a favor. Her voice was a whisper, like we were sharing a dirty secret. "We're missing one hundred dollars and a carton of cigarettes. Will you check Cyrus's coat and locker? Don't tell him I called."

I told her I'd look around, and I did, but I took Cyrus with me. His locker was a junkyard filled with pop cans, chip bags, and candy wrappers, but no money. Later I found out he spent all the money at the corner store by the bus stop, on candy and junk so the neighborhood kids would play with him.

"I'm sorry, Cyrus. Sorry you got hit." I say this to most of the kids who tell me they've been hurt. I figure no other adult is going to apologize for the bruises they've caused or the scars they've left.

Cyrus smiles in embarrassment and shrugs his shoulders like it's no big deal. He ducks his head and looks at me through his long black eyelashes. Cyrus is a big boy for the third grade, thick and stocky. He could have pounded Rayman into the dirt if he wanted to. We've been working on not fighting, but maybe we should discuss exceptions. Rayman and I have been working on social skills. He's a scrawny, foul-mouthed second grader with loads of charm and even more rage. Starting today, we'll add an anger management goal to his life.

THE GRAY DRESS PANTS CYRUS'S mother buys for him slide off his hips when he stands to go. He snatches the waist with one hand and bows his knees together to keep them up. Now I see why he wasn't embarrassed to take down his pants. A wide patch of bright red boxer shorts flashes me. Cyrus is smiling. I can tell he is proud of the flaming underwear and wants to show them off.

We walk back to catch the last minutes of computer class. He's munching on a graham cracker and is in no hurry. "I on level 4 in Space Invaders. You ha' ta gobble da numbers before meteors fall down from da sky and crush you." He's loud and excited now, no more whispering. He punches the air with his fist as he talks. He's completely moved on from those few shameful moments in my office. For a second I doubt his story, but how can I? I saw the marks.

"Neal call my house last night."

"That's great." I try to sound excited. This is a moment we've been waiting for, a friend from school has called and they didn't just say, "You're fat" and hang up.

"You mad at me?" he asks, not understanding my mood.

"No, I'm not mad at you. Go gobble numbers."

Back in my office I call the police. "Bring a camera," I tell them.

The telephone rings just as I set it down.

"Shit." I like to brood and kick my desk a few times after a child abuse report. Instead I put on my caring voice, "Social Work."

"Linda, can you talk to Jason? He called three girls penis suckers."

"Are they?"

"What?"

"Nothing, send him down." Social work humor is rarely appreciated by the real world. I don't see many laughing matters, so sometimes I make my own.

"Jason, it's not O.K. to call girls penis suckers."

"I didn't call them penis suckers. I said some girls suck penises and they thought I was talking about them."

"You were misunderstood."

"Yes, they misunderstood me."

"Well, you don't have to worry about that happening again today because you are going home."

"I am? Why?"

"He *is*? Why?" the principal asks.

"Because three little girls—until today—had never entertained the idea that a penis might be sucked. They will go home and imagine penis sucking when they should be thinking about Barbie and Ken and Skipper at the malt shop. These second grade girls now have a picture in their minds, not of riding a bicycle or learning to skate or painting their nails but of sucking a penis. They have Jason to thank for that."

"I'm suspended?"

"Go."

The secretary buzzes me from the front desk. She whispers, "Linda, the police are here. Do you know why?"

"I can't live with myself any longer. I've decided to confess. The bodies in my basement are starting to stink."

"Oh." There is a long pause and then she hangs up. My humor seems to be failing me today, or maybe it is failing everyone else.

When I walk into the office both secretaries, the assistant principal, and a first grade teacher all turn to watch. It is all that I can manage not to stick out my wrists and say, "Cuff me, Dano." Instead I smile politely and shake his hand. "My office is this way," I say. I'm so mature.

The cop is a little tough guy. He wants me to know that he fights crime and I'm wasting his precious time. He was probably just about to crush a million-dollar drug ring single-handedly and now he's sitting on a twelve-inch high plastic chair next to a dollhouse.

"I wish you would have called me later," he grumbles.

"I wish I never called you." I don't like his attitude.

"I haven't gotten to eat lunch in days."

"The bad guy business must be pretty good."

"Nah, all week I've been having root canal just before my shift. My mouth feels like a dead fish afterward. This is the first day I can actually eat, and I been dreaming about the roast beef with the 'awe juice' at Old Country Buffet."

"Do you want me to analyze your dream or give you some Honey Nut Cheerios to eat while you're here? I don't have any milk."

"I think I'll wait."

"You won't get an offer like that again. Do you want me to get the boy?"

"Nah, I'll just do the paperwork first. Kid probably needs to be in class. Probably needed a whippin' too, am I right? I used to hit my kids and not a one of them are on drugs. But it's different now. Yeah, I have to keep telling myself it's different now. Don't mind if I help myself to one of your candy bars, do you? Of course, you don't need to use a belt. I always thought my hand did a fine job of making my point."

I look out the window as he talks. The sky is gray all the way down to the ground. One set of holes are punched through the icy layer of snow. One person has struggled up the hill, through three feet of crust, looking for a shortcut. "There are no shortcuts," my brain screams. "There's no free lunch. Life isn't a picnic."

Over the intercom the secretary says, "ATTENTION, ATTENTION, ALL TEACHERS, THERE WILL BE NO OUTSIDE RECESS TODAY. PLEASE SEND YOUR STUDENTS TO THE CAFETERIA WITH SOMETHING TO DO."

"We are making the kids at this school into weather wimps."

"What?" says the little cop, looking up from his seat on my little chair, and wiping his nose on his police jacket sleeve, "I don't get it."

"It's nothing, something the secretary told me. I'll go get Cyrus now. You'll need to take some pictures."

"Right, damn. I hate that part. Makes me feel like a pervert."

"Just keep thinking about roast beef and 'awe juice'; you'll be out of here in a flash. Maybe two flashes."

He's unwrapping a red licorice stick and looking through my *Where's Waldo* book. I consider asking him to stay for Friendship Group. He'd fit right in, taking candy without asking first. He doesn't seem like a quick cure, so I keep my silly ideas to myself.

Cyrus's smile slips only a little when he sees the police. He's getting used to the routine. He's walking wide-legged next to me, holding up his pants with one hand and tripping over his shoelaces. Kids go without shoelaces to imitate prison fashion. Cyrus has missed the point.

The cop shakes Cyrus's hand and asks, "Your daddy named Ruddy?"

"Yeah," says Cyrus, confused.

"I know Ruddy. He visits us down at the jail every three or four months. Your daddy have a couple beers last night?"

"Yeah." Cyrus looks to me for help.

"It was his mother that hit him."

"Yowch! That must a hurt. I've seen Ruddy after she's taught him a lesson. Your mama's a wrecking ball. Can you drop your drawers for me there, Cyrus?"

He does, and I tell the officer there are more marks on his back. The feisty crime fighter lets out a big breath, "Jesus, what did you do, Cyrus? Set the house on fire?"

"Rayman hit me." And that was the truth, the whole truth.

I found out the facts by the end of the day. Rayman had cornered Cyrus in the stairwell and demanded money. Cyrus didn't have any, so Rayman asked for his belt. Cyrus handed it over and Rayman beat him with it. Beat him until the buckle broke off. Cyrus got yelled at by his mom for losing his belt, getting blood on his shirt and letting a little kid beat him up. His big brother laughed at him, hurt his feelings, said he was a "fat baby" and a "chicken." Cyrus came to school looking for a little sympathy.

Rayman is one of my kids, along with Cyrus and Jason, Dickie and Antoine. I see Neal sometimes because he rips up his work as soon as he finishes it. Antoine sets fires and Dickie wants to be a girl. Three girls come to my office because they're too shy to speak in class. It's a quiet group. I'll see them this afternoon. Maybe one of the girls will talk to me if I stand on my head or juggle or read white elephant jokes. You know the kind: "What do you do if you see a white elephant in a tree?"

"Yell, Timberrrrrr!"

In that way, it's a normal day.

Linda Kantner lives and writes in St. Paul, Minnesota. Her work has been included in many short story collections, including *Sacred Ground* (Milkweed 1996) and the *Use of Personal Narratives in the Helping Professions* (Haworth 2002). Kantner is currently working on her first book about teaching teenage immigrants English through creative writing.

Kantner has worked as a waitress in a donut shop, a maid in a fancy hotel, a canner in a corn-canning factory, and a night worker in a halfway house for women just out of prison. Kantner notes that "these were good jobs for starting out and even better to leave behind. I can't imagine a lifetime of this work, but for so many immigrants without adequate language skills, this is their future."

After September 11, 2001, Kantner decided she didn't know enough about the rest of the world, so she went to visit a friend's English as a Second Language class and met kids from Somalia, Ethiopia, and Laos. "It is the best of life when your work, your values, and your passion can come together in one place. That is what teaching writing to those who have no voice is for me."

Kantner's twenty years as a social worker led to "One Woman Watching." "I wish that it was fiction," she writes.

"One Woman Watching" originally appeared in *The Heartlands Today*, vol. 12 (2002). Copyright © 2002 by Linda Kantner. It is reprinted here by permission of the author.

Jobbed

Philip Levine

IN THE SUMMER OF 1944 the war was almost five years old, my older brother was in England with the Eighth Air Force, but home life went on as though it were all that mattered. I was sixteen, about to enter my junior year of high school, and working for an automotive parts manufacturer and jobber on Detroit's Grand River Avenue. I needed the job in order to earn money to clothe myself for the coming school year, and since I had become aware of the presence of girls in my classes I yearned for clothes that would make me attractive. I also had to feed another passion I'd discovered two years earlier: horse racing, at which I did only slightly better. It wasn't a great job, but it was the best I could do, for I was small for my age, not much over five foot four, and I weighed less than a hundred and thirty-five pounds. The boss assigned me to work under the direction of Andrew Griffin, the truck driver and general handyman around the shop, which employed fewer than two dozen people, half of them women who assembled universal joints, work that required quick and precise hands rather than brute strength.

Andy Griffin was unlike anyone else I'd ever known. In truth, in the fifty years since then, I don't think I've met anyone who resembled Andy. He was not that much taller than I, perhaps five foot ten, and I would guess he weighed about a hundred and eighty-five pounds. He wore coveralls or overalls to work and always long-sleeved shirts, even on blazing days, but it was easy enough to see he was powerfully built. Though thick through the shoulders and thighs, he moved with the grace and ease of someone much more slender. In physique and in his physical bearing he reminded me of the young Eric Hawkins, the great dancer. His skin was dark brown; his hair, just beginning to show touches of gray, was worn short. I would guess he was in his late thirties or early forties. His teeth were very regular and a sparkling white, and because he frequently smiled, one saw a lot of them. His eyes were dark brown and very bright. With his long oval face, the skin of which was very smooth, and his compact, neat features, he was truly beautiful, although I doubt he knew it, for he never showed the least trace of vanity. By Fridays his handsomeness was somewhat obscured by his graying stubble, for he shaved only on weekends.

The truck he drove was a two-and-a-half-ton stake truck, a Chevy, built in the late thirties, and for smooth operation it required double clutching, which Andy performed so rapidly he had to slow the process so that I could get a clear sense of what he was doing. Once I'd mastered that, he showed me how to back up through the most intricate mazes. Often, we visited the larger auto or auto parts factories to buy scrapped material, and the truck had to be maneuvered down narrow aisles of machines and the men who worked them. "Always go in backwards so you don't have to think about getting out," Andy advised me. In order to accomplish this, he'd put the truck in reverse, and with the clutch depressed with his left heel, he'd face backwards on the running board while he steered with his left hand, propelling the truck backwards by delicately letting the clutch out. He was both inside and outside the truck and driving it with great precision. The first time I saw him drive this way I was utterly stunned, and later when I asked him where he'd learned this method he said he couldn't remember. He probably taught it to himself, for I've never seen anyone else do it.

A great deal of what we did together involved the movement of large and often very heavy wooden crates that Andy and another employee, Eugene Watkins, created out of scrap wood. The shop had no forklift, and this was before trucks were equipped with hydraulic lifts on the tail, so I had to learn how to lift and carry in tandem with a man much stronger than I. I had to learn to balance a crate on one knee and turn so that I could face forward if we were going upstairs: Andy, bearing the brunt of the weight, could thus propel the crate and me together. When we descended, he would go first, the crate resting on his broad back as I scampered behind as fast as I was able. So precise and careful was he that not once during the long summer did I mash a finger or bruise an elbow. Every few days he would cheer me up by assuring me I was growing stronger and more adept, and after a few months passed it was clear even to me that he was right.

Andy created the rhythm of those days we spent together. If the driving wasn't difficult and he was tired, he'd let me take the wheel. If we had dozens of boxes and crates to load, he would choose the order in which we handled them and the configuration they made in the truck. He would work steadily and almost always in silence, and I would have to hop to it to keep up with him. When he sensed my exhaustion, he would call for a cigarette break. I remember once I took out a pack of matches just as he did and was about to tear one off when he said, "Save it. You don't know when you'll need it." (That moment was a sudden vision into his history and character.)

When Andy was hungry, or sensed I was, we'd break for lunch, which on pleasant days we took in the back of the truck, having brought our brown bags with us. Our allotted lunchtime was thirty minutes, and though no one was watching over us, that was exactly the time we took. Once, as we were smoking before returning to work, two men approached us. They were both dressed in ill-fitting gray suits and wore fedoras. We were parked just off West Warren near the Kelsey Hayes plant, which was our next stop. One of the men called out, "Boy, do you know what time it is?" He seemed to be looking at Andy, who stood slowly and flicked his cigarette past the man and stood in silence for a long moment. "You shouldn't call my partner a boy," he said, "he's doing a man's work." Then he looked at his pocket watch and said, "About one." The man thanked him, and they went on their way. "Most people would be nice," Andy said, "if they just knew how."

In late August, just before the end of the summer vacation, the boss called me into his office and questioned me about a missing carton of very costly aircraft bearings. "Most of what goes in and out of the back door of this place goes through your hands," he said, "or Andy's." I suggested that someone could have misplaced it. No, he'd searched everywhere, and it wasn't here. I didn't believe him; the place was huge, maybe twenty thousand square feet. There were aisles of clutch plates, used bearings, drive shafts, and ancient Packard grills that no one ventured down for days at a time. "I can assure you it didn't go out the front door," he said. That left Andy and me on the loading dock at the rear. He dismissed me and told me to send Andy to the office. When he called me in again the next day, he threatened me with a phone call to the police. I assured him I had no idea where they were or even how one would go about selling such things. The boss, a less than totally Americanized immigrant from the Ukraine, ran a hand through his thick mane of white hair. "It's the nigger," he said. I was far more surprised by his lack of knowledge of Andy's character than by his language.

"Funny," Andy said less than an hour later, after a long session in the office. "Worked nine years for the man and he still don't trust me. Something's missing; it's got to be me. If I wanted to, I could take half the place out that back door," he added, gesturing toward the loading dock. We were in the back of the shop where I had been counting junk bearings out of a burlap sack. Beside me on the long wooden workbench, Andy was assembling his possessions slowly and placing them with great care into a large paper sack: a suit of coveralls, a pair of high lace-up boots for bad weather, a zip-up windbreaker, a few tools of his own—a claw hammer, a nail puller, pliers, and a large clasp knife. It was obvious he was leaving, but if he'd been fired or if he'd quit he didn't say. "Phil, you'll be OK," he said without looking my way. The single bare bulb that hung above us was so weak I could barely make out his features. "Some other driver will show you things I never had time to—maybe things I never learned." I'd never seen him move with such deliberation nor stand so erectly; it was as though he were on parade. When all his personal items were stowed, he turned to me, and I could see that his eyes were clear. We shook hands, and he walked out of my life. Less than a week later, the missing bearings turned up in the trunk of the boss's car.

Philip Levine was born in 1928 in Detroit. A twin and the second son of Russian-Jewish immigrants, Levine attended public schools and Wayne State University (then the city university of Detroit). Later he studied with Robert Lowell and John Berryman at the Iowa Writer's Workshop and Yvor Winters at Stanford University. Levine worked construction on US 99, sold Fuller Brushes, worked at Chevy Gear & Axle in the forge room, drilled little holes in Cadillac transmissions, drove a truck for Railway Express (the UPS of the Stone Age), rewired damaged electric motors, re-asbestosized pipes for Wyandotte Chemical, loaded box cars with cases of Mavis-Nu-Icy soda pop, reground universal joints for Automotive Supply, packed cartons for McKesson & Robbins, tended the pickling tanks at a metal plating plant, and, at age thirty, began teaching at the college level. He now spends half the year in Brooklyn and half in Fresno, California. He is the Distinguished Poet-in-Residence at New York University.

Levine, whose subject matter is often work, is the author of two collections of essays and seventeen books of poetry. A winner of two National Book Awards, two Guggenheim Fellowships, the National Book Critics Award, and the Pulitzer Prize, Levine says he wrote "Jobbed" for the same reason that he writes most things: "I've written about what I was moved by."

"Jobbed" originally appeared in *DoubleTake* (2000). Copyright © 2000 by Philip Levine. It is reprinted here by permission of the author.

Things You Need to Know about Your Boss

Elizabeth Kerlikowske

His grandma always let him win at cards
so he thought he deserved to.
None of his father's sisters and brothers
speak to each other.
He claims he's bald because
his football helmet was too tight.
Black sheets in college
so he wouldn't have to wash.
He denounced the establishment
living off his first wife's trust fund—
lobster with food stamps.
His parents stole the little ladles
from Chinese restaurants:
"They want us to have them."
Turning back the odometer
taken for granted.
He ate until he puked at the all-you-can-eat
and then went back for more.
Slipped at the top and bounced
a naked flight, big fart on the bottom stair.
His second wife only marries Mikes.
His dick: like a baby ear of corn
in a Szechuan stir-fry.
More hair on his shoulders than head.
He's become Native American
and discovered his Celtic roots,
house done in Feng Shui.
He's tried everything once
first blue-green algae in a sweat lodge
now cigars at brew pubs.
Clinically it's apnea.
Nights he tries to choke himself to death
because there's a spark of good in everyone.

Elizabeth Kerlikowske's first job was cleaning movie theater popcorn machines. She moved from there to go-go dancing, which morphed into cataloging serials for a library. After that, she was the first woman television stagehand in Canada, then she did PR for a shopping center and read annual reports on tape for blind stockholders. She managed a bed-and-breakfast in Colorado and then settled in Michigan, where she played ragtime piano concerts and worked as a Poet in the Schools. Most recently, Kerlikowske earned her PhD in English, and she currently teaches at Kellogg Community College in Battle Creek.

"When I was young, I was fascinated by the backs of book covers and the interesting lives some authors appeared to have led. I did not realize at the time that I was leading one," she writes. Her fifth book is *Dominant Hand* (Mayapple 2008).

Of "Things You Need to Know about Your Boss," Kerlikowske says, "The masks of perfection that bosses wear belie their real lives. At the time I wrote this poem, my boss was having a meltdown. . . . This is the poem I wanted to distribute to his employees."

Copyright © Elizabeth Kerlikowske

The Trouble with Guidebooks

J. C. Ross

It was fall in Pasadena, or what passed for fall—the leaves didn't turn so much as they dried like parchment and fell from the trees. So much exhaust from the 210 freeway, so much pollution. From the windows of the shop, she could watch as they blew about the street, thin and brown as lunch bags, whirling against the door, pausing against the wheels of a car, collecting in the decorative cement work at the base of a tree. Decorative cement work, a Southern California route to civic rejuvenation. Eject the secondhand clothing stores and pawn shops, install a Banana Republic and Baby Gap, pour decorative cement, and presto! a hot new shopping district, "Old Town" Pasadena.

Old is right, Mariah thought. She was twenty-nine, suddenly too old to be working in a bookstore. She knew this because of other people's reactions: at a recent party, when a woman raised one Botoxed eyebrow and said, *Riillly*, and grabbed her hand, *no kidding?* In the store, a customer patronizing her, spelling *Mal-dives*, slowly, telling her where it was—as though she'd never seen a map of the world, hadn't shelved the *Lonely Planet* guidebook to India, and didn't know someone who'd gone scuba diving there just last year. They'd begun to treat her and the shop like mascots for all things simpler. With the mega-chain bookstore stuffed into a former olive oil warehouse just past Pottery Barn and a twenty-screen multiplex, this was the only independent bookstore left in the city.

Destination: Kathmandu, the store was called, because Nepal seemed to represent, for their customers, the ultimate—the highlight of their travel lives. They came into the store with pictures to prove they'd gone. *Here's me at the market, me with an orange-robed monk, me trekking with Sherpas.* Or they chatted up Mariah, who complied. *I'd love to go to the market, see monks, go trekking with Sherpas!*

"Do you have *Lonely Planet Nepal*?" they'd ask, and she knew they were waiting for her to say, "Are you going?" and then it would begin, the complete itinerary. Even Ireland and Prague, the previous hot spots in the industry, couldn't compete. What were a few cathedrals, compared to the snow-capped Himalayas, shaggy yaks, colored prayer flags, tinkly bells, and all those supplications to the gods?

And maybe there was something to that, all those prayers bringing all those tourists. Perhaps it could work for the shop—it was very slow, the lull before what she hoped would be the storm of Christmas rush. Right now, people were buying back-to-school pens and markers, not taking back-to-school trips. She made a note on a Post-it: *back-to-school destinations?* It was an idea to flesh out with the co-manager, Jeff, when he got back from biking in Belize.

Outside, a business-suited man stopped to take in her Fall Getaways display, a poster of the Napa Valley with winery guides stacked strategically next to B&B directories. She paused in her counting of the morning newspapers.

Come IN to the store, she thought, making mental tractor beams in his direction. *Come IN and buy Where to Sleep–Northern California.*

This really worked sometimes; it was a trick she had discovered. You didn't *watch* the customers, you put your head down and busied yourself, but mentally, you thought in their direction. You pictured them in a wool sweater, hand-in-hand with a significant other, strolling the streets of a New England village; you joined all your travel wishes to theirs and sometimes they did indeed open the door to the shop and tell you they wanted a guidebook to Vermont. One very slow Saturday in March, she and Jeff and Monica, the part-time girl with all the piercings, had tried, as a joke, to draw in every customer who passed the shop with tractor beams. It had worked so well that they'd done $9,000 of business in one day—an absurd amount for March, the slowest month of the year. She'd made Jeff go with her to the night deposit because she didn't want to carry that much cash.

Jeff—when was he coming back again?

A mental lapse in her tractor beam. The man outside paused to look at the other window display, which by store policy was always of Nepal or other mountainous regions, and walked away.

And that was the downside of practicing tractor beams. If people didn't come into the shop, if they lingered with one hand on the door, talking animatedly with a friend in front of the shop, asking—you could hear them through the glass—*Should we go in? Do you want to go in?*—if it didn't work, it was easy, especially if receipts were down, to find yourself thinking something uncalled for and unproductive.

Mariah logged the newspapers, slid the papers into their display case, and checked the door sign. It said "OPEN."

Come IN to the store, she thought, in the direction of a jogger leaning against the tree outside to inspect her shoe. *Come IN and buy Spa Retreats 2007.*

The woman, in a baseball cap and an expensive fleece jacket over shiny jogging tights, scraped her shoe against the decorative concrete and jogged away.

Giving up, Mariah headed for the back room to bring out the Random House order; she could check books in at the counter while keeping an eye on the door. On a Post-it, she wrote, *alternatives to autumn???!!,* and stuck it in the pocket of her green store apron. Maybe she'd change the window even before Jeff got back. It was clear that fall foliage wasn't packing them in out here in Southern California, and she *was* co-manager.

Hefting the box onto a stool, she drew out her safety razor and sliced the tape cautiously, careful not to ruin the inventory. She pulled the flaps back and peered inside: books shrink-wrapped in hard, thick plastic. Slicing cleanly through, she exposed the books: *Fodor's Paris, Fodor's Madrid*, all Fodor's, it looked like—the slim ones with the gorgeous full-color photos. They sold like hotcakes, like tickets to Kathmandu.

Nepal. She'd been working the holidays at the mega-bookstore and moonlighting at Crate & Barrel, wrapping wine glasses for people with Platinum Visas. She had noticed the combination of Annapurna and London in the windows of the shop and decided that if she couldn't actually *be* in a Buddhist monastery or *at* Harrods for Christmas, she wanted to quit shelving the autobiographies of business moguls and start shelving the kinds of things she imagined they sold at Destination: Kathmandu. She confirmed her suspicions by drifting into the shop one evening after her Crate & Barrel shift, pretending to look for something on Rome. They had a ton of stuff: *Bella Tuscany, A Village in Italy*, and more obscure things put out by small English presses—the accounts of some vicar who'd lived there during the war, the autobiography of a widow who'd married a Venetian boatman, and an Italian guidebook to all the Madonnas with Children in the Uffizi as well as the Ravenna mosaics.

"If I can help you find anything, just ask," Jeff had said, speaking strictly about the guidebooks, although it seemed to her that *was* the central question—what was she looking for? And because she was too embarrassed to admit what she wanted was a job application, she'd only been faking an interest in Rome—not faking, truly, but faking on this particular occasion—she'd had to sneak back to the store on a lunch break the next day and ask for an application from a young college girl with a pierced tongue and fake black hair. Then she'd interviewed with Jeff, who was looking for someone to become co-manager because he had a fall cycling trip planned in Central America, and she'd gotten the job, Destination: Kathmandu. Not Nepal yet, precisely, but somewhere. Somewhere else, co-managing, anyway.

So while most of the retail workers in Old Town had to live in Glendale or Eagle Rock, she now made enough on the co-manager salary for an apartment just south of the 210, noisy but still a few blocks into the good side of town. More coffee shops, less gang graffiti. "It's rare here," Jeff said, "the area is very well-policed," and then he told her, on her first day as co-manager, to hire guys to clean up the mess where someone had spray-painted across store windows, "Destination: Fuck You."

She pulled open the plastic and extracted the guidebooks.

The first thing she noticed, after the graffiti, was that a travel bookstore seemed to attract people suffering from an ambiguity of direction. Customers came in all the time looking for a guidebook to Iran and picked up Iraq, as though there were no difference between the two countries, because both started with an "I" and were located in the Middle East. She saw them stepping off a plane with carry-on bags, in a different country than the one they'd planned, having to sort things out with gun-toting border guards, humorless in khaki, because things were even hotter and dustier and problematic in that country than the customer knew.

She tried to save people from this fate, sometimes, by engaging them in conversation. *So you have family in Iraq? Are they okay?*

After which the person—let's say a man in an expensive shirt and silk tie, browsing after a business lunch—might say, *Oh no, it's business, things are liberalizing there, and I guess I meant to pick up the guidebook for Teheran.*

She was between things herself, so she could understand the confusion.

Sometimes on her break, while microwaving a veggie burrito in the back room and keeping an ear out for customers, she'd skim through books that Jeff had left on the table. He was always rock climbing in Costa Rica or something like that, coming back with massive foot problems that meant he had to sit on a stool at the cash register for weeks. He'd log books into inventory and set aside the ones that interested him. She looked at some of them occasionally, especially *Ireland: Country Roads*; she was one-eighth Irish. Mostly, though, if the store was quiet, she read *Chemistry Today*, because she'd been a chemistry student at Caltech and was thinking of going to graduate school. Even though she'd taken a couple of years off, she wanted to be up on the literature when she was ready to take the plunge. She only had a few more years to decide, after which it might be too late to get the recommendations. She knew that *Fodor's Baghdad* was not the guidebook to the capital of Iran, and she knew there were few middle-aged graduate students winning research fellowships in chemistry.

She studied the book in her hand, *Around Boston with Kids*. It was weird, most of her classmates had gone directly to doctoral programs at places like MIT. And this seemed connected to a fact even stranger: after she engaged people in conversation over their travel plans—*What will the weather be like that month? Have you been there before?*—they went ahead and bought the wrong guidebook as well, as though this new one interested them more than the correct book, which they bought merely for logistics. As though the book itself exercised some sort of strange fascination over them.

She didn't get it. But she couldn't travel much herself; she was paying off student loans and saving for graduate school, and she didn't like the tropics, which was where a lot of package tours seemed to go. Jeff had gone rafting in Guatemala, and to visit a banana plantation, from which he had brought her a t-shirt that said "I'm the Top Banana" on the front and "Auger Family Plantations" on the back. She didn't know whether this was a joke or not, because they *were* co-managers. She always felt a little uncertain when she wore it in the store. When she wore it at all, in fact.

The back door bell rang. UPS. She glanced out front; still no customers. It was possible this time of year to go several days without making enough to pay the electric bill. She went to sign for the delivery. Monday morning, it would be a huge order; she'd have to find a place to stack it all. They had way too much inventory.

Come IN to the store and buy a book, she thought, a tractor beam sent to round up all the other store workers whose shops were slow this morning, those who could get away for coffee, for browsing displays in other stores. *Come IN and buy Underground Seattle.*

She signed for the UPS order and was left, surrounded by cartons, standing in the back room of the shop. Where to start!? The doorbell rang—a large, heavy Tibetan prayer bell hung around the knob. *Customer!* she thought. *Thank Buddha and any and all Tibetan gods.*

Later, she would find this hilarious—her premature thanks. It wasn't as though she'd never thought about it, working nights with a full drawer of cash, checks, and credit card slips, about the possibility of getting robbed. She'd just expected it to come, if it did, at Christmas, when huge amounts of cash traded hands. Tourists who'd just been to the ATM before boarding a plane and arriving at LAX would peel off bills in amounts much more visible and enticing, and Jeff would be in the store to hand it over to the robber, professionally, coolly, since none of them wanted any trouble.

She imagined that Jeff would say this exact thing: *We don't want any trouble*, and she imagined saying this very thing herself, right now, to the guy in the khaki jacket and expensive hiking boots with the large blue gun who had locked the front door behind him and told her to get into the back room.

Where she now sat along the wall, surrounded by boxes full of the *Rough Guide to Nepal.*

"We don't want any trouble," she said. She tried to be sure she was saying it out loud.

The guy with the gun peered around the doorframe into the shop and out onto the street, all the while training the gun on her. He looked back, appraising her. "What?"

"I said, uh, it's a very slow time of year and we don't have a lot of money in the store. But you're welcome to take whatever's there. I mean," she added, "we just work here." She hoped to imply that there were others in the store—perhaps out on an errand and returning soon. And she hoped to imply solidarity with all the little people, the suffering and disenfranchised workers of the world, including people who had been reduced to robbing travel bookstores.

He stared at her, and appeared to take in this invitation. For the first time, he surveyed the back room: the floor-to-ceiling shelves stacked twenty feet in the air with shiny-covered books, the rolling ladder, the receiving bench with its miniature TV and office supplies, the mounds of books in open boxes, in various stages of coming into the shop or being shipped out as returns.

"Anybody in there?" He nodded to the door of the employee restroom.

She shook her head. "But the, uh, co-manager went down the block for coffee. He, uh, will probably be right back."

"Is that so?" Backing up, he pulled the restroom door open, and stuck the gun inside. He turned on the light. Empty. Turning back, he waved the gun at the TV. "Turn that on," he said, "and kick that strapping tape over here."

She sat against the wall, against one of the giant W. W. Norton boxes, the kind that came in at sixty pounds, taxing even the brawny thighs of the UPS guy. She was wishing for a second delivery or for a customer to come to the shop and find it closed, to go next door to the Pretzel Shoppe and ask, *Isn't the travel bookshop open?* And for Rahim, who owned the Pretzel Shoppe, to get suspicious and call the police. She could smell pretzels baking through the common heating/air conditioning ducts up close to the ceiling.

"Breaking News," TV commentators were saying, "In Pasadena, police are looking for a fugitive, wanted on an outstanding warrant for drug trafficking."

The fugitive, whose description matched that of the guy standing in her shop, changed channels. "I hate Channel 4," he said. "That's messed up." Mindy Burbano, from Channel 5, appeared.

"Chuck," she said, "it looks like the police are going door-to-door in a twelve-block residential area near Caltech, looking for the suspect, Robert J. Whittlesworth. He was said to be attending his mother's birthday party in what's really a very nice neighborhood just south of the 210 freeway, when he was surprised by police, who'd received a tip about his possible appearance."

"Mindy," Chuck said, "This guy is supposedly—we're getting word that this guy is the head of a drug-trafficking network that runs from Colombia to Vancouver. With so many police staking out the house and schoolchildren just blocks away, how did this apparently violent fugitive, Whittlesworth, escape?"

"Chuck, we don't know at this point, but police feel they are moments away from apprehending the suspect. They are warning all Pasadena residents in the affected areas to stay indoors, though, until the fugitive is caught."

"So," Robert J. turned away from the TV, "let's just stay indoors, shall we?"

Robert J. Whittlesworth, aka Jazzy Jim, aka the Whittler, for reasons she did not want to know, was more than a little pissed at having had to leave his mother's party without so much as a piece of cake. They could both smell sugary pretzel wafting through the ductwork.

"You got no Coke machine here, no em-ploy-ee fridge?"

"I go out for lunch." When Monica comes on at 2, she thought. It was a quarter past noon.

According to the news—all the stations had gone to live coverage—police were expanding the search towards the freeway. Not yet in the direction of the shop, although periodically she could hear a helicopter overhead. Police? Or news?

"The co-manager—he's taking his time with the coffee." Robert J. settled himself on a stool and looked at her, moving the gun to the other hand.

"It's just the other guy who works here," she said, in an attempt to explain her missing co-worker's apparent flakiness. "Sometimes when we're slow he goes down the block and plays video games. I'm supposed to call if I need him."

"So *is* there a manager?" He got up and began to poke behind boxes. *As if looking for a safe,* Mariah thought.

"The co-manager, and me. I'm co-manager." She did not know why she established this fact, established that sitting there in strapping tape, she might have the combination to a safe. "In Belize," she said. "He's, uh, bicycling." What would *Jeff* do in this situation? Would Jeff have strapped his own ankles at the point of a gun with the giant tape dispenser they used to seal boxes? Would he have convinced Robert J. that he wasn't going to make any noise—*please, I won't scream, I, um, have asthma*—so he didn't need his mouth taped? And would he have allowed his wrists to be strapped in front of him?

Or would he—when the guy put the gun down to work the tape—would he have gone for the gun?

She hadn't.

She wondered whether the *L.A. Times* and the *Pasadena Weekly* and Channel 7 would speculate, in the future, *Why do you think, Mindy and Chuck, that she allowed herself to be tied up? Why is it that Rahim, owner of the Pretzel Shoppe next door, didn't hear any screams?*

Robert J. turned back to the television. Police had cleared the local elementary school, sent the children home for the day.

"Well, baby," he said, "if he's on vacation, and you here, then you co-manager of nothin'. You his bitch."

The helicopter droned overhead and Mariah slumped along the wall, her head beginning to pound to the pulsing of the chopper. Was this true? She opened and closed the store alone, made the bank deposits, and wrote out the payroll checks. She ordered books, met with the card company reps, and spoke up for the bookstore at evening meetings of the Downtown Association. Still, Jeff made all the decisions on budget, the final decisions on staffing—although she did the initial interviews—and held all the meetings with book reps. And when Jeff went on vacation, she and Monica split taking over his shifts. By comparison, when Mariah had taken a week to go visit a friend in Tucson who'd just had a baby, Jeff had found the money for a part-timer, someone who usually came in only at Christmas, so he hadn't needed to double his shifts.

She was still thinking over this bit of co-management news when the phone rang. First faintly out front and then a second time, loudly, on the receiving bench next to her. She dropped the security razor she'd re-found, which she'd been holding for the last half hour or so; it hit the concrete with a small, metallic thunk. She looked at Robert J., who was staring at the phone.

"I'd better answer that," she said. "We're supposed to be open. If we're not open on a normal business day, people might begin to wonder."

She wanted him to think not just about the phone but about the locked front door, and she wanted to believe that they were going to have—perhaps already had—at least one bright and suspicious customer who would have heard about the fugitive search on a car radio. Maybe they would note the locked door on the shop where they had come to buy discount tickets to Sea World, and put the fugitive news and the locked door together and called the police?

Come IN to the store, she thought, a feeble tractor beam out to the police, who were searching a neighborhood north of the 210. *Please, please, come IN to the store and pick this guy up and we'll give you wholesale on purchases for the rest of your lives.*

"Answer that," Robert J. finally instructed her. She slid the razor behind a box along the floor as she rose, and she stuck her strapping-taped wrists to one side.

"Can you undo these?" The phone rang again, loudly.

He crossed the back room, picked up the receiver, and put it to her ear. With the other hand, he cocked the gun at her.

"Hu-llo?" She stammered into the phone.

"Is this Destination: Kathmandu?" A woman's voice. "The travel bookstore?"

"Yes," Mariah said, "yes it is." She cleared her throat and tried to think. "What can I—assist you with?"

"I'm looking for a guide to Spain," the woman said. "Maybe a general guide, and then one for the capital."

"Yes," Mariah said, "we have several volumes you might be interested in." Volumes, where did *that* come from? "We have the *Insight Guide: Turkey* and also Istanbul. As well as, um, the islands in the Adriatic." She was trying to think of the island from *Midnight Express* or something else jail-related. How astute was this woman and did she watch midday news?

"Spain, dear." Mariah could hear a man murmuring in the background. "We want Madrid. One of those slim guides with the fold-out sections of the city with the color photos of places to eat, the little pictures of the meals. That's the one we want."

"Yes," Mariah said, "and we also have the other capitals. Londonderry. Glasgow. Uh, Milan." She was trying to name cities that weren't the capital of anything; in her mind, she could see the multicolored maps of Europe and the Middle East that had hung at the front of every grade-school classroom she'd ever been in. "Some of them have travel restrictions, um, unrest," she said. "You should check with the State Department. In Bergen, Norway, for instance," she named the safest Western non-capital city she could think of.

"Norway!?" She heard the woman sigh. "Do you have Spain or do you not?"

"Hang up, hon'," said the man in the background. "These bookstore employees today don't know anything."

Mariah eyed the gun. "You should come in on Sunday, when the manager is here to help you." She wondered, could the woman not hear the pounding of helicopters overhead? Where did she live, pricey and distant La Cañada?

"I thought you were closed on Sunday."

"Yes, we *are*," Mariah tried to convey with her tone that there was something odd about this. It's a fucking *clue*, she wanted to scream. Had this woman seen none of the movies put out in the last twenty years, where victims used this tactic? Where had she been, Junior League?

"Thank you anyway, dear." The woman hung up.

"They hung up," she said to Robert J. He replaced the receiver.

"Against the wall," he motioned with the gun.

He turned the TV up; the police seemed to be focusing their attention now on the corridor along the freeway that led to Old Town. They were evacuating City Hall, the public library, and the Episcopal church.

City Hall? Mariah thought. The public library? The giant Mexican-style buildings with cupolas and corridors and the Old Southwest maze of a floorplan? Those buildings were massive; it would take the SWAT team weeks to search them. She and Robert J. could take a steamer to the Holy Land and back before the police got to Destination: Kathmandu.

She needed a better plan—something better than trying to fake out a con or sending clues to the clueless. And she needed to pee, badly. She cleared her throat and tried to adopt the tone of voice she imagined one would use at a border checkpoint somewhere in the Third World staffed by nervous young men, high on some local leaf, with black-market Uzis and not much to lose.

"Could I use the restroom?" she asked, in utter deference to his position as the man with the gun. She expected argument or a negotiation over something like a requirement that she leave the door open.

To her surprise, he looked at her, made a little pointing gesture with the gun, *try something and I'll shoot you*, and waved her towards the john.

Struggling up, she indicated, once again, her hands; he picked a boxcutter out of a caddy and cut the tape in two.

"Just so you know," he said, "I ain't here to make trouble." He waved the boxcutter in her face. "But I *will* shoot you, so don't be tryin' anything."

"I won't," she promised. She hopped towards the door, and felt him watch her go. If she locked the door, both of them knew he could shoot it open—although he might not want to risk the noise. She considered this, and she considered making him mad. To this point he had shown, primarily, a desire to wait out the manhunt and get some lunch.

She closed but didn't lock the door, and got her khakis down—first things first. She had to pee to survive—and how amazing to have hands again, to be able just to form the intent to do something and be able to do it with one's hands! And then she began to cry. She hoped she would get to keep not only her hands but everything, that Robert J. would leave the shop, just exit right out the back door like a box of returns—WE DON'T NEED THESE, WE CAN'T SELL THEM, THANKS FOR THINKING OF US.

Struggling up, she flushed, and wiped her nose.

All right, she thought. *I may not be full co-manager of anything, but I am not staying here while Robert J. decides what to do.* What if the police *did* finish searching City Hall and moved into Old Town? She saw herself negotiating by phone with some helmeted mediation specialist, with Robert J. asking for sandwiches and the opportunity to speak to his mother. Or would it occur to him to put a pair of scissors, or a razor—there was one on the front counter, in plain sight—or the gun to her head and walk her into the front window, between the poster of Everest and the Cheap Sleeps guides, to request a helicopter to LAX and a pilot to fly him to Mazatlan?

Not that she thought he would get these things—in all the Breaking News she'd ever seen, the police eventually shot the guy. She did not want to be anywhere in proximity to such an occurrence. This was the very reason, she thought, that she not only avoided the tropics, she avoided traveling in Kashmir and Yemen and other hostage-happy countries. This was somehow the reason that at twenty-nine, she was still working in a bookstore. She had never believed the guidebooks that said you had a better chance of being killed by someone you knew, in the warm and cozy confines of your usual life, than by a stranger in a distant land. Even their statistics were not compelling to the scientist in her. Here in Pasadena, there was usually nothing but joggers. People headed for business meetings in outlying suburbs. Squirrels.

She surveyed the ceiling overhead. In the movies, a person could sometimes climb from the toilet to the sink to the ceiling, push aside ceiling tiles, hoist themselves into a heating/air conditioning duct, and crawl away before the terrorists even knew they were gone. She'd seen Bruce Willis do this at least three times.

"How we doin' in there?" Robert J. called. She could hear the TV, and helicopters again, directly overhead.

"Fine," she yelled. "Almost done. Sorry." Above her, all she could see was solid sheetrock—no acoustical tiles, and only one tiny duct, far too small for her head. She opened the medicine cabinet above the sink—bandages, more adhesive tape, Motrin, a pair of Jeff's nose-hair scissors. Yes, those would be a lot of help. She closed the cabinet and looked around, her brain cells revving up. She needed a plan; she needed a precise escape plan, not some vague hope for a soft landing. *Hurry up*, she thought, *hurry up and think*.

In one corner stood a mop and bucket. *Mop vs. gun*, she thought, *not a good fight*—unless she could get him to open the door and surprise him with the mop. How hard could she hit? She hadn't intentionally hit anyone since third-grade dodgeball. Hard enough to actually stun him? Or knock the gun away? Or would the angle be wrong—would he grab the mop and hit her with it? Surely big-time drug lords routinely bludgeoned people or pistol-whipped them. *What else*, she thought, *what else*.

In the other corner of the tiny bathroom, on open metal shelving, sat paper products—toilet paper and towels—and on the top shelf, the cleaning supplies. Glass cleaner and 409 and crystal hydrochloride, a toilet bowl cleaner that was to be used in a well-ventilated space.

He opened the door, gun in hand.

"Git outta there," he said. "Let's go," and he motioned her, with the gun, out into the room.

Overhead, she heard multiple choppers, louder, and on the news, she could see police on foot searching storefronts along Colorado. That was past City Hall and headed for Old Town. That was blocks away.

Resuming her position against the wall, she spotted the razor tucked behind a giant box from Tibetan Supplies, New York. Wall hangings, and maybe slides—they used Nepal for theme nights in the store, showing slides of good-looking climbers surmounting Everest, serving baklava and wine. She shifted her feet, which were cramping up, and bumped the box; it rang faintly.

Robert J. looked over.

"Tibetan prayer bells," she said. He stared at her with suspicion. *Yes, right*, she thought, *I'm going to get hold of some non-interventionist, Buddhist prayer bells and whack you with them.* "For display," she added. "We, uh, put them out by the front counter." Her voice was foreign, oddly perky, as if to say, *if you're done shopping, sir, I can ring you up and you can be on your way.* She formed a tractor beam in reverse, like a nudge in his direction. *Go out and run your empire. Go out and prosper in the new chemically assisted youth economy.*

He looked away, tensing his grip on the gun, and scowled at the TV. The police appeared to be headed south, toward a park that bordered downtown. For the first time, she realized that Robert J. was confused, that he had no escape plan. Indeed, this appeared to *be* his escape plan. Now that he was here, instead of, say, on the interstate headed for Bakersfield, he appeared ready to hide out in the store's backroom until when—dark?—with the smell of sugar pretzels and mariachi music wafting through the ducts, hoping that no one would notice the shop's unusual closing.

Shit, she thought, *it was going to be an under-1,000 day, way under.* And for some reason, this forced deprivation, this closure of the store of which she had finally attained co-manager status, bent something inside. Even if they put Christmas lights around the poster of Everest in the window, early, this weekend, it wouldn't be enough. The unexpected closing would bring down the wrath of the owner and of Mitchell Stark, president of the Downtown Association. She realized she was weeping, silently, gulping in air like someone practicing Lamaze.

Something else, try something else. Not for nothing had she been Team Associate of the Month twice at the mega-store. Not for nothing had she read Fielding's *The World's Most Dangerous Places*, one of the books Jeff had left out, cover-to-cover on her breaks. Stockholm Syndrome, the guide had said, can be used against your captors. Appear to be on their side; make friends with them and help them see you as a person. It is harder to torture or execute someone you know.

She looked down at her still un-taped hands. "Do you mind," she sniffed, and composed herself, "if I read?" She gestured to one of the books beside her.

"Whatever," he said, his eyes trained on the TV. She opened the box, peered inside, and pulled out an obscure guide to shopping the bazaars of Kathmandu. She looked up; the news chopper showed the police searching park restrooms with a tiny robot, which seemed to amuse Robert J., as though he himself was cast in a *Star Wars* movie, the cagey opponent of clueless drones. The gun rested lightly in his lap.

She riffled the pages of the book. "So you travel a lot in your business?" She tried to ask the way she'd asked thousands of other customers, *You must go to London quite a bit?*

He looked at her. "Damn right." He waved the gun loosely in the direction of an open box. "I got your *Rough Guide* to Colombia, know what I'm sayin'?"

"You bought it here?" She did not remember him as a customer, but then, when Jeff had been planning his trip, they'd had an entire window display on South America, which sold so well they re-ordered twice.

"Damn right, I bought it here. Why you think I picked *your* store? You think I'm goin' in some pretzel shop, to hide in their *bathroom* and get hit over the head by some asshole playin' out his little fantasy of bein' a hero? No, you and the little girl with the piercings."

Monica? It was certainly past noon. In some ways, Robert J. had been like any other demanding customer who had tied up her entire morning—like the woman who wanted to take the Siberian Express, who had spent four hours loudly comparing guidebooks on Russia, asking her opinion on Russian politics and critiquing it, finally condescending to her experience with riding trains. Granted, he had commandeered her attention at the point of a gun. But she did not need Monica to arrive to give him further ideas, to waylay him from his original intention of laying low.

She glanced at the safety razor, lying wedged against the box. *Find weapons,* the guidebook had said, *but keep in mind that if you aren't used to handling weapons, trying to do something with them might very well get you killed.* As an undergrad, she had taken a self-defense course, in which they'd done a lot of stomping on the kneecaps of a guy in a padded suit. She tried to work the equation: none of his so-called vulnerable areas—groin, eyes, throat—were easily accessible. No way did she think she could slash the back of his neck with enough force to disable him—to prevent him from grabbing the razor, slashing her face, shooting her. She could see it in bold, four-color photo, as though flipping the slender pages of a Fodor's: him turning, arm plus razor shorter than the reach of a gun, sound, flash, herself blown across a length of the floor.

She abandoned the razor idea and thought. On TV, the police packed up their robot, the reporter in the chopper saying, ". . . found nothing in this heavily-trafficked area." Where was Robert J.'s mother? Wasn't this the point in a search where one of the stations got the mother on camera, pleading with him

by name, telling him they all knew he was misunderstood and that whatever
he'd done, there was a way to undo it. Things didn't need to get any worse.
Robert J. looked like a boy who was capable of understanding that if they caught
him in a locked storefront with a hostage, he would be doing additional time.
She wondered about the three-strikes law—how many did he have? Was the
warrant for a third offense, so that it didn't matter to him whether he went back
for drug trafficking—or kidnapping, or murder?

What else had that book said?

Don't piss off the border guards, for one thing. "Be cool, smile, pass out
the trinkets and just keep talking." Indeed, she'd been trying, since Robert J.
had entered the store, to do what the guidebook said. She had been "calm and
compliant," avoiding argument. She had communicated to him that she wanted
to stay alive. She had tried to take control of her mental and physical state. She
hoped he would not be here long enough for her to need to develop a routine—
she couldn't imagine them holed up here for days, her greeting the UPS man
in days-old clothes, with Robert J. behind the door holding a gun. She pictured
herself sleeping on cardboard, eating old Halloween candy as Jeff and the police
negotiated with the drug kingpin through a bullhorn: "Okay, you can keep the
girl and the hardcover photo book of *Ansel Adams' Yosemite*, just give us the
store back."

She had tried to follow hostage etiquette. Relax and breathe, "remain
inconspicuous," avoid "direct eye contact and the appearance of observing your
captors' actions." Although it was hard to miss—he was a little too much like Jeff,
the way he commandeered the workbench and the TV, making all the decisions,
just because he had the gun. Jeff always took his lunch first, even if they opened
the shop together; if she wanted to go first, she always had to ask. She had to tell
him if she was taking a bathroom break or just a break-break, a break from the
customers to hide out in the back of the store for a few minutes' reprieve.

She wished she'd asked Jeff for a vacation, a real vacation this past summer.
Maybe a week just to drive up to Tahoe and sit on the beach in the sun at Meeks
Bay, with the *San Francisco Chronicle* and a sandwich from the Tahoma Market
deli. Mariah did not think she would ever be in the mood for a veggie burrito
eaten in the backroom again.

And it was questionable whether she would get out of this at all, because
there was stuff that, according to the guidebook, she had blown. She had failed
to establish a dialogue with him—Robert J., that is; she had failed to create
rapport by asking things like, *Your mother, does she like to travel?* While she
had avoided "political discussions and other confrontational subjects," she
could have tried to engage him in a chemist's tête-à-tête about the fine points of
manufacturing the product of his empire. And when he'd questioned her, she
hadn't kept her answers short; she had volunteered unnecessary information, so
he knew she was an idiot, no one was coming, help was not on the way, and he
was in control.

She thought about Jeff—about how he'd dismissed the idea, personally, of traveling to Nepal, saying it was full of English accountants dressed up in Patagonia trekking garb, choking on the smoke of yak dung fires and trying desperately to forget their sordid workaday lives. Mariah had felt small and rebellious—had felt, not for the first time, a desire to go herself, maybe just stay there and work in a refugee camp. It was all unclear to her, everything was unclear, and this was what guidebooks did not help with, the kind of thing they did not say—only what and where, only the possibilities, but never really why, or how, or especially when. They never told you when to go, except for the time of year, and here it was, fall.

"Shut up," he said, half turning, and Mariah became aware that she was crying for real, softly. She shifted along the wall and wiped her nose on the apron, very quietly. She did not want him to re-tape her hands. *Avoid a sense of despair,* the book had recommended. "Put yourself in a mode of passive cooperation," "think positive," and "rely on your inner resources." She tried to think for a moment what these were—aside from window display and a kind of cultivated retail patience that was not true patience per se but which needed to seem, to the customer, as though it was. She wondered, which of them, she or Robert J., had the longer fuse? "Remember," the book said, "that you are a valuable commodity. It's important to them to keep you alive and well."

I am a valuable commodity, she thought, telepathy to the gunman, despite the fact that she was not sure he would agree. *Trade me for a trained police hostage substitute, or a reporter, or a helicopter to Rio,* and here she threw in a tractor beam; she saw him shoving her away at the last second as he and a helicopter pilot took off from the middle of a beautified Pasadena street. *Get out of this store,* she thought. *Go now. Get out of Destination: Kathmandu.*

Someone knocked, loudly, at the front door. Mariah jumped, and Robert J. picked up the gun. She peered over at the running clock on the TV screen: 1:38. Monica was never on time, much less early. Whoever it was knocked again. "I'd better answer that," she said, automatically, with no specific plan and no idea whether this was right or wrong, according to the guidebook. Wait—yes, it was right, hostages were supposed to increase their demands.

"I should answer the door," she said, "and tell them something—like our computers are down and we're having a power outage so we had to close. Otherwise the CLOSED sign might attract attention."

And this was stupid, she realized, because of *course* the sign would attract attention if Monica showed up, having watched the news while getting ready for work. If Rashid came next door to exchange a ten for a roll of quarters, which he frequently did. If the police ever quit searching parks and decided to search downtown. She shouldn't have mentioned it.

"Forget it." He was tense again, changing the channel, turning the TV up.

Whoever it was at the front door seemed to have gone away.

Mariah could feel her ankles, still taped together, begin to rebel, like passengers on a transcontinental flight, belted too long into seats, elbows bumping, unable to get away. The small bones on the inside of her feet—the reticulus dorsi—felt like the horns of two rhinos locked in a very small cage.

On Channel 4, Bob Crum was standing in front of the Baby Gap. "Jane," he said, "the police aren't saying what they'll do next. There have been no confirmed sightings of this very dangerous felon. They have evacuated the Norton Simon museum, which was full of schoolchildren today, but we're hearing now that they may not search the museum. So we're all in a wait and see mode." He gestured to his cameraman. "We just have to wait right now and see what everyone else does."

Like hell, Mariah thought. One thing she now remembered well was that the most dangerous times for a hostage were at the beginning—and at the end. "At the moment of possible rescue." Your captor might go ahead and kill you, either so that you couldn't identify him or because he wanted to say "fuck you" to the police. Or the police themselves might kill you, inadvertently, a bullet careening off a wall, zinging towards you through a tear gas haze.

And yet she'd been counting on this, she realized. She had been counting on highly-trained men in black jumpsuits and helmeted visors bursting into the shop to save her. She had been counting on her tractor beams and all the forces of good in the universe drawing rescuers through the labyrinth of downtown, past the eight-story parking garage, its many deserted stairwells, past the movie theater with its maze of corridors and restrooms, down the alley behind Banana Republic, its changing rooms empty. She imagined them right at the door of the Pretzel Shoppe, their arrival coinciding with Monica's, so that her co-worker could huddle in the doorway and tell them there was something very strange indeed, that Mariah must be inside, unable to act on her own because she would never otherwise have closed the shop in the middle of the day.

As quietly as she could, Mariah leaned against the box as if fatigued, picked up the razor, and slit the tape around her ankles from the back. "If you think you can escape, do so," the book said, "but stop if you are under threat of death or being shot."

Robert J. returned the set to Channel 5, which appeared to have the best view from a chopper. She heard the THWACK THWACK THWACK.

Pressing the loosened tape to the backs of her legs, she put the tip of the razor against the box and pushed. The blade went in, and she drew it down along the ridges in the cardboard, then pulled it slowly back. Robert J. appeared fixed on the screen, where police were searching the museum after all.

"Chuck, they have evacuated the Ralph's supermarket as a precaution."

Mariah moved the blade four inches to the left and repeated the cut, top to bottom, the blade slicing silently through the box; she pushed tentatively against the cardboard, which flexed.

"You can see the shoppers coming out, they're exiting the store according to police instructions."

"Mindy, do the police think the suspect is inside, or among the shoppers?"

"They don't know, Chuck. You might remember the school shooting where the fear was that the suspect might hide amongst the shoppers, so that's why you see the hands up . . ."

And now Mariah began to wonder why he hadn't just left—why he hadn't just donned one of the safari hats they sold, with a pair of sunglasses from the Customer Lost & Found box under the front counter, and strolled out of Old Town with a book under his arm. Was he waiting to use her as a bargaining chip? A newscaster was likely to suggest this, if it hadn't already occurred to him.

She felt a sudden urge to abandon her previous plan, which had been to cut out a space in the side of the Tibetan supplies box after all and procure one of the large, heavy, metal bells, the kind they shipped in wrappings separate from the ringers so as not to drive the UPS carriers mad. Her plan had been to procure one of these, to wrap its long, heavy chain around her hand, and to swing it with all her might in the direction of his head. *Find weapons,* the guidebook said. *But only if you were sure you could use them successfully.*

She slid the razor behind some Styrofoam and cleared her throat.

"Ralph's is at least a dozen blocks away." Her voice came out creaky, like the voice of a little old lady trying to negotiate with a door-to-door salesman. "That's a ways away," she tried again. "We have sunglasses. Under the front counter out there. And hats. We sell hats. We could put some books in a bag, and you'd look like any other shopper." She gestured to the boxes and boxes of books that separated them, as if to indicate that despite his hostage-taking of the past few hours, surely this, a disguise and some directions to the freeway, were what he was really after. "There's a bus stop at the corner," she lied. She looked at the clock, which read eleven minutes to one. "The bus comes on the hour and takes you to Burbank. It goes to the airport." She felt strangely liberated by this embellishment, which was true in the vaguest of ways; there was in fact an airport in Burbank, to which buses surely ran.

"We have cash," she improvised. "Enough for a plane ticket to Mexico." She knew she was way out on a limb here; he might decide to kill her as a witness to a robbery, but she figured he might shoot her as a witness, period. "It's not my store," she added, "I just work here," and she hoped he might appreciate this kingpin-employee distinction and not fault her for siding in favor of her own skin. Surely, he had a boss—a mob boss? An overbearing associate in Florida to whom he occasionally wished to stick it?

And for the first time, Robert J. seemed to take in where he really was. A store, a place with a weepy and annoying sales clerk, but also a place with a cash register and who knew what else. He surveyed the receiving bench where he sat; he set the gun down on the workbench and, leaning forward, he extracted a pair of long, black, industrial scissors from a canister full of pens, and held onto them, opening and closing them slightly. He put his left hand on the TV and peered into it, as if to see more clearly.

"Police say they have yet to search the back rooms and freezers of the supermarket . . ." The newscaster pressed one finger to her ear. "That's right, Chuck, they're being guided in this search by the dogs; they're saying they will evacuate the Mercedes dealership and check under those cars, and then they may take the dogs back to the suspect's mother's house and retrace their steps to see if they can recover a scent."

"Hasn't she refused to cooperate with the police?"

"Yes, but this situation is changing rapidly and the word we have is that she is now concerned for her son's safety and cooperating with police."

"You have to wonder, don't you, Mindy, why suspects run in situations like this," Chuck said. "We see this time and again with car chases . . ."

"That's right, Chuck, the police are confident this suspect could not have gotten far on foot, and they are looking for any and all indications that he is in the area. They are continuing to advise area residents to stay inside if they are within a ten-block perimeter of the supermarket."

Ten blocks, Mariah thought. "We're twelve blocks away," she said, and this was the truth, just in case he knew Old Town, and because it was the truth and she wanted him to go, her plan was for him to go out the front door, with his hat and sunglasses and fake purchases and his real gun. When the door closed behind him she planned to flee out the back to the pretzel shop, where Rahim could call 911. She realized that Robert J. probably knew this, that he would probably tie her hands again and tape her mouth. If this happened, she planned to peel the tape off against one corner of the counter, which stuck out and was a little sharp; they were always hitting themselves against it.

"You have time," she said, "if you go now."

He got up off his stool, scissors in hand, and threaded his way through the boxes towards her. He leaned down and cut the front of the tape around her feet. The scissors were long and pointy. Scissors beat razor, even if she could grab the razor quickly, even with the element of surprise.

"Get the cash," he said. "All of it. And sunglasses."

"I might need to turn on the lights." For some reason she couldn't name, she wanted to turn on all the lights; she wanted to plug in the Mr. Coffee and turn on all the electrical appliances so that the shop was as bright as she could make it, like a bazaar at night, like Christmas.

He gestured with the scissors towards the gun in his other hand. "No lights," he said, "and don't try anything. I don't want to have to shoot you." He said "shoot" the way bad guys in Saturday afternoon westerns said it, like it was something they had done, albeit regretfully. Something about the way he said it made her believe he would do it—that he had done it before and probably pretty easily. You didn't get to be a drug kingpin the same way you became Associate of the Month, on the strength of your charming personality and excellent customer service.

"I'll get it," she said. And, at the time she said it, she meant it.

She intended to get up off the floor, dust herself off, go directly to the register and open it. To take out all the bills, lift the drawer and extract the fifties underneath, put all of it in a shopping bag with the first two books on the counter. Then she intended to gesture to the Lost & Found box, which would be slightly visible to him, standing in the doorway out of sight to the street but in range with his gun. She intended to slide the box out—it would be stuffed with lost leather gloves and twisty key rings and smudged sunglasses—and select the darkest, most eye-occluding pair. Then to get a hat, which hung from a display below the Tibetan prayer flags that ringed the shelves near the passage to the back room. But this, she realized, might encourage him to go out the back, while her plan depended on him going out the front, like any other customer, like any other day in Pasadena. Which was a safe place and not the Third World, not a place where you might go biking and expect to meet a man with a gun.

And while she was still thinking, she realized she did not need the lights to find the register keys that input her personal code. She had done it so often. You punched in the code and then the second button from the top. This was all familiar territory; the drawer slid open, bumping her slightly in the stomach. She was reaching for the twenties when there was a knock at the door.

Hand over the drawer, she paused and looked up.

It was Monica, in a crop top, belly piercings, and leather jeans. Early.

"Mariah," she called, from outside the door, "What's going on?" She stepped back and peered at the glass, as if to double check that she'd come to the bookstore in midday to find it dark and closed, but with Mariah inside and the register drawer open.

Mariah didn't move; she didn't dare look towards the back room, which might signal to Monica that someone was back there. She didn't know what to do.

This was like one of those moments where a chair was supposed to creak in the bar and the gunman was supposed to get distracted and the marshal would have a chance to rescue Miss Kitty. But nothing creaked in the shop; it was quiet. So quiet she wondered whether Robert J. had gone. She thought she could hear the wind just whistling down the Himalayas into empty space.

"Get the money, get the sunglasses. Bring them back here," he said quietly, from around the corner. "Then let her in."

And so in the exact same movement she'd made a million times, probably more than a million, although she had never spent her break adding it up, she slid out a medium-size sack, and began stuffing bills inside, one denomination on top of the other. *Go. Away. Monica.* she thought. *Go AWAY and find Rashid.* She wanted Robert J. not to overhear any of these thoughts, to find her cooperative; she took a chance.

"Computer's down," she called to Monica, "so I had to close the store. I'm just shutting down the register. I'll be right there. You should ask Rashid for quarters." She could see, in her peripheral vision, that Monica accepted this—the power outage had happened before, although usually in a thunderstorm—and had stepped away. Mariah wondered if she'd caught the thing about the quarters. Monica appeared to be surveying the block, to see if any other storefronts were dark. Just how far had this power outage gone?

Mariah closed the register and turned slightly toward the doorway. "Now I'm getting the glasses," she said. She reached beneath the counter into the box and felt around until she had put her fingers on what felt like the earpieces of some glasses. She brought them out—smallish women's Armanis.

Pushing them back, she felt around for something sturdier. Her fingers closed over thick, heavy plastic and she drew the frames out, checked them, and slipped them into the bag. She could hear her heartbeat and the blood in her temples, directly underneath the spot where glasses would go. She extracted a hat from the display as though she were stepping out for a walk under the possibility of light rain.

Just inside the backroom, he stopped her. "Let's see them."

"What?"

"The sunglasses."

She brought them out of the bag.

"I hate those," he said. "Get something else."

"They're men's Ray-Bans," she said. "You want to look like you fit in."

He put the gun against her chin. "Get . . . something . . . else," he repeated, very slowly.

She went back into the store. Through the glass, she could see Monica, arms crossed, huddled impatiently against the tree in the wind. She felt around in the Lost & Found box, but everything seemed small and plastic and broken, like parts of toys that children brought to the store and inadvertently crushed or left behind. In the movies, Mariah thought, good guys routinely escaped what seemed to be traps by hurling themselves off rooftops or out of windows. She was trying to remember what she knew about the chemistry of glass. Real glass, as opposed to stunt glass—its components, the temperature at which it formed, the force required to break it. She was trying to decide whether she could survive, whether Monica was near enough to be hit by flying shards. Trying to calculate whether Robert J. would follow her out, shoot them both, and walk away. Or whether he'd be smart enough to take off out the back, down the alley, and away. She'd have to get a running start; she'd have to commit to it, run full tilt directly at the door. And how would she get there? There was a counter in the way—the part that was just counter, nothing solid underneath, the part that flipped up if you needed to exit the counter area to work on a display or wait on a customer.

Her hand hit what felt like wool—gloves or mittens. And sunglasses.

She pulled them out. Men's.

"Get in here," he said, very low, insistent.

Autumn sun slanting in through the windows, she looked at the glasses.

They were Vuarnets, the favorites of her college boyfriend, the one who skied so much, the official glasses of the Tour de France. The kind Jeff owned and wore each afternoon as he rode away. Maybe they actually *were* Jeff's frames.

She intended to slip them into the bag and hand them to the drug kingpin and encourage him to be on his way. She gazed out the window at the empty street, prayer flags fluttering, the birch tree swaying in the wind. Sometimes, she realized, you looked back and wished you had traveled to a country while the borders were still open and there wasn't a war or natural disaster and things hadn't deteriorated enough to make the news. You wished you had gone before they looted the museums and blew up the treasures and acquired a dictator, before it was fall and everyone ate burgers and breathed First World smog.

She pulled on one glove, one mitten, and then she slid on the Ray-Bans, the bag heavy with bills and rolls of quarters in her other hand. She felt herself going now, over the edge, as though she had slid all the way to the end of a glacier, and beneath her, the steep and rocky moraine beginning to give.

"You should *go*," she said, into the breathy silence of the shop and without waiting for an answer, she shoved the Vuarnets into the bag, threw it in his direction, slipped under the edge of the counter and ran.

J. C. Ross was born in Sacramento and reared in Fresno, California. Her work has appeared in *The Dalhousie Review, Antietam Review, The Alabama Literary Review, The Brownstone Review, Tusculum Review,* and *Working Woman.* Her first short story collection, *My Crush on Tony Blair and How I Overcame It,* was released in 2006 by Popular Ink.

Ross has taught philosophy, humanities, and writing at colleges from Penn State to the University of Arizona and the University of Southern California. She has also worked as a journalist for the Associated Press and metropolitan newspapers. She has toasted grilled cheese sandwiches at a drive-in restaurant, arranged displays in a card shop, scheduled concert halls, and scripted a radio show for a U.S. senator. She currently teaches at Colorado Mountain College.

"The Trouble with Guidebooks" was inspired by Ross's work in four different bookstores, from a large chain near the beach to a tiny one-person store on the shore of a mountain lake. She has also lived in Pasadena, California (where the story is set); there, she watched many a live police pursuit on television.

Ross's writing often revolves around workplace. "It's not deliberate, but work matters a lot to the characters I'm interested in. I'm endlessly curious about the way we spend the majority of our waking hours—about the way work shapes us, warps us, pressures us, and reveals us to ourselves. And I like to examine the ways larger forces, from the socioeconomic to the psychological, play out in the intimacy—or torture—of a cubicle or office or bookstore."

Copyright © J. C. Ross

Debt

Will Watson

So I can sit here typing
granddad had to find out
what Weirton Steel had in mind
for Mingo County migrants
blacklisted out of coal:
seven-day-84-hour weeks
mingling molten steel and sweat
how a cracked steam line smells
just before she busts
how a metal-scalded man sounds
how he feels even.

To get Sheet and Tube to stitch
my dad's double rupture free
a dozen brothers and sisters paid
the heaviest damned union dues
in the history of Gary, Indiana
their lives nothing less
on Memorial Day, 1937
the lead in their backs
bought with Republic Steel gold
and because ten thousand more
turned out for picket next day
we got the union in Little Steel
and I can speak of this
can yell for something more
than number eight crane or my piss break.

To get me books and time enough
to figure how the Gold Coast
stays Gold while our world goes to rust
my Homestead Gary East Chicago Youngstown
had to scrap, scrape and pray
for any day's work
the suits would sell us
and because not many round here

came through in one piece
(hell, even in the fat times
not many came through in one piece)
I think
I feel
just a little prick, sir, is due:
this ain't over no way this is over
not by a long shot.

Will Watson was born in 1954 in Wheeling, West Virginia. The men in Watson's family had been steelworkers since the early 1900s, and Watson spent his teens and twenties working in steel mills and various other blue-collar environments around northwest Indiana. Before starting college at the age of twenty-six, he worked as a production laborer, forklift and overhead crane operator, tin mill feeder, road maintenance worker, longshoreman, and electricians' apprentice. His poetry and essays about working-class culture and life have appeared in *Labor, Minnesota Review, Blue Collar Review, New Laurel Review, College Literature,* and *Women's Studies Quarterly,* among other journals.

"The question of how I came to write 'Debt'," Watson says, "strikes to the heart of who I am and where I come from. There's a distilled history of three generations of Rust Belt steelworkers in the poem." Watson credits the Center for Working-Class Studies at Youngstown State University for helping him recover a poetic vocation that had been stifled, he says, for almost twenty years, "because I never felt I had anything to write about. I went to the second bi-annual conference at Youngstown State, back in 1995, and met all these academics and artists from working-class backgrounds. When I came home, all these poetic ideas suddenly started clamoring for expression. They were not polite about it, either." Will Watson is currently Associate Professor of English at the University of Southern Mississippi, Gulf Coast.

"Debt" was first published in *Living Forge,* vol. 1, no. 1 (Fall 2003). Copyright © 2003 by Will Watson. It is reprinted here by permission of the author.

The Suicidal Freezer Unit

Tom Wolfe

THE FREEZER WAS A WAREHOUSE within a warehouse, a vast refrigerated chamber down at one end of the building behind a wall covered in sheets of galvanized metal studded with rivets. A door, big as a barn's, covered in the same galvanized metal and battered as an old bucket, hung from a track. It had been opened for the start of the shift, revealing a curtain of heavy-gauge vinyl clouded by oily smears and shales of ice. The curtain had a slit up the middle so that the workmen could go in and out without too much of the cold air escaping. The freezer was maintained at dead zero Fahrenheit.

Inside, there were no windows. The chamber remained in an eternal frigid gray dusk, twenty-four hours a day. Stacks of cartons, tons of them, many of them packed with meat and fish, reached up three stories high on metal racks. Way up on the ceiling you could make out lengths of gray galvanized metal air-conditioning ducts doubling back and forth upon themselves like intestines. Between the ducts, strips of fluorescent tubing emitted a feeble bluish haze. The extreme cold seemed to congeal the very light itself and remove every trace of color.

Kenny, Conrad, and some thirty other pickers stood about just inside the entryway, waiting for the shift to start. They were clad in the lumpish, padded metal-gray Zincolon gloves and freezer suits with Dynel fur collars the warehouse issued. On the backs of the jackets was written CROKER in big yellow letters that looked lemony in the fluorescent light. Beneath the freezer suits they wore so many combinations of long johns, shirts, jerseys, sweaters, insulated vests, and sweatsuits, they were puffed up like blimps or the Michelin Tire Man. Kenny had the hood of a sweatshirt pulled up over his head, with just the bill of his baseball cap sticking out, upturned and emblazoned SUICIDE. His wild eyes seemed to be beaming out from within a shadowy hole. Three of the freezer pickers were black, three were Chinese, one was Japanese, and one was Mexican, but most were Okies, like Kenny, and half the Okies had adopted Kenny's SUICIDE regalia. They were known as the crash'n'burners, and they called the freezer the Suicidal Freezer Unit, a term Conrad couldn't get out of his head.

The way the jets of breath fog streamed from their noses and mouths was the first indication of how cold it actually was, but any picker foolish enough to try to work without his gloves on would soon have another. Each of them operated a pallet jack, a small but heavy electric vehicle with which you could jack up a loaded pallet and move it to another part of the warehouse. You stood on the back of the jack, behind its metal motor housing. It was simple to use. But if you touched the levers or handlebars with your bare hands in this ice box, your flesh would freeze to the metal. (And just try pulling it loose.)

To one side of the entrance was a wooden table manned by the night foreman, Dom, an old fellow—in the freezer, forty-eight was old—who looked a mile wide in his plaid Hudson Bay jacket. He wore a navy watch cap pulled down over his forehead and ears, which made the top half of his big round head look ridiculously tiny. Bursts of mouth fog pumped out of his mouth as he studied the printout order sheets in front of him. He had a little cylindrical remote microphone clipped to the collar of his jacket.

The boys were beginning to feel the cold creep in. It made your nose run even more. A chorus of sniffles, sneezes, snufflings, hawkings, coughs, and spitting welled up. Every now and then some picker would spit right on the floor, which made Conrad's flesh crawl.

Dom's deep voice sounded out over the wall speaker system:

"Okay, men! Before we get started, just a couple things. There's good news and bad news. First, the bad news. We been getting complaints from over at Bolka Rendering that somebody here's been using their parking lot for tailgate parties . . . Kenny."

"Ayyyyyyyyyyyy," said Kenny. "Why you looking at me?"

"Why?" said Dom. "Because two nights ago—or it was in the morning—the sun was up—and they're coming to work over there, and not only's there a buncha guys sprawled shit-faced all over their parking lot, but there's some kinda boom box playing this song where they're screaming, 'Eat shit.' Guy tells me that's all you could hear over half a Contra Costa County, 'EAT SHIT, EAT SHIT, EAT SHIT.' That's really terrific, that's very high class."

"Ooooooooo, oooooooo, oooooooooo!" whooped the crash'n'burners.

" 'Eat Shit'?" asked Kenny in a pseudo-startled voice. "Iddn'at by the Child Abusers?"

"Whoever it's by, it's disgusting," boomed Dom's voice over the speaker system. "There's a lotta women go to work at Bolka in the morning. I hope you realize that."

"Ooooooooooo, oooooooooooo, ooooooooooooooooo!" Now the pickers really let out whoops. Dom's concern for the tender sex, especially in the form it took at the Bolka Rendering works, struck them as a howl, worthy of maximum derision.

Dom shook his head. "Okay, you can laugh, but if it don't stop, somebody over *here's* gonna get child-abused. Capeesh? . . . Okay?" Lest the whoops start again, he hurried on. "All right, now here's the good news. We got a good turnout, and this is the end a the month, and so it looks like a light night. So whenever you men complete the orders, you can get outta here." Dom always said "you men" when he was appealing to their better natures.

More whoops, only now with a note of honest elation. Light nights they loved. Toward the end of the month, many of the hotels and the institutional kitchens that operated on monthly budgets—the prisons, hospitals, nursing homes, company cafeterias—cut back on their orders. On top of that, there had been a general falling off of business. The result was nights like tonight, on which the pickers could work five, six, seven hours and get paid for eight, so long as they got the orders out.

The boys converged on the foreman's table to pick up the order printouts, which were stacked in a wire basket. Now the great dreary chamber was filled with the squeals of rubber-soled boots pivoting on the concrete slab, the whines of the pallet jacks' electric motors starting up, the jolts of power hitting the driveshafts, the rumble of the wheels rolling over the concrete floor.

Conrad had slipped his order sheet onto the clipboard on his handlebars before he actually focused on what it was . . . Santa Rita . . . He ached a little more and rubbed his nose with the back of his glove. Santa Rita, down near the town of Pleasanton, was the Alameda County jail, one of eight prisons Croker supplied. Santa Rita orders always went on and on and included a lot of heavy cases of cheap meat. He scanned the sheet . . . twelve cases of beef shanks, Row J, Slot 12 . . . Each case weighed eighty pounds. In loading up a pallet the trick was to put the heaviest cases on the bottom and build up to the lightest. So that was how he'd have to start the night—lifting half a ton of frozen beef shanks in eighty-pound bricks.

He stood on the back of his pallet jack and squeezed the accelerator levers. With a whine and a jolt the machine came to life, and he headed down the aisle bearing an empty pallet on the blades before him. The boys were already plunging full-decibel into the frenzy of the light night . . . All over the freezer you could hear whining motors, squealing boots, cries, shouts, oaths, the crashing sound of pickers slinging heavy frozen cartons onto the pallets . . . They leaned into the racks' icy slots, waddled in, crawled in, swollen gray creatures with Dynel fur collars, and then they crawled back out, waddled back out, slithered back out, bearing frozen cartons of food, fat gray ice weevils swarming over the racks in a terribly diligent frenzy; and he was one of them.

His destination, Row J, Slot 12, was deep in the gloom of the freezer. He looked into the slot at floor level and sighed a long jet of breath fog. It was empty. He looked into the slot above it. It was about a quarter full, with the cartons stacked at the rear of the two pallets that formed the slot's floor. So he did the usual. He hopped up on top of the jack's motor housing and hoisted himself into the upper slot on his haunches. The slots were only four feet high. He duck-walked across a pallet toward the cartons stacked in the rear. The pallet's slats sagged in a weary, spongy way beneath his feet. He sank to his knees, hooked his hand over a carton in the uppermost row, let his body flop down on the icy blocks beneath him, and started pulling. It wouldn't budge; it seemed to be frozen fast between the cartons on either side. He started yanking on it . . . grunts . . . bursts of mouth fog . . . It was dark in here . . . inside this cliff of ice. He struggled to rock the carton free. The pressure on his fingers, his forearm, his elbow and shoulder was tremendous. His eyes started watering, and the rims of his eyelids began to burn.

Finally, with a hot burst of fog, he yanked the carton loose and began pulling it toward him. He got off his knees and rose up in a crouch once more. Then he went into a deep squat and tried to pick up this frozen eighty-pound dead weight without straining his back. Since he couldn't straighten up, he had to pull the carton in toward his midsection and duck-waddle to the mouth of the slot. Eighty pounds, frozen solid, more than half his own weight—already his shoulders, his arms, his hands, his lower back, the big muscles of his thighs were in agony. Despite the frigid temperature, his cheeks and forehead were hot from the exertion. At the edge of the slot he set the carton down, slid the four feet to the floor below, and grabbed the carton in a bear hug. For an instant he staggered before getting his feet squarely under the weight. Then he squatted again and lowered the carton onto the pallet on the front of his jack. When he stood up, a jolt of pain went through his lower back. He glanced down—

Blearily, in the periphery of his vision, he could see little glints and sparkles. Ice crystals were forming in his mustache. Sweat had run off his face, and mucus had flowed from his nose, and now his mustache was beginning to freeze up. He took the glove off his right hand and ran his fingers through his hair. There were little icicles in the hair on his head and in his eyebrows, and a regular little stalactite had formed on the end of his nose. He looked at his hand. He made a fist. Then he undid it and splayed his fingers out and turned them this way and that. They were extraordinarily broad, his fingers. From yanking, and carrying the eighty-pound carton, they were pumped up, bulging with little muscles. They were . . . stupendous . . . and grotesque at the same time. His hand looked as if it belonged to someone twice his size.

He stood still for a moment. The noise in the freezer had risen to a merry old ruckus. The whines of the jacks came from every direction . . . the crashes of product hitting the pallets . . . the shouts, the cries.

"Crash'n'burn!"—the unmistakable high nasal cry of Kenny himself somewhere a few rows away.

"Crash'n'burn!" sang Kenny's boys with the SUICIDE caps in a choral response.

Backing out of a slot nearby, here came a fat gray ice weevil wearing a Panzer helmet . . . Herbie Jonah was his name . . . He had a huge carton hugged into his abdomen. Jets of fog came out of his mouth with a regular beat. Conrad couldn't hear him, but he knew exactly what he was saying, because Herbie said the same thing all night long as he struggled with the frozen blocks: "Mother*fucker*, mother*fucker*, mother*fucker*." Over there, on the aisle, sailing past on his pallet jack at a real crash'n'burn clip came a wiry little crash'n'burner known as Light Bulb, his SUICIDE cap jammed down practically over his eyes, the hood of his sweatshirt sticking up with a funny point above the top of his head, as if he were an elf. For someone so small, he was amazingly strong. The pallet on the front of his jack was already piled high with product.

"Crash'n'burn!" Kenny sang out from somewhere, this time in falsetto.

And Light Bulb, perched on the back of his pallet jack, threw back his head and gave a falsetto yodel of his own—"Crash'n'burn!"—and zipped past.

Suddenly Dom's deep voice was bellowing over the speakers: "Cleanup! Cleanup! Betty 4! Betty 4! Cleanup! Chop chop!"

This meant a spill had occurred. "Betty 4" was Row B, Slot 4. Some product had slid off a pallet as it went around a curve; or some picker had dropped something from an upper slot; or an entire jack—picker, pallet, and all—had turned over, and product was spilled on the floor. Cleanup was not a verb but a noun, a job category. There were two cleanups, two Filipinos, known as Ferdi and Birdie, both of them too small to be pickers, who did nothing but clean up product that spilled or got smashed on the concrete slab. There would be plenty of spills tonight. There were plenty of them every light night, as the boys yahooed through the frozen phosphorescent haze in the name of the god of the Suicidal Freezer Unit, testosterone.

Conrad listened to the crazy din of his mates—and then caught himself. He was letting *No!* creep into his heart. What he was doing in this place had nothing to do with jacks and slots and pallets and product or with crashing and burning. It had to do with a new life for his young family. With a deep breath, a sigh, and a long jet of breath fog, he hopped back up on the motor housing of his pallet jack and hoisted himself back into the upper slot. A weevil with *Yes!* in his heart, he burrowed back into the cliff for eleven more eighty-pound blocks of frozen beef shanks. The evening had just begun.

BY THE TIME HE HAD loaded all twelve cartons onto the pallet on the front of his jack, his face was burning up, and his mustache was so full of ice he could feel its weight pulling at his skin. Quickly he scanned the printout again . . . Twenty-four cases of beef patties . . . Hadn't even noticed that . . . Row D, Slot 21 . . . fifty pounds apiece . . . Didn't help to dwell on it . . . He headed off on the jack, bearing the twelve cases of beef shanks on the pallet before him.

Down the aisle sailed Kenny, standing up on the back of his pallet jack. His eyes burned crazily in the shadow beneath his SUICIDE brim and the sweatshirt hood. The pallet on the front of his jack seemed to be more than half loaded already. As soon as he saw Conrad coming toward him, he broke into a big grin and yelled out, "Yo! Whoa!"

Conrad released his accelerator lever and drifted to a stop, and Kenny pulled up beside him. "Yo! Conrad! What the hell's happened to your *mus*tache?"

"Whattaya mean?" said Conrad. Kenny's own mustache was heavily flecked with frost.

"It's fucking turned to ice!" said Kenny. "You look like you got a couple a icicles hanging out your nose!"

Conrad pulled the glove off his right hand. It was true. His mustache was frozen solid from his nostrils to where it dropped down on either side of his mouth.

"I swear to God," said Kenny. "Looks exactly like a couple icicles hanging out your nose. Whattaya been doing?"

Conrad gestured toward the cartons of beef shanks on his pallet. "Santa Rita," he said.

Kenny said, "Like lifting the QE2, iddn'it?"

With that he shot a whining jolt of electricity to his driveshaft and sped on down the aisle.

Conrad burrowed on, a weevil with the best of them, into the Salisbury steaks, fishburgers, gravy stock, ice cream, orange juice, cut fava beans, American cheese, margarine, pepperoni pizza, chipped beef, bacon, and waffles, and the ruckus rose, and the cries rang out—*Crash'n'burn!*—and the product crashed, and the pickers yahooed, and Dom's big voice bellowed over the speakers: "Cleanup! Cleanup! Kilo 9! Kilo 9! Come on, Ferdi! You, too, Birdie! On the double!"—and the light-night frenzy ran through the chamber like a rogue hormone.

As soon as he retrieved the final item on the Santa Rita printout (a dozen cases of frozen buckwheat waffles), Conrad rubbed his nose with his glove to break up the rings of ice that had formed inside his nostrils. A thick, restless fog was beginning to roil around the tops of the racks from the heat of the machinery and the bodies of the struggling human beings. The fluorescent tubing gave off a wan tubercular-blue glimmer behind it. Conrad's pallet was piled perilously high with product. He eased the jack toward the freezer door. He pulled a handle hanging from a chain, and the door rolled open hydraulically. Slowly he drove through the slit in the vinyl curtain and out onto the dock's concrete apron.

As soon as he emerged from the freezer, he was engulfed, overwhelmed, by heat. The temperature out here was still well up into the eighties. The trucks were roaring and sighing; a few were already pulling out for the nightly delivery runs. All up and down the platform were great heaps of cartons, drums, canisters, sacks, resting on pallets the pickers had deposited. He could feel the ice melting from his hair and his eyebrows and his mustache and streaming down his face. What must he look like to the loaders and the drivers and everyone else out here in the real world? A poor encrusted weevil emerging from the polar depths, a mutant, bleary-eyed, blinking its way into a sweltering California night . . . He straightened up in an instinctive bid for dignity.

And yet when he deposited the pallet and its prodigious load at Bay 17, neither the checker nor the loaders nor the driver seemed to take any special notice of him. They were used to such creatures, the gray weevils who came crawling out from under the ice . . .

Before heading back into the freezer, Conrad got off the jack and stood and stretched. His long johns were soaked clear through from humping product for so long without a break.

He gazed out beyond the big white Croker trucks and the glare of the loading platform, out beyond the parking lot and the flatlands and the marshes. There was such a profusion of stars, they seemed to be swelling and surging in the sky. Below them, near the horizon, he could see other lights twinkling . . . San Francisco . . . Sausalito . . . Tiburon, he guessed it was . . . just across the bay . . . and so far off. Might as well be another continent. What were people his age, twenty-three, doing over there at this moment beneath that exuberant, starry sky? He couldn't even imagine it, and he steeled himself against submitting to such an idle exercise, for that would be inviting *No!* into his heart. The leafy town of Danville, in Contra Costa County, was as near to the fabled coast of California as he cared, or dared, to aspire.

With a great effort he beckoned *Yes!* back into his heart. It was slow in coming.

JUST BEFORE CONRAD REACHED THE entrance to go back into the freezer, there was a tremendous clatter. A picker from the warehouse's main section, Dry Foods, pulled up ahead of him driving an electric truck known as a tugger, pulling three metal wagons piled high with product . . . drums of detergent, canisters of tomato paste, sacks of pinto beans, huge jugs of red food dye . . . There was no end to it. The tugger had a seat like a golf cart's, and perched on it was a chubby redheaded fellow, no older than Conrad himself, wearing a short-sleeved sport shirt, work gloves, and crepe-soled boots. The Dry Foods pickers sometimes drew orders with one or two frozen items and were told to just go into the freezer and get them. They weren't dressed for it, but they could take it for the few minutes they might have to be in there.

This one, the chubby redhead, was studying the freezer's huge door. He couldn't figure out how to open it. Conrad drove up beside him and pointed to the chain and then pulled it for him. As the door rolled open, he gestured toward the slit in the vinyl curtain as if to say, "After you."

The redhead eased his tugger and his wagons on through, and Conrad entered behind him. The light-night ruckus had not died down for a moment. Shouts, oaths, crashing sounds, whines . . . and Kenny's voice singing out through the icy haze and the roiling fog:

"Crash'n'burn!"

"Crash'n'burn!" answered the crash'n'burners from every aisle, every row, every rack, every icy, hazy, fogbound corner.

Baffled, the boy on the tugger swiveled his head this way and that. All at once he took off for the racks, his tugger whining shrilly from all the juice he was feeding it.

Conrad drove his jack over to the foreman's desk. Kenny was standing there beside his jack studying a printout he had just picked up.

"Shit," he said to nobody in particular. Then he caught sight of Conrad and held up the sheet and said, "Nat'n'Nate's," and made a face. Nat'n'Nate's was a big old delicatessen in San Francisco just south of Market Street. The pickers hated Nat'n'Nate's orders because of the heavy cases of processed meat.

Conrad pulled a printout from the wire basket . . . Morden Rehabilitation, up in Santa Rosa . . . He scanned the sheet . . . Shouldn't be too bad an order. He got up on the pallet jack and drove into the canyons amid the ice cliffs.

He soon found himself humping product just one slot away from Kenny. He could hear Kenny grunting and swearing to himself. Conrad was loading a case of spareribs on his jack when Kenny emerged from the cliff embracing an eighty-pound carton of processed turkey. All at once, there was a sharp whine and a terrific clattering. Here came the redheaded Dry Foods picker, barreling out of a row on his tugger and pulling his three wagons full of product. He turned to go up the aisle. He was turning too fast. Instead of straightening out, he kept on turning in a huge crazy arc. The centrifugal force sent the wagons up on two wheels. They were going over. A massive gush of product hit the slick concrete of the aisle. A huge sack split open. *Pellets!* No, pinto beans, streaming in every direction. Hard and smooth and slippery as ball bearings they were. A loaded pallet jack came speeding up the aisle from behind . . . Panzer helmet . . . Herbie Jonah . . . Herbie veered to keep from crashing into the spill. His jack hit the streaming pinto beans, skidded, then went into a ferocious spin. Herbie, the jack, the loaded pallet—spinning, flinging frozen product in every direction, careening straight toward Kenny, who had his back turned with an eighty-pound block of frozen meat clutched to his midsection—

"Kenny!"

—Herbie, screaming, trying to keep his grip on the handlebars of the jack. Bango! He was thrown off. He hit the floor. The floor turned red. *Red!* Kenny turned his head. He could see Herbie's jack coming straight at him, but he was frozen by his own compulsive grip on the carton. Conrad sprang forward, dove at Kenny headfirst, bowled him over. A tremendous suffocating crash enveloped their bodies . . . a sea of red . . . They went sliding through a blood-red muck on the pinto beans . . . Kenny and Conrad . . . a tangle of arms and legs . . . racks and cartons wheeling overhead in the roiling fog . . . The moment stretched out endlessly and then stopped.

Conrad was upside down on his head and his right shoulder, looking up at his legs—which were *red!*—jackknifed over Kenny's body—*covered in—my blood?* Slowly, not at all sure that he could, he rolled his legs off Kenny. Everywhere—*red!* Hemorrhaging!—but he couldn't figure out where he was cut.

Kenny, lying next to him, contorted, seemed to be trying to roll over on his back. Cartons, drums, canisters, sacks were strewn about in the horrible red muck . . . A Panzer helmet, a body, a gray weevil, Herbie Jonah, smeared red . . . Herbie tried to sit up, but the heel of his hand skidded on the pinto beans, and he flopped back down into the red muck again. There was Herbie's pallet jack, smashed into Kenny's. The motor housing of Kenny's was ripped off its base. The levers of the two machines were twisted about each other. The slats on the two pallets were snapped into huge splinters. Both machines were jammed against one of the black metal uprights of the racks.

Out in the middle of the aisle all three of the Dry Food picker's wagons were turned over, but the tugger itself was still upright, nosed into the row on the other side, and the chubby redhead was still on his seat, slumped over toward his handlebars and moaning.

One of the black pickers, Tony Chase, came running toward Conrad and Kenny. Suddenly his legs went out from under him. The pinto beans. He landed in the red muck. Conrad managed to get up to a kneeling position. He could feel the pinto beans, hard as marbles, rolling underneath his knees. His Zincolon suit was dripping red—*blood!*

But wait a minute . . . Blood wouldn't look like this, couldn't possibly remain this bright . . . Then he saw them, two shattered ten-gallon jugs . . . red food dye . . . The jugs and the pinto beans . . . a flash flood of the stuff . . .

"Can't get my hand . . . can't get my hand . . ."

It was the Dry Foods picker, still hunched over the handlebars of his tugger, moaning, "Can't get my hand."

Somehow the boy had taken the glove off his right hand and neglected to put it back on before he took hold of the handlebars to steer his tugger into the turn, and his fingers and his palm had frozen to the metal.

Kenny was sitting up, staring at the wreckage of the two jacks. It was pretty obvious. If he had stayed where he was, squatting down beside his jack with the carton of frozen turkey in his arms, he would have been crushed. Conrad's diving tackle had knocked him toward the aisle. Conrad had thrown his own body directly into the path of Herbie's careening jack. Had his legs been six inches higher as he dove, they would have been crushed as the two motor housings smashed together. Had they been six inches lower, they would have been crushed by the scythe-like swing of Herbie's pallet.

The manic light had gone out in Kenny's wild blue eyes. Pickers were converging upon the spill. Kenny opened his mouth, but no words came out.

From above, Dom's voice, over the speakers: "Cleanup! Cleanup! Whiskey 8! Whiskey 8! Chop chop! Birdie! Ferdi! Both a you! On the double! Got a whole aisle out over here! Whiskey 8! Whiskey 8!"

And then Kenny, still sitting in the red muck, spoke more softly than Conrad had ever heard him speak before. "Jesus Christ, Conrad . . . you just saved my life."

THE TWO CLEANUPS, FERDI AND Birdie, earned their pay this time all right. There must have been a ton of product strewn about in the aisle and Row W, split open, staved in, mashed, crushed, all of it beginning to freeze to the floor in an icy red slush. It was a miracle that no one was badly hurt. The padded freezer suits saved them, probably, the suits and all the other stuff they swaddled themselves in. The worst off was the chubby redhead from Dry Foods who, sure enough, had ripped a chunk of flesh off his hand trying to remove it from the handlebar. The pickers who had hit the deck looked a lot worse than he did, however. They looked like survivors of a bomb explosion. There was red dye smeared all over their Zincolon jumpsuits, their gloves, their heads, their faces. Half of Conrad's hair was soaked with the dye; so was Herbie's. One side of Kenny's mustache was a sopping red. It looked as if he had been shot in the nostril.

Dom came over and took the whole bunch of them out to the loading platform to give them a break, let them warm up, and see if they were okay. Godalmighty! The checkers and the loaders looked at them now, all right! The muck had frozen to their freezer suits, and it was melting. The suits seemed to be oozing and festering blood. Every now and then a pinto bean would fall off, looking like a bloody clot. Conrad began to shiver, right out here in the stifling heat. He'd almost gotten killed, or maimed, him and Kenny both.

Kenny was abnormally quiet. He stuck by Conrad's side. He'd start to talk about what had happened, and he'd say, "I guess . . . I guess . . ." or something equally vague, and his eyes would look as if they were pinned on something a mile away.

And then Herbie came over and told Kenny he was truly sorry, but there had been no way he could control his jack once it hit the pinto beans. It seemed so strange, because nobody had ever heard Herbie express anything approaching a tender sentiment before.

"Oh, I know that," said Kenny. "I heard you yell, and I saw the goddamn thing coming at me, and I just froze. I had a goddamn carton of processed turkey in my hands, and I couldn't even drop it or nothing. I just froze. If this character here . . ." He nodded toward Conrad and smiled faintly and then that smile, too, died on his lips, and he got the far-off look again.

Dom came over and told the boys that the lunch break was coming pretty soon and they might as well stay out here until the horn sounded and go straight in to lunch. Then he drew Conrad aside and put his arm around his shoulders and said, "You okay? You showed us something in there, kid."

Conrad didn't know what to say except that he was, in fact, okay. He was still too shaken to take any pleasure in the compliment.

The lunch break was at 12:30 a.m. in what was known as the break room, which was nothing but a clearing in the main work bay, Dry Foods, with 4-by-8-foot sheets of raw plywood serving as walls. The freezer pickers had taken off their Zincolon freezer suits, the thermal vests, the hats and gloves and wadding and swaddling, and were sitting in plastic chairs at the break room's heavy-duty folding tables. Stripped down to shirts and jeans again, they looked whipped and clammy from lifting so much product at such a furious pace and sweating so much inside their insulation. Kenny was slumped back in a chair right across the table from Conrad. Conrad had just opened his paper bag and taken out one of the two meat-loaf sandwiches Jill had fixed him. A couple of dozen pickers, carrying their Igloo coolers, were lined up waiting to cook their lunches in the microwave ovens over by the plywood walls. They kept turning their heads and looking at him. He figured it was because he and Kenny presented such a spectacle, smeared red the way they were.

Light Bulb came over from the microwave with a steaming plastic picnic plate and sat down and said, "Jeeeeeesus Christ—how you guys doooooin'? You okaaaaaay?" Light Bulb stuttered, but he stuttered on the vowels rather than the consonants. By the time he reached the okaaaaaay, the little crash'n'burner was no longer looking at both of them but squarely at him, Conrad. He had a glistening look on his face. Conrad could feel himself blushing. For the first time he let the thought form in his mind: They all think I'm some kind of hero.

The notion was not exhilarating. On the contrary, he felt like a fraud. When he dove at Kenny, it had not been an act of calculated bravery in the teeth of dreadful, well-known odds. He had just . . . *done* it, in a moment of terror. And he was still terrified! *I could have been killed in there!* That he shared these guilty, submerged, utterly inexpressible feelings with most of the heroes of history, he had no way of knowing.

Just then, to his great relief, the warehouse's assistant night manager, Nick Derdosian, came into the break room with a burnt-orange manila folder cradled in his arms. In the folder would be the paychecks, and everybody would have something else to think about.

Derdosian was a swarthy man in his mid-thirties. The top of his head was bald, but the rest of him was remarkably hairy. A heavy crop of black hair emerged from the short sleeves of his shirt and ran all the way down his arms and out onto the backs of his hands. Thanks to Kenny, the freezer pickers all called him Nick Necktie. He and the other supervisory personnel and salesmen had offices up in the front of the warehouse, overlooking East Bay Boulevard. Kenny referred to them collectively as "the neckties." Most of the men up in the front office did, in fact, wear neckties, as did Derdosian—until recently. Every time he turned up in the break room or the work bays, Kenny had taken to yelling out, "Nick Necktie!" and some crash'n'burner or other would echo the cry in falsetto: "Nick *Neck*tie!" This finally so rattled Derdosian, a quiet, stolid man whom God had not designed for dealing with crash'n'burners, he had lately abandoned his necktie and started wearing open-necked shirts. But he was so hairy, a carpet of crinkly chest hairs was visible in the V of the open neck, and Kenny and the crash'n'burners had started calling him Harry No Tie. "Ha*rreeeeee* No Tie!" So this week he had put the necktie back on and taken to approaching the crew with a necktie and a tense, ingratiating grin.

Tonight, however, he came into the break room without any smile at all. Tonight he looked gloomy and wary, as if he thought perhaps Kenny had dreamed up some new way of making his life miserable.

Instead, Kenny merely nodded and said, "Hi, Nick." He looked every bit as glum himself.

Derdosian set the manila folder down on a nearby table, removed the stack of paychecks, and started calling out the names in alphabetical order. Conrad took his envelope without bothering to open it, folded it in two, put it in the pocket of his plaid shirt, and went back to the table.

Just then voices erupted at the next table. It was Tony Chase and the other two black pickers. Tony was showing them a white slip of paper and talking angrily. Light Bulb swung around to listen, then leaned forward again.

"Jesus Christ," he said, "Tohohohohohony just got nohohohohohotified. He's been laid off."

Conrad sat upright. Tony had been hired the same week he was.

Kenny and Light Bulb already had their envelopes out and were going through them to see if there was anything other than a check inside. Evidently they were safe. They hadn't been laid off. The same thing was going on all over the break room. From somewhere behind him Conrad heard a voice gasp out, "Fuck a *duck!*"

Slowly Conrad withdrew his envelope from his shirt pocket and slipped his big forefinger under the flap and ripped it open. There was the salmon-colored paycheck, as usual. Behind it was a white slip of paper.

He read the first few words: "Due to a necessary capacity reduction in this facility, your services . . ." Then he looked up. Kenny and Light Bulb were staring at him. He couldn't make himself speak. He could only nod up and down to tell them, "Yes, it's true."

"I don't fucking believe this," said Kenny. Lunging, he stretched his arm across the table and said, "Lemme see that," and snatched the slip of paper from Conrad's hand and studied it for a moment.

Then he bolted out of his seat. The chair hit the floor behind him with a loud plastic smack. Glaring at the retreating figure of Derdosian, he called out, "Yo! Nick!"

Derdosian stopped in the entryway to the break room. Immediately his head began to jiggle from side to side, as if to say, "I had nothing to do with it."

"What the hell's going on, *Nick!*"

Kenny's huge hands were pressed down on the surface of the table, supporting the weight of his upper body. His chin jutted forward. Every striation of the muscles of his great long neck stood out. He looked as if he were about to spring all the way from there to the opening in the plywood wall where the cowering assistant night manager stood. His wild-dog eyes bored in, demanding a response, and then they opened wide, and he screamed out:

"who's the bright boy thought this up, nick?"

You could still hear the clatter and banging of the Dry Foods bay beyond, but here in the break room there wasn't another sound. The crew froze stock-still, riveted by this outburst of crash'n'burner fury.

"WHO'S THE SHIT FER BRAINS, NICK? YOU'RE LAYING OFF CONRAD?
YOU'RE LAYING OFF THE BEST MAN IN THIS WHOLE FUCKING PLACE?"

Derdosian, transfixed, slowly lifted his shoulders and then the palms of his
hands and lowered his head, in the gesture that pleads, "It wasn't me! I don't
make these decisions!"

"HE WAS GONNA BUY A CONDO, NICK! HE'S GOT A WIFE AND TWO KIDS!
HE'S GOT HEART, NICK, HE'S GOT HEART! HE'S WORTH MORE'N THE WHOLE
BUNCHA YOU FUCKIN' NECKTIES PUT TOGETHER!"

The assistant night manager now had his palms up so high, and his head
down so low, he looked as if he were trying to disappear into his own thoracic
cavity.

"AW, I KNOW, NICK! YOU ONLY WORK HERE! YOU'RE SO FUCKIN' PATHETIC!
YOU KNOW THAT? SO WHYN'T YOU FUCKIN' GO GET LOST! WHAT'S THE NAME
OF THE ASSHOLE THAT OWNS THIS FUCKIN' COMPANY? SOMEBODY CROKER?
IS HE THE BRIGHT BOY? THEN HE'D BETTER FUCKIN' GET LOST, TOO, OR I'M
GONNA—"

Kenny's voice broke, and he lowered his gaze and looked not at Nick
Derdosian but at Conrad. He compressed his lips, which began to tremble, as
did his chin. His eyes opened wide, and then he closed them slowly. When he
opened them again, they were brimming with tears, which began to roll down
his cheeks. Still supporting himself on the table with one hand, he raised the
other and covered his face. He lowered his head, and his bony frame began
convulsing all the way from his shoulders down to his weight lifter's belt.

Conrad's eyes fastened on the most insignificant thing: Kenny's pale blond
hair, wet, stringy, matted down, was already thinning badly in the crown. All at
once the indomitable crash'n'burner looked so weak and weary.

Kenny raised his head and tried to wipe his tears away with his hand and
then with his forearm. He forced a smile.

"See? I was right, wasn't I, old buddy? They just ain't gonna let you do it. And
you were right, too. You said I got *No!* in my heart. And that's the truth. I got *No!*
in my heart." He clutched his throat with his forefinger and thumb. "I got it up to
here . . . from lapping up all that crap inside the rut they make you crawl in."

Tom Wolfe, an author and journalist, was born in Richmond, Virginia. He took his first newspaper
job in 1956 and eventually worked for *The Washington Post* and *The New York Herald Tribune,* among
others. He experimented with using fictional techniques in feature stories and is one of the founders
of the New Journalism movement of the 1960s and 1970s. Among his works are *The Kandy-Kolored
Tangerine-Flake Streamline Baby* (Farrar, Straus and Giroux 1965), *The Pump House Gang* (FSG 1968),
and *The Electric Kool-Aid Acid Test* (FSG 1968). In 1979 Wolfe published *The Right Stuff* (FSG), an
account of the pilots who became America's first astronauts. His first novel was *The Bonfire of the
Vanities* (FSG 1987).

"The Suicidal Freezer Unit" is from *A Man in Full* by Tom Wolfe (published in the United States by
Farrar, Straus and Giroux and in Great Britain by Jonathan Cape). Copyright © 1999 by Tom Wolfe. It is
reprinted here by permission of Farrar, Straus and Giroux, LLC, and by permission of The Random House
Group Ltd., Great Britain.

Photograph: Migrant Worker, Parlier, California, 1967

Larry Levis

I'm going to put Johnny Dominguez right here
In front of you on this page so that
You won't mistake him for something else,
An idea, for example, of how oppressed
He was, rising with his pan of Thompson Seedless
Grapes from a row of vines. The band
On his white straw hat darkened by sweat, is,
He would remind you, just a hatband.
His hatband. He would remind you of that.
As for the other use, this unforeseen
Labor you have subjected him to, the little
Snacks & white wine of the opening he must
Bear witness to, he would remind you
That he was not put on this earth
To be an example of something else,
Johnny Dominguez, he would hasten to
Remind you, in his chaste way of saying things,
Is not to be used as an example of anything
At all, not even, he would add after
A second or so, that greatest of all
Impossibilities, that unfinishable agenda
Of the stars, that fact, Johnny Dominguez.

Larry Levis was a professor of creative writing at Virginia Commonwealth University at the time of his death in 1996. A native of California, he had taught at California State College and directed the creative writing program at the University of Utah. His first book of poems, *Wrecking Crew* (University of Pittsburgh Press 1972), won the United States Award of the International Poetry Forum. His second book, *The Afterlife* (University of Iowa Press), won the Lamont Award of the American Academy of Poets in 1976. *The Dollmaker's Ghost* (Dutton 1981) was a winner of the Open Competition of the National Poetry Series. Among his other awards were three fellowships in poetry from the National Endowment for the Arts, a Fulbright Fellowship, and a Guggenheim Fellowship.

"Photograph: Migrant Worker, Parlier, California, 1967" originally appeared in Levis's last work, *Elegy*, which was published posthumously in 1997. Copyright © by Larry Levis. It is reprinted here by permission of the University of Pittsburgh Press.

After Cowboy Chicken Came to Town

Ha Jin

"I WANT MY MONEY BACK!" the customer said, dropped his plate on the counter, and handed me his receipt. He was a fiftyish man, of stout girth. A large crumb hung on the corner of his oily mouth. He had bought four pieces of chicken just now, but only a drumstick and a wing were left on the plate.

"Where are the breast and the thigh?" I asked.

"You can't take people in like this." The man's bulbous eyes flashed with rage. This time I recognized him; he was a worker in the nearby motor factory.

"How did we take you in?" the tall Baisha asked sharply, brandishing a pair of long tongs. She glared at the man, whose crown barely reached the level of her nose.

He said, "This Cowboy Chicken only sounds good and looks tasty. In fact it's just a name—it's more batter than meat. After two pieces I still don't feel a thing in here." He slapped his flabby side. "I don't want to eat this fluffy stuff anymore. Give me my money back."

"No way," Baisha said, and swung her permed hair, which looked like a magpie's nest. "If you hadn't touched the chicken, we'd refund you the money. But—"

"Excuse me," Peter Jiao said, coming out of the kitchen together with Mr. Shapiro.

We explained to him the customer's demand, which Peter translated for our American boss. Then we all remained silent to see how Peter, our manager, would handle this.

After a brief exchange with Mr. Shapiro in English, Peter said in Chinese to the man, "You've eaten two pieces already, so we can only refund half your money. But don't take this as a precedent. Once you've touched the food, it's yours."

The man looked unhappy but accepted the offer. Still he muttered, "American dogs." He was referring to us, the Chinese employed by Cowboy Chicken.

That angered us. We began arguing with Peter and Mr. Shapiro that we shouldn't have let him take advantage of us this way. Otherwise all kinds of people would come in to sample our food for free. We didn't need a cheap

"After Cowboy Chicken Came to Town" is from *The Bridegroom* by Ha Jin (published in the United States by Pantheon Books and in Great Britain by William Heinemann Ltd). It also appeared in *Tri-Quarterly* (2000). Copyright © 2000 by Ha Jin. It is reprinted here by permission of Pantheon Books, a division of Random House, Inc., and by permission of The Random House Group Ltd., Great Britain.

customer like this one and should throw him out. Mr. Shapiro said we ought to follow the American way of doing business—you must try to satisfy your customers. "The customer is always right," he had instructed us when we were hired. But he had no idea who he was dealing with. You let a devil into your house, he'll get into your bed. If Mr. Shapiro continued to play the merciful Buddha, this place would be a mess soon. We had already heard a lot of complaints about our restaurant. People in town would say, "Cowboy Chicken is just for spendthrifts." True, our product was more expensive and far greasier than the local braised chicken, which was cooked so well that you could eat even the bones.

Sponge in hand, I went over to clean the table littered by that man. The scarlet Formica tabletop smelled like castor oil when greased with chicken bones. The odor always nauseated me. As I was about to move to another table, I saw a hole on the seat the size of a soybean burned by a cigarette. It must have been the work of that son of a dog; instead of refunding his money, we should've detained him until he paid for the damage.

I hated Mr. Shapiro's hypocrisy. He always appeared goodhearted and considerate to customers but was cruel to us, his employees. The previous month he had deducted forty yuan from my pay. It hurt like having a rib taken out of my chest. What had happened was that I had given eight chicken breasts to a girl from my brother's electricity station. She came in to buy some chicken. By the company's regulations I was supposed to give her two drumsticks, two thighs, two wings, and two breasts. She said to me, "Be a good man, Hongwen. Give me more meat." Somehow I couldn't resist her charming smile, so I yielded to her request. My boss caught me stuffing the paper box with the meatiest pieces, but he remained silent until the girl was out of earshot. Then he dumped on me all his piss and crap. "If you do that again," he said, "I'll fire you." I was so frightened! Later he fined me, as an example to the seven other Chinese employees.

Mr. Shapiro was an old fox, good at sweet-talking. When we asked him why he had chosen to do business in our Muji City, he said he wanted to help the Chinese people, because in the late thirties his parents had fled Red Russia and lived here for three years before moving on to Australia; they had been treated decently, though they were Jews. With an earnest look on his round, whiskery face, Mr. Shapiro explained, "The Jews and the Chinese had a similar fate, so I feel close to you. We all have dark hair." He chuckled as if he had said something funny. In fact that was capitalist baloney. We don't need to eat Cowboy Chicken here, or appreciate his stout red nose and his balding crown, or wince at the thick black hair on his arms. His company exploited not just us but also thousands of country people. A few villages in Hebei Province grew potatoes for Cowboy Chicken, because the soil and climate there produced potatoes similar to Idaho's. In addition, the company had set up a few chicken farms in Anhui Province to provide meat for its chain in China. It used Chinese produce and labor and made money out of Chinese customers, then shipped its profits back to the

U.S. How could Mr. Shapiro have the barefaced gall to claim he had come to help us? We have no need for a savior like him. As for his parents' stay in our city half a century ago, it's true that the citizens here had treated Jews without discrimination. That was because to us a Jew was just another foreigner, no different from any other white devil. We still cannot tell the difference.

We nicknamed Mr. Shapiro "Party Secretary," because just like a party boss anywhere he did little work. The only difference was that he didn't organize political studies or demand we report to him our inner thoughts. Peter Jiao, his manager, ran the business for him. I had known Peter since middle school, when his name was Peihai—an anemic, studious boy with few friends to play with. Boys often made fun of him because he had four tourbillions on his head. His father had served as a platoon commander in the Korean War and had been captured by the American army. Unlike some of the POWs, who chose to go to Canada or Taiwan after the war, Peihai's father, out of his love for our motherland, decided to come back. But when he returned, he was discharged from the army and sent down to a farm in a northern suburb of our city. In reality, all those captives who had come back were classified as suspected traitors. A lot of them were jailed again. Peihai's father worked under surveillance on the farm, but people rarely maltreated him, and he had his own home in a nearby village. He was quiet most of the time; so was his wife, a woman who never knew her dad's name because she had been fathered by some Japanese officer. Their only son, Peihai, had to walk three miles to town for school every weekday. That was why we called him Country Boy.

Unlike us, he always got good grades. In 1977, when colleges reopened, he passed the entrance exams and enrolled at Tianjin Foreign Language Institute to study English. We had all sat for the exams, but only two out of the three hundred seniors from our high school had passed the admission standard. After college, Peihai went to America, studying history at the University of Iowa. Later he changed his field and earned a degree in business from that school. Then he came back, a completely different man, robust and wealthy, with curly hair and a new name. He looked energetic, cheerful, and younger than his age. At work he was always dressed formally, in a western suit and a bright-colored tie. He once joked with us, saying he had over fifty pounds of American flesh. To tell the truth, I liked Peter better than Peihai. I often wondered what in America had made him change so much—in just six years from an awkward boy to a capable, confident man. Was it American water? American milk and beef? The American climate? The American way of life? I don't know for sure. More impressive, Peter spoke English beautifully, much better than those professors and lecturers in the City College who had never gone abroad and had learned their English mainly from textbooks written by the Russians. He had hired me probably because I had never bugged him in our school days and because I had a slightly lame foot. Out of gratitude, I never spoke about his past to my fellow workers.

ON THE DAY COWBOY CHICKEN opened, about forty officials from the city hall came to celebrate. At the opening ceremony, a vice mayor cut the red silk ribbon with a pair of scissors two feet long. He then presented Mr. Shapiro with a brass key the size of a small poker. What's that for? we wondered. Our city didn't have a gate with a colossal lock for it to open. The attendees at the ceremony sampled our chicken, fries, coleslaw, salad, biscuits. Coca-Cola, ginger ale, and orange soda were poured free like water. People touched the vinyl seats, the Formica tables, the dishwasher, the microwave, the cash register, the linoleum tile on the kitchen floor, and poked their heads into the freezer and the brand-new restrooms. They were impressed by the whole package, shipped directly from the U.S. A white-bearded official said, "We must learn from the Americans. See how they have managed to meet every need of their customers, taking care of not only what goes in but also what comes out. Everything was thought out beforehand." Some of them watched us frying chicken in the stainless-steel troughs, which were safe and clean, nothing like a soot-bottomed caldron or a noisy, unsteady wok. The vice mayor shook hands with every employee and told us to work hard and cooperatively with our American boss. The next day the city's newspaper, the *Muji Herald*, published a lengthy article about Cowboy Chicken, describing its appearance here as a significant breakthrough in the city's campaign to attract foreign investors.

During the first few weeks we had a lot of customers, especially young people, who, eager to taste something American, came in droves. We got so much business that the cooked-meat stands on the streets had to move farther and farther away from our restaurant. Sometimes when we passed those stands, their owners would spit on the ground and curse without looking at us, "Foreign lackeys!"

We'd cry back, "I eat Cowboy Chicken every day and gained lots of weight."

At first Mr. Shapiro worked hard, often staying around until we closed at ten-thirty. But as the business was flourishing, he hung back more and stayed in his office for hours on end, reading newspapers and sometimes chewing a skinny sausage wrapped in cellophane. He rested so well in the daytime and had so much energy to spare that he began to date the girls working for him. There were four of them, two full-timers and two part-timers, all around twenty, healthy and lively, though not dazzlingly pretty. Imagine, once a week, on Thursday night, a man of over fifty went out with a young girl who was happy to go anywhere he took her. This made us, the three men hired by him, feel useless, like a bunch of eunuchs, particularly myself, because I'd never had a girlfriend, though I was almost thirty. Most girls were nice to me, but for them I was merely a good fellow, deserving more pity than affection, as if my crippled foot made me less than a man. For me, Mr. Shapiro was just a dirty old man, but the girls here were no better, always ready to sell something—a smile, a few sweet words, and perhaps their flesh.

The day after Mr. Shapiro had taken Baisha out, I asked her about the date, curious to see what else besides money made this paunchy man so attractive to girls. What's more, I was eager to find out whether he had bedded them in his apartment after dinner. That was illegal. If he had done it, we'd have something on him and could turn him in when it was necessary. I asked Baisha casually, "How many rooms does he have?" My hands were busy pulling plates out of the dishwasher and piling them up on a table.

"How should I know?" she said, and gave me a suspicious stare. I must admit, she was smart and had a mind quick like a lizard.

"Didn't you spend some time with him yesterday evening?"

"Yes, we had dinner. That was all."

'Was it good?" I had heard he had taken the girls to Lucky House, a third-rate restaurant near the marketplace.

"So-so."

"What did you eat?"

"Fried noodles and sauteed beef tripe."

'Well, I wish somebody would give me a treat like that."

"What made you think it was his treat?"

"It wasn't?" I put the last plate on the pile.

"I paid for what I ate. I won't go out with him again. He's such a cheapskate."

"If he didn't mean to spend money, why did he invite you out?"

"He said this was the American way. He gave the waitress a big tip though, a ten, but the girl wouldn't take it."

"So afterward you just went home?"

"Yes. I thought he'd take me to the movies or a karaoke bar. He just picked up his big butt and said he had a good time. Before we parted on the street, he yawned and said he missed his wife and kids."

"That was strange."

Manyou, Jinglin, and I—the three male employees—talked among ourselves about Mr. Shapiro's way of taking the girls out. We couldn't see what he was up to. How could he have a good time just eating a meal with a girl? This puzzled us. We asked Peter whether all American men were so stingy, but he said that like us they would generally pay the bill in such a case. He explained, "Probably Mr. Shapiro wants to make it clear to the girls that this isn't a date but a working dinner."

Who would buy that? Why didn't he have a working dinner with one of us, the male employees? We guessed he might have used the girls, because if he had gone to a fancy place like the Four Seas Garden or North Star Palace, which had special menus for foreigners, he'd have had to pay at least five times more than a Chinese customer. We checked with the girls, and they admitted that Mr. Shapiro had asked them to order everything. So he had indeed paid the Chinese prices. No wonder he had a good time. What an old fox. Still, why wouldn't he take the girls to his apartment? Though none of them was a beauty, just the smell of the youthful flesh should have turned his old head, shouldn't it? Especially the two part-timers, the college students, who had fine figures and educated voices; they worked only twenty hours a week and wouldn't condescend to talk to us very often. Probably Mr. Shapiro was no good in bed, a true eunuch.

OUR BUSINESS DIDN'T BOOM FOR long. Several handcarts had appeared on Peace Avenue, selling spiced chicken on the roadside near our restaurant. They each carried a sign that declared, PATRIOTIC CHICKEN—CRISPY, TENDER, DELICIOUS, 30% CHEAPER THAN C. C.! Those were not false claims. Yet whenever we saw their signs, we couldn't help calling the vendors names. Most citizens here, especially old people, were accustomed to the price and taste of Patriotic Chicken, so they preferred it to ours. Some of them had tried our product, but they'd complain afterward, "What a sham! So expensive, this Cowboy thing isn't for a Chinese stomach." And they wouldn't come again. As a result, our steady clientele were mainly fashionable young people.

One day Mr. Shapiro came up with the idea of starting a buffet. We had never heard that word before. "What does it mean?" we asked.

Peter said, "You pay a small amount of money and eat all you can."

Good, a buffet would be great! We were all ears. Our boss suggested nineteen yuan and ninety-five fen as the price for the buffet, which should include every kind of Cowboy Chicken, mashed potatoes, fries, salad, and canned fruit. Why didn't he price it twenty yuan even? we wondered. That would sound more honest and also make it easier for us to handle the change. Peter explained that this was the American way of pricing a product. "You don't add the last straw to collapse the camel," he said. We couldn't understand the logic of a camel or a horse or an ox. Anyway, Mr. Shapiro fell in love with his idea, saying that even if it didn't fetch us enough customers, the buffet would help spread our name.

Peter wasn't enthusiastic about it, but we all said it was a brilliant idea and would definitely make us famous. Of course we knew it wouldn't work. We supported it because we wanted to eat Cowboy Chicken. Mr. Shapiro was such a skinflint that he would never give us a discount when we bought chicken for ourselves. He said the company's policy didn't allow any discount for its employees. On the other hand, our friends, when buying chicken here, often asked us to do them a favor—give them either some choice pieces or a discount—but we dared not break the rules for them. Now came an opportunity, so without delay we put out notices and spread the word about the buffet, which was to start the following week. For a whole weekend we biked around town in our free time to make sure the news would reach our relatives, friends, and whoever might benefit from it.

Two feet of snow fell on Sunday night, and traffic was paralyzed the next morning, but we all arrived at work on time. Mr. Shapiro was worried, fearing that the severe weather would keep people indoors. We assured him that they were not hibernating bears and would definitely show up. Still anxious, he stood outside the front door with the fur earflaps of his hat tied around his jaw, smoking and looking up and down the street at the people shoveling snow. Wisps of smoke and breath hung around his head. We all had on dogskin or quilted trousers in such weather, but he wore only woolen pajamas underneath jeans. It was glitteringly cold outside; the wind tossed the phone lines, which whistled like crazy.

With his protruding mouth pointed at Mr. Shapiro, Manyou said to us, "See how hard it is to be a boss in America. You have to worry about your business all the time."

"Boy, he's scared," I said.

"For once he's working," added Feilan, who, though a plump girl, had a pleasant apple face with two dimples on it. Unlike us, she hadn't gone to high school, because she had flunked two of the entrance exams.

We set the buffet stand in a corner and fried piles of chicken. Gradually people arrived. When about a dozen customers had sat down to their meals, Mr. Shapiro looked relieved, though he couldn't stop rubbing his cheeks and ears, which must have frozen numb. He retreated into his office for coffee, having no idea that this was just the first skirmish of a mighty battle. As the morning went by, more and more people came in, and we could hardly cook enough chicken and fries for them. The room grew noisy and crowded, undoubtedly reaching its maximum capacity, but still our boss was happy. Encouraged by the bustling scene, he even whistled in his office, where he, through bifocal lenses, was reading the *China Daily*.

My father and uncle were among the first dozen customers. Both could hardly walk when done with eating. After they left, my brother brought over six young men from his electricity station; they all had a soda or a beer in their pockets so that they wouldn't have to buy a drink. Without delay they began to attack the buffet; they ate as though this were their last supper on earth. I kept count of their accomplishment—on average they each finished at least a dozen pieces of chicken. Even when they were done and leaving, every one of them held a leg or a wing in his hand. Baisha's family had come too, including her father, uncles, and aunts. So had the folks of Manyou, Jinglin, and Feilan. The two part-timers had no family in town, but more than ten of their schoolmates turned up. In the back corner a table was occupied by five people, whose catlike faces showed that they belonged to Peter's clan. Among them was a young woman at least seven months pregnant; she was Peter's sister, and surely her unborn baby needed nutrition.

We all knew the buffet was headed for disaster, but we didn't care very much and just continued deep-frying chicken and refilling the salad and mashed-potato bowls. Once in a while we also went over to the buffet stand and picked a piece of chicken for ourselves, because today nobody could keep a record. At last we too could eat our fill. I liked the chicken better with soy sauce and slapped plenty on. The employees shared a bottle of soy sauce, which we kept under the counter.

By midday some people in the marketplace had heard of this rare bargain, and they came in, all eating like starved wolves. Most of them were from the countryside, in town selling and buying stuff; surely they had never dreamed that any restaurant would offer such an abundant meal.

Peter wasn't around most of the time. He had to be at the Tax Bureau in the morning, and in the afternoon he went to the bank to fetch our wages. When he returned at four o'clock, his face darkened at the amount of food consumed by the buffet. Twenty boxes of chicken and eighteen sacks of fries were gone— which should have lasted three days. He went to inform Mr. Shapiro, who came out of his office and looked disconcerted. Peter suggested we stop the buffet immediately. Our boss's face reddened, his Adam's apple going up and down as though he were guzzling something. He said, "Let's offer it a little while longer. We're not sure if we lost money or not."

We closed twenty minutes early that night in order to count the money. The result didn't surprise us: we lost seven hundred yuan, exclusive of our wages.

In spite of his misshapen face, Mr. Shapiro insisted on trying the buffet for another day. Perhaps he meant to show who was in command, reluctant to admit the buffet was a flop. This suited us fine, since not all of our people had come yet.

The next day Mr. Shapiro sat on a chair outside his office and watched the customers stuffing themselves. He looked like a giant bulldog, vigilant and sulky, now shaking his head, now smiling exaggeratedly. At times his face turned grim, his eyelids trembling a little. A few men from my father's office showed up, and two of them even attempted to chat with me in front of my boss. This scared me. I responded to their greetings and questions cursorily, for fear that Mr. Shapiro might detect my connection with them. Fortunately he didn't understand our language, so he noticed nothing.

After my father's colleagues left, a tall, thirtyish man in a buff corduroy jacket turned up. After paying for the buffet, he left his fur hat on a table, then walked across to the stand and filled a plate with drumsticks and breasts. As he was about to return to his seat, Mr. Shapiro stopped him and asked, 'Why did you come again?"

The man happened to know some English and said with a friendly grin, "First-time customer."

"You ate tons of chicken and mashed potatoes just now. How come you're hungry again so soon?"

"What's this about?" The man's face changed.

Peter came over, but he wasn't sure if the man had been here before. He turned to us and asked, "Is this his second time?"

Before we could answer, the man flared up, "This is my hundredth time. So what? I paid."

Manyou laughed and told Peter, "There was a fella here just now in the same kind of jacket, but that was a different man."

"That's true," I piped up. I knew the other man—he was an accountant in my father's bureau. This fellow fuming in front of us was a genuine stranger, with a beeper on his belt. He must be a cabdriver or an entrepreneur.

Peter apologized to the man, told him to go ahead and eat, then he explained the truth to Mr. Shapiro, who had become so edgy that some customers began to look identical to him. "How the hell could I tell the difference?" our boss said. "To me they all look alike—they're all real Chinese, with appetites like alligators." He laughed heartily, like a young boy.

Peter interpreted his words to us, and we all cracked up.

On the second day we lost about six hundred yuan, so that was the end of the buffet. Lucky for us, Mr. Shapiro didn't withhold our wages, which we all received the next day. This was the beauty of working for Cowboy Chicken—it was never late in paying us, unlike many Chinese companies, especially those owned by the state, which simply didn't have enough cash to pay employees their full wages. My mother often got only 60 percent of her salary from her weather station, which could not increase its clientele, or run a night school, or have any power over other companies. She'd sigh and say, "The longer I work, the more I lose."

At the sight of my monthly wages—468 yuan—my father became heartbroken. He'd had a drop too much that night, full of self-pity, and, waving a half-smoked cigarette, he said to me, "Hongwen, I've joined the Revolution for almost forty years, and I earn only three hundred yuan a month. But you just started working and you draw a larger salary. This makes me feel duped, duped by the Communist party I've served."

My youngest brother butted in. "It's never too late to quit, Dad."

"Shut up!" I snapped. He was such an idiot, he couldn't see the old man was really suffering. I said to my father, "You shouldn't think that way. True, you're not paid a lot, but your job is secure, like a rubber rice bowl that nobody can take away from you or smash—even a tank cannot crush it. Every day you just sit at your desk drinking tea and reading newspapers, or chatting away, and at the end of each month you take home a full salary. But I have to work my ass off for a capitalist who pays me by the hour."

"You make so much and always eat high-protein food. What else do you want?"

I didn't answer. In my heart I said, I want a job that pays a salary. I want to be like some people who go to their offices every morning for an eight-hour rest. My father kept on, "Cowboy Chicken is so delicious. If I could eat it and drink Coke every day, I'd have no need for socialism."

I wouldn't argue with him. He was beside himself that night. Indeed, I did often have some tidbits at the restaurant, mainly fries and biscuits. As a result, I seldom ate dinner when I came home, but mainly it was because I wanted to save food for my family. My father, of course, assumed I was stuffing myself with chicken every day.

After the disastrous buffet, Mr. Shapiro depended more on Peter, who in fact ran the place single-handedly. To be fair, Peter was an able man and had put his heart into the restaurant. He began to make a lot of connections in town and persuaded people to have business lunches at our place. This made a huge difference. Because their companies would foot the bill, the business people would order table loads of food to treat their guests to hearty American meals, and then they'd take the leftovers home for their families. By and by our restaurant gained a reputation in the business world, and we established a stable clientele. So once again Mr. Shapiro could stay in his office in the morning drinking coffee, reading magazines, and even listening to a tape to learn the ABCs of Chinese.

ONE AFTERNOON THE SECOND SON of the president of Muji Teachers College phoned Peter, saying he'd like to hold his wedding feast at our restaurant. I knew of this dandy, who had divorced his hard-working wife the year before; his current bride used to be a young widow who had given up her managerial position in a theater four years ago in order to go to Russia. Now they had decided to marry, and he wanted something exotic for their wedding dinner, so he picked Cowboy Chicken.

Uneasy about this request, Mr. Shapiro said to Peter, "We're just a fast-food place. We're not equipped to cater a wedding banquet."

"We must not miss this opportunity," said Peter. "A Chinese man would spend all his savings on his wedding." His owlish eyes glittered.

"Well, we'll have to serve alcoholic beverages, won't we? We have no license."

"Forget that. Nobody has ever heard of such a thing in China. Even a baby can drink alcohol here." Peter grew impatient.

Manyou, who could speak a few words of English, broke in. "Mr. Shapiro, Peter is right. Men of China use all moneys for wedding, big money." He seemed embarrassed by his accent and went back to biting his cuticles.

So our boss yielded. From the next day on, we began to prepare the place for the wedding feast. Mr. Shapiro called Cowboy Chicken's headquarters in Beijing to have some cheesecakes, ice cream, and Californian wines shipped to us by the express mail. Peter hired two temps and had the room decked out with colorful ribbons and strings of tiny light bulbs. Since it was already mid-December, he had a dwarf juniper and candlesticks set up in a corner. We even hung up a pair of large bunny lanterns at the front door, as the Year of Rabbit was almost here. Peter ordered us to wear clean uniforms for the occasion—red sweaters, black pants, and maroon aprons.

The wedding banquet took place on Thursday evening. It went smoothly, since most of the guests were from the college, urbane and sober-minded. The bride, a small woman in her mid-thirties, wore a sky-blue silk dress, her hair was permed, and her lips were rouged scarlet. She smiled without stopping. It was too bad that her parents hadn't given her beautiful eyes; she must have been altered by cosmetic surgery, which had produced her tight, thick double lids. Baisha said the woman owned two gift shops in Moscow. Small wonder she wore six fancy rings and a tiny wristwatch in the shape of a heart. With so many diamonds and so much gold on her fingers, she must be lazy, not doing any housework. From her manners we could tell she had seen the world. By comparison, her tall groom looked like a bumpkin despite his fancy outfit—a dark-blue western suit, a yellow tie studded with tiny magpies, and patent leather boots with brass buckles. He had a hoarse voice, often laughing with a bubbling sound in his throat. When he laughed, you could hardly see anything on his face except his mouth, which reminded me of a crocodile's. His gray-haired parents sat opposite him, quiet and reserved, both of them senior officials.

The man officiating at the banquet spoke briefly about the auspicious union of the couple. Next he praised the simple wedding ceremony, which had taken place two hours ago. After a round of applause, he turned to our boss and said, "We thank our American friend, Mr. Ken Shapiro, for providing us with such a clean, beautiful place and the delicious food. This is a perfect example of adapting foreign things to Chinese needs."

People clapped again. All our boss could say in Chinese was "Thank you." He looked a little shy, his cheeks pink and his hazel eyes gleaming happily.

As people were making the first toast, we began to serve chicken, every kind we had—crispy, spicy, barbecued, Cajun, and Cowboy original. An old woman opened a large paper napkin with a flowered pattern on it and studied it for a long time, as though it were a piece of needlework on lavender silk which she was reluctant to spoil. A bottle of champagne popped and scared the bridesmaid into screaming. Laughter followed.

"Boy, this is hot!" the groom said, chewing a Cajun wing and exhaling noisily.

They all enjoyed the chicken, but except for the champagne, they didn't like the American wines, which were too mild for them. Most women wouldn't drink wine; they wanted beer, Coca-Cola, and other soft drinks. Fortunately Peter had stocked some Green Bamboo Leaves and Tsingtao beer, which we brought out without delay. We had also heated a basin of water, in which we warmed the liquor for them. Mr. Shapiro raved to his manager, "Fabulous job, Peter!" He went on flashing a broad smile at everyone, revealing his white teeth. He even patted some of us on the back.

I liked the red wine, and whenever I could, I'd sip some from a glass I had poured myself. But I dared not drink too much for fear my face might change color. When the guests were done with the chicken, fries, and salad, we began to serve cheesecake and ice cream, which turned out to be a big success. Everybody loved the dessert. An old scholarly-looking man said loudly, "Ah, here's the best American stuff!" His tone of voice suggested he had been to the U.S. He forked a chunk of cheesecake into his mouth and smacked his thin lips. He was among the few who could use a fork skillfully; most of them ate with chopsticks and spoons.

That was the first time we offered cheesecake and ice cream, so all of us—the employees—would take a bite whenever we could. Before that day I had never heard of cheesecake, which I loved so much I ate two wedges. I hid my glass and plate in a cabinet so that our boss couldn't see them. As long as we did the work well, Peter would shut his eyes to our eating and drinking.

For me the best part of this wedding feast was that it was subdued, peaceful, and short, lasting only two hours, perhaps because both the bride and the groom had been married before. It differed from a standard wedding banquet, which is always raucous and messy, drags on for seven or eight hours, and often gets out of hand, since quarrels and fights are commonplace once enough alcohol is consumed. None of these educated men and women drank to excess. The only loudmouth was the bridegroom, who looked slightly retarded. I couldn't help wondering how come that wealthy lady would marry such a heartless ass, who had abandoned his two small daughters. Probably because his parents had power, or maybe he was just good at tricking women. He must have wanted to live in Moscow for a while and have another baby, hopefully a boy. Feilan shook her head, saying about him, "Disgusting!"

When the feast was over, both Mr. Shapiro and Peter were excited, their faces flushed. They knew we had just opened a new page in Cowboy Chicken's history; our boss said he was going to report our success to the headquarters in Dallas. We were happy too, though sleepy and tired. If business was better, we might get a bigger raise the next summer, Mr. Shapiro had told us.

That night I didn't sleep well and had to go to the bathroom continually. I figured my stomach wasn't used to American food yet. I had eaten fries and biscuits every day but had never taken in ice cream, cheesecake, red wine, and champagne. Without doubt my stomach couldn't digest so much rich stuff all at once. I was so weakened that I wondered if I should stay home the next morning.

Not wanting to dampen our spirit of success, I hauled myself to the restaurant at nine o'clock, half an hour late. As we were cutting vegetables and coating chicken with spiced flour, I asked my fellow workers whether they had slept well the night before.

"What do you mean?" Baisha's small eyes stared at me like a pair of tiny daggers.

"I had diarrhea."

"That's because you stole too much food, and it serves you right," she said with a straight face, which was slightly swollen with pimples.

"So you didn't have any problem?"

"What makes you think I have the same kind of bowels as you?"

Manyou said he had slept like a corpse, perhaps having drunk too much champagne. To my satisfaction, both Jinglin and Feilan admitted they too had suffered from diarrhea. Feilan said, "I thought I was going to die last night. My mother made me drink two kettles of hot water. Otherwise I'd sure be dehydrated today." She held her sides with both hands as if about to run for the ladies' room.

Jinglin added, "I thought I was going to poop my guts out." Indeed, his chubby face looked smaller than yesterday.

As we were talking, the phone rang. Peter answered it. He sounded nervous, and his face turned bloodless and tiny beads of sweat were oozing out on his stubby nose. The caller was a woman complaining about the previous evening's food. She claimed she had been poisoned. Peter apologized and assured her that we had been very careful about food hygiene, but he would investigate the matter thoroughly.

The instant he put down the phone, another call came in. Then another. From ten o'clock on, every few minutes the phone would ring. People were lodging the same kind of complaint against our restaurant. Mr. Shapiro was shaken, saying, "Jesus, they're going to sue us!"

What did this mean? we asked him, unsure how suing us could do the complainers any good. He said the company might have to pay them a lot of money. "In America that's a way to make a living for some people," he told us. So we worried too.

At noon the college called to officially inform Peter that about a third of the wedding guests had suffered from food poisoning and that more than a dozen faculty members were unable to teach that day. The bridegroom's mother was still in Central Hospital, taking an intravenous drip. The caller suspected the food must have been unclean or past its expiration dates, or perhaps the ice cream had been too cold. Mr. Shapiro paced back and forth like an ant in a heated pan, while Peter remained quiet, his thick eyebrows knitted together.

"I told you we couldn't handle a wedding banquet," our boss said with his nostrils expanding.

Peter muttered, "It must've been the cheesecake and the ice cream that upset their stomachs. I'm positive our food was clean and fresh."

"Maybe I shouldn't have gone the extra mile to get the stuff from Beijing. Now what should we do?"

"Don't worry. I'll explain to them."

From then on, whenever a complainer called, Peter would answer personally. He said that our food had been absolutely fresh and clean but that some Chinese stomachs couldn't tolerate dairy products. That was why more than two thirds of the previous night's diners had not felt anything unusual.

His theory of Chinese stomachs was sheer nonsense. We had all drunk milk before and had never been poisoned like this. Three days later, a twelve-hundred-word article appeared in the *Muji Herald*. Peter was its author. He wrote that there was this substance called lactose, to which many Chinese stomachs were allergic because our traditional diet included very little dairy food. He even quoted from a scientific journal to prove that the Chinese had different stomachs from the westerners'. He urged people to make sure they could endure lactose before they ate our dairy items. From now on, he declared, our restaurant would continue to offer ice cream, but also a variety of nonmilk desserts, like Jell-O, apple pie, pecan pie, and canned fruit.

I was unhappy about the article, because I had thought the company might compensate us for the suffering we'd gone through. Even a couple of yuan would help. Now Peter had blown that possibility. When I expressed my dissatisfaction to my fellow workers, Feilan said to me, "You're small-minded like a housewife, Hongwen. As long as this place does well, we'll make more money."

Bitch! I cursed to myself. But I gave some thought to what she said, and she did have a point. The restaurant had almost become our work unit now; we'd all suffer if it lost money. Besides, to file for compensation, I'd first have to admit I had pilfered the ice cream and cheesecake. That would amount to asking for a fine and ridicule.

Soon Peter had Cowboy Chicken completely in his clutches. This was fine with us. We all agreed he could take care of the restaurant better than Mr. Shapiro. We nicknamed him Number Two Boss. Since the publication of his article, which had quieted all complaints, more and more people ate here, and some came especially for our desserts. Young women were partial to Jell-O and canned fruit, while children loved our ice cream. Again we began to cater for wedding banquets, which gradually became an important source of our profits. From time to time people called and asked whether we'd serve a "white feast"—the dinner after a funeral. We wouldn't, because it was much plainer than a wedding banquet and there wasn't much money to be made. Besides, it might bring bad luck.

When the snow and ice had melted away from the streets and branches began sprouting yellowish buds, Mr. Shapiro stopped going out with the girls as often as before. By now most restaurants in town treated him as a regular customer, charging him the Chinese prices. One day Juju, the younger part-timer, said our boss had gotten fresh with her the previous evening when he was tipsy at Eight Deities Garden. He had grasped her wrist and called her "honey." She declared she wouldn't go out with him anymore. We told the girls that if he did anything like that again, they should report him to the police or sue him.

In late April, Mr. Shapiro went back to Texas for a week to attend his stepdaughter's wedding. After he returned, he stopped dating the girls altogether. Perhaps he was scared. He was wise to stop, because he couldn't possibly contain himself all the time. If he did something indecent to one of the girls again and she reported him to the authorities, he would find himself in trouble, at least be fined. Another reason for the change might be that by now he had befriended an American woman named Susanna, from Raleigh, North Carolina, who was teaching English at Muji Teachers College. This black woman was truly amazing, in her early thirties, five foot ten, with long muscular limbs and a behind like a small caldron. She had bobbed hair, and most of the time wore jeans and earrings the size of bracelets. We often speculated about those gorgeous hoop earrings. Were they made of fourteen-carat gold? Or eighteen-carat? Or twenty-carat? At any rate, they must have been worth a fortune. Later, in the midsummer, she took part in our city's marathon and almost beat the professional runners. She did, however, win the Friendship Cup, which resembled a small brass bucket. She was also a wonderful singer, with a manly voice. Every week she brought four or five students over to teach them how to eat American food with forks and knives. When they were here, they often sang American songs she had taught them, such as "Pretty Paper," "Winter Wonderland," and "Silent Night, Holy Night." Their singing would attract some pedestrians, which was good for business, so we were pleased to have her here. Mr. Shapiro gave them a twenty-percent discount, which outraged us. We wondered why he kept a double standard. We had a company policy against discounts, but it must apply only to Chinese employees. Still, we all agreed Susanna was a good woman. Unlike other customers, she gave us tips; also, she paid for her students' meals.

One afternoon in late May, Susanna and four students were eating here. In came a monkeylike man who had half-gray hair and flat cheeks. With a twitching face he went up to Peter, his fist clutching a ball of paper. He announced in a squeaky voice, "I'm going to sue your company for ten thousand yuan."

This was the first time I ever heard a Chinese say he would sue somebody for money. We gathered around him as he unfolded the paper ball to display a fat greenhead. "I found this fly in the chicken I bought here," he said firmly, his right hand massaging his side.

"When did you buy the chicken?" Peter asked.

"Last week."

"Show me the receipt."

The man took a slip of paper out of his trouser pocket and handed it to Peter.

About twenty people formed a half-circle to watch. As the man and Peter were arguing, Mr. Shapiro and Susanna stepped out of his office. Seeing the two Americans, the man wailed at Peter, "Don't dodge your responsibility. I've hated flies all my life. At the sight of this one I puked, then dropped to the floor and fainted. I thought I'd recover soon. No, the next evening I threw up again and again. That gave me a head-splitting migraine and a stomach disorder. My ears are still ringing inside, and I've lost my appetite completely. Since last Wednesday I haven't gone to work and have suffered from insomnia every night." He turned to the spectators. "Comrades, I'm a true victim of this capitalist Cowboy Chicken. See how skinny I am."

"Like a starved cock," I said. People laughed.

"Stop blustering," Peter said to him. "Show us your medical records."

"I have them in the hospital. If you don't pay me the damages, I'll come again and again and again until I'm fully compensated."

We were all angry. Feilan pointed at the man's sunken mouth and said, "Shameless! You're not Chinese."

Baisha said, "Ten thousand yuan for a fly? How could you dream of that? Even your life isn't worth that much."

When a student had interpreted the man's accusation to Mr. Shapiro and Susanna, our boss turned pale. He moved closer and managed a smile, saying, "Sir, if you have concrete evidence, we'll be willing to consider your demand."

The student interpreted those words to the man, on whose face a vile smile appeared. We were angry at Mr. Shapiro, who again was acting like a number one Buddha. If you run into an evil man, you have to adopt uncivil measures. Our boss's hypocrisy would only indulge this crook.

"Excuse me," Manyou cried, and arrived with a bowl of warm water. He put it on the counter and said to the man, "I'm going to give your fly a hot bath, to see if it's from our place." He picked up the insect with a pair of chopsticks and dropped it into the bowl. We were all puzzled.

A few seconds later, Manyou announced, "This fly is not from Cowboy Chicken, because, see, there isn't any oil on the water. You all know we sell only fried chicken."

Some spectators booed the man, but he wouldn't give way. He fished out the fly with his hand and wrapped it up, saying, "I'm going to take you to court no matter what. If you don't offer a settlement, there'll be no end of this."

With a false smile Jinglin said to him, "Uncle, we're one family and shouldn't be so mean to each other. Let's find a quiet place to talk this out, all right? We can't negotiate in front of such a crowd."

The man looked puzzled, flapping his round eyes. Jinglin hooked his heavy arm around the man's neck while his eyes signaled at me. Reluctantly the crook moved away with him.

I followed them out the front door. It was slightly chilly outside, and the street was noisy with bicycle bells, vendors' cries, and automobile horns. A few neon lights flickered in the north. After about fifty paces, we turned into a small alley and then stopped. Jinglin smiled again, revealing his rotten teeth, and he took out a small pocketknife and a ten-yuan note. He opened the knife and said to the man, "I can pay you the damages now. You have a choice between these two."

"Don't make fun of me! I asked for ten thousand."

"Then I'll let you taste this knife."

The man wasn't frightened by the two-inch blade. He grinned and asked, "Brothers, why help the foreign devils?"

"Because Cowboy Chicken is our company, and our livelihood depends on it," I answered.

Jinglin said to him, "You're the scum of the Chinese! Come on, choose one."

The man didn't lift his hand. Jinglin said again, "I know what you're thinking. I can't stab you with such a small thing, eh? Tell you what—I know your grandson who goes to the Second Elementary School, and I can catch him and cut off his little pecker with this knife. Then your family line will be gone. I mean it. Now, pick one."

The crook was flabbergasted, looking at me and then at Jinglin, whose fat face became as hard as though made of copper sheet. With a trembling hand he took the money and mumbled, "Foreign dogs." He turned and hurried away. In no time he disappeared in a swarm of pedestrians.

We both laughed and walked back to the restaurant. Across the street, three disheveled Russian beggars were playing the violin and the bandora. Unlike most Chinese beggars, who would cry woefully and accost people, those foreign musicians were reserved, with just a porkpie hat on the ground to collect money, as though they didn't care whether you gave or not.

We didn't tell our boss what we had done; we just said the man was satisfied with a ten-yuan note and wouldn't come again. Susanna and her students applauded when they heard the news. Peter reimbursed Jinglin the money on the spot. Still, Mr. Shapiro looked suspicious and was afraid the man would return.

"He won't trouble us anymore," Peter said, smiling.

"Why are you so sure?" asked our boss.

"I have this." With two fingers Peter pulled the crook's receipt out of his breast pocket.

We all laughed. Actually, even with the receipt in hand, that old bastard wouldn't have dared come again. He wasn't afraid of Jinglin exactly but feared his four brothers, who were all stevedores on the riverbank, good at fighting and never hesitant to use a club or a dagger or a crowbar. That was why Jinglin, unlike the rest of us, could get rid of him without fear of retaliation.

Later we revealed to Peter what we had done in the alley. He smiled and promised he would not breathe a word to Mr. Shapiro.

As our business became stable, Peter grew into a local power of sorts. For months he had been building a house in the countryside. We wondered why he wanted his home to be four miles away from town. It would be costly to ride a motorcycle back and forth every day. One Sunday morning, Baisha, Feilan, Manyou, Jinglin, and I set out to see Peter's new home. We pedaled abreast on the wide embankment along the Songhua River, humming movie songs and cracking jokes. Birds were crying furiously in the willow copses below the embankment, while on a distant jetty a team of men sang a work song as they unloaded timber from a barge. Their voices were faltering but explosive. It hadn't rained for weeks, so the river was rather narrow, displaying a broad whitish beach. A few boys fishing there lay on their backs; around them stood some short bamboo poles planted deep in the sand. When a fish bit, a brass bell on one of the poles would jingle. On the other shore, toward the horizon, four or five windmills were turning, full like sails; above them the gray clouds floated lazily by, like a school of turtles.

We knew Peter had a few American dollars in the bank, but we were unsure how rich he really was. His house, though unfinished, staggered us. It was a three-story building with a garage in its back; it sat in the middle of two acres of sloping land, facing a gentle bend in the river and commanding a panorama that included two islands and the vast landscape on the other shore.

Peter wasn't around. Six or seven workers were busy, rhythmically hammering something inside the house. We asked an older man, who looked like a supervisor, how much the house would cost.

"At least a quarter of a million yuan," he said.

"So expensive?" Manyou gasped, his large lashless eyes blazing.

"You know what? It could be even more than that. We've never seen a home like this before."

"What kind of house is this?" asked Feilan.

"It's called Victorian. Mr. and Mrs. Jiao designed it themselves. It has two marble fireplaces, both imported from Hong Kong."

"Damn! Where did he get so much money?" Baisha said, and kicked a beer bottle with her white leather sandal.

We were all pondering the same question, and it weighed down our hearts like a millstone. But we didn't stay long, fearing that Peter might turn up. On the way back we spoke little to one another, unable to take our minds off Peter's house. Obviously he made much more than we did, or he wouldn't have had the money for such a mansion, which was larger even than the mayor's. Before setting out, we had planned to have brunch together at a beer house, but now none of us had an appetite anymore. We parted company the moment we turned away from the quay.

After that trip, I noticed that my fellow workers often looked suspiciously at Peter, as though he were a hybrid creature. Their eyes showed envy and anger. They began learning English more diligently. Manyou attended the night college, working with a textbook called *English for Today*, while Baisha and Feilan got up early in the morning to listen to the study program on the radio and memorize English words and expressions. Jinglin wanted to learn genuine American English, which he said was more natural, so he was studying *English 900*. I was also learning English, but I was older than the others and didn't have a strong memory, so I made little progress.

At work, they appeared friendlier to Mr. Shapiro and often poured coffee for him. Once Baisha even let him try some scallion pancake from her own lunch.

One morning, when we were not busy, I overheard Baisha talking with Mr. Shapiro in English. "Have you a house in U.S.A.?" she asked.

"Yes, I have a brick ranch, not very big." He had a cold; his voice was nasal and thick.

"How many childs in house?"

"You mean children?"

"Yes."

"I have two, and my wife has three."

"Ah, you have five jildren?"

"You can say that."

Mr. Shapiro turned away to fill out a form with a ballpoint pen, while Baisha's narrow eyes squinted at his heavy cheek and then at the black hair on his wrist. She was such a flirt, but I was impressed. She was brave enough to converse with our boss in English!—whereas I could never open my mouth in front of him.

Because we had seen Peter's mansion, our eyes were all focused on him. We were eager to find fault with him and ready to start a quarrel. But he was a careful man, knowing how to cope with us and how to maintain our boss's trust. He avoided arguing with us. If we didn't listen to him, he'd go into Mr. Shapiro's office and stay in there for a good while. That unnerved us, because we couldn't tell if he was reporting us to the boss. So we dared not be too disobedient. Every night Peter was the last to leave. He'd close the shutters, lock the cash register, wrap up the unsold chicken, tie the package to the back of his Honda motorcycle, and ride away.

Ever since the beginning, the daily leftovers had been a bone of contention between Mr. Shapiro and us. We had asked him many times to let us have the unsold chicken at the end of the day, but he refused, saying the company's policy forbade its employees to have leftovers. We even offered to buy them at half price, but he still wouldn't let us. He assigned Peter alone to take care of the leftovers.

It occurred to us that Peter must have taken the leftovers home for the construction workers. He had to feed them well, or else they might jerry-build his mansion. Damn him, he not only earned more but also got all the perks. The more we thought about this, the more resentful we became. So one night, after he closed up the place and rode away, we came out of the nearby alley and pedaled behind him. Manyou was at the night college, and Jinglin had to look after his younger brother in the hospital, who had just been operated on for a hernia, so they couldn't join us. Only Feilan, Baisha, and I followed Peter. He was going much faster than we were, but we knew where he was headed, so we bicycled without hurry, chatting and laughing now and then.

In the distance Peter's motorcycle was flitting along the embankment like a will-o'-the-wisp. The night was cool, and a few men were chanting folksongs from their boat anchored in the river. We were eager to prove that Peter had shipped the leftovers home, so that we could report him to Mr. Shapiro the next morning.

For a long while the light of Peter's motorcycle disappeared. We stopped, at a loss. Apparently he had turned off the embankment, but where had he gone? Should we continue to ride toward his home, or should we mark time?

As we were discussing what to do, a burst of flames emerged in the north, almost two hundred yards away, at the waterside. We went down the embankment, locked our bicycles in a willow copse, and walked stealthily toward the fire.

When we approached it, we saw Peter stirring something in the fire with a trimmed branch. It was a pile of chicken, about twenty pieces. The air smelled of gasoline and burned meat. Beyond him, the waves were lapping the sand softly. The water was sprinkled with stars, rippling with the fishy breeze. On the other shore everything was buried in darkness except for three or four clusters of lights, almost indistinguishable from the stars in the cloudless sky. Speechlessly we watched. If there had been another man with us, we might have sprung out and beaten Peter up. But I was no fighter, so we couldn't do anything, merely crouch in the tall grass and curse him under our breath.

"If only we had a gun!" Baisha whispered through her teeth.

Peter was in a happy mood. With a ruddy face he began singing a song, which must have been made up by some overseas Chinese:

> I'm not so carefree as you think,
> My feelings never unclear.
> If you can't see through me,
> That's because again you waste
> Your love on a worthless man.
>
> Oh my heart won't wander alone.
> Let me take you along.
> Together we'll reach a quiet place
> Where you can realize
> Your sweetest dream . . .

For some reason I was touched by the song. Never had I known he had such a gorgeous baritone voice, which seemed to come a long way from the other shore. A flock of ducks quacked in the darkness, their wings splashing the water lustily. A loon let out a cry like a wild laugh. Then all the waterfowl turned quiet, and Peter's voice alone was vibrating the tangy air chilled by the night.

Feilan whispered, "What a good time he's having here, that asshole."

"He must miss his American sweetheart," Baisha said.

Feilan shook her chin. "Makes no sense. He's not the romantic type."

"Doesn't he often say American girls are better than Chinese girls?"

"Shh—" I stopped them.

When the fire almost went out, Peter unzipped his fly, pulled out his dick, and peed on the embers, which hissed and sent up a puff of steam. The arc of his urine gleamed for a few seconds, then disappeared. He yawned, and with his feet pushed some sand over the ashes.

"Gross!" said Feilan.

Peter leaped on his motorcycle and dashed away, the exhaust pipe hiccuping explosively. I realized he didn't mind riding four miles to work because he could use some of the gasoline provided by our boss for burning the leftovers with.

"If only I could scratch and bite that bastard!" Feilan said breathlessly.

"Depends on what part of him," I said.

Baisha laughed. Feilan scowled at me, saying, "You have a dirty mind."

The next day we told all the other workers about our discovery. Everyone was infuriated, and even the two part-timers couldn't stop cursing capitalism. There were children begging on the streets, there were homeless people at the train station and the ferry house, there were hungry cats and dogs everywhere—why did Mr. Shapiro want Peter to burn good meat like garbage? Manyou said he had read in a restricted journal several years ago that some American capitalists would dump milk into a river instead of giving it to the poor. But that was in the U.S.; here in China, this kind of wasteful practice had to be condemned. I told my fellow workers that I was going to write an article to expose Ken Shapiro and Peter Jiao.

In the afternoon we confronted Peter. "Why do you burn the leftovers every night?" Manyou asked, looking him right in the eye.

Peter was taken aback, then replied, "It's my job."

"That's despicable," I snapped. "You not only burned them but also peed on them." My stomach suddenly rumbled.

Feilan giggled. Baisha pointed at Peter's nose and said sharply, "Peter Jiao, remember you're a Chinese. There are people here who don't have enough corn flour to eat while you burn chicken every night. You've forgotten your ancestors and who you are."

Peter looked rattled, protesting, "I don't feel comfortable about it either. But somebody has to do it. I'm paid to burn them, just like you're paid to fry them."

"Don't give me that crap!" Jinglin cut in. "You're a capitalist's henchman."

Peter retorted, "So are you. You work for this capitalist company too."

"Hold on," Manyou said. "We just want to reason you out of this shameful thing. Why do you waste chicken that way? Why not give the leftovers to the poor?"

"You think I enjoy burning them? If I gave them away, I'd be fired. This is the American way of doing business."

"But you're a Chinese running a restaurant in a socialist country," said Jinglin.

As we were wrangling, Mr. Shapiro came out of his office with coffee stains around his lips. Peter explained to him what we were quarreling about. Our boss waved his hand to dismiss us, as though this were such a trifle that it didn't deserve his attention. He just said, "It's company policy; we can't do anything about it. If you're really concerned about the waste, don't fry too many pieces, and sell everything you've fried." He walked to the front door to have a smoke outside.

Peter said, "That's true. He can't change a thing. From now on we'd better not fry more than we can sell."

I was still angry and said, "I'm going to write to the *Herald* to expose this policy."

"There's no need to be so emotional, Hongwen," Peter said with a complacent smile, raising his squarish chin a little. "There have been several articles on this subject. For example, the *Beijing Evening News* carried a long piece last week about our company. The author praised our policy on leftovers and believed it would reduce waste eventually. He said we Chinese should adopt the American way of running business. In any case, this policy cannot be exposed anymore. People already know about it."

That silenced us all. Originally we had planned that if Mr. Shapiro continued to have the leftovers burned, we'd go on strike for a few days. Peter's words deflated us all at once.

Still, Jinglin wouldn't let Peter off so easily. When it turned dark, he pressed a thumbtack into the rear tire of the Honda motorcycle parked in the backyard. Peter called home, and his wife came driving a white Toyota truck to carry back the motorcycle and him. This dealt us another blow, because we hadn't expected he owned a brand-new pickup as well. No one else in our city could afford such a vehicle. We asked ourselves, "Heavens, how much money does Peter actually have?"

We were all anxious to find that out. On payday, somehow Mr. Shapiro mixed Peter's wages in with ours. We each received an envelope stuffed with a bundle of cash, but Peter's was always empty. JuJu said Peter got only a slip of paper in his envelope, which was called a check. He could exchange that thing for money at the bank, where he had an account as if he were a company himself. In Juju's words, "Every month our boss just writes Peter lots of money." That fascinated us. How much did he get from Mr. Shapiro? This question had remained an enigma ever since we began working here. Now his pay was in our hands, and at last we could find out.

Manyou steamed the envelope over a cup of hot tea and opened it without difficulty. The figure on the check astounded us: $1,683.75. For a good moment nobody said a word, never having imagined that Peter received an American salary, being paid dollars instead of yuan. That's to say, he made twenty times more than each of us! No wonder he worked so hard, taking care of Cowboy Chicken as if it were his home, and tried every trick to please Mr. Shapiro.

That night after work we gathered at Baisha's home for an emergency meeting. Her mother was a doctor, so their apartment was spacious and Baisha had her own room. She took out a packet of spiced pumpkin seeds, and we began chatting while drinking tea.

"God, just think of the money Peter's raking in," Jinglin said, and pulled his brushy hair, sighing continually. He looked wretched, as if ten years older than the day before. His chubby face had lost its luster.

I said, "Peter can afford to eat at the best restaurants every day. There's no way he can spend that amount of money."

Feilan spat the shells of a pumpkin seed into her fist, her eyes turning triangular. She said, "We must protest. This isn't fair."

Baisha agreed with a sigh. "Now I know what exploitation feels like."

"Peter has done a lot for Cowboy Chicken," Manyou said, "but there's no justification for him to make that much." He seemed still in a daze and kept stroking his receding chin.

"We must figure out a countermeasure," said Jinglin.

I suggested, "Perhaps we should talk with our boss."

"You think he'll pay each of us a thousand dollars?" Baisha asked scornfully.

"Of course not," I said.

"Then what's the point of talking with him?"

Manyou put in, "I don't know. What do you think we should do, Baisha?"

I was surprised that he could be at a loss too, because he was known as a man of strategies. Baisha answered, "I think we must unite as one and demand that our boss fire Peter."

Silence fell in the room, in which stood a double bed covered with a pink sheet. A folded floral blanket sat atop a pair of eiderdown pillows stacked together. I wondered why Baisha needed such a large bed for herself. She must have slept with her boyfriends on it quite often. She was such a slut.

"That's a good idea. I say let's get rid of Peter," Manyou said, nodding at her admiringly.

Still perplexed, I asked, "Suppose Mr. Shapiro does fire him, then what?"

"One of us may take Peter's job," said Manyou.

Feilan picked up, "Are you sure he'll fire Peter?"

To our surprise, Baisha said, "Of course he will. It'll save him fifteen hundred dollars a month."

"I don't get it," said Jinglin. "What's the purpose of doing this? Even if he fires Peter, he won't pay us more, will he?"

"Then he'll have to depend on us and may give us each a raise," answered Baisha.

Unconvinced, I said, "What if the new manager gets paid more and just ignores the rest of us?"

Manyou frowned, because he knew that only Baisha and he could be candidates for that position, which required the ability to use English. Feilan, Jinglin, and I couldn't speak a complete sentence yet.

"Let's draw up a contract," Feilan said. "Whoever becomes the new manager must share his wages with the rest of us."

We all supported the idea and signed a brief statement, which said that if the new manager didn't share his earnings with the rest of us, he'd be childless and we could get our revenge in any way we chose. After that, Baisha went about composing a letter addressed to Mr. Shapiro. She didn't know enough English words for the letter, so she fetched a bulky dictionary from her parents' study. She began to write with a felt-tip pen, now and again consulting the dictionary. She was sleepy and yawned incessantly, covering her mouth with her left palm and disclosing her hairy armpit. Meanwhile, we cracked pumpkin seeds and chatted away.

The letter was short, but it seemed to the point. Even Manyou said it was good after he looked it over. It stated:

Our Respected Mr. Kenneth Shapiro:

We are writing to demand you to fire Peter Jiao immediately. This is our united will. You must respect our will. We do not want a leader like him. That is all.

Sincerely,
Your Employees

We all signed our names and felt that at last we had stood up to that capitalist. Since I'd pass our restaurant on my way home, I took charge of delivering the letter. Before we left, Baisha brought out a bottle of apricot wine, and together we drank to our solidarity.

I dropped the letter into the slot in the front door of Cowboy Chicken. After I got home, for a while I was lightheaded and kept imagining the shock on Mr. Shapiro's pudgy face. I also thought of Peter, who, without his current job, might never be able to complete his outrageous mansion. But soon I began to worry, fearing that Baisha might become the new manager. Compared with Peter, she had a volatile temper and was more selfish. Besides, she couldn't possibly maintain the connections and clientele Peter had carefully built up, not to mention develop the business. Manyou wasn't as capable as Peter either. Sometimes he could be very clever about trivial matters, but he had no depth. He didn't look steady and couldn't inspire trust in customers. To be fair, Peter seemed indispensable to Cowboy Chicken. I wouldn't have minded if Mr. Shapiro had paid him five times more than me.

We all showed up at work at eight-thirty the next morning. To our surprise, neither Mr. Shapiro nor Peter betrayed any anxiety. They acted as if nothing had happened, and treated us the same as the day before. We were baffled, wondering what they had planned for us. Peter seemed to avoid us, but he was polite and quiet. Apparently he had read the letter.

We expected that our boss would talk with us one by one. Even if he wouldn't fire Peter, he might make some concessions. But for a whole morning he stayed in his office, as if he had forgotten us altogether. He was reading a book about the Jews who had lived in China hundreds of years ago. His calm appearance agitated us. If only we could have had an inkling of what he had up his sleeve.

When the day was at last over, we met briefly at a street corner. We were confused, but all agreed to wait and see. Feilan sighed and said, "I feel like we're in a tug-of-war."

"Yes, we're in a mental war, so we must be tough-minded and patient," Manyou told us.

I went home with a stomachache. Again my father was drunk that night, singing revolutionary songs and saying I was lucky to have my fill of American chicken every day. I couldn't get to sleep until the wee hours.

The next day turned out the same. Peter assigned each of us some work, and Mr. Shapiro still wouldn't say an unnecessary word to us. I couldn't help picturing his office as a giant snail shell into which he had shut himself. What should we do? They must have devised a trap or something for us. What was it? We had to do something, not just wait like this, or they would undo us one by one.

That night we gathered at Baisha's home again. After a lengthy discussion, we agreed to go on strike. Baisha wrote a note, which read:

Mr. Shapiro:
Because you do not consider our demand, we decide to strike at Cowboy Chicken. Begin tomorrow.

We didn't sign our names this time, since he knew who we were and what we were referring to. I was unsure of the phrase "strike at Cowboy Chicken," but I didn't say anything, guessing that probably she just meant we'd leave the place unmanned. Again I delivered the letter. None of us went to work the next morning. We wanted the restaurant to lose some business and our boss to worry a little so that he'd be willing to cooperate with his workers. But we had agreed to meet at one o'clock in front of Everyday Hardware, near Cowboy Chicken; then together we'd go to our workplace and start to negotiate with Mr. Shapiro. In other words, we planned to strike only for half a day.

After lunch we all arrived at the hardware store. To our astonishment, a squad of police was standing in front of Cowboy Chicken as if a fire or a riot had broken out. They wouldn't allow people to enter the restaurant unless they searched them. What was going on? Why had Mr. Shapiro called in the police? We were puzzled. Together we walked over as if we had just returned from a lunch break. The front of the restaurant was cordoned off, and three police were stationed at the door. A tall policeman stretched out his arm to stop us. Baisha asked loudly, "Hey, Big Wan, you don't remember me?" She was all smiles.

"Yes, I saw you," Wan said with a grin.

'We all work here. Let us go in, all right? We have tons of work to do."

"We have to search you before letting you in."

"I've nothing on me. How do you search?" She spread her arms, then lifted her long skirt a little with one hand, to show she didn't even have a pocket.

"Stand still, all of you," said Wan. A policewoman waved a black wand over Baisha, a gadget like a miniature badminton racket without strings.

"Is this a mine detector or something?" Jinglin asked the policewoman.

"A metal detector," she said.

"What's going on here?" Baisha asked Wan.

"Someone threatened to blow this place up—"

We were all horrified by that, hoping it had nothing to do with us.

The police let us in. The moment we entered, we saw an old couple standing behind the counter taking care of orders. Damn it, Peter had brought his parents in to work! How come he wasn't afraid a bomb might blow them to pieces? In a corner, Susanna and two student-looking girls were wiping tables and placing silver. They were humming 'We Shall Overcome,' but stopped at the sight of us. In the kitchen the two part-timers were frying chicken. Dumbfounded, we didn't know how to respond to this scene.

Mr. Shapiro came over. He looked furious, his face almost purple. He said to us, his spit flying about, "You think you can frighten me into obeying you? Let me tell you, you are all terminated!"

I didn't know what his last word meant, though I was sure it had a negative meaning. Manyou seemed to understand, his lips twitching as if he were about to cry. He gulped and couldn't say a word.

Peter said to us, 'We can't use you anymore. You're fired."

"You can't do this to us," Baisha said to Mr. Shapiro, and stepped forward. "We are founders of this place."

Mr. Shapiro laughed. "What are you talking about? How much stock do you have in this company?"

What did he mean? We looked at one another, unable to fathom his meaning. He said, "Go home; don't come anymore. You'll receive this month's pay by mail." He turned and walked off to the men's room, shaking his head and muttering, "I don't want any terrorists here."

Peter smiled at us with contempt. "Well, the earth won't stop spinning without the five of you."

I felt the room swaying like a lumbering bus. I never thought I could be fired so easily: Mr. Shapiro just said a word and my job was no more. The previous fall I had quit my position in a coal yard in order to work here. Now I was a total loser, and people would laugh at me.

The five of us were terribly distressed. Before we parted company on the street, I asked Manyou to spell for me the word Mr. Shapiro had used. With his fountain pen he wrote on my forearm, "Terminated!" There was no need for an exclamation mark.

At home I looked up the word in my pocket dictionary; it says "finished." My anger flamed up. That damned capitalist believed he was finished with us, but he was mistaken. We were far from terminated—the struggle was still going on. I would ask my elder brother to cut the restaurant's electricity first thing the next morning. Baisha had said she'd have one of her boyfriends create some problems in Cowboy Chicken's mail delivery. Manyou would visit his friends at the garbage center and ask them not to pick up trash at the restaurant. Jinglin declared, "I'll blow up Peter's Victorian!" Feilan hadn't decided what to do yet.

This was just the beginning.

Ha Jin came to the United States in 1985 from his native land, China, when he was twenty-nine. He has published in English three volumes of poetry, three books of short stories, and five novels. His most recent book is *A Free Life* (Pantheon 2007), a novel set in the United States and about the immigrant experience. He lives outside Boston and teaches at Boston University. Before moving to Boston, he lived in Georgia for nine years, where he taught at Emory University.

" 'After Cowboy Chicken Came to Town' started with an uncomfortable feeling after I had read an article in an official Chinese-language newspaper that reported that a U.S. fast-food restaurant in Beijing burned leftover chicken at night and would not give it away to its employees or to people who were hungry. The article praised the American way of doing business and insisted that eventually this practice would reduce the waste of food. Still, it troubled me. The unease kept bothering me for several years. Try as I might, I couldn't think of a way to justify the practice. Eventually I had to write about it to purge the uncomfortable feeling. I couldn't name the U.S. company in my story, so I used 'Cowboy Chicken' instead. The story has no plot, which was intended. I wanted to present a slice of life in the Chekhovian sense. The setting and the episodes are fictional on the whole, though I did once work at an American fast-food restaurant. Once the story was written, my unease was gone, as if to write it was to satisfy a physical need."

Job

Erika Meitner

My mother sold life insurance
for twenty-five years—
something you can't see or touch.

The first day I went to work—
Fifth Avenue in pumps
and a business suit—
I smelled the pretzel vendors
and thought of my father,
elevators carrying him up
to the sixty-third floor
for fifteen years; how, one day,
they escorted him down
with a box of paperweights
and picture frames. Every
childhood morning I'd wake
to the whir of his electric tie rack
circling outside my bedroom door.

For years that was all I wanted—
a machine I would never
have a use for. My ID badge
says I work at Bell Atlantic
this month. On the twelfth floor
we document old systems
that track tangible holdings:
file cabinets, phone poles,
things you can touch. SCATS,
the system I'm in charge of,
depreciates and retires assets.
Bob, my client, calls me
"Brooklyn," smiles with his
overwhelming moustache,
doesn't know we downsize.

He has a sign on his desk:
"It's nice to be important,
but it's more important
to be nice." He waves
over the cubicle walls,
shouts, *Hey Brooklyn,
you stayin' out of trouble?*

My mother sold life insurance
for twenty-five years—
not a morbid plan
for the death of a loved one,
she insisted, but fiscal reality.

Morning commute vertigo,
the rushing subway gears,
twin headlights blooming
from the anxious tunnel,
beautiful fifteen-year-olds
from the East Side projects
with lacquered hair, platform
sneakers, hoop earrings singing
their effortless downtown
strength and music rolling
like the train; fuck this
and fuck that, fuck this
and fuck that, fuck this
and fuck that, throttled forward.

The blank security guard
with the freckled face forgets me
when I forget my pass, claims
she's never seen me before.
I believe her. Express elevator,
slate blue cubicle near aisle B,
briefcase, blouse, slacks,
clips, staples, tacks. Fist of fire
in my stomach. This job
makes me want to frequent
upscale restaurants, devour
thermostats, bleed like a tattoo,
barter for angels. As if I have
nothing to lose.

My mother sold life insurance
for twenty-five years—
she was certified by the state
and always told me,
If you can sell that,
you can sell anything.

Some nights I work past ten
for the overtime, and so I can
return home in a taxi billed
to the company, sliding around
on the leather of the black
back seat, East River speeding by
to the rhythm of FDR Drive:
fuck this and fuck that,
endless buildings winking wealth,
shrinking slowly as we drive
the Brooklyn Bridge to my walk-up,
where I'll climb six flights to eat
lobster rescued from a client dinner
on my Salvation Army couch in pajamas,
watching the evening news
blaring the unstoppable market.

Erika Meitner's poems have appeared in *The Kenyon Review, Barrow Street, The American Poetry Review, Prairie Schooner, North American Review,* and on *Slate.com.* Her first book, *Inventory at the All-Night Drugstore,* won the 2002 Anhinga Prize for Poetry. She has taught creative writing and religious studies at the University of Virginia, the University of Wisconsin–Madison, and the University of California–Santa Cruz and is currently an assistant professor of English at Virginia Tech. She is also completing her doctorate in religion, as the first Morgenstern Fellow in Jewish Studies, at the University of Virginia.

Before diving into academia, Meitner worked as a lifeguard, a documentary film production assistant, a Hebrew school instructor, an office temp, a computer programmer, and a public middle school teacher in Brooklyn. Her poem "Job" came out of her year-long stint as a systems consultant for Andersen Consulting (now Accenture), where she was an Analyst in their Process Competency Group. "My parents both worked in the business world," Meitner writes, "and I took the job at Andersen to prove to myself (and them) that I could do that kind of corporate work. I'm still not sure I'm competent in processes of any kind, but it was my first job out of college, and I was working on a process-of-elimination plan to try to figure out what I wanted to be when I grew up. All I knew, at the end of that year, was that I no longer wanted to have a job that required pantyhose."

"Job" originally appeared in *The Madison Review* (2002) and was subsequently included in *Inventory at the All-Night Drugstore* (Aningha Press 2003). Copyright © 2002 by Erika Meitner. It is reprinted here by permission of Anhinga Press, Tallahassee, Florida.

Livelihood

Lou Fisher

I WALKED GINNY AROUND MY new neighborhood. Actually it was an old neighborhood; we passed boarding houses, BEWARE OF DOG signs, and fences with little padlocks on the gates. As we stepped across one of the gravel driveways, Ginny, in high heels, grabbed my hand for support.

"You gave up your nice apartment for *this*?"

"Had to," I said.

"You should have called me." Ginny was in real estate and this was right up her alley, so to speak. "I could have found you something better."

"But not cheaper," I said.

"Oh, maybe not. Listen, when you go back to work . . ." She paused to get my reaction. A few minutes in the moonlight had lifted her cheekbones, rustled her short light hair, and softened her business-day makeup. Her eyes had progressed, as they always did, from afternoon gray to evening blue. In her voice, though, I could still hear the duty and strain of closing a deal. "Jeff," she said that way, "everyone needs a job."

"Maybe selling houses is great fun," I said.

"Hardly. You want to try it?"

"No."

"Big commissions," she said. "And bonuses too. If I get that free trip to Hawaii—will you go with me?"

"I don't know. We'll see."

I pulled on her hand to halt the walk. She twirled in close, compressing for a hug, but I was just trying to figure out where we were. Almost around the block, was what I decided. And soon we'd be back at my furnished room with the slanted walls. I'd have to keep her from coming up.

"You think too much," Ginny said.

I didn't answer. I was thinking.

"At least I can afford to live decently. Can you say that?" She went on. "You need a haircut. And you look thinner than ever. When's the last time you had a full meal?"

"Well, you know," I said, not wanting to go into it.

Mostly, though, as she suspected, I ate peanut butter, bologna, corn flakes . . . and reused my tea bags until they were tattered. Tuna fish, in cans, on sale, would have fit my fortunes, but I was boycotting tuna to save the dolphins. I stayed firm on that. On the other hand, I sold my noisy old car. Got rid of the junker right away. A little cash went in the bank and better yet, no more gas, no oil changes. Then I cut my rent by more than half, and here I was: frugal. Hung out at City Park and the library. Washed my jeans, T-shirts, and underwear in the landlady's basement. Shaved forever with one blade. Even so, the money went fast. So fast that one day I thought about calling Mr. Dearing and asking for my job back. Instead I called the phone company and had the phone taken out.

GOOD OLD BIG-NOSED MR. DEARING, as staunch as the Harker Building itself. Yes. Tiled floors. Sprinkler system. A photo badge pinned to my suit jacket. Did I dare to loosen my tie?

In those days I shared a cubicle with a couple of guys from Finance. They didn't say much, those accountants. Chewed gum. Scratched the backs of their necks. One of the accountants had devised a system for beating the horses, based on wind, weight, and post positions, but the system had yet to prove itself, even on paper, even on his computer. The other guy was keeping track of lottery numbers until a pattern emerged. Within this crowded but quiet cubicle, from our three cross-angled desks, each of us faced a blank wall, and those walls, every year, were repainted beige. The year I was there I asked the painter, up on his ladder, why beige? and he said, "Hey, buddy, I use what they give me."

Right. Didn't we all.

Once every afternoon I snuck away and went down the far hallway to look out the window. That window, of course, didn't open. Couldn't ever. And there wasn't a whole lot to see from the fifth floor, maybe a few cars snaking by, this way and that. I suppose the people in the cars were only going off to other office buildings, to other jobs, but at the moment they were out in the sun and the air and the world, while I was stuck at the end of the hall.

Previously, at another company, my desk was fenced around by plastic panels. Seemed like a private office until I stood up. Or until the boss leaned in. *How's it going, Jeffrey?* he'd want to know, trying with every turn of his neck to see what was on my computer screen. And before that, at the downtown government job, my desk was meshed with a hundred others in a stadium-like fluorescent chamber. The big shots had the corner offices—windows, drapes, and adjustable vertical blinds.

Whenever Mr. Dearing caught me standing down at the hall window, he would come and stand beside me, not so much to share the view or to visualize himself out there, but more as to say, *I know where you are, you are not at your desk.*

SATURDAY MORNING ALAN CAME TROTTING through the park in a white nylon warm-up suit. A matching headband set off his dark curly hair and a couple of tight-strung racquets were nestled in the crook of his arm. I was already pushing at the net post, in my denim shorts, stretching. "Yo," I said.

We shook hands. His grip was firm, but quickly broken.

"One hour, Jeff, that's all I've got. But don't worry, I'll wear you out by then."

"Sure," I said, unconvinced. Alan, for an office worker—stocks and bonds and foreign equities—was a decent athlete, but he ate in a hurry, I thought, and drank that way too. Lately his stomach was sagging. And more lately he had taken to wearing loose tennis shirts, the kind that hung out over his shorts.

At the net we jogged lightly in place.

"Or maybe *I* ought to worry," he went on. "Now that you're not working, you must be full of extra energy." He grinned, as if it couldn't be so. "How are you getting along, anyway? We miss you at the tennis club. And the guy playing in your spot on Friday nights is a jerk."

"The club was nice," I said, "but the park is free."

"So what? If you'd let me handle your money, I'd get you—"

"What money?"

"Well, free is good then," he said, not looking around, intent on ripping open a new can of balls. Keeping two, he tossed one to me and hustled to the opposite side of the court. I was left facing the sun, where I wanted to be. The sun was mine. I'd still have it on Monday. On Tuesday. Alan was yelling, "C'mon, hit one."

When Alan first joined the club he wasn't that sharp a player. I spent a lot of evenings just hitting the ball with him—forehands, backhands, volleys, overheads—and even before he was quite good enough I urged him into the Friday night league. Then we started going out together, him with his wife, and I was attending to Ginny a bit more seriously then. Yes, a bit more . . . or a lot more . . . somewhere in that range. Anyway, it was at a cocktail party, months later, at Alan's house, that standing side by side with their martini glasses touching he and his thin, dark-haired wife announced their plans for divorce. A shock, like having your baseball team move out of town. Some of the women at the party thought the announcement was, well, pretentious. Me, I didn't comment, just had another drink. Or two. Ginny took it even harder. She kept saying, *Oh, I don't believe this.* I think if anything was the beginning of our end, it was that night, that party. Relationships were more fragile than we thought, of no good use, and not to be trusted.

"Good match," I said, meeting Alan at the net-post where our things were stacked. Yes, he'd won the set, but barely, and complaining all the while about my line calls. I asked, "How about again next week?"

Silently, he slipped his racquet into its cover. Then he put the used balls back in the can, offering them to me. I took the can and set it on the ground next to my racket. When I looked up again, Alan was already zipped into his warm-up suit.

"Jeff, you know I enjoy playing with you." He let that sink in. "But I pay a lot of money to play at the club. It doesn't make sense for me to play somewhere else, especially out on these concrete courts, on these *cracked* concrete courts, when I've got Har-Tru and beer and umbrella tables and windscreens."

"Okay," I said.

"You were there," he went on. "You know the difference. And I pay all that money. And the other guys . . ."

"Yeah, Alan. You're right."

"Look, you can come as my guest sometime." He tucked both racquets under his right arm, returning exactly to the image in which he'd arrived. He looked at his watch. "Will you come? I'll give you a call."

Actually, I didn't mind him inviting me, but I knew the guest fee was twenty dollars and the court time came on top of that. I didn't think he'd pay. He told me once, at the club, after a game, with a cold sudsy beer in his hand, about return on investment.

HOME FROM WORK, I'D HEAD straight for the kitchen—I had a separate kitchen then—and pour myself about two inches of scotch. Carry the glass to the recliner chair. Turn on the TV news. Lean back. Swallow. Much later I'd try to listen to some songs of the west, by Willie or Waylon, and while sipping warm scotch I'd go into tears. Not sobbing, you know. Just feeling the moisture in my eyes, maybe high on my cheeks. So I'd lean back again. Swallow. If I drank enough, around midnight I'd fall asleep, right there in the recliner, and not think anymore about the next day . . . about waking up at a quarter to seven, about putting on a suit and tie, about driving to work, about trudging with my shined black shoes into the Harker Building.

An older guy named Steve I used to work with kept a pint bottle of vodka, label removed, in the bottom right-hand drawer of his desk. Vodka, he advised me, has no color, no odor, costs not too much, and comes in all sizes. Good stuff for the office.

I never went that far.

But one afternoon Steve started tearing up invoices and stuffing them in the wastebasket. He must have gone through half the file before Mr. Dearing caught him and wrestled him to the floor. Then Steve went away for two months to dry out at Blaggin House. He said, afterward, that Blaggin House was nicer than the office. He said it was a hell of a lot nicer.

GINNY WANTED TO KNOW WHAT I was going to do for a health plan. I mentioned sunshine and exercise, but she was talking about insurance. Blue Cross. Blue Shield.

I got a feeling called the blu-u-es . . .

"That country music again," she said. "Can't you play anything decent?"

I knelt to the floor and fussed through a pile of cassettes. "You gave me some tapes . . ."

"New Age," she said. "Did you ever listen to them?"

"Sure."

"I'll bet."

"Well, they're in here somewhere."

"Never mind, Jeff," she said. "Just shut it off."

While I did, Ginny ran a hand across one of the stereo speakers. She showed me her fingertips. Dark dusty smudges. I nodded as if it were a discovery. Then I kicked the tapes back in a pile and reclaimed my seat on the unmade bed, scrunching both pillows behind my back. I stole a glance up at the skylight. The twin glass panes that were folded into the peak of the roof turned the plain ordinary wall-boarded attic into a penthouse, a spaceship, an observatory. At that moment, far beyond the glass, a thousand cool stars were blinking. Maybe more than a thousand. And the moon would pass by later.

When I looked down, Ginny had backed away to the only chair in the furnished apartment. Wasn't much of a chair, really, and I half expected the legs to give way.

"What's got into you?" she said. "You can't go on living like this, doing nothing."

"Well, I wouldn't say *nothing*."

"What would you say?"

"That I don't have a job."

"And is that good?"

"I guess not," I said, reading her eyes.

"There's no guesswork about it." Ginny, at the time, was working with a developer, selling his condos as fast as he built them. Actually, she sold them faster. The people expected to move in during, say, October, then hoped for December, and waited for summer . . . Well, delays were common in the working world.

"I'm thinking," I said, "about getting a dog."

Her eyes widened. "A dog? What kind of dog?"

I wiggled my hand uncertainly. "Haven't decided. But as soon as I get an idea . . ."

"They won't let you have a dog here."

"You'd be surprised. My landlady says, as long as I'm going to be home every day."

"Oh, wonderful." Ginny hunched forward in her blue linen suit, letting the soft collar rise to meet her trim-cut, blonde-dyed hair. "This room," she said in that earnest position, "is already a complete mess. Awful, in fact. Unlivable. Look at the bed, the books, the rug, the sink . . . Will you just look around? Dogs shed, you know. Tell me, do you want to have dog hair all over everything? And dogs poop too. I can just see you out in the yard in the middle of the night trying to housebreak it."

"Him," I said.

"*What?*"

"The dog would be a him, not an it."

"I don't care," she said. She shifted uncomfortably in the loose-legged wooden chair. "Listen, do you want to go out for a burger?"

I shook my head.

"My treat, Jeff."

I shook my head.

She stood up and pushed back the chair, though not too far because it came up against the sloped wall. "All right, we'll skip the food," she said. "We'll just skip everything and let the world go by." She looked at her watch, pinching the tiny jeweled face as if to hold the hour. "Well, I've got a closing at the bank, first thing in the morning. Better get home and do some paperwork."

My only door led down steep stairs to the side exit of the house. I walked her down. Before she stepped outside, she leaned back to me and I kissed her lightly on the mouth, a lot more lightly than I used to. But she turned and pressed into my arms, looking for something better.

"Keep in touch," she said, sighing.

"Sure," I told her. "Sure."

ONE MONDAY MORNING I BROUGHT a poster to work and pinned it ceremoniously to the wall opposite my desk. A window, in full color. Within its panes birds flew, trees leaved, sunbeams descended, and a narrow foot-bridged stream, reaching the rocks, turned from blue to frothy white. Sure, poster flat, all of it, but if I squinted or glanced a bit from the side, I could almost feel the breeze. Even the accountants looked up, tilted their heads, fought off smiles.

After lunch Mr. Dearing strolled into the office to converse as usual about my productivity. Or was it, that day, my attitude? Anyway, when he spotted the poster, he started to rock from side to side. He put a hand on his jaw. He cleared his throat. *Ur-r-r-ga*, it sounded like. He then turned to the three of us, the two accountants and me, and explained as crisply as he could that hanging such things on a business wall was not in touch with the spirit or the policies of the company.

The accountants were not happy that I got them in trouble. Red-faced and dark-eyed, they became more silent than ever.

"WHERE'S GINNY?" MY MOTHER ASKED, struggling up from the couch as I walked in the door.

I said, "She's not with me."

"I can see that, smart-ass. You used to bring her with you sometimes."

"She works on weekends. You know, real estate."

"But today's Tuesday." Mom looked around, her chin not lifted but her eyes darting, as if she had a calendar hanging somewhere low on the living-room drapes. She turned back to me. "I *think* it's Tuesday."

"I think so too," I said. I waited while she coughed. Then I took a step closer, close enough to touch her small bent shoulder, to kiss her hello on the cheek.

Her face felt dry; it looked corrugated. "Actually, Mom, the big romance is over. It's been over for a long while. Ginny still stops by, though. In fact, with the phone out, all she can do is stop by."

Mom coughed again, several times, clutching the front of her robe and pressing with both elbows to hold her ribs in place. When she was done, she dabbed her mouth with a tissue. "Well, I think Ginny's a nice girl. Isn't she?"

"Yeah. Sure. But she has her own kind of life. You know, she's more fussy, orderly. And she doesn't much appreciate country music—not even Alan Jackson, not even The Judds."

Mom sighed. "You always wanted to be a cowboy."

"When I was a kid?"

"Yes," she said. "From TV. When you were little."

"Kid stuff," I remarked. But I was aware that boots and saddles, and jeans and sweaters, still impressed me more than suits and ties. For that reason my work clothes were now hanging in a consignment store. Size 38s and 40s, blue, gray, with mild patterns. No one had yet made an offer. I supposed I could take them back. "Anyway," I said, "I'm going to get a dog."

"Instead of Ginny?"

"No, not instead of Ginny. Just . . . a dog."

"An *animal*." Mom's breath began to come in frightening wheezes. Or squeezes. Both. Leaning on me, she pointed to the couch. After I helped her shuffle back there and get comfortable, I covered her legs with a brown knitted afghan. "I have to go to the bathroom," she said, when I finally got her all tucked in.

ONE DAY I WENT TO the men's room and they had taken the doors off the stalls. Mr. Dearing said it was because some of the employees were using the place as a reading room.

Okay, how did he know?

At home I would tear pages out of a magazine and fold them into fourths, and before I left for work I would stash the wad in my pants pocket. I took articles, stories, classifieds, two or three items a day, whatever looked interesting. I had a few subscriptions going then just for that purpose.

Later in the morning, sitting on the toilet, I quietly unfolded one page at a time, tilted it to the best of the mediocre light, read it word for word, then refolded that page and flushed it away. I learned about opinion polls and exercise equipment and adultery. About boards of education and bankruptcies. About Charlotte, North Carolina. Once I even read how to build a worm box, from plywood and Plexiglas, with air holes. Why do I remember that? Anyway, by the time I left the stall each morning my jaw was relaxed and the pain had eased in my neck and shoulders. That's what you were supposed to get when you went to the bathroom. Temporary relief.

On my way back to the desk, Mr. Dearing would give me a look. I used to think, what could he do? The evidence was gone.

But so, from that day forward, were the doors.

ACCORDING TO MY SISTER, MOM'S age and ailments had her headed for a nursing home. I told Elaine that Medicaid probably handled those expenses, but she said she didn't think so, not really, that I shouldn't depend on it. Actually, my sister knew much more about Mom because she lived on the same street. When I rode the bus every week to see my mother, I always had to stop afterward and see Elaine too.

Probably I shouldn't have told her that I gave up my job.

"But what do you *do*?" Elaine wanted to know. She was pregnant again and her face, usually as thin as mine, had become as round and pale as the moon, though not nearly as swollen as the front of her sweat suit. Any day now. She once made me promise that I'd shoot her if she ever thought of having a third kid, but that was before my niece and nephew started school.

"How are you feeling?" I asked.

"Fine. Ready. How can a man have no job?"

"And no boss. No walls. No bells that ring at the beginning and end of lunchtime."

"Cut that out," she said. "Tell me."

From a chair at the kitchen table I watched her heat up the coffee. "Well, I've been sleeping late. Not much of an apartment, you know, but my bed's right under a skylight. Hey, what a feeling when I open my eyes."

"That's it, Jeff? You sleep late?"

"I read a lot too. The landlady downstairs lets me go out on her back porch and that's where I read. In a swing. I just finished *Lonesome Dove*. Had that book around for years."

"Love isn't lonesome," Elaine said. "If you'd give Ginny half a chance . . ."

"Not love. Dove. Like a bird."

"Oh, wasn't that on TV?" She filled my special mug with coffee and brought it to the table. Already there was an open cellophane package of Fig Newtons, one of which was between my teeth—three would be a midday meal. Standing over me, Elaine asked, "Don't you have a VCR?"

"I just kept my stereo," I told her.

She shrugged her shoulders.

"It's all I need," I said. "You wouldn't believe how my days fill up. The kind of street I live on . . . I pitch in where I can. One guy's overhauling the engine of a rusted '72 Chevy, and a man with no teeth is hauling deposit bottles to the supermarket. The woman next door is a sign painter and sometimes I go out with her and dig post holes. That kind of stuff. Then I run, I walk, I play tennis. There's a kid who comes to the park after school, plays tennis with me."

"This is ridiculous—you're a grown man."

I sipped the coffee. The brew was hot but tasted bitter, like yesterday's coffee. "And I want to get a dog. What kind should I get?"

"You're asking *me*?" Now she sat down at the table and put her hands over her eyes. "Jeff, how's any of this going to help Mom? And poor Dad, if he could see you . . ."

Yes, my father was a worker. Up and at 'em every morning. Overtime, all he could get. He worried constantly that the auto company would force him to retire at sixty-five or seventy. But he died at fifty-eight. At the time, his gloved hands were gripped on the welding torch—the shut-off switch was automatic or he'd have fried the guy working next to him. So that's how my mother, who thought she was one of those lucky women whose husbands didn't want to retire, ended up with no husband at all. Until then, Mom liked to say, *Jeff, you're just like your father*, but I never knew in what way she meant.

In fact, I saw him more in my sister. Elaine had that same way of crooking her nose when she got upset. Her husband was employed by the city to inspect restaurants, and she said his civil-service income couldn't begin to pay for a nursing home. She said also, when I visited her the next time, that I'd better face up to it.

NONE OF MY JOBS PAID very well.

And no wonder. At my first office job, the one for the government, I had nothing to do, nothing whatsoever. How slowly the time passed. I just sat there, day after day. No one talked to me. My phone didn't ring. My fax spewed no paper.

Dead silent blank.

Finally, one late Thursday afternoon when my head was fogged in and my hands felt deprived of all feeling, I approached my supervisor at his desk and asked him, plain as could be, for some work to do. Oh, he loved that. I remember how the corners of his mouth twisted, how his eyes looked to heaven for support. I definitely remember. Then he said, *listen, pal, you're only here for back-up, for when Kenline goes out of town.*

Kenline? Who was Kenline? He must have been sitting in one of the large corner offices—the ones with windows.

On my last job Mr. Dearing gave me some busy work, but by then I was out of the habit. He didn't pay much either, though I think he paid the best. Yes, I'm sure he did. How else did I save enough to quit?

SITTING ON THE BED, I went over a notice from the bank. My account had dropped below the minimum and from now on a service charge would be applied. Well, too bad, too late—the rent check had already closed the account. And there on the dresser was my wallet, folded thinly over a twenty-dollar bill. A single twenty-dollar bill.

I shut my eyes; in that darkness I began to bounce softly on the bed.

A job, I thought.

An office, a desk, a salary, a necktie . . .

Meetings, employee evaluations, bulletin boards, coffee machines, freezing blowing air-conditioning, badge-locked doors, walls . . .

Okay, where did I put Mr. Dearing's phone number?

Mr. Dearing. Mr. Dearing. Strange, I couldn't remember what he looked like. What came to mind instead was a square-faced Airedale, wheat brown, ears flapping, mouth panting, and a stubby tail that wagged whenever he saw me. Sure, I could get him free from the ASPCA. I'd name him Useless.

Here, Useless. Off to the park.

Dreamily I opened my eyes. At the far end of the attic, the window was showing me plenty of daylight, along with the tops of trees and a cloud that looked like a camel, while pouring in through the double slab of glass above my head, sunshine. Sunshine. Good on me, but a blinding glare on the white empty obsolete bank statement.

And in cash, just twenty dollars. For dog food, for corn flakes, for next month's rent . . . and, yes, for all the months after that.

I swung my feet off the bed. I started slowly, tucking in the edges of the sheets, feeling not a shade desperate, surprisingly calm. I fluffed the pillows. Placed them back like eggs on Formica. Then I smoothed over my one blue cotton blanket, again and again until every ripple was gone. As the day went on, I searched and destroyed cobwebs, scoured the sink, scrubbed the bathtub too, picked up the books, threw out the accumulated mail, reglued the chair, and even borrowed an old noisy vacuum cleaner from the landlady. Finally, early that night, as I stacked up the cassettes, I hid the country music behind the unused New Age tapes.

So I had a soft rag in my hand and was dusting the stereo speakers when I heard Ginny ring the bell downstairs. *Okay,* I thought. *Let her in.*

Lou Fisher received the *New Letters* Literary Award for Fiction. His stories have also appeared in two prize issues of *Mississippi Review* and in *The Crescent Review*, *The Florida Review*, and *Bridge,* among other journals and magazines. Fisher's work has been selected for several anthologies, including *Bar Stories* (Bottom Dog Press 2007). His novel *The Blue Ice Pilot* (Warner 1986) is a look at work in an imagined future.

Fisher writes that he now lives with his wife in downstate New York, "a rural, nicely wooded area with plenty of job opportunities that I can ignore. I play tennis instead. And I'm learning to play the piano. All that along with twelve continuing years of teaching fiction and nonfiction for the Long Ridge Writers Group."

"Most writers need day jobs," Fisher explains. "I wrote this story in first-person voice because I often yearned to do what the narrator does, and because during my years of office life in three corporations I often endured the frustrations and follies that are revealed truly herein."

"Livelihood" originally appeared in *Other Voices*, vol. 22 (Spring 1995). Copyright © 1995 by Lou Fisher. It is reprinted here by permission of the author.

The Fireman

Rick Bass

THEY BOTH STAND ON THE OTHER SIDE of the miracle. Their marriage was bad, perhaps even rotting, but then it got better. He—the fireman, Kirby—knows what the reason is: that every time they have an argument, the dispatcher's call sounds, and he must run and disappear into the flames—he is the captain—and while he is gone, his wife, Mary Ann, reorders her priorities, thinks of the children, and worries for him. Her blood cools, as does his. It seems that the dispatcher's call is always saving them. Their marriage settles in and strengthens, afterward, like some healthy, living, supple thing.

She meets him at the door when he returns, kisses him. He is grimy—black, salt-stained, and smoky-smelling. They can't even remember what the argument was about. It's almost like a joke—the fact that they were upset about such a small thing, any small thing. He sheds his bunker gear in the utility room and goes straight to the shower. Later, they sit in the den by the fireplace and he drinks a few beers and tells her about the fire. Sometimes he'll talk about it till dawn. He knows he is lucky—he knows they are both lucky. As long as the city keeps burning, they can avoid becoming weary and numb. Always, he leaves, is drawn away, and then returns, to a second chance.

The children—a girl, four, and a boy, two—sleep soundly. It is not so much a city that they live in but a town—the suburbs on the perimeter of the city— and it could be nameless, so similar is it to so many other places: a city in the center of the southern half of the country, a place where it is warm more often than it is cold, so that the residents are not overly familiar with fires—the way a fire spreads from room to room, the way it takes only one small errant thing in a house to invalidate and erase the whole structure, to bring it all down to ashes and send the building's former occupants—the homeowners, or renters, or leasers—out wandering lost and adrift into the night, poorly dressed and without direction. They talk until dawn. She is his second wife; he is her first husband. Because they are in the suburbs, unincorporated, his is a volunteer department. Kirby's crew has a station with new equipment—all they could ask for—but there are no salaries, and he likes it that way; it keeps things purer. He has a day job as a computer programmer for an engineering firm that designs steel girders and columns used in industrial construction: warehouses, mills, and factories. The job means nothing to him: he slips along through the long hours of it with neither excitement nor despair, his pulse never rising, and when it is over each day he says goodbye to his coworkers and leaves the office without even the faintest echo of his work lingering in his blood. He leaves it all the way behind, or lets it pass through him like some harmless silver laxative.

But after a fire—holding a can of cold beer and sitting there next to the hearth, scrubbed clean, talking to Mary Ann, telling her what it had been like—what the cause had been, and who among his men had performed well, and who had not—his eyes water with pleasure at his knowing how lucky he is to be getting a second chance, with every fire.

He would never say anything bad about his first wife, Rhonda—and indeed, perhaps there is nothing bad to say, no fault or failing in which they were not both complicit. It almost doesn't matter; it's almost water under the bridge.

The two children asleep in their rooms; the swing set and jungle gym out in the back yard. The security of love and constancy—the *safety.* Mary Ann teaches the children's choir in church, and is as respected for her work with the children as Kirby is for his work with the fires.

It would seem like a fairy-tale story; a happy marriage, one that turned its deadly familiar course around early into the marriage, that day he signed up to be a volunteer for the fire department six years ago. One of those rare marriages, as rare as a jewel or a forest, that was saved by a combination of inner strength and the grace and luck of fortuitous external circumstances—*the world afire.* Who, given the chance, would not choose to leap across that chasm between a marriage that is heading toward numbness and tiredness and one that is instead strengthened, made more secure daily for its journey into the future?

And yet—even on the other side of the miracle, even on the other side of luck—a thing has been left behind. It's almost a perfect, happy story; it's just this side of it. The one thing behind them—the only thing—is his oldest daughter, his only child from his first marriage, Jenna. She's ten, almost eleven.

THERE IS ALWAYS EXCITEMENT AND mystery on a fire call. It's as if these things are held in solution, just beneath the skin of the earth, and are then released by the flames; as if the surface of the world, and the way things are, is some errant, artificial crust—almost like a scab—and that there are rivers of blood below, and rivers of fire, rivers of the way things used to be and might someday be again—true but mysterious, and full of power, rather than stale and crusty.

It does funny things to people—a fire, and that burning away of the thin crust. Kirby tells Mary Ann about two young men in their thirties—lovers, he thinks—who, bewildered and bereft as their house burned, went out into the front yard and began cooking hamburgers for the firefighters as the building burned down.

He tells her about the man with a house full of antiques that could not be salvaged. The attack crew was fighting the fire hard, deep in the building's interior—the building "fully involved," as they say to one another when the wood becomes flame, air becomes flame, world becomes flame. It is the thing the younger firemen live for—not a smoke alarm, lost kitten, or piddly grass fire but the real thing, a fully involved structure fire—and even the older firemen's hearts are lifted by the sight of one. Even those who have been thinking of retiring (at thirty-seven, Kirby is far and away the oldest man on the force) are made new again by the sight of it, and by the radiant heat, which curls and browns and sometimes even ignites the oak leaves of trees across the street from the fire. The paint of cars that are parked too close to the fire sometimes begins to blaze spontaneously, making it look as if the cars are traveling very fast . . .

Bats, which have been out hunting, begin to return in swarms, dancing above the flames, and begin flying in dark agitated funnels back down into the chimney of the house that's on fire, if it is not a winter fire—if the chimney has been dormant—trying to rescue their flightless young, which are roosting in the chimney, or sometimes the attic, or beneath the eaves. The bats all return to the house as it burns down, but no one ever sees any of them come back out. People stand around on the street, their faces orange in the firelight, and marvel, hypnotized at the sight of it, not understanding what is going on with the bats, or any of it; and drawn too like somnambulists to the scent of those blood rivers, those vapors of new birth that are beginning already to leak back into the world as that skin, that crust, is burned away.

The fires almost always happen at night.

This fire that Kirby is telling Mary Ann about, the one in which the house full of antiques was being lost, was one of the great fires of the year. The men work in teams, as partners, always within sight or one arm's length contact of one another, so that one can help the other if trouble is encountered—if the foundation gives way or a burning beam crashes across the back of one of the two partners, who are not always men; more and more women are volunteering, though none have yet joined Kirby's crew. He welcomes them, since from what he's seen from the multiple-alarm fires he's fought with crews in which there are women firefighters, the women tend to try to outthink rather than outmuscle the fire, which is almost always the best approach.

Kirby's partner now is a young man, Grady, just out of college. Kirby likes to use his intelligence when he fights a fire rather than just hurl himself at it and risk getting sucked too quickly into its born-again maw and becoming trapped—not just perishing in that manner, but possibly causing harm or death to those members of his crew who might then try to save him—and for this reason he likes to pair himself with the youngest, rawest, most adrenaline-rich trainees entrusted to his care, to act as an anchor of caution upon them, to counsel prudence and moderation, even as the world burns down around them.

The fire in the house of antiques—Kirby and Grady had just come out to rest, and to change oxygen tanks. The homeowner had at first been beside himself, shouting and trying to get back into his house, so that the fire marshal had had to restrain him—he had the homeowner bound to a tree with a canvas strap—but now the homeowner was watching the flames almost as if hypnotized. Kirby and Grady were so touched by his change in demeanor, by his coming to his senses—the man wasn't struggling any longer, was instead only leaning slightly away from the tree, like the masthead on a ship's prow, and sagging slightly—that they cut him loose so that he could watch the spectacle of it in freedom, unencumbered.

He made no more moves to rejoin his burning house, only stood there with watery eyes—whether tears of anguish or irritation from the smoke, they could not tell—and, taking pity, Kirby and Grady put on new oxygen tanks, gulped down some water, and though they were supposed to rest, they went back into the burning building and began carrying out those pieces of furniture that had not yet ignited, and sometimes even those that had—burning breakfronts, flaming rolltop desks—and dropped them into the man's back-yard swimming pool for safekeeping, as the tall trees in the back yard crackled and flamed like giant candles, and floating embers drifted down, scorching whatever they touched; and the neighbors all around them climbed up onto their cedar-shingled roofs in their pajamas and with garden hoses began wetting down their own roofs, trying to keep the conflagration, the spectacle—the phenomenon—from spreading . . .

The business of it has made Kirby neat and precise. He and Grady crouched and lowered the dining room set carefully into the deep end (even as some of the pieces of furniture were still flickering with flame), releasing them to sink slowly, carefully to the bottom, settling in roughly the same manner and arrangement in which they had been positioned back in the burning house.

There is no longer any space or room for excess, unpredictability, or recklessness; these extravagances can no longer be borne, and Kirby wants Grady to see and understand this, and the sooner the better. The fire hoses must always be coiled in the same pattern, so that when unrolled, they can be counted upon; the female nozzle must always be nearest the truck, and the male farthest. The backup generators must always have fresh oil and gas in them and be kept in working order; the spanner wrenches must always hang in the same place.

The days go by in long stretches, twenty-three and a half hours at a time, but in that last half-hour, in the moment of fire, when all the old rules melt down and the new world becomes flame, the importance of a moment, of a second, is magnified ten thousandfold—is magnified to almost an eternity, and there is no room for even a single mistake. Time inflates to a density greater than iron. You've got to be able to go through the last half-hour, that wall of flame, on instinct alone, or by force of habit, by rote, by feel.

An interesting phenomenon happens when time catches on fire like this. It happens to even the veteran firefighters. A form of tunnel vision develops—the heart pounding two hundred times a minute, and the pupils contracting so tightly that vision almost vanishes. The field of view becomes reduced to an area about the size of another man's helmet, or face: his partner, either in front of or behind him. If the men ever become separated by sight or sound, they are supposed to freeze instantly and then begin swinging their pikestaff or a free arm in all directions; and if their partner does the same and is within one or even two arm's lengths, their arms will bump one another, and they can continue—they can rejoin the fight, as the walls flame vertical and the ceiling and floors melt and fall away. The firefighters carry motion sensors on their hips, which send out piercing electronic shrieks if the men stop moving for more than thirty seconds. If one of those goes off, it means that a firefighter is down—that he has fallen and injured himself or has passed out from smoke inhalation—and all the firefighters stop what they are doing and turn and converge on the sound, if possible, centering back to it like the bats pouring back down into the chimney.

A person's breathing accelerates inside a burning house—the pulse leaps to over two hundred beats a minute—and the blood heats, as if in a purge. The mind fills with a strange music. Sense of feel and the memory of how things *ought* to be become everything; it seems that even through the ponderous, fire-resistant gloves, the firefighters could read Braille if they had to. As if the essence of all objects exudes a certain clarity, just before igniting.

Everything in its place; the threads, the grain of the canvas weave of the fire hoses, is canted such that it tapers back toward the male nipples; if lost in a house fire, you can crouch on the floor and with your bare hand—or perhaps even through the thickness of your glove, in that hypertactile state—follow the hose back to its source, back outside, to the beginning.

The ears—the lobes of the ear, specifically—are the most temperature-sensitive part of the body. Many times the heat is so intense that the firefighters' suits begin smoking and their helmets begin melting, while deep within, the firefighters are still insulated and protected, but they are taught that if the lobes of their ears begin to feel hot, they are to get out of the building immediately—that they themselves may be about to ignite.

It's intoxicating; it's addictive as hell.

THE FIRE DOES STRANGE THINGS to people. Kirby tells Mary Ann that it's usually the men who melt down first—who seem to lose their reason sooner than the women. That particular fire in which they sank all the man's prize antiques in the swimming pool in order to save them—that man becalmed himself after he was released from the tree (the top of which was flaming, dropping ember-leaves into the yard, and even onto his shoulders, like fiery moths), and he walked around into the back yard and stood next to his pool, with his back turned toward the burning house, and began busying himself with his long-handled dip net, laboriously skimming—or endeavoring to skim—the ashes from the pool's surface.

Another time—a fire in broad daylight—a man walked out of his burning house and went straight out to his greenhouse, which he kept filled with flowering plants and where he held captive twenty or more hummingbirds of various species. He was afraid that the fire would spread to the greenhouse and burn up the birds, so he closed himself in there and began spraying the little birds down with the hose as they flitted and whirled from him, and he kept spraying them, trying to keep their brightly colored wings wet so they would not catch fire.

KIRBY TELLS MARY ANN ALL of these stories—a new one each time he returns—and they lie together on the couch until dawn. The youngest baby, the boy, has just given up nursing; Kirby and Mary Ann are just beginning to earn back moments of time together—little five- and ten-minute wedges of time—and Mary Ann naps with her head on his freshly showered shoulder, though in close like that, at the skin level, she can still smell the charcoal, can taste it. Kirby has scars across his neck and back, pockmarks where embers have landed and burned through his suit, and she, like the children, likes to touch these; the small, slick feel of them is like smooth stones from a river. Kirby earns several each year, and he says that before it is over, he will look like a Dalmatian. She does not ask him what he means by "when it is all over," and she holds back, reins back like a wild horse to keep from asking the question "When will you stop?" Everyone has fire stories. Mary Ann's is that when she was a child at her grandmother's house, she went into the bathroom and took off her robe, laid it over the plug-in portable electric heater, and sat on the commode; but as she did so, the robe quickly leapt into flame. The peeling old wallpaper caught on fire too—so much flame that she could not get past—and she remembers even now, twenty-five years later, how her father had to come in and lift her up and carry her back out, and how that fire was quickly, easily extinguished.

But that was a long time ago and she has her own life, needs no one to carry her in or out of anywhere. All that has gone away and vanished; her views of fire are not a child's but an adult's. Mary Ann's fire story is tame, it seems, compared to the rest of the world's.

She counts the slick, small oval scars on his back: twenty-two of them, like a pox. She knows he is needed. He seems to thrive on it. She remembers both the terror and the euphoria after her father whisked her out of the bathroom, as she looked back at it—at the dancing flames she had birthed. Is there greater power in lighting a fire or in putting one out?

He sleeps contentedly, there on the couch. She will not ask him—not yet. She will hold it in for as long as she can, and watch—some part of her desirous of his stopping, but another part not.

She feels as she imagines the street-side spectators must, or even the victims of the fires themselves, the homeowners and renters: a little hypnotized, a little transfixed; and there is a confusion, as if she could not tell you, or her children—could not be sure—whether she was watching him burn down to the ground or was watching him being born and built up, standing among the flames, like iron being cast from the earth.

She sleeps, her fingers light across his back. She dreams the twenty-two scars are a constellation in the night. She dreams that the more fires he fights, the safer and stronger their lives become.

She wants him to stop. She wants him to go on.

They awaken on the couch at dawn to the baby's murmurings from the other room, and soft sleep-breathings of their daughter, the four-year-old. The sun, orange already, rising above the city. Kirby gets up and dresses for work. He could do it in his sleep. It means nothing to him. It is its own form of sleep, and these moments on the couch and in the shells of the flaming buildings are their own form of wakefulness.

SOME NIGHTS HE GOES OVER to Jenna's house—to the house of his ex-wife. No one knows he does this: not Mary Ann, and not his ex-wife, Rhonda, and certainly not Jenna—not unless she knows it in her sleep and in her dreams, which he hopes she does.

He wants to breathe her air; he wants her to breathe his. It is a biological need. He climbs up on the roof and leans over the chimney and listens— *silence*—and inhales, and exhales.

THE FIRES USUALLY COME ABOUT once a week. The time spent between them is peaceful at first but then increasingly restless, until finally the dispatcher's radio sounds in the night, and Kirby is released. He leaps out of bed—he lives four blocks from the station—kisses Mary Ann, kisses his daughter and son sleeping in their beds, and then is out into the night, hurrying but not running across the lawn. He will be the first one there, or among the first, other than the young firemen who may already be hanging out at the station, watching movies and playing cards, just waiting.

Kirby gets in his car—the chief's car—and cruises the neighborhood slowly, savoring his approach. There's no need to rush and get to the station five or ten seconds sooner, when he'll have to wait another minute or two anyway for the other firemen to arrive.

It takes him only five seconds to slip on his bunker gear, ten seconds to start the truck and get it out of the driveway. There used to be such anxiety, getting to a fire: the tunnel vision beginning to constrict from the very moment he heard the dispatcher's voice. But now he knows how to save it, how to hold it at bay—that powerhousing of the heart, which now does not kick into life, does not come into being, until the moment Kirby comes around the corner and first sees the flames.

In her bed—in their bed—Mary Ann hears and feels the rumble of the big trucks leaving the station; hears and feels in her bones the belch of the air horns, and then the going-away sirens. She listens to the dispatcher's radio—hopefully it will remain silent after the first call, will not crackle again, calling more and more stations to the blaze. Hopefully it will be a small one, and containable.

She lies there, warm and in love with her life—with the blessing of her two children asleep there in her own house, in the other room, safe and asleep—and she tries to imagine the future: tries to picture being sixty years old, seventy, and then eighty. How long—and of that space or distance ahead, what lies within it?

KIRBY GETS HER—JENNA—ON WEDNESDAY NIGHTS, and on every other weekend. On the weekends, if the weather is good, he sometimes takes her camping and lets the assistant chief cover for him. Kirby and Jenna cook over an open fire; they roast marshmallows. They sleep in sleeping bags in a meadow beneath stars. When he was a child, Kirby used to camp in this meadow with his father and grandfather, and there would be lightning bugs at night, but those are gone now.

On Wednesday nights—Kirby has to have her back at Rhonda's by ten—they cook hamburgers, Jenna's favorite food, on the grill in the back yard. This one constancy—this one thing, small, even tiny, like a sacrament. The diminishment of their lives shames him, especially for her, she for whom the whole world should be widening and opening rather than constricting already.

She plays with the other children, the little children, afterward, all of them keeping one eye on the clock. She is quiet, inordinately so—thrilled just to be in the presence of her father, beneath his huge shadow; she smiles shyly whenever she notices that he is watching her. And how can she not be wondering why it is, when it's time to leave, that the other two children get to stay?

He drives her home cheerfully, steadfastly, refusing to let her see or even sense his despair. He walks her up the sidewalk to Rhonda's like a guest. He does not go inside.

By Saturday—if it is the off-weekend on which he does not have her—he is up on the roof again, trying to catch the scent of her from the chimney; and sometimes he falls asleep up there, in a brief catnap, as if watching over her and standing guard.

A million times he plays it over in his mind. Could I have saved the marriage? Did I give it absolutely every last ounce of effort? Could I have saved it?

No. Maybe. *No.*

IT TAKES A LONG TIME to get used to the fires; it takes the young firemen, the beginners, a long time to understand what is required: that they must suit up and walk right on into a burning house.

They make mistakes. They panic, breathe too fast, and use up their oxygen. It takes a long time. It takes a long time before they calm down and meet the fires on their own terms, and the fire's.

In the beginning, they all want to be heroes. Even before they enter their first fire, they will have secretly placed their helmets in the ovens at home to soften them up a bit—to dull and char and melt them slightly, so anxious are they for combat and its validations, its contract with their spirit. Kirby remembers the first house fire he entered. His initial reaction was "You mean I'm going in *that?*" But enter it he did, fighting it from the inside out with huge volumes of water, the water sometimes doing as much damage as the fire, his new shiny suit yellow and clean among the work-darkened suits of the veterans . . .

Kirby tells Mary Ann that after that fire he drove out into the country and set a little grass fire, a little pissant one that was in no danger of spreading, then put on his bunker gear and spent all afternoon walking around in it, dirtying his suit to just the right color of anonymity.

You always make mistakes, in the beginning. You can only hope that they are small or insignificant enough to carry little, if any, price—that they harm no one. Kirby tells Mary Ann that on one of his earliest house fires, he was riding in one of the back seats of the fire engine so that he was facing backward. He was already packed up—bunker gear, air mask, and scuba tank—so that he couldn't hear or see well, and was nervous as hell; and when they got to the house that was on fire—a fully involved, "working" fire—the truck screeched to a stop across the street from it. The captain leapt out and yelled to Kirby that the house across the street was on fire.

Kirby could see the flames coming out of the first house, but he took the captain's orders to mean that it was the house across the street from the house on fire that he wanted Kirby to attack—that it too must be burning—and so while the main crew thrust itself into the first burning house, laying out attack lines and hoses and running up the hook-and-ladder, Kirby fastened his own hose to the other side of the truck and went storming across the yard and into the house across the street.

He assumed there was no one in it, but as he turned the knob on the front door and shoved his weight against it, the two women who lived inside opened it so that he fell inside, knocking one of them over and landing on her.

Kirby tells Mary Ann that it was the worst he ever got the tunnel vision; that it was like running along a tightrope; that it was almost like being blind. They are on the couch again, in the hours before dawn; she's laughing. Kirby couldn't see flames anywhere, he tells her—his vision reduced to a space about the size of a pinhead—so he assumed the fire was up in the attic. He was confused as to why his partner was not yet there to help him haul his hose up the stairs. Kirby says that the women were protesting, asking why he was bringing the hose into their house. He did not want to have to take the time to explain to them that the most efficient way to fight a fire is from the inside out. He told them to just be quiet and help him pull. This made them so angry that they pulled extra hard—so hard that Kirby, straining at the top of the stairs now, was bowled over again.

When he opened the attic door, he saw that there were no flames. There was a dusty window in the attic, and out it he could see the flames of the house across the street, really rocking now, going under. Kirby says that he stared at it a moment and then asked the ladies if there was a fire anywhere in their house. They replied angrily that there was not.

He had to roll the hose back up—he left sooty hose- and foot-prints all over the carpet—and by this time the house across the street was so engulfed, and in so great a hurry was Kirby to reach it, that he began to hyperventilate and blacked out there in the living room of the nonburning house.

He got better, of course—learned his craft, his calling better, learned it well in time. No one was hurt. But there is still a clumsiness in his heart, in all of their hearts—the echo and memory of it—that is not that distant. They're all just fuckups, like anyone else, even in their uniforms, even in their fire-resistant gear. You can bet that any of them who come to rescue you or your home have problems that are at least as large as yours. You can count on that. There are no real rescuers.

KIRBY TELLS HER ABOUT WHAT he thinks was his best moment of grace—his moment of utter, breathtaking, thanks-giving luck. It happened when he was still a lieutenant, leading his men into an apartment fire. Apartments were the worst, because of the confusion; there was always a greater risk of losing an occupant in an apartment fire, simply because there were so many of them. The awe and mystery of making a rescue—the holiness of it, like a birth—is in no way balanced by the despair of finding an occupant who's already died, a smoke or burn victim, and if that victim is a child, the firefighter is never the same and almost always has to retire after that; his or her marriage goes bad, and life is never the same, never has deep joy and wonder to it again . . . The men and women spend all their time and energy fighting the enemy, *fire*—fighting the way it consumes structures, consumes air, consumes darkness—but then when it takes a life, it is as if some threshold has been crossed—it is for the firemen who discover that victim a feeling like falling down an elevator shaft, and there is sometimes guilt too, that the thing they were so passionate about, fighting fire—a thing that could be said to bring them relief, if not pleasure—should have this as one of its costs . . .

They curse stupidity, curse mankind, when they find a victim, and are almost forever after brittle rather than supple . . .

This fire, the apartment fire, had no loss of occupants, no casualties. It was fully involved by the time Kirby got his men into the structure, Christmas Eve, and they were doing room-to-room searches. No one ever knows how many people live in an apartment complex: how many men, women, and children, coming and going. It can never be accounted for. They had to check every room.

Smoke detectors—thank God!—were squawling everywhere, though that only confused the men further—the sound slightly less piercing than but similar to the motion sensors on their hip belts, so that they were constantly looking around in the smoke and heat to be sure that they were all still together, partner with partner.

Part of the crew fought the blazes while the others made searches: horrible searches, for many of the rooms were burning so intensely that if they did still house an occupant, no rescue could be made, and indeed, the casualties would already have occurred . . .

You can jab a hole in the fire hose at your feet if you get trapped by the flames. You can activate your ceased-motion sensor. The water will spew up from the hose, spraying out of the knife hole like an umbrella of steam and moisture—a water shield, which will buy you ten or fifteen more seconds. You crouch low, sucking on your scuba gear, and wait, if you can't get out. They'll come get you if they can.

This fire—the one with no casualties, the one with grace—had all the men stumbling with tunnel vision. There was something different about this fire— they would talk about it afterward—that they could sense as no one else could: that it was almost as if the fire wanted them, had laid a trap for them.

They were all stumbling and clumsy, but still they checked the rooms. Loose electrical wires dangled from the burning walls and from crumbling, flaming ceilings. The power had been shut off, but it was every firefighter's fear that some passerby, well-meaning, would see the breakers thrown and would flip them back on, unthinking.

The hanging, sagging wires trailed over the backs of the men like tentacles as they passed beneath them. The men blew out walls with their pickaxes, ventilated the ceilings with savage maulings from their lances. Trying to sense, *to feel*, amid the confusion, where someone might be—a survivor—if anyone was left.

Kirby and his partner went into the downstairs apartment of a trophy big-game hunter. It was a large apartment—a suite—and on the walls were the stuffed heads of various animals from all over the world. Some of the heads were already ablaze—flaming rhinos, burning gazelles—and as Kirby and his partner entered, boxes of ammunition began to go off: shotgun shells and rifle bullets, whole caseloads of them. Shots were flying in all directions, and Kirby made the decision right then to pull his men from the fire.

In thirty seconds he had them out—still the fusillade continued—and thirty seconds after that the whole second floor collapsed: an inch-and-a-half-thick flooring of solid concrete dropped like a fallen cake down to the first floor, crushing the space where the men had been half a minute earlier, and the building folded in on itself after that and was swallowed by itself, by its fire.

There was a grand piano in the lobby, and somehow it was not entirely obliterated when the ceiling fell, so that a few crooked, clanging tunes issued forth as the rubble shifted, settled, and burned; and still the shots kept firing.

No casualties. They all went home to their families that night.

Grace. One year Rhonda tells Kirby that she is going to Paris with her new fiance for two weeks and asks if Kirby can keep Jenna for that time. His eyes sting with happiness—with the unexpected grace and blessing of it. Two weeks of clean air, a gift from out of nowhere. A thing that was his and taken away, now brought back. This must be what it feels like to be rescued, he thinks.

Mary Ann thinks often of how hard it is for him—she thinks of it almost every time she sees him with Jenna, reading to her or helping her with something—and they discuss it often, but even at that, even in Mary Ann's great lovingness, she underestimates it. She thinks she wants to know the full weight of it, but she has no true idea. It transcends words, spills over into his actions, and still she, Mary Ann, cannot know the bottom of it.

Kirby dreams ahead to when Jenna is eighteen; he dreams of reuniting. He continues to take catnaps on the roof by her chimney. The separation from her betrays and belies his training; it is greater than an arm's length distance.

The counselors tell him never to let Jenna see this franticness—this gutted, hollow, gasping feeling. To treat it as casual.

As if wearing blinders, unsure of whether the counselors are right or not, he does as they suggest. He thinks that they are probably right. He knows the horrible dangers of panic.

And in the meantime, the new marriage strengthens, becomes more supple and resilient than ever. Arguments cease to be even arguments anymore, merely pulsings of blood, lung-breaths, differences of opinion, like the sun moving in its arc across the sky, or the stars wheeling into place—the earth spinning, rather, and allowing these things to be scribed into place. It becomes a marriage as strong as a galloping horse, reinforced by the innumerable fires and by the weave of his comings and goings, and by the passion of it. His frantic attempts to keep drawing clean air are good for the body of the marriage.

Kirby and Mary Ann are both sometimes amazed by how fast time is going by. She worries about the fifteen or twenty years she's heard get cut off the back end of all firefighters' lives: all those years of sucking in chemicals—burning rags, burning asbestos, burning formaldehyde—but still she does not ask him to stop.

The cinders continue to fall across his back like meteors: twenty-four scars, twenty-five, twenty-six. She knows she could lose him. But she knows he will be lost for sure without the fires.

She prays in church for his safety. Sometimes she forgets to listen to the service and instead gets lost in her prayers. Her eyes blur upon the votive candles. It's as if she's being led out of a burning building herself: as if she's remaining calm and gentle, as someone—her rescuer, perhaps—has instructed her to do.

She forgets to listen to the service. She finds herself instead holding in her heart the secrets he has told her, the things she knows about fires that no one else around her knows.

The way light bulbs melt and lean or point toward a fire's origin—the gases in incandescent bulbs seeking, sensing that heat, so that you can often use them to tell where a fire started, the direction in which the light bulbs first began to lean.

A baby is getting baptized up at the altar, but Mary Ann is still in some other zone—she's still praying for Kirby's safety, his survival. The water being sprinkled on the baby's head reminds her of the men's water shields, of the umbrella mist of spray that buys them extra time, time on earth.

As he travels through town to and from his day job, he begins to define the space around him by the fires that have visited it and that he has engaged and battled. The individual buildings—some charred husks, others intact—begin to link together in his mind. *I rescued that one, there, and that one,* he thinks. *That one.* The city becomes a tapestry, a weave of that which he has saved and that which he has not, with the rest of the city becoming simply all that which is between points, waiting to burn.

He glides through his work at the office. If he were hollow inside, the work would take a thing from him, would suck something out of him, but he is not hollow, is only asleep, like some cast-iron statue from the century before. Whole days pass without his being able to account for them. Sometimes at night, lying there with Mary Ann, both of them listening for the dispatcher, he cannot recall whether he even went into the office that day or not.

He wonders what she is doing, what she is dreaming of. He rises and goes in to check on his other children—simply to look at them.

WHEN YOU RESCUE PEOPLE FROM a burning building, the strength of their terror and panic is unimaginable: enough to bend iron bars. The smallest, weakest persons can strangle and overwhelm the burliest. They will always defeat you. There is a drill that the firemen go through on their hook-and-ladder trucks—mock-rescuing someone from a window ledge or the top of a burning building. Kirby picks the strongest fireman to go up on the ladder and then demonstrates how easily he can make the fireman—vulnerable up on that ladder—lose his balance. It's always staged, of course—the fireman is roped to the ladder for safety—but it makes a somber impression on the young recruits watching from below: the big man being pushed backward by one foot, or one hand, and falling backward and dangling, the rescuer suddenly in need of rescuing.

You can see it in their eyes, Kirby tells them, speaking of those who panic. You can see them getting all wall-eyed. The victims-to-be look almost normal, but then their eyes start to cross just a little. It's as if they're generating such strength within, such *torque,* that it's causing their eyes to act weird. So much torque that it seems they'll snap in half—or snap you in half, if you get too close to them.

Kirby counsels distance to the younger firemen. Let the victims climb onto the ladder by themselves when they're like that. Don't let them touch you. They'll break you in half. You can see the torque in their eyes.

Mary Ann knows all this. She knows it will always be this way for him—but she does not draw back. Twenty-seven scars, twenty-eight. He does not snap; he becomes stronger. She'll never know what it's like, and for that, she's glad.

Many nights he runs a fever, for no apparent reason. Some nights it is his radiant heat that awakens her. She wonders what it will be like when he is too old to go out on the fires. She wonders if she and he can survive that: the not going.

THERE ARE DAYS WHEN HE does not work at his computer. He turns the screen on but then goes over to the window for hours at a time and turns his back on the computer. He's up on the twentieth floor. He watches the flat horizon for smoke. The wind gives a slight sway, a slight tremor to the building.

Sometimes—if he has not been to a fire recently enough—Kirby imagines that the soles of his feet are getting hot. He allows himself to consider this sensation—he does not tune it out.

He stands motionless—still watching the horizon, looking and hoping for smoke—and feels himself igniting, but makes no movement to still or stop the flames. He simply burns, and keeps breathing in, detached, as if it is some structure other than his own that is aflame and vanishing; as if he can keep the two separate—his good life, and the one he left behind.

Rick Bass has worked for moving and storage companies, a valet parking service, a landscaping company, and as a biologist, a geologist, and a teacher of creative writing. About how "The Fireman" came to be, he writes, "For many years, my best friend Kirby was captain of a volunteer fire department. I was able to spend time with him and his crew while on assignment to write a nonfiction article about his work, but found the subject, along with the firefighters' complex lives, so rich that a nonfiction treatment alone was insufficient. I took a simple theme—hardly an original one—of fire being not only a destructive agent, but a rejuvenating one—and followed the story in the direction it wished to travel, as if following opportunities of fuel and wind, from there."

Bass is the author of twenty-four books of fiction and nonfiction, including a memoir, *Why I Came West* (Houghton 2008). He lives in northwest Montana's Yaak Valley, where he is a board member of the Yaak Valley Forest Council (*www.yaakvalley.org*).

"The Fireman" originally appeared in *Kenyon Review* (2000) and was reprinted in *Best American Short Stories*. It is also in the collection *Hermit Stories* (Mariner 2003). Copyright © 2000 by Rick Bass. It is reprinted here by permission of the author.

White Boots:
Ghost of the San Manuel Mine

William Pitt Root

for James G. Davis

As you know, Jim, I did work underground
in the same mine you've imagined
      in your studio: half a mile down, taking
wages enough to make it to California
and fool's gold enough to remind me
      I don't know much after all.

New guys like myself—still thrilled
by the dangers of fire or falling
      through the dark into a hole followed
by twenty tons of dusty rumbling ore—
we all tried to stay alert
      each minute of the eight-hour shift.

And for a week or two, alert we were,
then habit made us careless as the rest
      so we'd pocket our safety glasses,
let dust masks dangle from our necks
and sometimes catch each other
      stepping out across open shafts

without first snapping our lanyards
to the rusty cables overhead.
      The buddy system wasn't much observed,
so like the rest come break time
I'd kick back alone against the stone wall
      and light up, flicking my headlamp off

so the dark expanded, flooding gently
through my eyes. In the distance,
      sometimes, a solitary hunched figure

projecting its small wedge of light
would glide by my line's entrance
  tiny as a fly in a tear of amber

from where I watched, invisible
and isolate as a stone in outer space,
  or inner space. Just some guy.
Never saw old White Boots in those days
but often thought how all those men
  just lost in the Sunshine Mine
must have felt—poor bastards
who lived long enough to feel,
  long enough to lose everything
in their minds but hope
before their air was gone, long after
  their light. You'd have to kill your light

to keep from igniting whatever gasses
might be seeping from walls,
  so dark is where you'd be,
whether by yourself or in the company of others.
In such a dark I had no need of White Boots, my friend,
  but looking at this image, startling, almost comic,

you've drawn from the dark of blinding inks
and your own heart familiar with disaster,
  I'm reminded now of how it is
the living keep hold of the things
that bind them to those gone—
  how gypsies, when a loved one's dying,

will help the one failing stay just a little longer
by turning a wooden chair upside-down
  to hold between them. On one leg
a live hand, the dying on another,
until, ready, it falls free. But
  the thing is the clasp itself

across that final distance,
how it allows those last things
  that need saying to be said.

That's how it's always seemed
to me, with art I mean. Whether
        it's paint on canvas or ink on a page,

it's the chance for what knows it must die in us
to join what knows it will live forever.
        And knowledge from such a common depth
only survives in the light as shadow,
as White Boots, imago, as a way, meanwhile,
        to stay in touch while the sun burns on.

William Pitt Root lived between the Everglades and the Gulf until he was eleven, when his father was killed and the family estate went bankrupt. He then moved to his mother's home place in Minnesota, where he delivered papers and "discovered the sound bike tires made in pre-dawn snow at −40 degrees." En route to becoming a writer, Root was variously a boxboy at Safeway, a "puller" at a gun club, a pipe-fitter's assistant at a shipyard, a bouncer at a downtown bar in Seattle, a warehouse clerk, an experimental subject at the University of Washington and for NASA's earliest zero gravity research, a Teamster, a furniture mover, an oil company night manager, an underground miner, and a teacher. Root has taught as a writer for eighteen years at Hunter College in Manhattan.

Root was Tucson, Arizona's first Poet Laureate. His books include *The Storm and Other Poems* (Carnegie Mellon 2005), *Trace Elements from a Recurring Kingdom* (Confluence 1994), *Faultdancing* (University of Pittsburgh Press 1986), and *Reasons for Going It on Foot* (Atheneum 1981), among others. He has published in over three hundred magazines and literary journals, including *The Atlantic Monthly*, *The Nation*, *The New Yorker*, *Harper's Magazine*, *Poetry*, and *The American Poetry Review*. His work has been included in over one hundred anthologies, including three Pushcart Prize collections and *The New Yorker Book of Poetry* (Viking 1969).

Root writes, "This poem began when I read at Rancho Linda Vista just outside Oracle, Arizona, where the reading was announced previously at the local bars, gathering a few miners from the nearby San Manuel copper mine. One poem I read was about a cave-in at a construction site. Afterward, a man introduced himself as a foreman at the mine and asked if I'd like to visit underground and write about what I saw. I regretted not being able to take him up on it at the time, but when I came through the next year, I was broke and I asked him for a job underground instead, which I got.

"It was rough. Three of us trained together and the other two were both disabled within the first month—one with a crushed thigh, the other a broken shoulder. By then I'd begun my retirement account—sparkling 'gold' nuggets smuggled out of the mine in my lunch bucket, done just as everyone else was doing. By the time I learned all that ore in my car truck was fool's gold (I gave it to every kid I met for a few years), I knew I'd be an even worse fool to stick around any longer.

"But it took years to actually write about that experience, which was so foreign to my sensibility and so taken for granted by the miners—most of whom were third or fourth generation, permanently stoned, and coughing chronically by the time they hit forty. 'White Boots' is the name used in most American mines for the haunts, haints, spooks, spirits, ghosts of the dark underworld."

"White Boots" originally appeared in *Wildwood Review* (1988). It was reprinted in *Tucson Poet* (1998) and is the title poem of the book *White Boots: New and Selected Poems of the West* (Carolina Wren 2006). Copyright © 1988 by William Pitt Root. It is reprinted here by permission of the author.

The Dog

Nathan Alling Long

I'VE SPENT SO MANY HOURS on Greyhound buses, if I cashed them in for nickels I could buy the state of Tennessee. My friend Billy says he'd rather hitch than ride the Dog—that's his word for it. To hell if I'm going to stand in the cold and sleep out at night, just to get between jobs. I travel respectably.

Once Billy and I had to go from Myer's Orchard in Washington State to Southern California to harvest lettuce, and we decided to race—me in the Greyhound, him on the road.

"Why waste your money?" Billy said at the station. He'd gone with me to get my ticket. "Get there the same amount of time using your thumb."

"We'll see," I said back. It was a hot day, early summer, and the station's air wasn't running yet. The doors were wide open, and I could hear each bus pull up, the hiss of brakes, and doors opening and closing.

"Ray," he said, "there're places you can't get to by the Dog."

"No place I want to go," I said. You have to be pretty down and out to stick to the road, I thought. But I didn't tell Billy that. The guy has it rough—lost two toes to frostbite last year. And he drinks himself to death, 'til his nose gets purple. Though he always holds it somehow. Billy was probably drunk when he lost his toes, but I never asked him.

We looked around at the passengers sitting in the plastic seats and standing in line.

"Nicer people on the road," Billy said. He had a hard time letting a thing go. "I mean, if they pick you up, it means they want you. You're chosen."

"But these folks know exactly where they're going," I said. "It's written on the ticket in their hands."

YOU MEET THE DAMNEDEST PEOPLE and see the wildest things on the bus. People fuck, take drugs, steal. It's entertainment, I told Billy. Better than those grocery store newspapers. Once, I saw someone in the back pull a gun out, though he didn't shoot. At the next stop, the cops came on and hauled him away. And in Oklahoma one time, a guy punched out a side window with his fist, yelling about not getting any fresh air. They kicked him out right there on the side of the road.

I remember last year seeing a shaved-headed man boarding the bus outside of Asheville, North Carolina. He wasn't tall but he was well-built, with arms like river rocks, hard and smooth. He sat behind a white woman with brown hair in a feather cut, though her bangs hung heavily. He was a black man, but about as light as they get before they look white. The color of ash. What you really noticed, though, was his eyes. He had the eyes of a husky. Pale blue, as though the whites had bled into the center.

The man was fresh out of a penitentiary—I could tell from the blue issue shirt and pants. I don't think the feather-cut woman could tell though, or else she didn't care. They started talking the way people do all the time on the bus. I couldn't hear much, a little here and there.

"Florida," he said to her at one point. "To the West Coast, near Fort Myers, where my family is. How far you going?" She was twisted around, looking over the seat. I couldn't make out what she said.

Then later. "*Why?*" he said. "Because bald men are the best lovers. Don't tell me you never heard that?" He brushed his hand over his shaved head.

"I never heard that," she said.

"No one's ever told you that? Where are you from?" he asked. Then she got to talking all about her growing up. I looked out my window: We were crossing the Georgia line.

Later, when I looked back, his hand was brushing through her hair. "No, I like it like that," he said. His words were sounding sweet, but I kept staring at those arms. There were tiny white scars in his milky coffee skin, like the belly of a whale I'd seen once in Baltimore.

Two stops later, when the bus pulled out, I noticed that she was gone. Maybe it was her stop, I thought. It took me a moment to realize he was gone, too. Then I saw them out the window, walking up into a cemetery above the town, holding hands. Lucky them, I thought. It can happen that quick, on the bus.

ONE GUY IN A DINER, just outside the Dallas station, offered to pay for my cup of coffee—he was a bit funny, I think, but I was broke and stoned and he was loaded: wore a two piece suit, lots of rings, slicked-back hair. It was late at night, but he was eating a steak-and-egg breakfast. A business guy, I figured.

As I waited for the coffee, he asked me where I was going.

"Idaho," I said. "Potato season."

"You want a lift?" he asked and looked down at his plate.

"I'm taking the bus," I said. "Already have my ticket."

"You know," he said, turning to me, "there is no way I'll ever ride a Greyhound again. I rode it once, from Boston to New Orleans."

"It must have been one hell of a ride," I said.

"Well, you can just say, I've been *grey-hounded.*" He paused and looked at me. "That's a verb," he said—as if I wouldn't know.

The coffee came and I took a sip. "Well, I've ridden them everywhere," I said. "I like who you meet."

"See, I'm not saying Greyhounds aren't important. No, I mean, my God, they're classic." He dropped his napkin on the rest of his food. "I figure one day they'll have a museum for them. It'll have uncomfortable seats in the auditorium, and the whole place will smell like exhaust fumes and piss."

He was laughing.

I didn't say anything. What could I say? He went on a bit, about that Greyhound museum in the future, and kept looking at me like he wanted something. But I couldn't give him anything. He was the one with money.

I WON THE BET WITH Billy, by the way, though Billy didn't think so. I got to Escondido before him. It took me a while to get out to the actual fields, but that's because the farm trucks were late picking us up, and Billy'd gotten a ride straight there. He said we were counting from site to site, but I said, No, what counted was from region to region. He started fussing. I mean, we'd only bet ten dollars, and I wasn't going to fight over it. Not worth losing a friend. I said maybe it was best we both kept our money and called it a draw. He didn't say anything to that.

That was in late fall. After picking lettuce, I headed to Mississippi for oranges; Billy stayed on out West. Next spring, we hooked up to thin apples, up in Washington again. It was probably our eighth year out there together, Billy and I.

They say thinning is unskilled, but it's skilled. If you snap the wrong ones off, they could lose half their crop. You have to snap them off with a twist, so you don't end up tearing the bark. There's a lot of ladder moving, too. And you can damn near break a leg, tripping over the fallen fruit.

The best job is at Myer's, near Spokane—they're the largest in Washington State and we always show up there early, get the best cots in the barracks. They let us leave stuff there, too, for when we come back in the fall to harvest. Not that we have much to leave.

IT WAS THAT SPRING AFTER the bet that Susie showed up at Myer's. Billy and I had been working there for about a week when he spotted her one afternoon. She drove one of those golf carts the managers drive, and she had on tight jeans and a white shirt that wasn't tucked in at all.

Billy had just repositioned his ladder. He said to me, "Ray, I think Eve just showed up." He's always talking about the Myer's grove like it's Eden, because of the apple trees, I guess, and the rolling hills, and the lake. I turned around for a look.

Susie had this curly hair tied back in a ponytail. It was all gold in the sunlight. And her face was just like the skin of the best Georgia peaches, when they're too ripe to pick to sell and you have to eat them right there under the hot sun.

"That's *my* girl," I whispered down to Billy.

"You fall for them all the time," Billy said.

"No, this one I'm serious about," I said. "It'll happen."

"Start praying," Billy said, laughing at me.

Just then the foreman came out of nowhere. He watched us a couple minutes, inspected our tree. By the time he had gone, Susie's cart had disappeared too.

SUSIE HAD A SPECIAL JOB, sawing off the dead limbs and treating them with black tar, to keep the trees healthy. She worked by herself, but sometimes ended up at the same tree I was working at. I remember the first time she came to my tree, looking for any dead parts. She circled it twice, then set her ladder up near mine.

"Found a bad one?" I said, grinning.

"Yeah," she said, and started sawing. Behind her was the lake.

I wanted to give her something, but all I had with me was a joint. The limb fell to the ground and looked like a stiff hand lying in the grass.

"Want to get stoned?" I asked.

"Not while working," she said.

"After, I mean." I reached far in the branches to twist an apple off.

"I better not, thanks. It's hard enough getting up on time."

"Maybe on Friday," I said. I leaned back to look at her better.

"Maybe." She had cut another branch and I watched it drop to the ground. *There's so many good limbs left*, I thought, *if she just stayed here and cut them all off, we could talk for hours.*

When Susie pulled out the tar can, I said, "You like doing this work?"

"It's all right," she said. "I like being outside. What about you?"

"My friend Billy there says it's Eden." I pointed to him in the next tree.

"What do you say?" she asked and grinned.

"Feels that way at the moment," I said and grinned again.

"Well, good," she said, and began tarring the ends. I saw Billy shake his head at me. Susie didn't see him, though. "What?" I said to him, after she had gone.

THE CONVERSATIONS WERE ALWAYS SHORT like that, but over the weeks, I felt we were making a rapport. I asked Billy if he thought so.

"Keep dreaming," he said. Billy can be about as sour as anyone I know. Like he was about losing the Greyhound bet. But like I said, he doesn't have it so easy. It's no wonder, putting half his money in a bottle, that he can't afford to ride the bus. That probably makes him bitter.

"What do you know about these things?" I finally said to Billy.

"And what are you, Albert Einstein?" he asked.

"No," I said, "but I do pick up a lot of stuff on the bus, things you'd never learn about hitching."

Like once, I told him, in Nevada I sat next to this girl heading to Mount Shasta. She wore one of those Indian cotton dresses and sandals. She was a looker, but nothing compared to Susie. Her name was Star, or Moon—something like that. The whole trip she spent telling me about vortexes—said they were centers of energy that existed all around the world. The Grand Tetons was one, and Devil's Tower, South Dakota; Glacier Park, and Big Rock Candy Mountain—that's in Idaho, of all places. Star said vortexes were places aliens had picked out long before humans came. Later, certain natives figured them out, like the Aztecs, who built a temple on one of them. Star said she was going to visit all the sites, to collect the energy of the world. Somehow it would prepare her to be a warrior for life. She believed all that. Star was something. She must have been seventeen.

On the bus, I figure, you're not quite resting on the earth; you're suspended above it, and all kinds of things can seem real: vortexes, alien centers, energy for life battles. Why not?

Riding the Dog, I've learned about how to hook a phone up for free, why that helicopter fell into Crater Lake, how to heal wounds with lichen, and how weather satellites are heating up the planet. You could pay to read all about that stuff in a grocery store newspaper, but by riding the Greyhound, it's free.

I DIDN'T GET TO SEE Susie often, only every few days. Each time she seemed just as beautiful, even wearing jeans and carrying that leather tool belt around her hips. It hung down on the right like a gun belt and everyone kidded her about looking like a cowboy. Me and the others, we didn't have belts, we just had our hands.

"Where you from, originally?" I asked her once.

"Maine," she said. "Well, I was born in Vermont."

"That's pretty, up there." I snapped off a few apples and let them thump on the ground. I felt like God just then, dropping apples on the earth. "So, you'll be here next year, then?"

"Maybe," Susie said.

"Why's not?"

"I'm trying to get a real job."

"Real? Like what?" I asked. I looked down at all the golf-ball-sized apples I'd pulled, then out over the trees and the lake. This all seemed pretty real to me.

"I'm going to be a carpenter," she said.

I looked at her mouth and there wasn't any smile, so I knew she was serious. Still, I couldn't believe it. "A carpenter? Why you want to be a carpenter? Why not let a man be a carpenter, and you can have a house?" As soon as I said it, I wished I hadn't.

"What man?" she said. "I want to be a carpenter."

"Just because you got a saw?" I said, joking.

"No, not just because I got a saw." She shook her head. Her being mad though, didn't really take the sunlight off her hair, or make her skin look any less like peaches.

"I bet you'll be a good carpenter," I said.

"Yeah." Susie stepped down her ladder until her feet were on the ground. "See you."

THE NEXT MORNING I SPENT a long time thinking about Susie while I was in the showers, imagining she was under the water with me. I started singing that old Kris Kristofferson song about the carpenter and the lady taking a chance on him and having his baby.

I knew the words didn't fit right, but it didn't matter. It had carpenters in it and it was a love song. I would have gone on like that all morning, but Billy came in and told me to haul my ass out of there, I was late.

Billy left, then came back a few minutes later to say the last truck was about to leave for the site. "You miss it, you won't get paid for the day."

I hopped out and dressed fast. I didn't want to lose any money. I have to admit, Billy was good at reminding me of that.

I THINK SUSIE HAS TO be the beautiful-est person in America. Once when she was leaning over to snip a branch, hanging from a ladder just a few feet from mine, I looked down her shirt and I could see one of her tits, the shape of a strawberry, the color of a plum. It was perfect. I nearly fell over staring. She reached out and steadied me, her hand on my arm, just for a moment. That was all I needed. I snapped apples the rest of the day, imagining I was twisting her nipples.

Going on the Dog, I've probably seen more people than just about anyone has, except maybe the drivers. So when I say Susie is the beautiful-est person, it means a lot more than someone saying that about their wife, or daughter, or high school sweetheart.

Susie's hair was somewhere between red and blond, and so frizzy, when it wasn't held back, light would pour right through it.

"It's like a halo," I said once. It was near the end of the season. We had two days left. The foreman had stopped coming out to check on us.

"Well, I'm no angel," she said, grinning. She was on the ground, inspecting all the limbs she'd tarred up those past weeks.

"Prove it," I said. I watched her circle my tree.

She smirked and came back around to my side. "What do you plan to do with yourself?" she asked.

I have to admit, I was surprised at that. I stopped picking a moment and wiped my brow. I used to think about plans. Then after a couple years of following the seasons—planting, pruning, picking—it got hard to think about it. "I like moving," I said, "seeing the country." I could tell she wanted more, so I said, "I like working with my hands, too, like you."

Susie nodded, gave me a smile. "That's good." She gathered her tools. "This tree's done," she said.

"See you later," I said, as she got in her cart, but she didn't say anything back.

I didn't see Susie again that season. I hoped she'd be there in the fall, when Billy and I came back to Myer's to pick, but the foreman said she wasn't due back until spring. I thought of her all the time, though, while I was in the trees, filling bushels. As I worked, I'd sing Susie's song really loud.

Billy would hit me on the head with a bad apple. "Your singing is about the worst-assed thing I could think of for a hangover, Ray."

I laughed. I liked Billy for that, being honest. "Well, now we've both got headaches," I said.

"Look at us," he said, "we don't have nothing." And he was right.

It was nearly November when I left Washington State and took the Dog to Phoenix, to pick cotton. Most people don't know it, but that county around Phoenix grows a lot of cotton. For some reason, they don't like black folks picking it, so they give it to us and the Mexicans to pick.

I was waiting in the Flagstaff station for a connection, drifting off to sleep, sort of stoned, when a man came up and said to me, "Hey, Ray."

I didn't recognize him at all, but he said he'd met me a year ago, in that same place.

"You a picker, too?" I asked. I could tell he wasn't by his hands, and how clean his glasses were.

"No, I'm hiding," he said and slapped his knees. "The police are after me, the whole town really. It's hard. Especially if you have the bankers after you. Then how do you get your money, Ray? Tell me that?"

"I don't know," I confessed. The man wasn't all there.

"My home," he said, looking at the floor, "the bankers sold it."

"I'm sorry," I said, and thought of Billy for some reason, wondered where he was just then.

"Tell me, Ray," he said, "tell me something about yourself, so I know that you are not a banker."

It was Sunday and I had nothing to do but wait for the bus, so I told him a little about farm work, and even about Susie, because I'd been thinking about her. I said we'd met in Washington working apples.

"I live by the I-10 bridge," he said. "But you know, Ray, they're kicking us out and building a Wendy's." He stopped suddenly and slapped his lap again.

"That's awful," I said. I didn't know what else to say.

"Yes it is, Ray, it's awful." He looked so worried. "There's just one thing I want to know, Ray."

"What's that?" I asked.

"Well, Ray, what I want to know is why there're not more housing duplexes for all of us? Why do they keep building Wendy's and not duplexes?"

"I don't know," I said.

He slapped his thighs and laughed this time. "Of course, you don't. That would be too simple. You have to ask Susie. Ask your friend Susie, the carpenter."

He talked as though he knew her. It made me think about when Susie asked me what I planned to do. I felt then that I had a plan. I would go back to

Myer's, ask Susie to join me. Together, we would build buildings. Hell, we could build duplexes, if we wanted. Then maybe we'd get married and build a house together. She'd probably like that. I fell into that dream then, like some story they read to you in fourth grade, about living happily ever after, that you never forget.

I GOT THROUGH THAT WINTER and the early spring, traveling from crop to crop, always taking the Dog. Finally, it was late spring and I was heading back to Myer's from the East Coast, to thin apples again. I hadn't seen Billy since the fall. He'd be there, if he wasn't drunk in some ditch. I sensed Susie would be there for sure. I would tell her about what the Flagstaff man said and she would see we were meant to be together. I would even let her be the lead carpenter, I guess.

There were those two days crossing Missouri and Kansas. In Pueblo, a young guy from Minnesota named Joel sat beside me. I was hoping to be by myself, sleep through the next stint, but then I figured he might have some weed to share. I'd been out for a week. I remember waking up as we pulled into Grand Junction, Colorado. The sky was layered with purples and blues, like it was bruised, and I wasn't certain if it was sunset or dawn. Even after I stumbled into the station and stood there a moment, I couldn't tell. The clock read six forty-five. It was cold, but when Joel asked me if I wanted to take a walk, I knew just what we were going to do.

Joel and I stood behind a brick wall along some dirt road—I swear they don't pave the roads in Colorado if they don't have to. Joel loaded the pipe and handed it to me. When I flicked the lighter, I saw that its eyes were made of small green stones. The bowl had a face on it that stared right at you and its mouth came out along the stem as though it was smoking me.

"Mean pipe," I said.

"I made it myself," Joel said.

"It looks like the devil," I said and took another hit.

He smiled at that. "It's just a face I came up with when I was stoned."

"I bet," I said and took another drag before handing it back to him. We smoked a long while. Joel kept looking at me funny, but maybe it was the dope. If it was day coming on, I thought, I wanted to be stoned, to get through the flat lands that were coming.

BACK AT THE TERMINAL, WE tried to warm up by walking back and forth between the restaurant and the lobby. If I'd had more money, I'd have bought coffee. Joel finally sat in one of those TV chairs and took a nap, and I went over and stared at the map of the U.S. on the wall.

All the roads looked like veins. I got to thinking of a woman at some hot springs outside of Eugene, Oregon, who had varicose veins so bad her legs looked like the hills of West Virginia. That got me to thinking about all the hippie chicks up there who'd be all naked in the pool. I'd spend the day there, sweating half to death, just so I could watch those girls with their ratty hair and tattoos and rings in their noses. Sometimes rings in their tits, too. There were some damn nice girls—still, none got close to Susie.

"God, this is good shit," I said to myself, meaning the dope. I looked away from the map a second and out the windows. It was pitch black, so I finally knew we were going into night. I went back to staring at the map and the highways began to lift off the paper again, like they were 3-D. They looked like wire mesh I'd seen in a warehouse window once somewhere. Chicago, I think, the South Side—just outside of the Greyhound Station on 95th Street. I remember the driver had said don't leave the station, that a man had had his face cut in two a week before, near a church just a block away. But I walked around anyway—what did I have to lose?

In my mind I was still there in Chicago when some voice said, "Which way you heading?"

I nearly jumped against the chairs behind me. There was a short man who wore a black cowboy hat drawn down to his eyes. I must have stared at him a minute before I said, "West." And then I thought some more and said, "And you?"

"I just came from there," he said. He was rocking a bit and steadied himself with one hand on the wall. "You going through Salt Lake, or up Idaho?"

I could smell whiskey at the end of his question and it made me think of Billy.

"Idaho," I said.

"That'll be fifty, then."

"Huh?" I said.

"Route 50, that's it right here." He jabbed his index finger at the map. I was surprised it landed right on the line.

"Loneliest highway in the world," he said.

"Why do you say that?"

"That's what they call it, that's all." Then he fell backward a bit, walked off, and dropped into a seat.

When our bus came, it looked like it was going to be crowded. I took the back seat, hoping to get it all to myself, but Joel asked to sit there, too, and I couldn't say no after he'd given me smoke. The bus lights went out and we jerked forward.

At the corner I saw a Wendy's and thought of the Flagstaff guy, him warning me about bankers. We passed the building where Joel and I had smoked. I was going to say something to him but he already looked asleep. In a few minutes his head began dropping toward my shoulder, like it was an old door hinge. But I didn't care. It was almost nice, and I was so high, in the dark, I could imagine he was Susie. I leaned further back, and he did too. In my head I began singing those Kristofferson lyrics.

I was thinking about Susie's hair, the warmth of sun on those days, and of course I was thinking about what I'd seen down her shirt the day she'd bent over to clip that branch. I guess that's why I didn't do anything when I felt Joel's hand fall into my lap. It moved a bit, and then some more. Soon, he was rubbing and I didn't know what to do. I hadn't stopped him when I should have. So, I imagined it was Susie again, her touching me. Joel was about her size.

We were in the back, so no one could see. And it was pure dark in there. I'm not that way, but I guess I was just too stoned to stop him or care. I remember feeling like I wasn't inside the bus anymore. I was soaring above it, like a large bird, a hawk or something. There was all this wind around me. I saw the bus below, like prey, traveling on the highway. I thought of vortexes then and wondered if we were traveling toward someplace special.

The city was far behind us, and not even a farmhouse light shined in through the tinted windows. The small golf-ball vent above us was blowing air on my neck like Susie's breath. It was easy, floating there in the night air, imagining it was her. Susie was saying in my head, *Baby, I want you.* She was right there in front of me, her lips like every fruit I'd ever picked, and I kissed her and kissed her.

Then I got so high, the bus disappeared altogether. I was no longer a hawk either, but something smaller and white. Like a dove, or just a feather, being sent way up through the air.

AFTER WE STOPPED AT A town just in that corner of Utah you go through before you hit Idaho, Joel got up and changed seats. He knew not to stay beside me. It had been five or six hours, we'd both slept right through them, and I was coming down. I had never guessed him to be funny that way, or else I wouldn't have sat with him. I was in the last seat by myself now, alone, and I couldn't get back to sleep. I kept wondering if it had really happened, but I knew it had. Maybe Joel had gotten me high just so he could do it. It was better not to think about it. Instead, I tried to think of Susie, but no image of her would come.

When I got to Spokane, I stepped off the bus, not realizing how stiff I was. I just wanted to be at the site. I was running late this year. I walked around the town, waiting for the Myer's truck to pick me up. A young Asian guy wanted to sell me a quarter bag for a hundred bucks. He must have been desperate, though, because I talked him down to fifty, the last of my money. It was a deal.

When I got to Myer's, I went straight for the barracks. I saw Billy lying on a cot.

"I tried to save you a good one, pal," he said, "but no dice."

"That's all right," I said.

"Welcome back to Eden." He laughed.

"Is Susie here?" I asked, throwing my bag on the last free bed.

"Haven't seen her. Think she'll come?"

"I have a feeling."

Billy had been hiding a bottle by the foot of his bed, and he lifted it up for a swig. "Keep praying," he said. I wanted to punch him, but not really.

The next morning we got up with the others and worked through the day.

I kept looking around for Susie, but she didn't appear. It was one of those rare cloudy days during late spring. That meant we could work later, without the sun killing us, but Billy and I were talking so much, we still barely made quota.

That night we sat off by ourselves, Billy and me, near the campfire they light every evening, him getting drunk and me getting high. I was keeping the quarter bag in my shoes; there were over forty guys there in the barracks, and I only trusted about three of them. If your stash is stolen, you can't really go to the foreman and tell him about it.

Billy said he'd slipped by his folks' house for a while—in Arkansas—then went to Michigan for a job. To get to Myer's he'd hitched across Montana. It took four days. I would have told him how it'd have taken half the time by bus, but there was no point. That night he went through a liter of Beam by himself. Around eleven-thirty, I stood up to go to bed and nearly blacked out. I was stoned good. Billy said he was going to take a walk, which meant going into town for more, and when I watched him head off toward the road into town, I wondered if it was him or me who seemed to not be standing up straight.

WE WERE ALL WOKEN BY sirens at two in the morning. For a second I thought we were being attacked. But then I got up and peered out the window. Three cop cars parked at different angles, like they never learned what a straight line was, and five cops stood in front of them, talking to each other. Our foreman was there.

Just about everyone in the barracks had some reason to be afraid of the police. A few Mexican fellows talked rapidly at the end of the building. They were probably talking to Jerry—their white buddy who spoke Spanish—about what they should do. One Mexican unlocked the window above his bed and looked out to see if they could escape that way. I thought about the quarter in my shoe, then looked around and noticed Billy's bed was empty.

Finally, a cop came in with a flashlight, sweeping it back and forth like it was a sword.

"Sorry to bother you gentlemen," he said. He walked slowly around the room.

I get suspicious when a cop acts friendly. It means he wants something and if he doesn't get it, he'll just switch tactics. Once a cop told me he'd found a bag of dope laced with arsenic and was just trying to prevent people from killing themselves—did I know anyone who had tried to sell me some recently? I said no, kept saying no, and by the time I figured out that wasn't the answer he wanted, he'd already thrown me on the ground, searched me, and found a reason to put me in jail for a week.

"Does anyone know a William Denton here?" the cop asked.

Billy.

"He was found on the side of the road with blood alcohol poisoning and the foreman said some of you all here might be his friends. We just need someone to go down to the hospital and answer questions."

No one said anything. It was the questions that scared us. Besides, everyone was sleepy and didn't want to miss work. Me, he was my friend, but I couldn't go. I felt bad, but I had enough grass in my shoe for them to get me good. There's no reason they'd search me, but you never know how things can turn. And I wasn't going to leave the quarter there in the barracks. It was all I had. Plus, what good could I do?

"If your foreman has to go, he'll be pissed," the cop said, and began shining the light in one face after another. I saw it coming, he was shifting over to mean.

No one stepped forward. A couple people looked over at me. I felt like a dog for not speaking up.

"I guess we'll have to turn on the lights," the cop said, "and check everyone's ID."

"I'll go," a guy said in the back, where it was dark. The cop shone his light down that end so the guy could walk up. It was Jerry. He already had his shoes and clothes on.

"Thank you, buddy," the cop said. "Good to see there's a decent man in the bunch."

A couple guys rolled their eyes. I said, "Thanks, Jerry," as he passed.

Once the cops and Jerry left, I checked my shoe and went back to bed, but I couldn't sleep, worrying about Billy. I felt bad, but what could I've done?

THE NEXT DAY I DIDN'T see Jerry or Billy. I had a dope hangover, plus the interrupted sleep. And I was worried. Everyone was, I guess. I would have asked the foreman about Billy, but he knew we were best friends and I didn't want him asking me why I hadn't volunteered. Work was slow. I'd given up thinking about Susie just then. She hadn't shown up anyway.

That evening, by the fire again, Jerry showed up and everyone gathered around to hear. He held a loose fist up to his mouth and looked into the fire.

"He's not going to make it," Jerry said. "He went into shock this morning and doctors said his liver was crumbling like an old sponge."

Some guys were asking questions, but I just walked off. It sounds strange, but hearing what Jerry said made me want to drink. Just that night. To get as drunk as Billy, and maybe feel a little what he'd been feeling.

I WAS LATE FOR CREW the next day, missed the second truck run and had to walk across the orchard to the site. The grass was wet and all the clouds had disappeared; there was only a line of pink along the horizon. On the way, I thought a long while about Billy lying in a hospital bed. I wished, way back, I had paid him the ten bucks for that bet. Then I thought how he would have just spent it on booze.

The air was cool still. Walking between the trees, I breathed out—glad I was alone. I could see for quite a distance rows and rows of trees, and I thought how Billy called Myer's Orchard Eden. What a joke.

I saw the foreman walking toward me, one row over. He was carrying a wrench and a bucket. When he was near enough he said, "You're late, Ray."

"I know," I said. He passed me without expression. He was an ordinary man, I thought. Nothing special.

For a moment, I almost ran back and asked the foreman about Susie, but I knew what his answer would be. She wasn't coming. It made me sick then to think Joel's hand was the closest I'd ever get to her. She was probably off becoming a carpenter, making good money. And here I was still in an orchard.

Instead of heading to the site, I went down to the lake and looked out into the water. A couple of spring apples had rolled down to the edge, and I tossed them, one at a time, across the surface of the lake. Then I turned and walked back toward the barracks. I wasn't going back to work. I'd head into town and say goodbye to Billy. Then I'd take off somewhere new, somewhere the Dog couldn't go.

Nathan Alling Long was born in Washington, DC., in 1964. He has been the recipient of a Truman Capote Literary Scholarship, a Virginia Commission of the Arts Fellowship, Bread Loaf Writers' Conference Fellowships, and a Mellon Foundation Fellowship. His work—fiction, poetry, drama, and essays—have appeared in many literary journals, including *Glimmer Train, Indiana Review, Story Quarterly, Tin House,* and *The Sun.*

Long has worked playing Frosty the Snowman at a local town mall, making sandwiches at a food co-op, driving a recycling truck, selling South American clothing on the street, packaging English muffins, building and cleaning houses, loading boxes for a Clorox factory, acting as an extra in a Vietnam War film, moving furniture, counting traffic patterns, conducting bus surveys, caring for the mentally ill and the deaf, baking, and cooking at an organic restaurant, as well as tutoring, editing, writing, and teaching. Currently, he is a professor of creative writing at Richard Stockton College of New Jersey. He recently completed a collection of short stories, *Conveyance,* about people in motion.

Long considers himself a consummate traveler, having traversed the continental United States over twenty-five times. " 'The Dog,' " he says, "began with the desire to use the images I'd collected over years of travel. My friend Jean, who also frequently took Greyhound, coined the phrase 'the Dog,' and my sister Kathryn's experience picking apples in Washington State helped form the description of Myer's Orchard. Many of the events and details in this story are inspired by what I have witnessed exploring the United States, but the story and the central character, Ray, are complete invention."

Long has been interested in migrant farm work for years, since reading the book *American Pictures* by Jacob Holdt, a Danish traveler and author, which illuminates how the underclass live (those who work below minimum wage and are often not reported in the census or in employment figures). Long says, "The incredibly low cost of our food is dependent on this work force, but few know much about it. I met many migrant farm workers while I lived in Oregon, mostly when I visited free public hot springs in the Cascades. 'The Dog' was an attempt to imagine some of the differences within the migrant farm worker community, to hopefully, then, understand them better."

"The Dog" is part of Long's collection *The Last Hot Day of Summer & The Dog* (Popular Ink 2006). Copyright © 2006 by Nathan Alling Long. It is reprinted here by permission of Popular Ink.

After Garbage Men

Jay Snodgrass

They staggered the brown and orange garbage trucks
in rows and lifted their backs like they were dumping trash
so we could wash them.
They looked like colossal dung beetles venting
on the tarmac, which cooked in the sun and
reflected heat back up to the trucks
so the rotten innards of them steamed.
The stench of diesel and milk-splatter
sweltered. The scraps and leavings of other peoples' lives
were easy enough to blow off with a pressure hose.
Flies clouded everywhere, tickling our necks
like sweat and demons. The exhaust choked
and clung to the hose's mist like slobber.

We used degreaser on the crankshafts. The drivers
were meticulous about this, even though they left their
windshield wipers clogged with cat litter
six days of the week. We cleaned up after garbage men.
In our van we had a white plastic fifty-five gallon drum of degreaser,
with a foot of clear liquid visible through the bottom.
The OSHA label read: *caustic*, in words nobody paid attention to.
I had to crawl into the van, cooked also in the sun
and maneuver the drum to pour a measure
into the soap tank. Settling the drum as gently as I
could, a slosh drop peeked through the one-inch
nozzle and trajectoried right into my eye.

Over the grumble of diesels, over the howl
of the two-stroke water pump inside the van,
the yard boss heard me scream.
In the garbage-truck shop I leaned over the eye wash
for half an hour. Outside the grumbling
of truck washing went on, grease and garbage water
riveting into grates already rainbowed with oil.
I was glad to be inside, though I felt
weak for not being out with the others as they worked.

The smell of landfills was already in my clothes,
in my sweat. When I looked in the mirror
to check the redness of my eye, a thick fluid
discharged like milk-splatter.

Jay Snodgrass was born in Florida and grew up on an Air Force base in Japan. He is the author of two books of poetry, *Monster Zero* (Elixir 2002)—poems about Godzilla—and *The Underflower* (Cherry Grove 2007), described as "Ponce de Leon meets Paul Celan in the nether regions of Biscayne Boulevard." He is currently completing his PhD at Florida State University in Tallahassee, where he lives with his wife and daughter.

Snodgrass writes, "'After Garbage Men' was written when I lived in Richmond, Virginia, and worked as a mobile truck washer. Washing trucks is grueling and horrific. It is auto detailing on an industrial scale. The work took place at night and on weekends when the machinery of the world could be accessed for service. Because of the struggle to make art out of my life, I tried to imagine that I was involved in the effort to make something decent out of the world in which I found myself—that there was real virtue in spit-polishing garbage trucks. The poem was written after an eighteen-hour stint washing the grease from the chassis of garbage trucks. Although I was nearly blinded by the circumstance of the poem, I feel, like Odin, that I gained at least the vision of the poem. I worked at that job for six more months until I had to clean out the backs of trucks which carried pigs to slaughter. At that point, the exchange of life for work, even under the auspices of art, became unsustainable."

Copyright © Jay Snodgrass

The Women Who Clean Fish

Erica Funkhouser

The women who clean fish are all named Rose
or Grace. They wake up close to the water,
damp and dreamy beneath white sheets,
thinking of white beaches.

It is always humid where they work.
Under plastic aprons, their breasts
foam and bubble. They wear old clothes
because the smell will never go.

On the floor, chlorine.
On the window, dry streams left by gulls.
When tourists come to watch them
working over belts of cod and hake,
they don't look up.

They stand above the gutter. When the belt starts
they pack the bodies in, ten per box,
their tales crisscrossed as if in sacrament.
The dead fish fall compliantly.

It is the iridescent scales that stick,
clinging to cheek and wrist,
lighting up hours later in a dark room.

The packers say they feel orange spawn
between their fingers, the smell of themselves
more like salt than peach.

Erica Funkhouser's books of poems include *Earthly* (2008), *Pursuit* (2002), *The Actual World* (1997), and *Sure Shot and Other Poems* (1992), all published by Houghton Mifflin, and *Natural Affinities* (1983), published by Alice James Books. Included in *Sure Shot* is a trio of dramatic monologues in the voices of three hard-working American women: Sacagawea, Louisa May Alcott, and Annie Oakley. The Oakley poem was adapted for the stage and produced by the Helicon Theatre Company in Los Angeles. Funkhouser's work on Sacagawea led her to become involved with the production of Ken Burns's PBS documentary on the Lewis and Clark expedition, and her essay on Sacagawea appears in Ken Burns and Dayton Duncan's *Lewis and Clark*. A 2007 recipient of a Guggenheim Fellowship in Poetry, Funkhouser currently teaches at MIT and lives on Cape Ann, near Gloucester, where "there are now a lot less fish to clean than in the 1980s, when this poem was written."

"The Women Who Clean Fish" is from *Natural Affinities*. Copyright © 1983 by Erika Funkhouser. It is reprinted here by permission of Alice James Books.

Appointed Route

Ben Satterfield

SANDERS GOT OUT OF BED slowly so as not to disturb his wife, put on his robe and slippers, and went out the back of the house. Standing on the patio, he scanned the heavens for any ominous sign, but found none; the morning sparkled like champagne in a crystal glass, and he knew exactly what he was going to do.

It was Friday, the last day of his vacation. His wife would sleep at least another hour, he knew, exhausted from "tromping all over Cuernavaca," as she put it. But walking didn't bother Sanders at all; he was used to it. And today he was going to do something he had done a thousand times, yet had never done before.

He went back inside and put coffee on, then washed his face and shaved. Moving quietly in the bedroom, he selected the clothes he wanted—khaki pants, blue chambray shirt, deerskin shoes—and dressed. Softly he closed the door behind him, returned to the kitchen and began making a breakfast of eggs scrambled with mushrooms and onions. He sliced a tomato and made toast, humming a tune from some musical he had seen while in New York on another vacation a decade ago.

As he ate, he made a list for the weekend shopping. Sanders printed in block letters, compiling a neat list in two columns, with fruit and vegetables making up one column and staples the other. He had an orderly mind and liked making lists. He even enjoyed shopping and found it easy to remember where items were in the supermarket.

After eating, he put his plate and utensils in the sink, had another cup of coffee, and wrote his wife a note: *Went out for a while. Be back for lunch.* Looking at what he had written, he was struck by the stark simplicity, the flatness, the lack of detail. He thought about elaborating but his mind blanked, and he added only *late* in front of *lunch*. He tore the sheet from the tablet, put the paper on the refrigerator door, and secured it with a magnetized ornament colored and shaped like a banana.

Utilitarian, he thought as he pulled away from the house. Driving across town, he wondered how much of his life had become merely useful, how much pleasure and delight—even joy—had been sacrificed in favor of utility. How could he know? Every choice cancels the possibility of other choices, each decision leads to another decision like links in a chain, on and on, until one day we find ourselves hobbled and struggling against a fetter of our own making. Sanders wondered: Was he chained?

He had begun thinking about the substance of his life when he was on vacation in Puebla as he observed the Mexican custom of closing up business for siesta. In America, of course, only a catastrophe could shut the doors of commerce, and he was American from scalp to toenail. Still, he had begun to wonder.

He thought back twenty years, then shook his head. The past was unalterable; no point in playing out a line in dead water. Meaning, in whatever form, would have to be found in the present and the possible. His quest was before him.

He parked his car at the corner of Montrose and Wilson, looked at his watch, then walked eight blocks to the end of Wilson where it met Gramercy in a T. He crossed to the other side and walked back down Wilson, then took Montrose to Cleveland. On Cleveland he strode along the east side to Gramercy, then back down the west side to Montrose, repeating the jaunt. One block on Montrose to Harrison, then—again—down the east side.

The streets in this section of the city had been named after U.S. presidents and statesmen, but not in any order that Sanders understood, although he knew their sequence perfectly. "Wilson, Cleveland, Harrison, Polk," he recited, trying to discern a pattern that made sense. "McKinley, Adams, Fillmore, Pierce." He shook his head, doubtful that after five years of running the names through his head he would discover any logic in the arrangement. "It must be random," he said to himself for the hundredth time. Yet he continued to search for some evidence of method in the signs marking the avenues he knew so well, as if believing not only that logic and order rule absolutely, but that the "city fathers" or whoever had decided upon the names of the streets would have had the wisdom to recognize this immutable fact and act accordingly. "Harding, Monroe, Jackson, Tyler." He suspected that if there had been any reasoning behind the order, it was of so arcane a nature that he would never fathom it.

About halfway down Harrison he saw five boys, who looked scruffy and cool in a practiced way, standing around a red Ford Fiesta, its headlights on but growing dim. The boys were talking and watching the lights with interest. One of them Sanders recognized. "The Farley boy," he said to himself, trying to remember his first name. "It ends in 'o'—Milo, Waldo, Hugo—" He couldn't recall, but he had seen the name before; not often, certainly, or he would have remembered it.

Sanders looked at his watch as he approached the boys. "Why don't you turn the lights off?" he asked.

The Farley boy looked at him sullenly. "Locked," he said, snapping the word like a rubber band. He was large and shaggy, just out of high school, with time and boredom hanging on his burly frame like a millstone. He slouched, smoking a black cigarillo as if it were a prop and he was trying out for a part. One of the others shook a cigarette from a pack of Kools and lit it with a disposable lighter.

"Know whose car it is?" Sanders asked.

A couple of the kids snickered, but the Farley boy held his sullen look.

"Yeah," he said, exhaling smoke. "It belongs to the guy who's in there"—he jerked his thumb toward a white frame house that had all the blinds drawn—"having fun with Miz Divorcée."

The woman he referred to, Sanders knew, was a pretty brunette, recently divorced and with two young children. Moore was her name. He looked at the house. A small bicycle with training wheels was chained to one of the posts of the stoop. "I'm sure he would appreciate your telling him—"

"He don' wanta be disturbed," the Farley boy said, looking at him closely, letting the thin cigar hang from the corner of his mouth. "You live around here?"

"No, I don't."

"What's it to you?"

"I'd hate for my battery to run down because nobody would let me know I'd left the lights on."

"It ain't your batt'ry."

"I meant—"

"Hey, man, I don' care. What I mean is, this ain't your car. This ain't your neighborhood. This ain't your business."

"Still," Sanders said pleasantly, "I think it's a shame to let it happen."

"A shame?" the Farley boy said as if the word were one he did not recognize or could not understand. He took the prop out of his mouth and spat in the street. "A shame?" He looked around at his companions, shook his head in mock disgust, and threw the cigar past Sanders onto the sidewalk.

"I mean it's needless."

"Hey, it's not our fault the guy is so hot and bothered that he drives around in broad daylight with his lights on, and can't take the time to turn 'em off." The Farley boy made a circle with the thumb and fingers of his left hand, then stabbed the rigid index finger of his right hand into the circle several times while rolling his eyes and lolling his tongue. The other boys laughed nervously. "Furthermore, we got a bet on the lights."

"A bet?"

"Yeah, we all guessed how long the batt'ry would last. Whoever gets the closest wins."

"And the owner loses."

"Not my fault, man. Just like it's not your business. Bug off."

Sanders marched up the walk to the white frame house and rang the bell. A Raggedy Ann doll was lying on its back in the gutter, legs propped against the cement steps of the tiny stoop, its dirty skirt inverted. Behind him he heard the boys cursing and calling him names. He turned to watch them straggle away from the car, arguing about how to settle their bets and grumbling about "nosy bastards." Mrs. Moore came to the door in a faded blue housecoat and looked at him questioningly, pushing errant strands of hair from her face. When he told her about the car, she called someone named Harry to talk to him. Moments later a barefooted man appeared wearing gray slacks and a T-shirt, and Sanders assumed that was all. "For Christ's sake," he snarled, giving Sanders a dark look as he stamped past and out to the car, a thick scent of cologne hanging in his wake. He jerked open the door and shut off the lights. "What're they doing on?" he asked angrily. To Sanders the question sounded like an accusation.

"I'm sorry, I thought it was locked."

"For Christ's sake," the man said again. He went back inside and slammed the door.

Sanders looked at his watch and resumed walking down the street.

After Harrison, he went up and down Polk, greeting only one person, a plump housewife who had just returned home with a carload of groceries. "Good morning, Mrs. Howard," he called, but she did not answer, casting him only a curt glance as she unloaded her car. A black and white cat crouching on the sidewalk stared at him as he passed by. Overhead a helicopter chuffed its way across the sky and disappeared.

On McKinley he saw deaf Ira Wingard sitting on his small porch, whiling away the morning as he usually did. Sanders waved without speaking, but the shriveled man only peered at him through thick lenses, guarded and suspicious, thrusting his head forward like a turtle looking out of its shell.

Very few people moved about or were even visible, and Sanders thought that residents stayed indoors more than they used to, that people were neighbors only in name, and neighborhoods merely districts marked by the boundaries of common streets. Despite the similarity of the houses, there was no feeling of community, no sense of anything shared beyond property lines, not even an impression of belonging. Many homeowners lived for years, Sanders believed, within shouting distance of others who remained strangers, as though exiled. Suburbia. Even the name sounded alien.

He began looking for something.

Old Mrs. Argun was sweeping a few leaves from her walk on Adams Avenue when Sanders approached. He smiled at her and nodded, but she went inside. He could feel her watching him as he continued down to Gramercy and then back on the other side of the street. He knew her reputation for always being on the watch. One of the people who lived next door to her, a well-educated man frequently out of work, had once said, "She should've been named Argus, not Argun."

By the time he reached Fillmore a police car had arrived and moved slowly behind him. The driver seemed to linger, watching, before pulling up beside Sanders and stopping. The officer, a young man with short dark hair and a moustache, both neatly trimmed, moved briskly from the car to the sidewalk. "Excuse me, sir," he said, politely but firmly.

Sanders stopped and looked at his watch. "Yes?"

"Could I see some identification, please?"

Sanders took out his wallet, removed his driver's license and handed it over. The policeman took it and read aloud, "Sheldon Allister Sanders," as if checking the name against some mental file. He wore a plastic nameplate over his right shirt pocket that read "J. Willis." Over his left pocket he wore the badge of authority, and Sanders thought that one identified him as much as the other.

"Is this your correct address?"

"Yes, it is."

"It's on the other side of town. Are you visiting someone in this area?"

"No, not exactly."

"I'll be blunt, Mr. Sanders: what exactly are you doing here?"

"Just walking. That's certainly not a crime."

"A complaint came in about a strange man prowling around this locale."

"Prowling? You can see for yourself that I'm simply walking."

"I was using the complainant's terminology," the patrolman said in an official tone. "What I see is that you're quite a ways from home and with no apparent purpose in this area." He looked steadily at Sanders, letting him know that because his behavior was unusual, it was therefore suspicious.

"My purpose," Sanders began with a flash of anger, but suddenly felt foolish and stopped, thinking to himself, in a free society, why should he need a purpose to walk on public property or have to justify his movements to any authority? He slowly took a laminated card from his pocket and handed it to the policeman. "This is my Postal Service ID," he said. "I'm a mail carrier."

Officer Willis studied the card, looked back at Sanders quizzically. "A postman?"

"Yes, and this is my route." He swept his right arm out in a semicircle. "Like you have a beat, I have a route."

"But you're not delivering mail."

"I'm on vacation, actually. But I've been on this particular route for over five years. Today I was walking it empty just to see how it felt, and to find out how long it would take."

"You mean you're timing yourself?"

Sanders nodded.

Officer Willis stared at him, frowning. "What difference does it make how long it takes when you're not carrying mail?"

Sanders looked away. "Well, I wanted to know," was all he could think of to say.

"Kind of a busman's holiday, you mean?"

"Not exactly," Sanders said, feeling awkward and embarrassed, as if he had been caught naked. He found his "purpose"—which he felt earlier was as clear as the sunshine itself—hazy and impossible to explain. "But something like that."

"Busman's holiday I can understand," Willis said, nodding his head slightly. "I have a friend who's a mechanic—guy just loves to work on cars, can't get enough. I mean, this guy is a mechanic. Over at his house he has a den, and the walls are covered with mounted parts from automobiles, like animal trophies. They're all named and dated—'Voltage regulator, 1969 Rambler American, August 18,

1982'—like that. Carburetor, starter, alternator, fuel pump, you name it, it's on his wall, parts from every kind of automobile I know of, on plaques. It's something to see, but I figure, what the heck, it's his room. He surrounds himself with stuff he knows. Makes him feel comfortable, I guess."

Sanders nodded, although he didn't feel that he was at all like the mechanic.

"Me, I'm not that way. Nosiree. I go home, I take off the uniform, that's it. I don't even watch cop shows on television."

"I thought it would be different," Sanders said. "You see, I can tell you the names of the people in every house around here. It's kind of like, well, my neighborhood too—except that nobody knows me. The people who've seen me today just stared at me. Not one person has recognized me."

"That's understandable. You're not wearing your uniform. "

"But I talk to these people. They see me more often than they do most of their relatives."

"Except they don't see you, really."

Speechless, Sanders gazed at the young man.

"Like I say, it's nothing personal. They don't see you."

"But they must."

"When I went through the academy," the officer said, "I learned first thing not to get personally involved. The instructor told us that outsiders don't see us as people. What that means is, when civilians look at me, they don't see a person, they see a cop. Has nothing to do with me."

"That's terrible," Sanders said.

The officer shrugged. "Part of the job. You get used to it."

"No."

"Hey, look, I can see you're not doing anything wrong," Willis said, returning the identity cards. "But at the same time, maybe it'd be better if you just went on home."

"That's not an order, is it?"

"Well, no, just a suggestion. I mean, it's not like you have to make a point or anything, is it?"

Sanders looked down the street, feeling more than ever that a point was exactly what he had to make. "I don't know," he said.

Willis pursed his lips, hitched up his gunbelt, and checked his own watch. "Well," he said hesitantly, as if uncertain of his authority, "I'd recommend that you go home. Don't upset the people here." He turned and went to his car.

Sanders walked on down the street, quickly calculating the time he had just lost and adding it to what he had wasted with the youths on Harrison. A minute later, the police car passed him, moving slowly, the officer holding a microphone to his lips. Sanders thought he was scowling.

He finished his walk on Fillmore, then Pierce and Harding, without incident. He spotted only a few people, and those went inside when they saw him coming. No one recognized him or even spoke to him. He began saying the names of the occupants as he passed the houses. Newton, 4726, lots of bills, American Express, Visa, Transamerica, Beneficial Finance, on and on. Lambert, 4728, *Reader's Digest*, Book-of-the-Month, Sears.

He went on.

Monroe and Jackson were eventless too. Behind the chain link fence of the Finley house on Tyler a German shepherd barked and watched him closely. When he was in front of the house, he stopped and stood by the gate facing the dog. "Hello, Durwin," he said, and the animal cocked its head and looked at him, ears straight. "Remember me?" When the shepherd growled, Sanders, looking for recognition in the thick eyes, said, "You know me, don't you?" and put his hand on the mailbox attached to the outside of the fence. As if in answer the dog snarled and leapt at the gate, causing Sanders to draw back. *Well, that was something.*

Mrs. Finley, a wooden spoon in her hand and a white chef's apron over her housedress, opened the front door and stared at him in much the same manner as the dog. Only she frowned, her face a study of puzzlement as she squinted and leaned forward toward him. "What are you doing?" she snapped, moving onto the little porch and brandishing her spoon as if it were a weapon.

"Nothing," Sanders beamed at her, raising his arms and holding them open. In a frenzy, the shepherd threw himself against the fence. Sanders stopped smiling as he looked straight at the dog, its front paws hooked in the mesh of the fence, its yellow teeth bared.

"Quiet, Durwin!" Mrs. Finley yelled. Then to Sanders, "And, you, get away. Go do nothing somewhere else. Better yet, get a job!" She shook her head and went back inside.

Sanders squatted on his heels in front of the dog. The animal stared at him with its forelegs straining against the wire that separated them, a low and vicious growl in its throat. "I've got a job," Sanders said to the dog. "And you know what it is, don't you?"

The dog growled louder. Sanders growled back.

Ben Satterfield's biography is unknown. Since he submitted his piece for consideration, the editors have made extensive efforts to track him down, without success.

Copyright © Ben Satterfield

The Basement

Paula Champa

RIGHT NOW, I DO NOT think of them as familiar or human. Not fat or ducts or flesh. Not even a part of me. They're oranges one week, grapefruits the next, and cantaloupes the rest of the month. They're especially cantaloupes today, with the temperature above ninety.

I'm thinking about them too much.

They're not that big. They've never been as big or as small as I wanted them to be. Not as firm as Kelly Mulligan's in the showers after swim class—that sculpted muscular wall, the proof of her perfect butterfly. Not as high as Brenda Joley's—that continental shelf she carried around, solid and proud as America.

Hasn't every saleslady since my first training bra insisted I am average?

I'm thinking about them too much. What I should be doing is buying a new pair of shoes. These soles are getting worse. Flapping all the way through Downtown Crossing. And now *they* kick in—bouncing against my blouse all the way down the steps into women's accessories, past the sunglasses, the jewelry, the discount travel agency, into the Designer Corner, past the bins full of bras and panties, racks crammed with raincoats—women everywhere, digging and calculating. Filene's Basement world famous automatic markdown plan: 25% discount after one week, 50% the next, 75% after the third. Just read the price tags: *Markdowns taken at the cash register. Dates on the back.*

I wonder if a double-breasted jacket will cover them? Wonder if anything could protect them from the daily scrutiny of Jerry Hanrahan. He's a pervert.

No, he's the boss.

And you are a Temp, with a Temp's salary, working your way through a rack of special discounts. A Temporary person. An Almost person. Almost—if the job in accounting comes through—a permanent employee at Colony Insurance. Almost—after our conversation in the elevator today—the girlfriend of mutual-funds manager Rick Milton. Almost. Like these clothes: always slightly damaged or irregular, cut differently than whatever shape is popular.

I should be buying something to wear to dinner tonight with Rick Milton. Something sexy from those racks of cocktail suits on the back wall. Why didn't I suggest tomorrow night instead? Sweating in the elevator after lunch, talking to him about mutual funds until the doors opened at his company's floor. *Why don't we discuss it over dinner?* Another few floors and I could have suggested tomorrow night, so I could find something to wear.

I never speak up fast enough. I pause, but not to listen to myself. Not to say what I really want to say. *You didn't speak until late*—doesn't she remind me of that constantly? *Not for years after you could walk.* I learned to speak late and I never caught up.

More cotton blazers back there, if I could get past all these women pulling pants up under their skirts, getting pinched by surveillance tags, stuck with pins, eyed by guards. *Just getting a look at what you've got there.*

Did Jerry Hanrahan really say that? He said that to me. So casually. Coming up behind me and leaning over my shoulder, pretending to study the report on my computer screen. *Just getting a look at what you've got there.* Breathing his rotting lunch down my neck.

You wanted big ones! Ever since you were a kid!—She had to remind me of that on the phone when I complained to her about Jerry Hanrahan, about the way he always stares and leans. *Don't you think you might be imagining it?* She thinks it's funny. *You wanted them to be huge.* Watching the Miss America pageant in my bra, stuffing oranges into the tiny elastic triangles and parading around the house.

Did I push them out when I was talking to Rick Milton in the elevator? *It's sweating out there today.* Rick Milton, so cool with his suit jacket over his shoulder, his sleeves rolled up. *Just getting a look at what you've got there.* Rick Milton, smiling. A container of fruit salad in his hand. ·

The average price for jackets is $50, even with the 25% discount. The same price as shoes.

Shoes or jacket?

Jacket.

Shoes?

I can take these shoes to the cobbler and get them reglued. What I need is something to wear to dinner tonight with Rick Milton. Something to make them feel natural and fleshy and connected to me, so I won't think about them so much. No, the one who is thinking about them too much is Jerry Hanrahan. But I can't prove anything, really. I can only sense.

Sequins and Lycra. Sleeveless and strapless and backless. Forget it. Forget even trying to wear a bra with these. I'm not small enough for these. I'd need a reduction of at least 50%. Oh, God, she would laugh at that! She'd say, *I'll show you a reduction of 50%.* She'd unzip her bathrobe and show me her huge brassiere, that one deflated cup. Grab a handful of the empty fabric in her fist and shake it around. She would.

What about this? No. No. Low-cut, plunging—I'm not big enough. I'd have to be at least 25% bigger to fill up the empty space in between. I'd need a miracle to fill that.

Why aren't they like dicks? They should be like dicks. They should get bigger when you're having sex and stay small when you have to get work done. Then I wouldn't have to think about them when I'm trying to concentrate on a report and Jerry Hanrahan is leaning over me. *Just trying to see what you've got there.*

Tits, Boobs, Honkers . . . What else? Go through the list. Go through the whole list and think about the debasement. The way you can cheapen them: Tits—25% cheaper. Boobs—50%. Honkers—75%. *Discounts taken at the register.*

Jugs, Knockers, Hooters . . .

Which word does Rick Milton use? *It's sweating out there today.*

Which one does Jerry Hanrahan say to himself when he stands there in front of my desk? *Is the air conditioning up too high for you?*

What does *she* call them—with that thick purple scar stretching all the way under her armpit like a fault line? *I'll show you a reduction of 50%!*

What do all these women call them, twisting themselves, pulling dresses over their heads, swarming around with clothes piled over their arms, purses around their necks, lined up to get in front of the mirrors.

Jerry Hanrahan looks at them combined. Not one, then the other, but both of them together. Never at my face.

Rifling through the racks now. Because if I find something sexy I can relax about dinner. I can relax and talk about mutual funds with Rick Milton. Maybe go out with him again. Maybe.

If I find something to cover them, I won't have to think about them when I ask Jerry Hanrahan again, *Can you recommend me for this position opening up in accounting?*

Let's discuss it over dinner.

This jacket isn't bad for 75% off, except for the makeup stain on the collar. It's long enough to cover my butt, too, in case he's been staring at that. I've bought stuff with stains before. And with the 75% markdown, I can still afford shoes. I have to look at the combined savings. Now there's a line at the mirror again . . .

—*It's cute, but it's a work thing. I have enough work things.*

Even with the 50% discount, this yellow top by itself would cost more than a pair of shoes upstairs in the shoe salon. Upstairs, where the sales floor is neat and quiet, like the accounting department at Colony Insurance. Upstairs, where they have private dressing rooms with chairs and three-way mirrors, and motherly salesladies who reassure you, *They're not that big.*

Not like here, in the Basement, where it's all confusing. Where you can't slow down and think about what you really want.

I'd like to ask you about this job opening up in accounting.

Let's discuss it over dinner.

Why don't we discuss it now, in the office? That's what I was thinking. That's what I should have said to Jerry Hanrahan. *You didn't speak until late.* I could have shook my head, at least, instead of sitting there like a piece of fruit until he finally walked away.

Maybe I should block out the things I hear wrong. The things I take the wrong way. *Is the air conditioning up too high for you?* Who said anything about my nipples? I'm paranoid, because I can't control them. I can't keep them from shrinking or swelling or sticking out or growing weird-shaped cells.

Let's discuss it over dinner. Rick Milton never said anything about a date, really. We're just going to talk about mutual funds. There's no reason to buy this sexy yellow top for $100 to talk about mutual funds with Rick Milton, when for that much money I could probably get a jacket and a pair of shoes for the interview in accounting.

These shoes should really be thrown out. Even without the loose soles, the heels are grated from the bricks. But this yellow top is beautiful. The label isn't even cut out. It would fit perfectly, too. Just low enough in the front. Just narrow enough on the sides.

—*Hide it until tomorrow, when it goes down to 75%.*

Hide it until tomorrow. Tomorrow is too late. Tomorrow wouldn't have been too late if I had I suggested it to Rick Milton in the elevator. But I could buy it now, and bring it back tomorrow.

Just wear it temporarily.

Buy it now, tape the price tag down, and bring it back tomorrow at lunch. Exchange it for a jacket and a pair of shoes . . .

Put it on in one of the dressing rooms upstairs, where the salesladies nod when I show them I've paid for it in the Basement, when I tell them I have a date and I just need to change quickly. Who don't notice when I take a little piece of Scotch tape off the roll next to the cash register, bring it into the dressing room and tape the price tag down under the armhole. Who smile and tell me how nice it looks when I come out.

Who expect me to spray myself with a tester of nice perfume, because women always walk through the store after work and spray themselves on their way out to dinner . . .

Just looking at what you've got there. But he's talking about the food, leaning over my plate. Stop laughing and explain to Rick how awful it is being a Temp. *Just wear it temporarily.* Eat slowly. Be careful. Don't get anything on the yellow top and make a stain.

Wear it tonight and bring it back tomorrow.

Wear it back to Rick Milton's place and don't spill the melon liqueur in the little glasses. Try to sit still. Don't spill it on his sofa. We're on his sofa and we've talked about everything except mutual funds. I don't care, and I don't think he cares either. But I don't know—I can only sense.

It's sweating out there.

Shit. The Scotch tape is coming loose. Every time I lift my glass the price tag moves and cuts into the side of the left one.

Ignore it. Try to ignore the scraping.

Is the air conditioning up too high for you?

Because they feel good when the price tag isn't cutting into them. *Dates are on the back.* Like they're connected to what I feel in the rest of my body. *I know you're looking at them and thinking about them.* As if all those other feelings are concentrated in them. *You wanted them to be huge!* Leaning back on the sofa, tasting melon inside Rick Milton's mouth. Tasting melon and moving with him as he shifts and starts to ease the zipper down.

Just getting a look at what you've got there.

Wait—what happened?

Discounts taken at the register

Shit. The price tag is caught on the zipper.

Dates on the back

He's trying to ease the zipper down, but the corner of the tag is caught. It's cutting into me.

I'll show you a reduction of 50%

The tag and the zipper are jammed.

Don't you think you might be imagining it?

Say something.

You didn't speak until late.

He's tugging at the zipper now.

Not for years after you could walk.

He's pulling it.

Say something.

Because if anything happens to this shirt, I can't take it back tomorrow and buy a jacket . . .

Buy it now and bring it back tomorrow

. . . or shoes for the interview in accounting.

You're average

And if I don't get the job in accounting, I will still be Temporary.

Just wear it temporarily

Tell him about the price tag. Tell him . . .

I know you're looking at them and thinking about them

Before he pulls too hard—

Dates are on the back

and the tag flies loose—

Just say something

and the zipper rips away from the fabric—

You wanted them to be huge!

and the fabric tears in a long jagged line across my—

Paula Champa was born in Providence, Rhode Island. Her short fiction and poems have appeared in *Iron Horse Literary Review, Yemassee, Thirteenth Moon, The Tusculum Review,* and other journals. In 1998, she was awarded an individual artist's grant from the Virginia Commission for the Arts for her short story manuscript *Everything Must Go,* which includes "The Basement." Popular Ink released an edition of her short story "Admissions" in the fall of 2006.

Champa has worked carrying newspapers for *The Providence Journal-Bulletin,* selling bread and pastries at a neighborhood bakery, processing clothing at a dry cleaners, alphabetizing credit card statements, modeling junior fashions, creating travel CD-ROMs, and compiling presentations for an ad agency in Boston. For the past two decades, she has been a writer and editor for magazines on design and culture, including *I.D., Print, Intersection,* and *Surface,* where she is a contributing editor. Champa is currently based in Brighton, England.

Champa began writing "The Basement" out of a desire to capture the gestalt of a department store in downtown Boston where workers shopped for discounts during their lunch breaks. "I'd seen how many people go there trying to stretch their small income," she says. "And I knew from experience the financial and psychological pressures of being a 'temp' employee. I created a female character who had to operate within this context while trying to handle a threatening situation with her boss. The story unwound itself as an internal monologue that overlays workplace issues with the cultural and fashion-industry dictates that influence women's body images."

"The Basement" was first published in *Thirteenth Moon,* vol. 16 (2000). Copyright © 2000 Paula Champa. It is reprinted here by permission of the author.

Labor #1

Clay Blancett

Six weeks of framing gives you a kind of springy
soreness that gets you out of bed after four hours sleep.
You may be a little stiff there in the dark dressing, lashing
your boots to you. The coffee helps,
as does the music, to get you across the bridge—
to get you ready for another day of framing. The soreness wears off
after the second or third piece of plywood, or the fifth rafter
handed up to the lead man. If you didn't get any
breakfast, you feel that all day.

I had given myself a mohawk that summer, the heat made me
do it. We'd lay up the hollow forms that made the walls all week
and on Friday the pump truck would show up at the top of the hill,
a stream of cement trucks lined up to feed concrete into the back of it.
The pumper would run the stuff down a pipe on its giant boom to the boss,
who would fill the forms. Maybe it was the sound of the fifty-dollar-an-hour
pumper idling, maybe it was the boss, but on Friday we would run
fifth gear all day, hardly speaking, only the sound of the truck
and the clinking of our belts. I always stood my mohawk up on Friday.

I don't want this to be about how I hated the lead because he reminded
me of my father. Or how I disrespected my boss because he was
so fat and clever. Or how every day, after Larry died,
    I almost threw down my tools
in disgust—the rest of the crew almost being gentle with me then.
Or how I spent days busting rebar and left work not noticing I looked like
a coal miner until I got home—my friends letting me wear my filth
like a kind of badge. Maybe I want this to be about the pump truck and
its belly full of concrete, its arm reaching out to us on the Ho Chi Minh
network of scaffolding, raining cement down on me as I scurried underneath.
The pumper being the cause and the reason for that summer.

Clay Blancett was born in Chattanooga, Tennessee, in 1971. Blancett, who earns his living as a restoration carpenter, has been featured in *GoodFoot, CaKe: A Journal of Poetry, La Fovea, Curious Rooms,* and *The Indelible Kitchen.* He is the co-founder of *The Shambling Darkness Project.* His blog, *Fig. 1 – Worm Drive (blancett.blogspot.com),* features writing and art about his work as a carpenter, among other things.

Blancett has worked as a landscaper, dishwasher, busboy, line cook, tile-setter, finish carpenter, framer, and furniture maker. Blancett writes, "I keep hoping my writing will get me out of doing this line of work. The summer in which 'Labor #1' occurs was the same that my friend and teacher Larry Levis died and also the first summer that I learned to truly despise working in the trades. The only problem is, after fifteen years, I have yet to come upon any other occupation that I'd rather be doing. Also, on a good day, I figure I am fortunate to have the opportunity to give a voice to the people who build the places other people live in."

Copyright © Clay Blancett

Senior's Last Hour

(ALCOA Aluminum, North Plant, Alcoa, TN)

Richard Joines

They shift—streaming out
and in, lunch pails empty,
full. Car doors slam.
The horizon gives mountains,
speckled horses, bulls. Once,
before I knew him,
my grandfather aimed his rage
at that factory window:
"I didn't throw the first brick," he said,
"but I threw the second." His father
drove shine through the foothills;
mine peddles radiation. Steel toes shuffle—
hunger dreams what it wants.
There is no accounting for this.

Richard Joines was born in Alcoa, Tennessee, and the landscape of his earliest memories is the intersection at ALCOA Aluminum's North Plant, the setting of "Senior's Last Hour." "To go anywhere," Joines writes, "it seemed, one had to pass through this intersection bounded by a factory, a church, fields of livestock, and, in the distance, the Smoky Mountains. 'Senior's Last Hour' is a kind of family history. The concept of 'Senior's last hour' comes from Karl Marx's *Capital*, where he critiques Nassau W. Senior's economic theory that during the worker's day, all but the last hour of labor produces the worker's wages while the 'last hour' alone produces surplus, or profit, thus justifying the capitalist's demand for a longer workday."

Joines's grandfather worked at that aluminum plant all his life, organizing workers and occasionally busting windows. Joines's father moved on and out to become a road tech and then a seller of road testing equipment and author of ASTM standards for road construction. "Thanks to this history of hard work," Joines himself has been able to spend most of his life either attending school or teaching it, in Tennessee, Kentucky, Japan, Kansas, Florida, Alabama, and Texas.

"Senior's Last Hour" was originally published in *The Tusculum Review* (2006).
Copyright © 2006 by Richard Joines. It is reprinted here by permission of the author.

At Work

Mary Malinda Polk

I work for two attorneys. One partner and one associate. Both male. But I work among women. Secretaries. There are two male legal secretaries at our firm, but they both sit in other areas of the office.

The associate just bought himself a new motorcycle, and waited until he picked it up to tell his mother.

The partner received his AARP card in the mail for the first time and bristled.

The women who work in my area often shop. The woman who works next to me sometimes does not leave her desk to eat her lunch because "if I go out, I'll shop."

My lack of privacy at work has made me even less tolerant of crowds. I now shop almost exclusively through the mail.

The associate stops by and tells me about the ongoing sagas of his pro bono clients. Even though I always volunteer, he goes to the hospitals and courts to get their records himself. A nice break from sitting in his office doing research.

The partner likes to call me "Paralegal Polk," as though asking me to find a Web site for him is a sign of his respect for my intelligence.

Two women in my area often speak in baby talk. When they do this at me, I know they expect me to find it endearing. One is easily one of the smartest secretaries in our firm; the other is probably the hardest working. They are both good-hearted, generous people. As much as it grates on my nerves when they address me in baby talk, I want to put my head through my computer screen when I hear them addressing male attorneys that way.

When I've been sleeping well and exercising regularly, I don't tend to wear makeup beyond a smear of lipstick—if there is a lipstick in my tote bag. If I have been up nights at all that week and am feeling lucky that I managed to put on my shoes (usually slip-on clogs at that), I don't get to the lipstick. When I have been getting no sleep, eating like crap, and feeling too lazy to exercise, I'm disciplined about putting on at least mascara and lipstick and even a stripe of eye shadow, and sometimes I think about investing in base. It is only when I have made this effort that I notice I am the only secretary in my immediate area who does not wear serious, daily makeup.

For Christmas and my birthday, the associate gave me generous gift certificates to a bookstore because he had seen me reading, often with my back turned to a conversation, in the lunchroom.

The partner gives me an extravagant bunch of flowers and a card that contains liberal amounts of cash. This year, the day before my birthday, the partner handed me a memo from HR announcing the death of another partner's father. He asked me to run down to the shop in the lobby to pick out a card. The next day, the very card I had selected was the cash-containing card the partner gave me for my birthday. He said, "I wanted to make sure you got a card you liked this year." I smiled; he expected me to be pleased. He had written something very complimentary inside. But I kept thinking, "He couldn't even pick out a card. He had me pick out my own card." Which may not have been fair. I know he picked the flowers for the bouquet himself.

After we had been working side by side for four months, my cubicle neighbor asked, "Do you ever wear heels?"

Before this job, I taught composition at a small college. I averaged a hundred students a semester, and at least half of my students were considered "remedial" by testing standards. I found most of them were bright enough, but were overwhelmed when faced with the task of learning everything they should have learned in high school *plus* what I was supposed to teach them about writing at "the college level." It takes more than twice as long to grade a poor paper than a polished paper. Most of their papers, especially at the beginning of the semester, were poor. With the raise I received at the end of my first year at the firm and the overtime I do, I am now making literally twice what I made teaching.

If the only job he was guaranteed in a very tight job market hadn't required that he become a Jesuit priest, the associate was going to get his PhD and become a philosophy professor.

Sometimes around 3:00 or 3:30, the partner needs a mocha chip cookie to get him through the afternoon. I go to the café in the lobby to get it for him.

The secretaries in my area organize potlucks every now and then. Someone usually has a dish of candy up on her counter for anyone who is walking by. If someone cuts up an apple, we all usually walk the row to see who wants a piece. No one ever eats anything without talking about the fat content, a skipped meal earlier that day, an exercise program, or how thin she used to be.

The associate has been classified as a "hottie" and there is a single woman who "really likes him." The one time I went out for a drink with "the gang" after work, the associate and I talked for the first time away from the office, and it was a nice, relaxed conversation. After a while, another secretary interrupted and started whispering in my ear. The woman who "really likes" the associate was "really upset" and it was "because of" me. Apparently, the associate and I had been talking for "too long." I consider both of these secretaries buddies. I also consider the area they sit in "grudge row" because I've seen how they treat people who get on their bad sides. I threw back the rest of my beer and weaved my way home. I'm careful not to step into conversations between the "hottie" associate and this other secretary now, even when they are just talking about this and that.

My job with the partner became available because he and his previous secretary were indiscreetly dating. When I started working for him, people would ask me what I knew. I would say I knew nothing, even though I answered the phone when she called. I would say, "I don't talk about that." I overheard an attorney and a secretary talking about my not talking and coming to the conclusion that I was "weird about that."

Most of the secretaries around me can type over 80 words per minute. On the last round of optional testing, two of them typed *over* 110.

Without spellcheck, I would have flunked out of college; I never would have gotten into graduate school. My first week of being a legal secretary, I learned that Microsoft Word could do 30 things that I never knew it could do. After almost two years, I'm still averaging one new computer trick a week.

The only time I corrected grammar in a letter by my associate, he changed it back.

Every now and then, the partner gives me an outline of what he needs a letter to say and tells me what tone he is going for. He lets me write a rough draft for him to edit. Most of his edits have to do with legal language or giving more details. He is usually complimentary about my writing. This is my favorite part of my job.

One of the secretaries organized a book club that lasted for about a year. We read a few Oprah picks, a romantic comedy set in an office (at which meeting I had to remind everyone that I didn't want to talk about my boss's social life). One of the last books we read was by John Grisham. I couldn't imagine what we would say about it. It was one of our better discussions.

Two nights a week I take classes. I'm, slowly, earning a Master's in American Studies. One thing American Studies examines is how the power structures in our culture, which seem natural to us, have actually been constructed. I have become increasingly aware that other power structures are possible.

When the associate sees me reading in the lunch room, I am usually cramming for school. Sometimes, unprompted, he asks me how it is going.

The partner remembers not to ask me to stay late on school nights and likes to say, "I am sensitive to the plight of the student." So, when there is work to do on a deadline, I leave at 5:00 to get to class. To compensate, I show up to work early the next morning. I also come in early in the morning when the partner calls me at home—sometimes after 9:00 p.m.—the night before.

The woman who sits at the far end of grudge row only says hello when somebody else says it first. When she doesn't have work to do, she studies French and reads papers in a manila folder. She has the highest score on the skills test of anyone in the office. She never participates in potlucks. She never comes out for drinks. She doesn't seem to need any of us as friends, or even friendly acquaintances. Grudge row hates her.

She is doing what I meant to do. Show up, do the job, go home to the things that really matter. But I joined the book club. When the partner "asks" me to go downstairs to get his cookie or the associate "corrects" my grammar correction, I remember all of my education. When I slice up an apple, I walk the row to see who wants any. It is eight hours of my day, five days a week. Sleeping is the only thing I spend as much time doing in a week. I don't know how not to let that much of my week matter. And I wish I did.

Mary Malinda Polk has worked as a telemarketer, a commercial real estate property manager, a "book doctor," a receptionist, an assembly worker at an electronic transducers company, a server at McDonald's, a legal secretary, and a teacher. Her fiction has appeared in *Thema* and *Bent Spoon*. She is currently Assistant Professor of English at Fisher College in Boston.

Polk wrote this piece when she was working as a legal secretary by day and pursuing a master's degree in American Studies at night. She was reading feminist theory about body image for a Popular Culture class. She writes, "I was having a hard time reconciling the theory in the book with the behavior around me. Specifically, the book kept talking about certain stereotypes as though our society had 'outgrown' them, and I was eating lunch with, making copies for, giving paperclips to, and answering the phone amongst them every day." While Polk was working in this particular situation, she was also struck by how differently the two attorneys she worked for treated her. Polk says, "While they confirmed many gender stereotypes, they also subverted some generational stereotypes. I learned a lot working at the law firm, and the thing that I think about a lot now that I am teaching full time is this: the two legal secretaries with the best grammar, spelling, and general knowledge base had never gone to college, but they had both graduated from high school more than twenty-five years ago."

Copyright © Mary Malinda Polk

If Language Was a House of Being

Darren Morris

I was a poor editor
of state curriculum materials
for the office of Career
and Technical Education.
I'll admit it. Yet, once, for an entire
month, I stayed in the catatonic
fit of high efficiency.
Still, I could not overcome
the *Supplementary Manual*
for Advanced Database Design
and Management. I vanished
within its village of scripting
languages that were
clearly understood by computers.
I built a rickety house
of being and when
I awoke, there it sat
at the edge of my desk:
a dog-eared manifesto
with tabbed corrections.
"Thou Shalt Not" scribbled
on each yellow petal.
I ripped them off one by one
and, in the end, it loved me not.
It shipped for approval
like a cut of meat
and was handled by a woman,
on the other end, who lived
in an empty apartment,
ironing old blouses, perpetually
two years from retirement.

Darren Morris gets paid for his work as a writer/editor, instructional designer, and trainer for a non-profit, grant-funded office in Richmond, Virginia. Morris writes, "I value all the things that do not pay, such as poetry, short fiction, screenwriting, love, and baseball—not necessarily in that order. Occasionally, I teach a class that barely pays, which is of uncertain value to me, but I hope it's valuable to others. My poem included in this anthology places an individual dreamer within a bureaucratic context that compromises his humanity by decimating the language."

Morris is completing a volume of short fiction titled *American Sporting Events,* in which he examines how leisure, rather than work, is defining the emerging Rx Generation. He has published poems in *American Poetry Review, Diner, River Styx, Rattle, Bitter Oleander*, and *Best New Poets 2006.* His fiction was awarded a fellowship from the Virginia Commission for the Arts and his short story "Paper Airplane Engineer" won second prize in *Style Weekly's* annual fiction contest. Most recently, he co-wrote a screenplay for Richmond's first 48-Hour Film Project that was awarded "Best in City."

Copyright © Darren Morris

He's at the Office

Allan Gurganus

Till the Japanese bombed Pearl Harbor, most American men wore hats to work. What happened? Did our guys—suddenly scouting overhead for worse Sunday raids—come to fear their hat brims' interference? My unsuspecting father wore his till yesterday. He owned three. A gray, a brown, and a summer straw one, whose maroon-striped rayon band could only have been woven in America in the 1940s.

Last month, I lured him from his self-imposed office hours for a walk around our block. My father insisted on bringing his briefcase. "You never know," he said. We soon passed a huge young hipster, creaking in black leather. The kid's pierced face flashed more silver than most bait shops sell. His jeans, half down, exposed hat racks of white hipbone; the haircut arched high over jug ears. He was scouting Father's shoes. Long before fashion joined him, Dad favored an under-evolved antique form of orthopedic Doc Martens. These impressed a punk now scanning the Sherman tank of a cowhide briefcase with chromium corner braces. The camel-hair overcoat was cut to resemble some boxy-backed 1947 Packard. And, of course, up top sat "the gray."

Pointing to it, the boy smiled. "Way bad look on you, guy."

My father, seeking interpretation, stared at me. I simply shook my head no. I could not explain Dad to himself in terms of tidal fashion trends. All I said was "I think he likes you."

Dad's face folded. "Uh-oh."

By the end, my father, the fifty-two-year veteran of Integrity Office Supplier, Unlimited, had become quite cool again, way.

We couldn't vacation for more than three full days. He'd veer our Plymouth toward some way-station pay phone. We soon laughed as Dad, in the glass booth, commenced to wave his arms, shake his head, shift his weight from foot to foot. We knew Miss Green must be telling him of botched orders, delivery mistakes. We were nearly to Gettysburg. I'd been studying battle maps. Now I knew we'd never make it.

My father bounded back to the car and smiled in. "Terrible mixup with the Wilmington school system's carbon paper for next year. Major goof, but typical. Guy's got to do it all himself. Young Green didn't insist I come back, but she sure hinted."

We U-turned southward, and my father briefly became the most charming man on earth. He now seemed to be selling something we needed, whatever we needed. Traveling north into a holiday—the very curse of leisure—he had kept as silent as some fellow with toothaches. Now he was our tour guide, interviewing us, telling and retelling his joke. Passing a cemetery, he said (over his family's dry carbon-paper unison), "I hear they're dying to get in there!" "Look on the bright side," I told myself: "We'll arrive home and escape him as he runs—literally runs—to the office."

Dad was, like me, an early riser. Six days a week, Mom sealed his single-sandwich lunch into its Tupperware jacket; this fit accidentally yet exactly within the lid compartment of his durable briefcase. He would then pull on his overcoat—bulky, war-efficient, strong-seamed, four buttons as big as silver dollars and carved from actual shell. He'd place the cake-sized hat in place, nod in our general direction, and set off hurrying. Dad faced each day as one more worthy enemy. If he had been Dwight Eisenhower saving the Western world, or Jonas Salk freeing kids our age from crutches, okay. But yellow Eagle pencils? Utility paperweights in park-bench green?

Once a year, Mom told my brother and me how much the war had darkened her young husband; he'd enlisted with three other guys from Falls; he alone came back alive with all his limbs. "Before that," she smiled, "your father was funnier, funny. And smarter. Great dancer. You can't blame mustard gas, not this time. It's more what Dick saw. He came home and he was all business. Before that, he'd been mischievous and talkative and strange. He was always playing around with words. Very entertaining. Eyelashes out to here. For years, I figured that in time he'd come back to being whole. But since June of forty-five it's been All Work and No Play Makes Jack."

Mom remembered their fourth anniversary. "I hired an overnight sitter for you two. We drove to an inn near Asheville. It had the state's best restaurant, candlelight, a real string quartet. I'd made myself a green velvet dress. I was twenty-eight and never in my whole life have I ever looked better. You just know it. Dick recognized some man who'd bought two adding machines. Dick invited him to join us. Then I saw how much his work was going to have to mean to him. Don't be too hard on him, please. He feeds us, he puts aside real savings for you boys' college. Dick pays our taxes. Dick has no secrets. He's not hurting anyone." Brother and I gave each other a look Mom recognized and understood but refused to return.

The office seemed to tap some part of him that was either off limits to us or simply did not otherwise exist. My brother and I griped that he'd never attended our Little League games (not that we ever made the starting lineup). He missed our father-son Cub Scout banquet; it conflicted with a major envelope convention in Newport News. Mother neutrally said he loved us as much as he could. She was a funny, energetic person—all that wasted good will. And even as kids, we knew not to blame her.

Ignored, Mom created a small sewing room. Economizing needlessly, she stayed busy stitching all our school clothes, cowboy motifs galore. For a while, each shirt pocket bristled with Mom-designed embroidered cacti. But Simplicity patterns were never going to engage a mind as complex as hers. Soon Mom was spending most mornings playing vicious duplicate bridge. Our toothbrush glasses briefly broke out in rashes of red hearts, black clubs. Mom's new pals were society ladies respectful of her brainy speed, her impenitent wit; she never bothered introducing them to her husband. She laughed more now. She started wearing rouge.

We lived a short walk from both our school and his wholesale office. Dad sometimes left the Plymouth parked all night outside the workplace, his desk lamp the last one burning on the whole third floor. Integrity's president, passing headquarters late, always fell for it. "Dick, what do you do up there all night, son?" My father's shrug became his finest boast. The raises kept pace; Integrity Office Supplier was still considered quite a comer. And R. Richard Markham, Sr.—as handsome as a collar ad, a hat ad, forever at the office—was the heir apparent.

DAD'S WAS INTEGRITY'S FLAGSHIP OFFICE: "Maker of World's Highest Quality Clerical Supplies." No other schoolboys had sturdier pastel subject dividers, more clip-in see-through three-ring pen caddies. The night before school started, Dad would be up late at our kitchen table, swilling coffee, "getting you boys set." Zippered leather cases, English slide rules, folders more suitable for treaties than for book reports ("*Skipper, A Dog of the Pyrenees*, by Marjorie Hopgood Purling"). Our notebooks soon proved too heavy to carry far; we secretly stripped them, swapping gear for lunchbox treats more exotic than Mom's hard-boiled eggs and Sun-Maid raisin packs.

Twenty years ago, Dad's Integrity got bought out by a German firm. The business's vitality proved somewhat hobbled by computers' onslaught. "A fad," my father called computers in 1976. "Let others retool. We'll stand firm with our yellow legals, erasers, Parker ink, fountain pens. Don't worry, our regulars'll come back. True vision always lets you act kind in the end, boys. Remember."

Yeah, right.

My father postponed his retirement. Mom encouraged that and felt relieved; she could not imagine him at home all day. As Integrity's market share dwindled, Dad spent more time at the office, as if to compensate with his own body for the course of modern life.

HIS SECRETARY, THE ADMIRED MISS Green, had once been what Pop still called "something of a bombshell." (He stuck with a Second World War terminology that had, like the hat, served him too well ever to leave behind.)

Still favoring shoulder pads, dressed in unyielding woolen Joan Crawford solids, Green wore an auburn pageboy that looked burned by decades of ungrateful dyes. She kicked off her shoes beneath her desk, revealing feet that told the tale of high heels' worthless weekday brutality. She'd quit college to tend an ailing mother, who proved demanding, then immortal. Brother and I teased Mom: poor Green appeared to worship her longtime boss, a guy whose face was as smooth and wedged and classic as his hat. Into Dick Markham's blunted constancy she read actual "moods."

He still viewed Green, now past sixty, as a promising virginal girl. In their small adjoining offices, these two thrived within a fond impersonality that permeated the ads of the period.

Integrity's flagship headquarters remained enameled a flavorless mint green, unaltered for five decades. The dark Mission coatrack was made by Limbert— quite a good piece. One ashtray—upright, floor model, brushed chromium— proved the size and shape of some landlocked torpedo. Moored to walls, dented metal desks were as gray as battleships. A series of forest green filing cabinets seemed banished, as patient as a family of trolls, to one shaming little closet all their own. Dad's office might've been decorated by a firm called Edward Hopper & Sam Spade, Unlimited.

For more than half a century, he walked in each day at seven-oh-nine sharp, as Miss Green forever said, "Morning, Mr. Markham. I left your appointments written on your desk pad, can I get you your coffee? Is now good, sir?" And Dad said, "Yes, why, thanks, Miss Green, how's your mother, don't mind if I do."

FOUR YEARS AGO, I RECEIVED a panicked phone call: "You the junior to a guy about eighty, guy in a hat?"

"Probably." I was working at home. I pressed my computer's "Save" function. This, I sensed, might take a while. "Save."

"Exit? No? Yes?"

"Yes."

"Mister, your dad thinks we're camped out in his office and he's been banging against our door. He's convinced we've evicted his files and what he calls his Green. 'What have you done with young Green?' Get down here A.S.A.P. Get him out of our hair or it's nine-one-one in three minutes, swear to God."

From my car, I phoned home. Mom must have been off somewhere playing bridge with the mayor's blond wife and his blond ex-wife; they'd sensibly become excellent friends. The best women are the best people on earth; and the worst men the very worst. Mother, overlooked by Dad for years, had continued finding what she called "certain outlets."

When I arrived, Dad was still heaving himself against an office door, deadbolt—locked from within. Since its upper panel was frosted glass, I could make out the colors of the clothes of three or four people pressing from their side. They'd used masking tape to crosshatch the glass, as if bracing for a hurricane. The old man held his briefcase, wore his gray hat, the tan boxy coat.

"Dad?" He stopped with a mechanical cartoon verve, jumped my way, and smiled so hard it warmed my heart and scared me witless. My father had never acted so glad to see me—not when I graduated summa cum laude, not at my wedding, not after the birth of my son—and I felt joy in the presence of such joy from him.

"Reinforcements. Good man. We've got quite a hostage situation here. Let's put our shoulders to it, shall we?"

"Dad?" I grabbed the padded shoulders of his overcoat. These crumpled to reveal a man far sketchier hiding in there somewhere—a guy only twenty years from a hundred, after all.

"Dad? Dad. We have a good-news, bad-news setup here today. It's this. You found the right building, Dad. Wrong floor."

I led him back to the clattering, oil-smelling elevator. I thought to return, tap on the barricaded door, explain. But, in time, hey, they'd peek, they'd figure out the coast was clear. That they hadn't recognized him, after his fifty-two years of long days in this very building, said something. New people, everywhere.

I saw at once that Miss Green had been crying. Her face was caked with so much powder it looked like calamine. "Little mixup," I said.

"Mr. Markham? We got three calls about those gum erasers," she said, faking a frontal normality. "I think they're putting sawdust in them these days, sir. They leave skid marks, apparently. I put the information on your desk. With your day's appointments. Like your coffee? Like it now? Sir?"

I hung his hat on the hat tree; I slid his coat onto its one wooden Deco hanger that could, at any flea market today, bring thirty-five dollars easy, two tones of wood, inlaid.

I wanted to have a heart-to-heart. I was so disoriented as to feel half-sane myself. But I overheard Father already returning his calls. He ignored me, and that seemed, within this radically altered gravitational field, a good sign. I sneaked back to Miss Green's desk, and admitted, "I'll need to call his doctor. I want him seen today, Miss Green. He was up on four, trying to get into that new headhunting service. He told them his name. Mom was out. So they, clever, looked him up in the book and found his junior and phoned me to come help."

She sat forward, strenuously feigning surprise. She looked rigid, chained to this metal desk by both gnarled feet. "How long?" I somehow knew to ask.

Green appeared ecstatic, then relieved, then, suddenly, happily weeping, tears pouring down—small tears, lopsided, mascaraed grit. She blinked up at me with a spaniel's gratitude. Suddenly, if slowly, I began to understand. In mere seconds, she had caved about Dad's years-long caving-in. It was my turn now.

Miss Green now whispered certain of his mistakes. There were forgotten parking tickets by the dozen. There was his attempt to purchase a lake house on land already flooded for a dam. Quietly, she admitted years of covering.

From her purse, she lifted a page covered in Dad's stern Germanic cursive, blue ink fighting to stay isometrically between red lines.

"I found this one last week." Green's voice seemed steadied by the joy of having told. "I fear this is about the worst, to date, we've been."

If they say "Hot enough for you?," it means recent weather. "Yes indeed" still a good comeback. Order forms pink. Requisition yellow. Miss green's birthday June 12. She work with you fifty-one years. Is still unmarried. Mother now dead, since '76, so stop asking about Mother, health of. Home address, 712 Marigold Street: Left at Oak, can always walk there. After last week, never go near car again. Unfair to others. Take second left at biggest tree. Your new Butcher's name is: Al. Wife: Betty. Sons: Matthew and Dick Junior. Grandson Richie (your name with a III added on it). List of credit cards, licnse etc. below in case you lose walet agn, you big dope. Put copies somewhere safe, 3 places, write down, hide many. You are 80, yes, eighty.

And yet, as we now eavesdropped, Dick Markham dealt with a complaining customer. He sounded practiced, jokey, conversant, exact.

"Dad, you have an unexpected doctor's appointment." I handed Dad his hat. I'd phoned our family physician from Miss Green's extension.

For once, they were ready for us. The nurses kept calling him by name, smiling, overinsistent, as if hinting at answers for a kid about to take his make-or-break college exam. I could see they'd always liked him. In a town this small, they'd maybe heard about his trouble earlier today.

As Dad got ushered in for tests, he glowerèd accusations back at me as if I had just dragged him to a Nazi medical experiment. He finally reemerged, scarily pale, pressing a bit of gauze into the crook of his bare arm, its long veins the exact blue of Parker's washable ink. They directed him toward the lobby bathroom. They gave him a cup for his urine specimen. He held it before him with two hands like some Magus's treasure.

His hat, briefcase, and overcoat remained behind, resting on an orange plastic chair all their own. Toward these I could display a permissible tenderness. I lightly set my hand on each item. Call it superstition. I now lifted the hat and sniffed it. It smelled like Dad. It smelled like rope. Physical intimacy has never been a possibility. My brother and I, half-drunk, once tried to picture the improbable, the sexual conjunction of our parents. Brother said, "Well, he probably pretends he's at the office, unsealing her like a good manila envelope that requires a rubber stamp—legible, yes, keep it legible, legible, now speed-mail!"

I had flipped through four stale magazines before I saw the nurses peeking from their crudely cut window. "He has been quite a while, Mr. Markham. Going on thirty minutes."

"Shall I?" I rose and knocked. No answer. "Would you come stand behind me?" Cowardly, I signaled to an older nurse.

The door proved unlocked. I opened it. I saw one old man aimed the other way and trembling with hesitation. Before him, a white toilet, a white sink, and a white enamel trash can, the three aligned—each its own insistent invitation. In one hand, the old man held an empty specimen cup. In the other hand, his dick.

Turning my way, grateful, unashamed to be caught sobbing, he cried, "Which one, son? Fill which one?"

FORCIBLY RETIRED, MY FATHER LIVED at home in his pajamas. Mom made him wear the slippers and robe to help with his morale. "Think *Thin Man*. Think William Powell." But the poor guy literally hung his head with shame. That phrase took on new meaning now that his routine and dignity proved so reduced. Dad's mopey presence clogged every outlet she'd perfected to avoid him. The two of them were driving each other crazy.

Lacking the cash for live-in help, she was forced to cut way back on her bridge game and female company. She lost ten pounds—it showed in her neck and face—and then she gave up rouge. You could see Mom missed her fancy friends. I soon pitied her nearly as much as I pitied him—no, more. At least he allowed himself to be distracted. She couldn't forget.

Mom kept urging him to get dressed. She said they needed to go to the zoo. She had to get out and "do" something. One morning, she was trying to force Dad into his dress pants when he struck her. She fell right over the back of an armchair. The whole left side of her head stayed a rubber-stamp pad's blue-black for one whole week. Odd, this made it easier for both of them to stay home. Now two people hung their heads in shame.

At a window overlooking the busy street, Dad would stand staring out, one way. On the window glass, his forehead left a persistent oval of human oil. His pajama knees pressed against the radiator. He silently second-guessed parallel parkers. He studied westerly-moving traffic. Sometimes he'd stand guard there for six uninterrupted hours. Did he await some detained patriotic parade? I pictured poor Green on a passing float—hoisting his coffee mug and the black phone receiver, waving him back down to street level, reality, use.

One December morning, Mom—library book in lap, trying to reinterest herself in Daphne du Maurier, in anything—smelled scorching. Like Campbell's mushroom soup left far too long on simmer. Twice she checked their stove and toaster oven. Finally, around his nap time, she pulled Dad away from the radiator: his shins had cooked. "Didn't it hurt you, Dick? Darling, didn't you ever feel anything?"

Next morning at six-thirty, I got her call. Mom's husky tone sounded too jolly for the hour. She described bandaging both legs. "As you kids say, I don't think this is working for us. This might be beyond me. Integrity's fleabag insurance won't provide him with that good a home. We have just enough to go on living here as usual. Now, I'll maybe shock you and you might find me weak or, worse, disloyal. But would you consider someday checking out some nice retreats or facilities in driving distance? Even if it uses up the savings. Your father is the love of my life—one per customer. I just hate to get any more afraid of him!"

I said I'd phone all good local places, adding, giddy, "I hear they're dying to get in there."

This drew a silence as cold as his. "Your dad's been home from the office— what, seven months? Most men lean toward their leisure years, but who ever hated leisure more than Dick? When I think of everything he gave Integrity and how little he's getting back . . . I'm not strong enough to *keep* him, but I can't bear to put him anywhere. Still, at this rate, all I'll want for Christmas is a nice white padded cell for two."

I wished my mother belonged to our generation, where the women work. She could've done anything. And now to be saddled with a man who'd known nothing but enslavement to one so-so office. The workaholic, tabled. He still refused to dress; she focused on the sight of his pajamas. My folks now argued with the energy of newlyweds; then she felt ashamed of herself and he forgot to do whatever he'd just promised.

On Christmas Eve, she was determined to put up a tree for him. But Dad, somehow frightened by the ladder and all the unfamiliar boxes everywhere, got her into such a lethal headlock she had to scream for help. Now the neighbors were involved. People I barely knew interrupted my work hours, saying, "Something's got to be done. It took three of us to pull him off of her. He's still strong as a horse. It's getting dangerous over there. He could escape."

Sometimes, at two in the morning, she'd find him standing in their closet, wearing his pj's and the season's correct hat. He'd be looking at his business suits. The right hand would be filing, "walking" back and forth across creased pant legs, as if seeking the . . . exact . . . right . . . pair . . . for . . . the office . . . today.

I TRIED TO KEEP MISS GREEN informed. She'd sold her duplex and moved into our town's most stylish old-age home. When she swept downstairs to greet me, I didn't recognize her. "God, you look fifteen years younger." I checked her smile for hints of a possible lift.

She just laughed, giving her torso one mild shimmy. "Look, Ma. No shoulder pads."

Her forties hairdo, with its banked, rolled edges, had softened into pretty little curls around her face. She'd let its color go her natural silvery blond. Green gave me a slow look. If I didn't know her better, I'd have sworn she was flirting.

She appeared shorter in flats. I now understood: her toes had been so mangled by wearing those forties Quonset-huts of high heels, ones she'd probably owned since age eighteen. Her feet had grown, but she'd stayed true to the old shoes, part of some illusion she felt my dad required.

Others in the lobby perked up at her fond greeting; I saw she'd already become the belle of this place. She let me admire her updated charms.

"No." She smiled simply. "It's that I tried to keep it all somewhat familiar for him. How I looked and all. We got to where Mr. Markham found any change a kind of danger, so . . . I mean, it wasn't as if a dozen other suitors were beating down my door. What with Mother being moody and sick that long. And so, day to day, well . . ." She shrugged.

Now, IN MY LIFE I'VE had very few inspired ideas. Much of me, like Pop, is helplessly a company man. So forgive my boasting of this.

Leaving Miss Green's, I stopped by a huge Salvation Army store. It was a good one. Over the years, I've found a few fine Federal side chairs here and many a great tweed jacket. Browsing through the used-furniture room, I wandered beneath a cardboard placard hand-lettered "The World of Early American." Ladder-back deacon's chairs and plaid upholstered things rested knee to knee, like sad and separate families.

I chanced to notice a homeless man, asleep, a toothless white fellow. His overcoat looked filthy. His belongings were bunched around him in six rubber-banded shoeboxes. His feet, in paint-stained shoes, rested on an ordinary school administrator's putty-colored desk. "The Wonderful World of Work" hung over hand-me-down waiting rooms still waiting. Business furniture sat parlored—forlorn as any gray-green Irish wake. There was something about the sight of this old guy's midday snoring in so safe a fluorescent make-work cubicle.

Mom now used her sewing room only for those few overnight third cousins willing to endure its lumpy foldout couch. The room had become a catchall, cold storage, since about 1970. We waited for Dad's longest nap of the day. Then, in a crazed burst of energy, we cleared her lair, purging it of boxes, photo albums, four unused exercise machines. I paint-rolled its walls in record time, the ugliest latex junior-high-school green that Sherwin-Williams sells (there's still quite a range). The Salvation Army delivers: within two days, I had arranged this new-used-junk to resemble Integrity's workspace, familiarly anonymous. A gray desk nuzzled one wall—the window wasted behind. Three green file cabinets made a glum herd. One swivel wooden chair rode squeaky casters. The hat rack antlered upright over a dented tin wastebasket. The ashtray looked big enough to serve an entire cancer ward. Wire shelves predicted a neutral "in," a far more optimistic "out." I stuffed desk drawers with Parker ink, cheap fountain pens, yellow legal pads, four dozen paper clips. I'd bought a big black rotary phone, and Mom got him his own line.

Against her wishes, I'd saved most of Dad's old account ledgers. Yellowed already, they could've come from a barrister's desk in a Dickens novel. I scattered "1959-62." In one corner I piled all Dad's boxed records, back taxes, old Christmas cards from customers. The man saved everything.

The evening before we planned introducing him to his new quarters, I disarranged the place a bit. I tossed a dozen pages on the floor near his chair. I left the desk lamp lit all night. It gave this small room a strange hot smell, overworked. The lamp was made of nubbly brown cast metal (recast war surplus?), its red button indicating "on." Black meant "off."

That morning I was there to help him dress. Mom made us a hearty oatmeal breakfast, packed his lunch, and snapped the Tupperware insert into his briefcase.

"And where am I going?" he asked us in a dead voice.

"To the office," I said. "Where else do you go this time of day?"

He appeared sour, puffy, skeptical. Soon as I could, I glanced at Mom. This was not going to be as easy as we'd hoped.

I got Dad's coat and hat. He looked gray and dubious. He would never believe in this new space if I simply squired him down the hall to it. So, after handing him his briefcase, I led Dad back along our corridor and out onto the street.

Some of the old-timers, recognizing him, called, "Looking good, Mr. Markham," or "Cold enough for you?" Arm in arm, we nodded past them.

My grammar school had been one block from his office. Forty years back, we'd set out on foot like this together. The nearer Dad drew to Integrity, the livelier he became; the closer I got to school, the more withdrawn I acted. But today I kept up a mindless overplentiful patter. My tone neither cheered nor deflected him. One block before his office building, I swerved back down an alley toward the house. As we approached, I saw that Mom had been imaginative enough to leave our front door wide open. She'd removed a bird print that had hung in our foyer hall unloved forever. A mere shape, it still always marked this as our hall, our home.

"*Here* we are!" I threw open his office door. I took his hat and placed it on its hook. I helped him free of his coat. Just as his face had grown bored, then irked, and finally enraged at our deception, the phone rang. From where I stood—half in the office, half in the hall—I could see Mom holding the white phone in the kitchen.

My father paused—since when did he answer the phone?—and, finally, flushed, reached for it himself. "Dick?" Mom said. "You'll hate me, I'm getting so absentminded. But you did take your lunch along today, right? I mean, go check. Be patient with me, okay?" Phone cradled between his head and shoulder, he lifted his briefcase and snapped it open—his efficiency still water-clear, and scary. Dad then said to the receiver, "Lunch is definitely here, per usual. But, honey, haven't I told you about these personal calls at the office?"

Then I saw him bend to pick up scattered pages. I saw him touch one yellow legal pad and start to square all the desktop pens at sharp right angles. As he pulled the chair two inches forward I slowly shut his door behind me. Then Mother and I, hidden in the kitchen, held each other and, not expecting it, cried, if very, very silently.

When we peeked in two hours later, he was filing.

EVERY MORNING, SUNDAYS INCLUDED, DAD walked to the office. Even our ruse of walking him around the block was relaxed. Mom simply set a straw hat atop him (after Labor Day, she knew to switch to his gray). With his packed lunch, he would stride nine paces from the kitchen table, step in, and pull the door shut, muttering complaints of overwork, no rest ever.

Dad spent a lot of time on the phone. Long-distance directory-assistance charges constituted a large part of his monthly bill. But he "came home" for supper with the weary sense of blurred accomplishment we recalled from olden times.

Once, having dinner with them, I asked Dad how he was. He sighed. "Well, July is peak for getting their school supplies ordered. So the pressure is on. My heart's not what it was, heart's not completely in it lately, I admit. They downsized Green. Terrible loss to me. With its being crunch season, I get a certain shortness of breath. Suppliers aren't where they were, the gear is often second-rate, little of it any longer American-made. But you keep going, because it's what you know and because your clients count on you. I may be beat, but, hey—it's still a job."

"Aha," I said.

Mom received a call on her own line. It was from some kindergarten owner. Dad—plundering his old red address book—had somehow made himself a go-between, arranging sales, but working freelance now. He appeared to be doing it unsalaried, not for whole school systems but for small local outfits like day care centers. This teacher had to let Mom know that he'd sent too much of the paste. No invoice with it, a pallet of free jarred white school paste waiting out under the swing sets. Whom to thank?

Once, I tiptoed in and saw a long list of figures he kept meaning to add up. I noticed that, in his desperate daily fight to keep his desktop clear, he'd placed seven separate five-inch piles of papers at evened intervals along the far wall. I found such ankle-level filing sad till slowly I recognized a pattern—oh, yeah, "The Pile System." It was my own technique for maintaining provisional emergency order, and one which I now rejudged to be quite sane.

Inked directly into the wooden bottom of his top desk drawer was this:

Check Green's sick leave ridic. long. Nazis still soundly defeated. Double enter all new receipts, nincompoop. Yes, you . . . eighty-one. Old Woman roommate is: "Betty."

Mom felt safe holding bridge parties at the house again, telling friends that Dad was in there writing letters and doing paperwork, and who could say he wasn't? Days, Mom could now shop or attend master-point tournaments at good-driving-distance hotels. In her own little kitchen-corner office, she entered bridge chat rooms, e-mailing game-theory arcana to well-known French and

Russian players. She'd regained some weight and her face was fuller, and prettier for that. She bought herself a bottle-green velvet suit. "It's just a cheap Chanel knockoff, but these ol' legs still ain't that bad, hmm?" She looked more rested than I'd seen her in a year or two.

I cut a mail slot in Dad's office door, and around eleven Mom would slip in the day's *Wall Street Journal*. You'd hear him fall upon it like a zoo animal, fed.

SINCE DAD HAD TRIED TO break down the headhunters' door I hadn't dared go on vacation myself. But Mother encouraged me to take my family to Hawaii. She laughed. "Go ahead, enjoy yourself, for Pete's sake. Everything's under control. I'm playing what friends swear is my best bridge ever, and Dick's sure working good long hours again. By now I should know the drill, huh?"

I was just getting into my bathing suit when the hotel phone rang. I could see my wife and son down there on the white beach.

"Honey? Me. There's news about your father."

Mom's voice sounded vexed but contained. Her businesslike tone seemed assigned. It let me understand.

"When?"

"This afternoon around six-thirty our time. Maybe it happened earlier, I don't know. I found him. First I convinced myself he was just asleep. But I guess, even earlier, I knew."

I stood here against glass, on holiday. I pictured my father facedown at his desk. The tie still perfectly knotted, his hat yet safe on its hook. I imagined Dad's head at rest atop those forty pages of figures he kept meaning to add up.

I told Mom I was sorry; I said we'd fly right back.

"No, please," she said. "I've put everything off till next week. It's just us now. Why hurry? And, son? Along with the bad news, I think there's something good. He died at the office."

Allan Gurganus writes that he has "worked hard since June 11th 1947, with major help that day from Mom." His hunches and preoccupations finally fused into "the oddest of odd jobs, the manual art of writing fiction." Gurganus has earned his living "walking dogs, selling art reproductions at the Harvard Coop, teaching writing to college kids, painting neoclassical murals, and, once, as a male prostitute (when some guy left two fifties on a hotel's bedside table and inexplicably left before breakfast)."

"He's at the Office" tries to show how Americans use work as their very frame of being. Gurganus writes, "If Europeans define themselves by where they spend their indolent holiday Augusts, Americans often prefer nine-to-five over anything personal. We are Calvinists; we need nine-to-five, suspecting the vices awaiting us in horny leisure."

The present story was inspired when Gurganus saw a homeless man asleep amid a grouping of thrift-shop office-furniture.

The author, reared Presbyterian, accustomed to long hours and an artist's low pay, "thrives on poor work conditions and the terrible difficulty of minting all of human experience into a mere twenty-six letters. It is grueling work, but certain masochists in basement apartments have to do it, apparently."

Gurganus lives and works in a small town in his native North Carolina. His books include *Oldest Living Confederate Widow Tells All* (Knopf 1989), *White People* (Knopf 1991), *Plays Well With Others* (Knopf 1997), and *The Practical Heart* (North Carolina Wesleyan 1993). He is laboring on a long novel, a companion to *Widow* titled *The Erotic History of a Southern Baptist Church*.

"He's at the Office" originally appeared in *The New Yorker* (February 15, 1999) and will be included in *Assisted Living*, Gurganus's forthcoming collection of stories. Copyright © 1999 by Allan Gurganus. It is reprinted here by permission of the author.

By Appointment

Lisa K. Buchanan

RETURNING TO THE KITCHEN, I see by the drawstring pucker of my daughter's lips that a stealth perusal of my appointment book has convinced her I am a hypochondriac: Dr. G. this morning; Dr. F. this afternoon; Dr. C. next Friday. Ashley is mad because of the onslaught of medical appointments that prevent me from witnessing her moments of glory, such as today's rehearsal for the school play, the Wizard of Oz. And she is mad because she is eleven and her hair is sticking to her head on such a significant day. Not 8:00 a.m. and the forces have conspired against her.

She pinches her Slavic brows and glares down into her cereal, hides behind her voluminous black hair to eliminate the possibility of eye contact with me. I return my appointment book to my purse and fuss about the kitchen, wiping up spills and wishing I could make things better for her—or at least attend her dress rehearsal.

But today while Ashley is pacing and scowling, and calling forth the winged monkeys, I will be waiting for Dr. F. at a posh hotel near Union Square. When he arrives at Suite 1108, I will be sitting in the jet-powered tub the way he likes, posed amid sweat and steam, my hair teased and wavy around my face, toes curled over the rim of the tub. He will edge toward me sideways, deliberately, as if to withhold his touch, torment me with anticipation. He will ease his body down to join me, pull me close for our long-awaited meeting, a cherished consummation of illicit passion.

My name is Clare, but for the next three hours he will call me Vanessa or Nessa or Beautiful or Darling. He will gush: *Oh Baby Oh Vanessa how are you how have you been my darling I have missed you so.* He will kiss my neck and I will pull back as if to say we really mustn't. He will insist, then take me in the tub. After, we will nuzzle, and he will smile, moved, sentimental. We will clink glasses of brandy, hand-feed each other Belgian chocolates. I will roll a mocha buttercream slowly around my mouth and gaze into his eyes; it's a cheap trick but it works for Dr. F. He will lunge and I will resist. We will dry off and wear cheap Chinese robes to bed, and he will talk to me about my beauty, comparing me to some movie or song or billboard advertisement. *I thought of you the other day when . . .* He will lunge again and tear fabric from my body. I will fake orgasms and topple into his arms. He will stroke my hair and apologize for all the time he cannot spend with me.

Though I am not his mistress, Dr. F. likes to think of me this way, his crisp bills as a little sugar for my purse. Dr. F. likes to indulge, to throw off the mighty burden of being an orthopedic surgeon and giving, giving, giving all day long. He comes home at night to a renovated Victorian in Ashbury Heights and a wife who has been suffering from a degenerative disease for the last half of their 29-year marriage. Dr. F. is lonely—lonely enough to hire me each week for an afternoon at this hotel, lonely enough to posit that someday we might see each other outside, lonely enough to pretend that we are making love.

Of course, my daughter knows none of this, only that today while she is reciting the slow, eloquent demise of Dorothy and friends, I will not be there to witness her witchly powers.

She builds mountains in the soggy bran in front of her, mashes them with the flat side of her spoon, and asks me for the fourth time why I can't come to the rehearsal like I did the year before. "Nobody else's mom goes to nine billion doctor appointments," she says. "What's wrong with you anyway?"

My daughter has asked more questions this month than in all her prior years combined. The same kid who picks raisins out of her cereal wants to know if the Pill makes a girl fat. She wants to know why her mother is still going to school to learn how to work a camera, when Debby's mother has had a swanky gift shop for years. She wants to know how I get my hair "all perfect and everything." She wants to know why her father moved to a loft in the city and why he sends envelopes addressed to her with no letter, but a support check written to me. And she wants to know why today's medical appointment takes precedence over the most important event of her life.

My explanations do not suffice. She knows that her father and I met while working together—he, a photographer, and I, his model and assistant. She knows that he and I were in love when we created her; and that after she was born, I worked in his studio, airbrushing lines and moles and personality from young faces of women like myself. I have told her of a November day when I had pulled too many shiny-lip smirks and naive pouts from the fixer tank and hung them up to dry—faces frozen and glaring with a glossy finish, faces I had worn. I have told her that instead of developing his award-winning photos, I had to leave the man, take my own photos and let the faces breathe.

But Ashley was nine years old then. She knows now that I go to school three days a week and that Thursdays and Fridays are my days for personal business. She knows that I no longer spend long, weepy nights in the kitchen, holding buoyant tea bags under hot water with my fingers and worry about how to make ends meet. And she has heard that the Pill adds water-weight but doesn't make a girl nearly as heavy as pregnancy.

Still, Ashley is mad. Mad that her father lives 25 minutes away and rarely calls; mad that her mother cannot be there today; mad that her body seems to have gone spongy but for her bony knees. She is mad, too, because in addition to her hair sticking to her head, the fog will make it frizz. And though she hopes she'll be as smart and pretty as me when she's 34, she says, would I please drop her off a block from school instead of right up front?

So I tell her, once again, that things will get better when I graduate next year. This, followed by the usual dose of morning nags: Pack your lunch. Be home by 5:00. Bring your homework. And now, eat your cereal. Ashley returns my nagging with one sigh and two rolling eyeballs, scoops the goopy grains into her mouth to satisfy me.

Our kitchen window frames an immense tree whose shadow looms darkly this morning across our window. A mile down the road in a foggy parking lot, two or three bikers sit quietly, sipping coffee from foam cups and blowing steam while they wait for the Highlight Club to open. Our town has the only biker-bar I know where the burgers are grass-fed and the bikers don't smoke cigarettes. They have ridden the empty mountain roads through the night, crouched by a beach fire at sunrise. They are waiting for the gray-faced man to open the door; they are waiting to order Bloody Marys, pump quarters into the pool table and tap their feet to Johnny Cash. Some morning I will wait too, with a zoom lens next to a tree in the distance.

But for now, I pull up my stockings, adjust my skirt and pack my purse with the proper gear. In an hour, my daughter will be squirming in a wooden schoolchair, multiplying decimals. I will be reclined in Dr. G.'s acrylic chair although his downtown practice is closed on Fridays. For several minutes I'll be waiting, while he shuffles papers down the hall. I'll stare at his corny wallpaper— sky blue with clouds—and listen to the drone of New Age music. He will walk in from behind, wash his hands, flick on the overhead lamp like he did fourteen times the day before—his silhouette towering in the glare.

Open, he says. So I do, and he puts his mouth to mine. Dr. G. is nothing like Dr. F. His kiss is bland and wooden—a tongue depressor. I lie still and look straight ahead as he observes me from various angles. He watches my eyes blink, runs a thumb along the depression above my collar bone, presses his fingertips flat against the side of my neck, reaches under the plastic drape where I am naked, but for the pair of lacy turquoise panties he has provided. He presses one breast in circles, then the other, probes and prods the tender places around my ribs, belly, on down, in a strange combination of touching female skin and examining tissue.

He sets the drape aside so that it hangs from the chair and remains fastened around my neck. He hangs his trousers on a jacket peg, unzips his white, fluid-resistant smock, then snips the panties from my body with dainty, sterile scissors. He climbs into the chair on top of me, presses hard into my belly, likes for me not to moan or grind; no words or sighs. We look directly at each other as he moves; no expression. After the release he buries his face in my neck for a moment, but doesn't linger. He washes, dresses, and leaves a blank file on the Formica counter. I take the file—cash and the appointment card—and leave.

Dr. G.'s light glows from beneath his office door. I'll see him again in three weeks.

I know nothing about Dr. G. except that he got my name from Dr. S. and leaves messages with my service. In the seven months I have been working with him, we have spoken only once, by phone for basic arrangements: His office, 9:00 a.m., Fridays, sporadic, $400, half-hour maximum, stairwell entrance.

With just a few essential words—here, like this, open, close, again—Dr. G.'s communication is sparse and mostly tactile. He is a handsome man, tall and lanky, probably runs the Marina Green pathway every morning. He has a cool, square jaw. As an orthodontist he spends his days with restless, frightened kids and hovering parents, names and faces and demands for attention. From me he wants none of this.

From me he wants eye to eye, skin on skin.

"Maaaaaahm, your toatht is ready!"

Intrigued with a boy who has a lisp, Ashley has recently developed one of her own. She reads three plays a week, flunks grammar, cries often and is embarrassed by the strangeness protruding from her chest. Incredulous at having survived the drama of another day, she monopolizes the phone each night—Debby or Amber or Katy or Mandy—to deliver the grand news. Leaning against the doorframe, I watch her dip her spoon in and out of the cereal swamp, forming pools, tributaries, faults and crannies. For the moment, she has forgotten her mother's alleged hypochondria. Ashley is the Wicked Witch of the West, determining the fate of vulnerable trespassers on the fallen, granular land before her. She spies from the watchtower of her castle, upon Dorothy and pitiful crew as they scale the treacherous slope. She presses her thin, vicious lips together, pushes out a sneer, narrows her eyes and strokes her long, knobby chin with two warted fingers. My daughter is steeped in malice, obsessed over a braided brat from Kansas and her sparkling, accursed shoes. It is a moment I want forever. With a finger on the shutter, I am already gloating over the photo I am about to take.

"Mom, are you dying?" she asks, still staring into her bowl.

"Ashley, no. What makes you think that?"

"Would you tell me if you were?"

"No. I mean, of course . . . Yes, I would. I mean, I'm fine, honey."

"Well then, what do they do, those doctors, when you see them?"

"They're just looking after me, that's all."

And that's when she looks up.

Click.

This is not the candid daughter-at-breakfast photo I intended to take, but rather, a picture of us both. This is a girl looking at one parent who left the other; a girl whose mother used to attend dress rehearsals for school plays but has become arbitrarily cruel and possibly sick inside. And this is my daughter using a modeling trick I taught her, staring into the air above my head; her expression, vague and dispassionate.

Soon, I hope to be taking a different kind of picture—a clean image with a clear focus, a girl playing an artful role on stage rather than an expedient one at home. For the moment, however, the cunning cackler has all but melted; this is a picture of my daughter striking a pose; my daughter learning, despite her best efforts, to be like me.

Fiction and essays by **Lisa K. Buchanan** have received awards from *The Missouri Review* and *Glimmer Train* and have appeared in *Mid-American Review, Natural Bridge, Quick Fiction, Cosmopolitan,* and *Redbook*, among other publications. Her work has also been featured on public radio. She lives in San Francisco and at *lisakbuchanan.com.*

As an editor for a women's health magazine, Buchanan urged readers to take time for themselves, develop personal interests, maintain a nutritious diet, and not smoke. "I was, however, writing these prudent words on a Wednesday night between bits of pizza brought into the office for a 'working dinner.' On the long commute home, candy and cigarettes kept me awake, pacified and distracted from the absurdity of living in an exciting city I rarely saw." She notes that her "strongest skills and interests—eavesdropping, sloth, the crafting of illusion—are not in high demand from employers."

At the time of writing "By Appointment," Buchanan had a roommate "whose pretty boyfriend did protest too much that men were always hitting on him, a refrain that kept me thinking about ways we design, frame, and project images of ourselves. The story's protagonist, too, is selling an image, one tailored to each client. Her other professions—modeling, photography and even motherhood—all entail the projection of image." Buchanan's stories are also conceived on a "sonic level by which a phrase or fragment ('faces I had worn') whispered, asserted, or casually uttered by someone else will hang pleasantly in my ears and become a portal for a story."

"By Appointment" originally appeared in the Irish publication *U Magazine* (1992).
Copyright © 1992 by Lisa K. Buchanan. It is reprinted here by permission of the author.

"Spinner, Cotton Mill, 1908–1909"
Photograph by Lewis Hine

Jorn Ake

She is too young
to have hands that read
the spinning machinery
and the calloused cast cement of the window's sill
with the fluent touch of bathing
her own body before unlit and cold
tenement dawn, before the coal and brick
of the mill, dipping down into the gray water
to reach for the washcloth
and rub skin from bones that grow
though the body has become disconnected.

This morning spills into her room
as cold air steals lowly into warmth.
Perhaps, she catches herself looking
into some shiny trap,
some oil slick skim.
Sees the glass of her eye move
the woman of her hip
into the girl in her side
and thinks of something not named as simply
as "warm" or "man"
that makes her hands soften down, pull
a strand from the dresser's back drawers
to her hair, a dress from the darkness
of a closet to her shoulders. Something
she could walk towards with hands
laid out before herself.

Come here child. In the mill
she turns towards the sound.
She sees a body's white phosphorescence,
float calmly through grimy walls,
and waltz over the seeping floor
to her.

The light of a cigarette rises
in the feathery movement of a hand
winding a bobbin—
Turn around, turn around.
She feels the small black dot reach
into her eyes, butt its head
against the socket's smooth back wall.
Fill her head with its one
hard blink.

She does not remember her eyes
rolling up white and blind.

Or her tongue
arcing inward upon itself
as if to taste the sudden light.

She does not feel her hand
slip from the window sill
her body lurch into the air
before her
as her other hand falls
quietly, simply
into the clicking machinery,
the sharp, bright point of the spinner
piercing bone and flesh straight through
her palm's sweet center line,
holding her closely for a second.
Then
letting go.

Jorn Ake has worked as a bicycle mechanic, a travel agent, a manager of outdoor equipment stores, an animal shelter caretaker, a house painter, a carpenter's assistant, a theater set technician, a commissioned salesman, a waiter, a dishwasher, a hot dog vendor, a gardener, and a professor of English composition and creative writing. His first book of poetry, *Asleep in the Lightning Fields* (Texas Review 2002), won the 2001 X. J. Kennedy Award. He is currently self-employed as a writer and photographer, "though only barely." He lives in New York City.

Ake wrote "Spinner" after reading the book *What Work Is* by Philip Levine. Ake says, "The photo of the girl in my poem, taken originally by Lewis Hine, is on the cover of Levine's book. When I first read the book, I was working as a bicycle mechanic during the week, spending weekends in my painting studio, and watching my marriage fall apart. I had always thought of manual labor as the work most honorable. But Levine disabused me of my romantic notions without dishonoring those who work, as Lewis Hine helped disabuse the country of its notion that child labor was acceptable in modern society. The girl photographed by Hine staring out at me from Levine's book cover was trapped forever. I just tried to imagine her for a moment, freed."

Copyright © Jorn Ake

Jane

Ambur Economou

FATIGUE FROM 36 HOURS ON call makes the three-mile bike ride home dangerous. In the dark I think I see moving shapes in my peripheral vision. I get home too tired to eat, almost too tired to go to the bathroom—but I do manage to walk numbly down the hall to take care of that. I say hi to my husband. I'm too tired to tell him how my day (and night and day) was.

I head to the bedroom and lie on top of the covers, still in my scrubs. Ahhh, it feels so good. Rachel runs in the room and jumps on the bed. "Mommy!" she squeals. "We went on a walking trip to the store and . . ." She chatters on. I try to listen. I sit up. Shake my head hard. Cuddle her on my lap to listen. She smells good, feels alive and full of energy—in stark contrast to the death and illness that seems to hang on my scrubs and sweaty body. I feel like I should wash before I hold her.

But I am so tired. I am just going to lay my head down for a minute. I'm not going to sleep yet. I'll just listen to Rachel talk and rest my head.

An hour later I wake up to find myself surrounded by stuffed animals. They are set up in a semi circle. There is a cup from a play tea set in my hand. Rachel is talking for me. She has been moving me around like one of her animals. Pretending she has a mommy who talks, and plays, and listens to her.

IN THE HOSPITAL SOMEONE ELSE'S daughter is dying. Her name is Jane. She is my age, 24. She is a psychology PhD student who probably ate the wrong thing at a restaurant and had a severe asthma attack on the subway. By the time the paramedics could get air into her lungs, her brain had been turned to the "salt and pepper" we saw on the CT scan.

The ICU waiting room is next to my locker. Jane's family is from another city, across the country. They are camping in the waiting room. Her father talks to me when I go to my locker.

He is intelligent, a professor of English. He wants to learn what we are doing with his daughter. What do the lines on the EEG machine mean? What do they actually measure? How is her potassium? Her sodium? Is she overbreathing the ventilator? What is the level of intracranial pressure that is dangerous? He follows me down to the candy machine. It is two in the morning and I need a Snickers to stay awake.

He asks me about medical school. What is it like? How long before I become a doctor? When did I last get to sleep? He acts concerned. Fatherly.

IN JANE'S ROOM, I LOOK at her body. The top of her head is shaved and there is a "bolt" in place to monitor the pressure inside. Her face is pale and waxy. She looks dead. A tube in her mouth breathes for her. A tube in her nose sucks out her stomach contents. Soon we will have to consider feeding her. Her body is thin, covered with patches and catheters and wires. Her toenails, painted pink, have grown out a bit. She needs a pedicure. Her mother has washed her hair, braided it. Perhaps she will fix her toenails.

AS A MEDICAL STUDENT I HEAR both sides. The family accepts me amongst them and has discussions about what they think and feel and see. The medical team has discussions about what they think and feel and see. The two perspectives are so different that it seems unreal.

HER UNCLE ASKS BLUNT QUESTIONS. "Is she going to be a vegetable? What are the chances she will wake up? Should we just stop all of this?" The attending physician answers, "There is a less than one percent chance she will wake up, based on how she is doing now." But I read the paper he is quoting from. The authors listed less than one percent when in fact there were none. No one in the study who was as bad off as Jane ever woke up.

WE DO EVERYTHING. WE ADJUST HER electrolytes, urine output, and intracranial pressure. In fact, she is stabilizing. Her brainstem seems relatively intact. She will likely be able to breathe on her own soon. But still she does not wake up. There is no brainwave activity to suggest that she is going to.

AFTER WEEKS HER FATHER TELLS ME in the hallway, "We don't have much hope, but if there is a one in a hundred chance she will wake up we need to keep going. Besides, nothing we are doing is hurting anyone. We have everything to gain and nothing to lose."

I usually just listen. But today I am tired and have been thinking too much. Feeling too much. Perhaps empathizing too much with Jane. I tell him what I see. What the members of the physician team say amongst themselves, but not to the family. "Jane is not likely to wake up. But in a week or so, if it is decided to stop the life support, she may live without it. She may live just as she is now but without the breathing machine or monitors. She may live like this for a long time. That is the risk of continuing." My heart pounds as I realize what I have said.

"Nobody told me that," he says quietly. "I was just thinking that we could keep trying until there was no hope, and then she would die quietly, peacefully. I don't think she would want to live like this."

The next morning Jane's uncle confronts the attending doctor about what I have said. He does not say where he got the information. The attending tells him it is true. Her uncle asks him what should be done. "That is up to you," he says. He seems angry and cuts the meeting off abruptly when his beeper sounds. The team rounds on Jane but the family's questions are not discussed. I feel like everyone knows it was me who betrayed some sort of awful secret.

Two days later the attending changes services as scheduled. The job of talking to the family daily is assigned to me by the new attending "because they know you better than they know me." No one comes with me when I do this. The intern says, "I don't do that family stuff."

Four days later the family decides to withdraw life support.

I AM SO WRACKED WITH guilt, I can barely stand to be with myself. I obsessively read books on death and dying. I need to know that what I said to Jane's father was the right thing. But I don't think that it was. I think I have stolen their hope. I am so ashamed that I cannot talk to anyone about it. And all along I am taking call every third night—36 hours with only occasional sleep. I have insomnia even when I am allowed to sleep.

JANE'S FATHER HAS BEEN TALKING to me about Jane. Who she is, what she has done, her likes and dislikes, what she was like as a little girl. He and his wife clean out her apartment, close her checking account, move her things back to their house. More family comes. They are waiting for a last family member to come from India and then they want to stop the breathing machine. I can feel their hope that she will wake up before the grandfather is able to travel.

JANE HAS BEGUN TO POSTURE. She coughs when the tube is suctioned and draws her arms into her body in an unnatural way. The residents have been spending less and less time on her. Aside from me, no one talks to the family.

IT IS THE LAST DAY of my rotation, and my last night on call. The grandfather arrives and seems to pull the family together. "It is time to let Jane die. She is ready," he tells me. I get the resident on call, who calls the attending. The attending isn't coming. We are to have the respiratory therapist "pull the vent." But the family wants all the tubes off of her and the bolt out of her head. The neurosurgery resident is busy and doesn't have time to come take it out. He has patients who may live to attend to. We wait for hours until the nurses start paging him with trivial questions, over and over again. He removes the bolt at 11 p.m. The respiratory therapist withdraws the ventilator.

Jane coughs, and postures, and makes terrible noises. I back into the corner. Her mother swoons. Jane's brother takes their mother from the room. The nurse administers morphine and Jane quiets. I stand in the corner next to a silent television for a long time. Finally I ask Jane's father if he would like me to stay. He shakes his head no. "We'll call a nurse," he whispers, "if we need anything."

I get a Snickers and a Pepsi and sit at the nurses' station, watching the door. Two hours later Jane's father drifts out like a sleepwalker. "She died an hour ago. I don't know if you need to know that or not." He moves toward the waiting room with his family. The nurses start making calls. The resident arrives and listens with a stethoscope in order to "pronounce death." I think, "You don't need to do that, her father already did." Absurdly, this strikes me as funny. I feel I am losing my mind.

The body is cleaned; the IV removed. I watch and realize that she did not look dead before. Now I know what dead really looks like. It is not as disturbing as the way she looked weeks ago. This is just an empty shell. It is a cadaver, like the ones I dissected in anatomy. Something I am comfortable with. I watch the aides put her into a bag and zip it up over her face. It is close to 3 a.m. and I have a final exam tomorrow. I need to sleep.

I walk past the waiting room and Jane's uncle, the one who always asked the blunt questions, rushes out at me. "Now what do we do?" he asks. "Are there papers or something to sign? Where is the body? What will they do with her?" I answer his questions but he keeps asking them over and over, seemingly not hearing the answers. I am beginning to feel frustrated. What does he want from me? I am tired. I just want to sleep. I have given all I have and he seems to want more of me. Need more.

Eventually I realize he is asking a deeper question. One I have no way to answer. What do they do now that their young, bright, hopeful, funny Jane is dead? What do they do now?

I HAVE TERRIBLE NIGHTMARES THAT I am dying. That they are pulling the tube from my throat and I cannot breathe but I am alive. I am awake but cannot move. I see everyone in the room and I feel myself dying and I somehow know it is going to hurt terribly. I wake up sweating and shaking.

RACHEL IS IN THE KITCHEN chatting with her father. I hear her voice accelerating to a whine. "But she has been sleeping for a long time. I want Mommy."

I drag myself out of bed and shuffle to the kitchen. Rachel is sitting on the floor with her ratty, pink teddy bear and her favorite Little Mermaid doll. Her legs are extended stiffly, petulantly. Her muscles are tense, ready for a kicking tantrum.

"Here I am." I fake brightness for my daughter, who is alive. "Here's Mommy."

I hug Rachel and press my check against hers—such smoothness. I press Rachel back into her father's arms. Already her legs are going rigid again. Stiffening into the succession of rapid little kicks she now releases. "But you just got here. I want to play. You never play."

"Mommy can't play now. She has to go to school, to take a test," I smile—

another fake smile. Then I try to make up for it. I look directly into Rachel's brown eyes, but she looks away and resumes her kicking.

I leave her like that—kicking and crying—and bike to school. For the first time in my life, I flunk an exam.

Ambur Economou is a family medicine physician, practicing in a small town in southern Missouri. She lives with her two children, Rachel and Jackson. "Jane" was her first published work.

Economou writes, " 'Jane' is about an experience I had while in medical school. For me, my work has never been very separate from my life, so it is as natural to write about work as it is to write about anything. My work wakes me up in the middle of the night, and I take my children with me on hospital rounds. My son has waited in the lounge while I delivered the baby sister of his neighborhood friend. I see my patients at the grocery store, and they see me at my home or my children's school. There doesn't ever seem to be a separate entity of Ambur v. Doctor."

"Jane" was first published in the anthology *This Side of Doctoring: Reflections from Women in Medicine*, edited by Eliza Lo Chin (Sage 2001). Copyright © 2001 by Ambur Economou. It is reprinted here by permission of the author.

Quitting the Paint Factory

Mark Slouka

Love yields to business. If you seek a way out of love,
be busy; you'll be safe, then.
—Ovid, *Remedia Amoris*

I DISTRUST THE PERPETUALLY BUSY; always have. The frenetic ones spinning in tight little circles like poisoned rats. The slower ones, grinding away their fourscore and ten in righteousness and pain. They are the soul-eaters.

When I was young, my parents read me Aesop's fable of "The Ant and the Grasshopper," wherein, as everyone knows, the grasshopper spends the summer making music in the sun while the ant toils with his fellow *formicidae*. Inevitably, winter comes, as winters will, and the grasshopper, who hasn't planned ahead and who doesn't know what a 401K is, has run out of luck. When he shows up at the ant's door, carrying his fiddle, the ant asks him what he was doing all year: "I was singing, if you please," the grasshopper replies, or something to that effect. "You were singing?" says the ant. "Well, then, go and sing." And perhaps because I sensed, even then, that fate would someday find me holding a violin or a manuscript at the door of the ants, my antennae frozen and my bills overdue, I confounded both Aesop and my well-meaning parents, and bore away the wrong moral. That summer, many a wind-blown grasshopper was saved from the pond, and many an anthill inundated under the golden rain of my pee.

I was right.

In the lifetime that has passed since Calvin Coolidge gave his speech to the American Society of Newspaper Editors in which he famously proclaimed that "the chief business of the American people is business," the dominion of the ants has grown enormously. Look about: The business of business is everywhere and inescapable; the song of the buyers and the sellers never stops; the term "workaholic" has been folded up and put away. We have no time for our friends or our families, no time to think or to make a meal. We're moving product, while the soul drowns like a cat in a well. [*"I think that there is far too much work done in the world,"* Bertrand Russell observed in his famous 1932 essay *"In Praise of Idleness,"* adding that he hoped to *"start a campaign to induce good young men to do nothing." He failed. A year later, National Socialism, with its cult of work (think of all those bronzed young men in Leni Riefenstahl's* Triumph of the Will *throwing cordwood to each other in the sun), flared in Germany.*]

A resuscitated orthodoxy, so pervasive as to be nearly invisible, rules the land. Like any religion worth its salt, it shapes our world in its image, demonizing if necessary, absorbing when possible. Thus has the great sovereign territory of what Nabokov called "unreal estate," the continent of invisible possessions from time to talent to contentment, been either infantilized, rendered unclean, or translated into the grammar of dollars and cents. Thus has the great wilderness of the inner life been compressed into a median strip by the demands of the "real world," which of course is anything but. Thus have we succeeded in transforming even ourselves into bipedal products, paying richly for seminars that teach us how to market the self so it may be sold to the highest bidder. Or perhaps "down the river" is the phrase.

Ah, but here's the rub: Idleness is not just a psychological necessity, requisite to the construction of a complete human being; it constitutes as well a kind of political space, a space as necessary to the workings of an actual democracy as, say, a free press. How does it do this? By allowing us time to figure out who we are, and what we believe; by allowing us time to consider what is unjust, and what we might do about it. By giving the inner life (in whose precincts we are most ourselves) its due. Which is precisely what makes idleness dangerous. All manner of things can grow out of that fallow soil. Not for nothing did our mothers grow suspicious when we had "too much time on our hands." They knew we might be up to something. And not for nothing did we whisper to each other, when we *were* up to something, "Quick, look busy."

Mother knew instinctively what the keepers of the castles have always known: that trouble—the kind that might threaten the symmetry of a well-ordered garden—needs time to take root. Take away the time, therefore, and you choke off the problem before it begins. Obedience reigns, the plow stays in the furrow; things proceed as they must. Which raises an uncomfortable question: Could the Church of Work—which today has Americans aspiring to sleep deprivation the way they once aspired to a personal knowledge of God—be, at base, an anti-democratic force? Well, yes. James Russell Lowell, that nineteenth-century workhorse, summed it all up quite neatly: "There is no better ballast for keeping the mind steady on its keel, and saving it from all risk of crankiness, than business."

Quite so. The mind, however, particularly the mind of a citizen in a democratic society, is not a boat. Ballast is not what it needs, and steadiness, alas, can be a synonym for stupidity, as our current administration has so amply demonstrated. No, what the democratic mind requires, above all, is time; time to consider its options. Time to develop the democratic virtues of independence, orneriness, objectivity, and fairness. Time, perhaps (to sail along with Lowell's leaky metaphor for a moment), to ponder the course our unelected captains have so generously set for us, and to consider mutiny when the iceberg looms.

Which is precisely why we need to be kept busy. If we have no time to think, to mull if we have no time to piece together the sudden associations and unexpected, mid-shower insights that are the stuff of independent opinion, then we are less citizens than cursors, easily manipulated, vulnerable to the currents of power.

But I have to be careful here. Having worked all of my adult life, I recognize that work of one sort or another is as essential to survival as protein, and that much of it, in today's highly bureaucratized, economically diversified societies, will of necessity be neither pleasant nor challenging nor particularly meaningful. I have compassion for those making the most of their commute and their cubicle; I just wish they could be a little less cheerful about it. In short, this isn't about us so much as it is about the *Zeitgeist* we live and labor in, which, like a cuckoo taking over a thrush's nest, has systematically shoved all the other eggs of our life, one by one, onto the pavement. It's about illuminating the losses.

We're enthralled. I want to disenchant us a bit; draw a mustache on the boss.

Infinite Bustle

I'm a student of the narrowing margins. And their victim, to some extent, though my capacity for sloth, my belief in it, may yet save me. Like some stubborn heretic in fifth-century Rome, still offering gifts to the spirit of the fields even as the priests sniff about the *tempa* for sin, I daily sacrifice my bit of time. The pagan gods may yet return. Constantine and Theodosius may die. But the prospects are bad.

In Riverside Park in New York City, where I walk these days, the legions of "weekend nannies" are growing, setting up a play date for a ten-year-old requires a feat of near-Olympic coordination, and the few, vestigial, late-afternoon parents one sees, dragging their wailing progeny by the hand or frantically kicking a soccer ball in the fading light, have a gleam in their eyes I find frightening. No outstretched legs crossed at the ankles, no arms draped over the back of the bench. No lovers. No behatted old men, arguing. Between the slide and the sandbox, a very fit young man in his early thirties is talking on his cell phone while a two-year-old with a trail of snot running from his nose tugs on the seam of his corduroy pants. "There's no way I can pick it up. Because we're still at the park. Because we just got here, that's why."

It's been one hundred and forty years since Thoreau, who itched a full century before everyone else began to scratch, complained that the world was increasingly just "a place of business. What an infinite bustle!" he groused. "I am awaked almost every night by the panting of the locomotive. It interrupts my dreams. There is no Sabbath. It would be glorious to see mankind at leisure for once. It is nothing but work, work, work." Little did he know. Today the roads of commerce, paved and smoothed, reach into every nook and cranny of the republic; there is no place apart, no place where we would be shut of the drone of that damnable traffic. Today we, quite literally, live to work. And it hardly matters what kind of work we do; the process justifies the ends. Indeed, at times it seems there is hardly an occupation, however useless or humiliating or downright despicable, that cannot at least in part be redeemed by our obsessive dedication to it: "Yes, Ted sold shoulder-held Stingers to folks with no surname, but he worked so *hard!*"

Not long ago, at the kind of dinner party I rarely attend, I made the mistake of admitting that I not only liked to sleep but liked to get at least eight hours a night whenever possible, and that nine would be better still. The reaction—a complex Pinot Noir of nervous laughter displaced by expressions of disbelief and condescension—suggested that my transgression had been, on some level, a political one. I was reminded of the time I'd confessed to Roger Angell that I did not much care for baseball.

My comment was immediately rebutted by testimonials to sleeplessness: two of the nine guests confessed to being insomniacs; a member of the Academy of Arts and Letters claimed indignantly that she couldn't remember when she had *ever* gotten eight hours of sleep; two other guests declared themselves grateful for five or six. It mattered little that I'd arranged my life differently, and accepted the sacrifices that arrangement entailed. Eight hours! There was something willful about it. Arrogant, even. Suitably chastened, I held my tongue, and escaped alone to tell Thee.

Increasingly, it seems to me, our world is dividing into two kinds of things: those that aid work, or at least represent a path to it, and those that don't. Things in the first category are good and noble; things in the second aren't. Thus, for example, education is good (as long as we don't have to listen to any of that "end in itself" nonsense) because it will presumably lead to work. Thus playing the piano or swimming the 100-yard backstroke are good things for a fifteen-year-old to do *not* because they might give her some pleasure but because rumor has it that Princeton is interested in students who can play Chopin or swim quickly on their backs (and a degree from Princeton, as any fool knows, can be readily converted to work).

Point the beam anywhere, and there's the God of Work, busily trampling out the vintage. Blizzards are bemoaned because they keep us from getting to work. Hobbies are seen as either ridiculous or self-indulgent because they interfere with work. Longer school days are all the rage (even as our children grow demonstrably stupider), not because they make educational or psychological or any other kind of sense but because keeping kids in school longer makes it easier for us to work. Meanwhile, the time grows short, the margin narrows; the white spaces on our calendars have been inked in for months. We're angry about this, upset about that, but who has the time to do anything anymore? There are those reports to report on, memos to remember, emails to deflect or delete. They bury us like snow.

The alarm rings and we're off, running so hard that by the time we stop we're too tired to do much of anything except nod in front of the TV, which, like virtually all the other voices in our culture, endorses our exhaustion, fetishizes and romanticizes it and, by daily adding its little trowelful of lies and omissions, helps cement the conviction that not only is this how our three score and ten must be spent but that the transaction is both noble and necessary.

Ka-Chink!

Time may be money (though I've always resisted that loathsome platitude, the alchemy by which the very gold of our lives is transformed into the base lead of commerce), but one thing seems certain: Money eats time. Forget the visions of sanctioned leisure: the view from the deck in St. Moritz, the wafer-thin TV. Consider the price.

Sometimes, I want to say, money costs too much. And at the beginning of the millennium, in this country, the cost of money is well on the way to bankrupting us. We're impoverishing ourselves, our families, our communities—and yet we can't stop ourselves. Worse, we don't want to.

Seen from the right vantage point, there's something wonderfully animistic about it. The god must be fed; he's hungry for our hours, craves our days and years. And we oblige. Every morning (unlike the good citizens of Tenochtitlan, who at least had the good sense to sacrifice others on the slab) we rush up the steps of the ziggurat to lay ourselves down. It's not a pretty sight.

Then again, we've been well trained. And the training never stops. In a recent ad in *The New York Times Magazine*, paid for by an outfit named Wealth and Tax Advisory Services, Inc., an attractive young woman in a dark business suit is shown working at her desk. (She may be at home, though these days the distinction is moot.) On the desk is a cup, a cell phone, and an adding machine. Above her right shoulder, just over the blurred sofa and the blurred landscape on the wall, are the words "Successful entrepreneurs work continuously." The text below explains: "The challenge to building wealth is that your finances grow in complexity as your time demands increase."

The ad is worth disarticulating, it seems to me, if only because some version of it is beamed into our cerebral cortex a thousand times a day. What's interesting about it is not only what it says but what it so blithely assumes. What it says, crudely enough, is that in order to be successful, we must not only work but work *continuously*; what it assumes is that time is inversely proportional to wealth: our time demands will increase the harder we work and the more successful we become. It's an organic thing; a law, almost. Fish gotta swim and birds gotta fly, you gotta work like a dog till you die.

Am I suggesting then that Wealth and Tax Advisory Services, Inc. spend $60,000 for a full-page ad in *The New York Times Magazine* to show us a young woman at her desk writing poetry? Or playing with her kids? Or sharing a glass of wine with a friend, attractively thumbing her nose at the acquisition of wealth? No. For one thing, the folks at Wealth and Tax, etc., are simply doing what's in their best interest. For another, it would hardly matter if they did show the woman writing poetry, or laughing with her children, because these things, by virtue of their placement in the ad, would immediately take on the color of their host; they would simply be the rewards of working almost continuously.

What I am suggesting is that just as the marketplace has co-opted rebellion by subordinating politics to fashion, by making anger chic, so it has quietly underwritten the idea of leisure, in part by separating it from idleness. Open almost any magazine in America today and there they are: The ubiquitous tanned-and-toned twenty-somethings driving the $70,000 fruits of their labor; the moneyed-looking men and women in their healthy sixties (to give the young something to aspire to) tossing Frisbees to Irish setters or tying on flies in midstream or watching sunsets from their Adirondack chairs.

Leisure is permissible, we understand, because it costs money; idleness is not, because it doesn't. Leisure is focused; whatever thinking it requires is absorbed by a certain task: sinking that putt, making that cast, watching that flat-screen TV. Idleness is unconstrained, anarchic. Leisure—particularly if it involves some kind of high-priced technology—is as American as a Fourth of July barbecue. Idleness, on the other hand, has a bad attitude. It doesn't shave; it's not a member of the team; it doesn't play well with others. It thinks too much, as my high school coach used to say. So it has to be ostracized. [*Or put to good use. The wilderness of association we enter when we read, for example, is one of the world's great domains of imaginative diversity: a seedbed of individualism. What better reason to pave it then, to make it an accessory, like a personal organizer, a sure-fire way of raising your SAT score, or improving your communication skills for that next interview. You say you like to read? Then don't waste your time; put it to work. Order* Shakespeare in Charge: The Bard's Guide to Leading and Succeeding on the Business Stage, *with its picture of the bard in a business suit on the cover.*]

With idleness safely on the reservation, the notion that leisure is necessarily a function of money is free to grow into a truism. "Money isn't the goal. Your goals, that's the goal," reads a recent ad for Citibank. At first glance, there's something appealingly subversive about it. Apply a little skepticism though, and the implicit message floats to the surface: And how else are you going to reach those goals than by investing wisely with us? Which suggests that, um, money is the goal, after all.

The Church of Work

THERE'S SOMETHING UN-AMERICAN ABOUT SINGING the virtues of idleness. It is a form of blasphemy, a secular sin. More precisely, it is a kind of latter-day antinomianism, as much a threat to the orthodoxy of our day as Anne Hutchinson's desire 350 years ago to circumvent the Puritan ministers and dial God direct. Hutchinson, we recall, got into trouble because she accused the Puritan elders of backsliding from the rigors of their theology and giving in to a Covenant of Works, whereby the individual could earn his all-expenses-paid trip to the pearly gates through the labor of his hands rather than solely through the grace of God. Think of it as a kind of frequent-flier plan for the soul.

The analogy to today is instructive. Like the New England clergy, the Religion of Business—literalized, painfully, in books like *Jesus, CEO*—holds a monopoly on interpretation; it sets the terms, dictates value. [*In this new lexicon, for example, "work" is defined as the means to wealth; "success," as a synonym for it.*]

Although today's version of the Covenant of Works has substituted a host of secular pleasures for the idea of heaven, it too seeks to corner the market on what we most desire, to suggest that the work of our hands will save us. And we believe. We believe across all the boundaries of class and race and ethnicity that normally divide us; we believe in numbers that dwarf those of the more conventionally faithful. We repeat the daily catechism, we sing in the choir. And we tithe, and keep on tithing, until we are spent.

It is this willingness to hand over our lives that fascinates and appalls me. There's such a lovely perversity to it; it's so wonderfully counterintuitive, so very Christian: You must empty your pockets, turn them inside out, and spill out your wife and your son, the pets you hardly knew, and the days you simply missed altogether watching the sunlight fade on the bricks across the way. You must hand over the rainy afternoons, the light on the grass, the moments of play and of simply being. You must give it up, all of it, and by your example teach your children to do the same, and then—because even this is not enough—you must train yourself to believe that this outsourcing of your life is both natural and good. But even so, your soul will not be saved.

The young, for a time, know better. They balk at the harness. They do not go easy. For a time they are able to see the utter sadness of subordinating all that matters to all that doesn't. Eventually, of course, sitting in their cubicle lined with *New Yorker* cartoons, selling whatever it is they've been asked to sell, most come to see the advantage of enthusiasm. They join the choir and are duly forgiven for their illusions. It's a rite of passage we are all familiar with. The generations before us clear the path; Augustine stands to the left, Freud to the right. We are born into death, and die into life, they murmur; civilization will have its discontents. The sign in front of the Church of Our Lady of Perpetual Work confirms it. And we believe.

ALL OF WHICH LEAVES ONLY the task of explaining away those few miscreants who out of some inner weakness or perversity either refuse to convert or who go along and then, in their thirty-sixth year in the choir, say, abruptly abandon the faith. Those in the first category are relatively easy to contend with; they are simply losers. Those in the second are a bit more difficult; their apostasy requires something more . . . dramatic. They are considered mad.

In one of my favorite anecdotes from American literary history (which my children know by heart, and which in turn bodes poorly for their futures as captains of industry), the writer Sherwood Anderson found himself, at the age of thirty-six, the chief owner and general manager of a paint factory in Elyria, Ohio. Having made something of a reputation for himself as a copywriter in a Chicago advertising agency, he'd moved up a rung. He was on his way, as they say, a businessman in the making, perhaps even a tycoon in embryo. There was only one problem: he couldn't seem to shake the notion that the work he was doing (writing circulars extolling the virtues of his line of paints) was patently absurd, undignified; that it amounted to a kind of prison sentence. Lacking the rationalizing gene, incapable of numbing himself sufficiently to make the days and the years pass without pain, he suffered and flailed. Eventually he snapped.

It was a scene he would revisit time and again in his memoirs and fiction. On November 27, 1912, in the middle of dictating a letter to his secretary ("The goods about which you have inquired are the best of their kind made in the . . ."), he simply stopped. According to the story, the two supposedly stared at each other for a long time, after which Anderson said: "I have been wading in a long river and my feet are wet," and walked out. Outside the building he turned east toward Cleveland and kept going. Four days later he was recognized and taken to a hospital suffering from exhaustion.

Anderson claimed afterward that he had encouraged the impression that he might be cracking up in order to facilitate his exit, to make it comprehensible. "The thought occurred to me that if men thought me a little insane they would forgive me if I lit out," he wrote, and though we will never know for sure if he suffered a nervous breakdown that day or only pretended to have one (his biographers have concluded that he did), the point of the anecdote is elsewhere: Real or imagined, nothing short of madness would do for an excuse.

Anderson himself, of course, was smart enough to recognize the absurdity in all this, and to use it for his own ends; over the years that followed, he worked his escape from the paint factory into a kind of parable of liberation, an exemplar for the young men of his age. It became the cornerstone of his critique of the emerging business culture: To stay was to suffocate, slowly; to escape was to take a stab at "aliveness." What America needed, Anderson argued, was a new class of individuals who "at any physical cost to themselves and others" would "agree to quit working, to loaf, to refuse to be hurried or try to get on in the world."

"To refuse to be hurried or try to get on in the world." It sounds quite mad. What would we do if we followed that advice? And who would we be? No, better to pull down the blinds, finish that sentence. We're all in the paint factory now.

Clearing Brush

AT TIMES YOU CAN ALMOST SEE it, this flypaper we're attached to, this mechanism we labor in, this delusion we inhabit. A thing of such magnitude can be hard to make out, of course, but you can rough out its shape and mark its progress, like Lon Chaney's Invisible Man, by its effects: by the things it renders quaint or obsolete, by the trail of discarded notions it leaves behind. What we're leaving behind today, at record pace, is whatever belief we might once have had in the value of unstructured time: in the privilege of contemplating our lives before they are gone, in the importance of uninterrupted conversation, in the beauty of play. In the thing in itself—unmediated, leading nowhere. In the present moment.

Admittedly, the present—in its ontological, rather than consumerist, sense—has never been too popular on this side of the Atlantic; we've always been a finger-drumming, restless bunch, suspicious of jawboning, less likely to sit at the table than to grab a quick one at the bar. Whitman might have exhorted us to loaf and invite our souls, but that was not an invitation we cared to extend, not unless the soul played poker, ha, ha. No sir, a Frenchman might invite his soul. One expected such things. But an American? An American would be out the swinging doors and halfway to tomorrow before his silver dollar had stopped ringing on the counter.

I was put in mind of all this last June while sitting on a bench in London's Hampstead Heath. My bench, like many others, was almost entirely hidden; well off the path, delightfully overgrown, it sat at the top of a long-grassed meadow. It had a view. There was whimsy in its placement, and joy. It was thoroughly impractical. It had clearly been placed there to encourage one thing—solitary contemplation.

And sitting there, listening to the summer drone of the bees, I suddenly imagined George W. Bush on my bench. I can't tell you why this happened, or what in particular brought the image to my mind. Possibly it was the sheer incongruity of it that appealed to me, the turtle-on-a-lamppost illogic of it; earlier that summer, intrigued by images of Kafka's face on posters advertising the Prague Marathon, I'd entertained myself with pictures of Franz looking fit for the big race. In any case, my vision of Dubya sitting on a bench, reading a book on his lap—smiling or nodding in agreement, wetting a finger to turn a page—was so discordant, so absurd, that I realized I'd accidentally stumbled upon one of those visual oxymorons that, by its very dissonance, illuminates something essential.

What the picture of George W. Bush flushed into the open for me was the classically American and increasingly Republican cult of movement, of busy-ness; of doing, not thinking. One could imagine Kennedy reading on that bench in Hampstead Heath. Or Carter, maybe. Or even Clinton (though given the bucolic setting, one could also imagine him in other, more Dionysian scenarios). But Bush? Bush would be clearing brush. He'd be stomping it into submission with his pointy boots. He'd be making the world a better place.

Now, something about all that brush clearing had always bothered me. It wasn't the work itself, though I'd never fully understood where all that brush was being cleared from, or why, or how it was possible that there was any brush still left between Dallas and Austin. No, it was the frenetic, anti-thinking element of it I disliked. This wasn't simply outdoor work, which I had done my share of and knew well. This was brush clearing as a statement, a gesture of impatience. It captured the man, his disdain for the inner life, for the virtues of slowness and contemplation. This was movement as an answer to all those equivocating intellectuals and Gallic pontificators who would rather talk than do, think than act. Who could always be counted on to complicate what was simple with long-winded discussions of complexity and consequences. Who were weak.

And then I had it, the thing I'd been trying to place, the thing that had always made me bristle—instinctively—whenever I saw our fidgety, unelected President in action. I recalled reading about an Italian art movement called Futurism, which had flourished in the first decades of the twentieth century. Its practitioners had advocated a cult of restlessness, of speed, of dynamism; had rejected the past in all its forms; had glorified business and war and patriotism. They had also, at least in theory, supported the growth of fascism.

The link seemed tenuous at best, even facile. Was I seriously linking Bush—his shallowness, his bustle, his obvious suspicion of nuance—to the spirit of fascism? As much as I loathed the man, it made me uneasy. I'd always argued with people who applied the word carelessly. Having been called a fascist myself for suggesting that an ill-tempered rottweiler be put on a leash, I had no wish to align myself with those who had downgraded the word to a kind of generalized epithet, roughly synonymous with "ass-hole," to be applied to whoever disagreed with them. I had too much respect for the real thing. And yet there was no getting around it; what I'd been picking up like a bad smell whenever I observed the Bush team in action was the faint but unmistakable whiff of fascism; a democratically diluted fascism, true, and masked by the perfume of down-home cookin', but fascism nonetheless.

Still, it was not until I'd returned to the States and had forced myself to wade through the reams of Futurist manifestos—a form that obviously spoke to their hearts—that the details of the connection began to come clear. The linkage had nothing to do with the Futurists' art, which was notable only for its sustained mediocrity, nor with their writing, which at times achieved an almost sublime level of badness. It had to do, rather, with their ant-like energy, their busy-ness, their utter disdain of all the manifestations of the inner life, and with the way these traits seemed so organically linked in their thinking to aggression and war. "We intend to exalt aggressive action, a feverish insomnia," wrote Filippo Marinetti, perhaps the Futurists' most breathless spokesman. "We will glorify war—the world's only hygiene—militarism, patriotism, the destructive gesture of freedom-bringers. . . . We will destroy the museums, libraries, academies of every kind. . . . We will sing of great crowds excited by work."

"Militarism, patriotism, the destructive gesture of freedom-bringers," "a feverish insomnia," "great crowds excited by work" . . . I knew that song. And yet still, almost perversely, I resisted the recognition. It was too easy, somehow.

Wasn't much of the Futurist rant ("Take up your pickaxes, your axes and hammers and wreck, wreck the venerable cities, pitilessly") simply a gesture of adolescent rebellion, a FUCK YOU scrawled on Dad's garage door? I had just about decided to scrap the whole thing when I came across Marinetti's later and more extended version of the Futurist creed. And this time the connection was impossible to deny.

In the piece, published in June of 1913 (roughly six months after Anderson walked out of the paint factory), Marinetti explained that Futurism was about the "acceleration of life to today's swift pace." It was about the "dread of the old and the known . . . of quiet living." The new age, he wrote, would require the "negation of distances and nostalgic solitudes." It would "ridicule . . . the 'holy green silence' and the ineffable landscape." It would be, instead, an age enamored of "the passion, art, and idealism of Business."

This shift from slowness to speed, from the solitary individual to the crowd excited by work, would in turn force other adjustments. The worship of speed and business would require a new patriotism, "a heroic idealization of the commercial, industrial, and artistic solidarity of a people"; it would require "a modification in the idea of war," in order to make it "the necessary and bloody test of a people's force."

As if this weren't enough, as if the parallel were not yet sufficiently clear, there was this: The new man, Marinetti wrote—and this deserves my italics—would communicate by *"brutally destroying the syntax of his speech. He wastes no time in building sentences. Punctuation and the right adjectives will mean nothing to him. He will despise subtleties and nuances of language."* All of his thinking, moreover, would be marked by a *"dread of slowness, pettiness, analysis, and detailed explanations. Love of speed, abbreviation, and the summary. 'Quick, give me the whole thing in two words!'"*

Short of telling us that he would have a ranch in Crawford, Texas, and be given to clearing brush, nothing Marinetti wrote could have made the resemblance clearer. From his notorious mangling of the English language to his well-documented impatience with detail and analysis to his chuckling disregard for human life (which enabled him to crack jokes about Aileen Wuornos's execution as well as mug for the cameras minutes before announcing that the nation was going to war), Dubya was Marinetti's "New Man": impatient, almost pathologically unreflective, unburdened by the past. A man untroubled by the imagination, or by an awareness of human frailty. A leader wonderfully attuned (though one doubted he could ever articulate it) to "today's swift pace"; to the necessity of forging a new patriotism; to the idea of war as "the necessary and bloody test of a people's force"; to the all-conquering beauty of Business.

Mark Slouka is the author of the novel *God's Fool* (Knopf 2002), which was named a Best Book of the Year by *The San Francisco Chronicle*; the short story collection *Lost Lake* (Knopf 1998), a *New York Times* Notable Book; and, most recently, the novel *The Visible World* (Houghton Mifflin 2007). A contributing editor for *Harper's Magazine*, he has had his essays selected for inclusion in *Best American Essays* in 1999, 2000, and 2004. His short story "The Woodcarver's Tale" won the National Magazine Award for Fiction. A recipient of Guggenheim and NEA fellowships, Slouka is currently Professor of English Language and Literature and Chair of Creative Writing at the University of Chicago.

"Though I've always worked," Slouka writes, "I've also always questioned the priorities of a culture that elevates work, or business, more precisely, to the status of a religion. Most if not all of life's value, after all, lies outside work's domain; sometimes money costs too much. Ironically, less than a year after I published 'Quitting the Paint Factory,' I accepted a job at the University of Chicago, which, though undeniably a superb university, stands in the same relation to The Church of Work as Rome does to Catholicism."

At this writing, Slouka is currently on sabbatical, "working hard at splitting wood for the winter, reading all the novels of Henry Green, and spending time with my wife and kids."

"Quitting the Paint Factory" first appeared in *Harper's Magazine* (2004). Copyright © 2004 by Mark Slouka. It is reprinted here by permission of the Denise Shannon Literary Agency, Inc.

W . . .

Shirlee Sky Hoffman

womb
work
wage
war

weary
wight

Born in Toronto, Canada, **Shirlee Sky Hoffman** has lived in Chicago since 1971. The poem "W . . ." reflects her ambivalence about having children in the mid-1970s, "a time when employers saw motherhood as a defect." Hoffman writes that, after the birth of her son (1976) and daughter (1980), "I achieved the peace of flexibility in 1983 by founding Marketscope, a marketing consulting, facilitating, and training firm that now works primarily with environmentally concerned organizations." Hoffman's previously published works include "The Dreadlock Suite: Tales to Relieve a Mother's Distress" and "Pesach on Wheels."

Copyright © Shirlee Sky Hoffman

HD6957.U6 W29 2008
The way we work :
contemporary writings from
the American workplace